Japanese Buddhist Pilgrimage

Japanese Buddhist Pilgrimage

Michael Pye

SHEFFIELD UK   BRISTOL CT

Published by Equinox Publishing Ltd.

UK: Office 415, The Workstation, 15 Paternoster Row, Sheffield S1 2BX
USA: ISD, 70 Enterprise Drive, Bristol, CT 06010
www.equinoxpub.com

First published 2015

© Michael Pye 2015

All rights reserved. No part of this publication may be reproduced or transmitted in any form or by any means, electronic or mechanical, including photocopying, recording or any information storage or retrieval system, without prior permission in writing from the publishers.

ISBN 978-1-84553-916-0 (hardback)
ISBN 978-1-84553-917-7 (paperback)

British Library Cataloguing-in-Publication Data
A catalogue record for this book is available from the British Library.

Library of Congress Cataloging-in-Publication Data

Pye, Michael.
Japanese Buddhist Pilgrimage / Michael Pye.
   pages cm
Includes bibliographical references and index.
ISBN 978-1-84553-916-0 (hb) — ISBN 978-1-84553-917-7 (pb)
1. Buddhist pilgrims and pilgrimages—Japan. 2. Japan—Religious life and customs. I. Title.
BQ6450.J3P935 2014
294.3'4350952—dc23
                2013038065

Edited and Typeset by Queenston Publishing, Hamilton, Ontario, Canada

Printed and bound in the UK

Contents

LIST OF FIGURES	viii
LIST OF TABLES	xi
PREFACE	xiii

1 INTRODUCTION   1

   Circulatory pilgrimages in Japan   1
   The principle of circulation   6
   Single-goal pilgrimages in Japan   8
   Various theories of pilgrimage   11
   Defining und understanding pilgrimage   16
   Materials and methods   24

2 GOING ROUND TO VISIT KANNON-SAMA   29

   Saikoku 33—the classic sequence   29
   Bandō 33 and Chichibu 34   46
   Other Kannon-sama routes   53
   The Izumo, Kamakura and Izu Kannon routes   59
   Miniature Kannon-sama routes   65
   Denominational spread of Kannon-sama routes   69
   Completing the pilgrimage routes   72

3	THE SHIKOKU PILGRIMAGE	75
	Introducing the Shikoku pilgrimage	75
	The temples of the 88 spiritual places	82
	Imitations of the Shikoku route	92
	Miniature Shikoku pilgrimages	96
	Concluding the Shikoku route	101
4	MORE BUDDHIST ROUTES	103
	More Buddhas and more pilgrimages	103
	Visiting the Thirteen Buddhas	106
	36 Fudō Myōō and 49 Yakushi Nyorai	109
	Linked visits to Jizō Bosatsu	114
	In the tracks of saintly founders	120
	Pilgrimage in Shin Buddhism	127
	Temples within temples	130
	More enumeration and circulation	134
	Pilgrimage and circumambulation	136
5	GOING ROUND TO OTHER DIVINITIES	141
	Buddhist pilgrimage and the wider field of Japanese religion	141
	The Seven Gods of Good Fortune	147
	Shintō circulatory pilgrimages	159
	Patriotic shrine pilgrimages	162
	Various Shintō shrine circuits	169
	Shintō pilgrimage considered	177
6	THE PILGRIM'S TRANSACTION	181
	A religious transaction in three steps	181
	The pilgrim deposits evidence of the visit	187
	The pilgrim performs a devotional act	193
	The pilgrim acquires evidence of the visit	197
	Hanging scrolls as proof of pilgrimage	200

Contents

7 THE MEANING OF JAPANESE BUDDHIST PILGRIMAGE 207
    Divergent meanings and Buddhist meaning 207
    Chinese and Indian perspectives 212
    Clothing, staff, hat 218
    Instructions for the route 224
    Four stages in the Shikoku pilgrimage 226
    Buddhist recitations 230
    Sūtras, *wasan* and *go-eika* 237
    Kannon-sama and the *Kannon Sūtra* 244
    The *Heart Sūtra* 254

8 GENERAL CONCLUSIONS 259
    Are the pilgrimages Buddhist? 259
    Postscript on the general theory of pilgrimage 263

BIBLIOGRAPHY 269

INDEX OF TEMPLES AND SHRINES 279

GENERAL INDEX 287

List of Figures

FRONTISPIECE Iconic depiction of Nyoirin Kanzeon Bosatsu from Temple No. 1 of the Saikoku Pilgrimage, starting at Kumano Nachi.

1.1	Simplified map of the Saikoku Kannon Pilgrimage.	2
1.2	A popular map of the Shikoku Pilgrimage.	7
1.3	Notice showing combined approach to Nachi Shrine and Saikoku Temple No. 1.	23
2.1	Modern map of the Saikoku Kannon Pilgrimage.	30
2.2	Iconic depiction (*miei*)[a] of Tokudō Shōnin, reputed founder of the Saikoku Kannon Pilgrimage.	31
2.3	Iconic depiction (*miei*) of Kannon Bosatsu (Nyoirin Kanzeon) from Saikoku No.14.	36
2.4	Iconic depiction (*miei*) of standing Shō Kannon as shown in a pilgrim's book from Mitakesan Kōsanji, Chita.	37
2.5	Iconic depiction (*miei*) of Jūichimen Kanzeon from Saikoku No. 33 (Kegonji).	37
2.6	Iconic depiction (*miei*) of Senju Kanzeon from Saikoku No. 19 (Gyōganji).	38
2.7	Iconic depiction (*miei*) of Fukūkensaku Kanzeon from Saikoku No. 9 (Kōfukuji, Nan'endō).	39
2.8	Iconic depiction (*miei*) of Batō Kanzeon from Shikoku No. 70 (Motoyamaji).	40

List of Figures

2.9	Iconic depiction (*miei*) of Juntei Kannon from a Chita pilgrim's commemoration booklet.	40
2.10	A worn-out signpost on the Saikoku Pilgrimage pointing right to Kannonshōji (temple No. 32) and left to nearby railway stations and a bus stop.	44
2.11	Diagram of a Kannon 33 pilgrimage route in Tokyo showing modern infrastructure.	56
2.12	Pilgrims' slips (cf. Chapter Six) of the Izumo Kannon Pilgrimage.	60
2.13	Traditional map of the Saikoku Kannon Pilgrimage, probably nineteenth century: detail showing the last few temples.	73
3.1	Traditional map of the Shikoku Pilgrimage with railways (reduced).	77
3.2	Traditional map of the Shikoku Pilgrimage with railways: detail showing the beginning and the end (temples 1–23 and 71–88).	83
3.3	Iconic depictions (*miei*) from the Shikoku pilgrimage, showing nos. 1–6.	89
3.4	Iconic depiction (*miei*) of Dainichi Nyorai from Shikoku No 4.	89
3.5	Iconic depiction (*miei*) of Yakushi Nyorai from Shikoku No 6.	90
3.6	Iconic depiction (*miei*) of Amida Nyorai from Shikoku No 7.	90
4.1	Iconic depiction of Fudō Myōō from No. 4 of the Kinki Fudō Circuit.	111
4.2	Iconic depiction of Fudō Myōō from No. 11 of the Kinki Fudō Circuit.	111
4.3	Map for visits to the Six Jizō in modern Kyōto with public transport.	118
4.4	Map of twenty-five spiritual places connected with Hōnen Shōnin.	125
5.1	Iconic depiction (*miei*) of Myōon Benzaiten at Demachi, Kyōto.	143
5.2	Map of Kamakura Enoshima Shichifukujin circuit.	157
5.3	Notice for sixteen shrines in Kyōto as a New Year's pilgrimage.	171
6.1	Pilgrim's shirt with Saikoku seals and calligraphy. The central calligraphy appears reversed because it shows through from the back of the shirt.	184
6.2	Pilgrim slips from the Saikoku Kannon Pilgrimage (right); and the Izumo Kannon Pilgrimage (personal name deleted) (left).	188
6.3	Unused pilgrims' slips for the Shikoku pilgrimage.	190
7.1	Popular sketch of mannequin with pilgrim's attire.	219

7.2	Map of the Shikoku pilgrimage showing four provinces and four spiritual stages.	228
7.3	Dainichi Nyorai as illustrated in a guidebook.	233
7.4	Paper amulet showing Kōbō Daishi in traditional pose.	238
7.5	A *shingon* formula (mantra) in a book of pilgrim's devotions.	239
7.6	Traditional book of the Saikoku go-eika, opened at temples 8 and 9.	240
7.7	Handwritten pilgrim's song pinned on temple entrance of Saikoku No. 19.	243
8.1	Iconic depiction of Nyoirin Kannon Bosatsu from Saikoku No. 18 (Rokkakudō, Kyōto).	262
8.2	Traditional illustration of pilgrims with details of Saikoku No 1.	266

a) An "iconic depiction" (*miei* 御影, literally a "respected image") is printed on thin paper and acquired at the temple for commemorative purposes.

© All Illustrations including photos where applicable by Michael Pye 2014. All of the items shown here are from the author's personal collection.

List of Tables

2.1	The most frequent iconographic forms of Kannon-sama.	35
2.2	The Saikoku temples with the iconographical types of Kannon/Kanzeon.	42
2.3	Current denominational affiliation of the Saikoku temples.	44
2.4	Temples of the Bandō pilgrimage.	47
2.5	Bandō list showing iconographical types and temple denominations.	50
2.6	Temples of the Chichibu pilgrimage.	51
2.7	Chichibu list showing iconographical types and temple denominations.	52
2.8	Names and denominations of the Izumo Thirty-three temples (simplified).	61
2.9	The Kamakura 33 Kannon showing alternative numerations.	63
2.10	Denominational spread of the leading Kannon-sama routes.	69
3.1	The eighty-eight temples of the Shikoku pilgrimage with their main objects of reverence.	83
3.2	Statistics of central objects of reverence in the 88 Shikoku temples.	92
4.1	Thirteen Buddhas and mourning anniversaries.	107
4.2	Temples of the Thirty-six Fudō of the Kinki Region.	112
4.3	Temples of the Six Jizō in Kyōto.	117
4.4	Sixteen head temples of Nichirenite Buddhism in Kyōto.	123

4.5	Twenty-five Spiritual Places of Hōnen Shōnin.	126
4.6	Six linked Amida temples in Kyōto.	135
5.1	Kanpei Taisha appearing on a pilgrim's scroll.	163
5.2	The Tokyo Ten Shrines Pilgrimage and locations in city Wards.	167
5.3	Eight shrines of good fortune, Tokyo.	169
5.4	Sixteen linked shrines in Kyōto.	172
5.5	Kyōraku Hassha: Eight Shrines of Central Kyōto.	173
5.6	Sub-shrines of Imamiya Jinja.	173
5.7	Shimozuke Eight Shrines and their benefits.	176

Preface

These pages provide a general account of the Buddhist pilgrimages of Japan in modern times. The special feature of these pilgrimages is that they involve visiting a long string of different temples in sequence. The Japanese term for this is *o-meguri*, meaning "going round," and so they are referred to here as "circulatory pilgrimages."

In the classic pilgrimage route of this kind, the pilgrims visit 33 specially designated temples to pay devotion to the compassionate bodhisattva known in Japan as Kannon-sama. This reflects an idea found in the Lotus Sūtra, where we read that the bodhisattva appears in 33 different forms in order to bring salvation to living beings in their various situations. Another famous example is the pilgrimage to 88 different temples on Japan's fourth largest island, Shikoku. Here the temples are devoted to various buddhas and bodhisattvas, but the famous Shingon Buddhist teacher Kōbō Daishi is also revered at each one, since he is reputed to have founded the pilgrimage. In other cases devotion is paid to divinities such as Fudō-son, Jizō-sama, or the Seven Gods of Good Fortune, and recently there has been a trend, as yet hardly documented, for Shintō shrines to form links in the same manner. Information about the latter will also be found below. However the main subject of this book is the circulatory pilgrimages of Japanese Buddhism. Going beyond a description of the routes as such, attention will be given to the ritual activities of the pilgrims and the various levels of meaning which are involved.

In some cases I have carried out the pilgrimage myself in person, temple by temple, as a participant observer. At other times I remained behind longer at selected temples in order to speak with the various people passing through. I would like to express my heartfelt thanks, therefore, to all those anonymous pilgrims who kindly found a few minutes—in their busy travel schedule—to talk to me about what they were doing. I am also very grateful for information provided by temple priests and their assistants, whose role is, among other things, to complete the pilgrims' books and scrolls with their temple seal and some impressive calligraphy.

While I have been taking note of various Japanese religions since first residing in the country from late 1961, my observations of Buddhist pilgrimages cover a period of nearly forty years, from 1973 to the time of the final touches to this book in 2013. In 1973 I began observations of the Saikoku 33 Pilgrimage, and in 1979 and 1980, while a visiting lecturer at Tsukuba University, I visited various temples of the related Bandō, Edo, Izumo and Sendai Kannon circuits. The Shikoku Pilgrimage had been undergoing a major revival of interest during the 1970s, as evidenced in the media, but my first personal visit to Shikoku had to wait until 1982. This was followed by later, shorter visits. The last one was in 2010 in the company of a bus-load of pilgrims who braved most unusual rains, in late April, to get their pilgrimage well launched around the first seven temples.

In 1979 I also began to appreciate the importance of miniaturization, abbreviation and variation in many areas of Japanese religious culture. This can be seen, for example, in mini-versions of Mount Fuji which one can climb symbolically in just a few steps, or even by jumping over them. In the same way, it is common to find compact groups of thirty-three stone statues of Kannon-sama, or symbols of the eighty-eight temples of the Shikoku pilgrimage, which can be visited in an hour or less. Being aware of such things made me seek a very wide variety of relevant information, including materials related to Shintō as well as to Buddhism. I would like to thank all those who have incidentally facilitated this.

In 1983 and 1985 I carried out a detailed study of the Chichibu Pilgrimage of 34 Buddhist temples linked to Kannon-sama, and was able to complete it. Here I would like to record my especial thanks to the Sonoda family, the hereditary Shintō priests in charge of Chichibu Shrine. They gave most kindly and practical support in my exploration of what is after all a Buddhist pilgrimage. Among other things, they lent me their traditional English bicycle for the purpose. Following this I reported on "The interpretation of Japanese Buddhist pilgrimage" at the 1987 conference of the British Association for the Study of Religions in Oxford, which thematized pilgrimage, and enjoyed some feed-back. In 1993 I benefited from a travel grant from the British Academy which enabled me to make visits to those sites of the Saikoku 33 Pilgrimage with which I was not already familiar, and also to explore a number of less well known variations. This assistance is gratefully acknowledged here.

Information about the many other pilgrimage routes referred to below was collected during further research journeys to Japan, down to the time of writing. Some of these have been facilitated in particular by a long-standing association with Ōtani University. For this I have been

Preface

particularly grateful, since in the Shin Buddhist background of many who teach at Ōtani the ideas of merit-making and self-determined progress, which are inherent in much pilgrimage activity, are somewhat frowned upon. After all, they can be regarded as an expression of "self-power" (*jiriki* 自力), as opposed to the "other power" (*tariki* 他力) of Amida Buddha which is central in Shin Buddhism. It is no accident that the Japanese for bicycle is *jitensha* 自転車, being a wheel or wheels which one has to turn by one's own power.

Another fascinating aspect of Japanese religious culture is the sheer complexity of the source material, which includes many ephemeral documents and artefacts. Over the years I have been able to bring such material into use in teaching and in small exhibitions and publications. Some of this material is documented in the catalogues *O-meguri, Pilgerfahrt in Japan* (1987), from an exhibition mounted in the University Library of the University of Marburg and *Pilgerfahrt visuell. Hängerollen in der religiösen Alltagspraxis Japans* (2011 with Katja Triplett), from an exhibition in the Marburg Museum of Religions which ran from 2009. These publications show typical materials relating to pilgrimage, but much else has also enriched the following pages. Step by step the relevant material is being lodged in the Museum of Religions (*Religionskundliche Sammlung*) at the University of Marburg, Germany. Almost all of it was collected by myself, but occasionally others have added to it, and I am very grateful for such kindnesses.

In this connection I was fortunate to discover a completed scroll of the Saikoku Pilgrimage in a so-called "recycle shop" in Kyōto in 2005, and to acquire it for a negligible price. This was a cause for joy, thanks to the efforts and merits of an anonymous pilgrim, because it dramatically complements the more modest book of seals which I had completed myself while going the rounds. Other scrolls and interesting items from second-hand sources include a complete book of seals for the Shikoku pilgrimage made by a pilgrim who visited all 88 temples twice. I would like to thank all these unknown pilgrims, somehow, from the bottom of my heart. Their prayers for the transfer of merit to other living beings have been answered.

For very helpful comments on particular details of this book in the later stages I would like to thank in particular Brian Bocking, Graham Harvey, Peiying Lin, Satō Naomi, Elizabeth Tinsley, Christopher Triplett and Yoshie Takami.

It is frequently noted that pilgrimages in Japan have a close relationship to the travel industry. Even so, they are often surprisingly arduous and require steady enthusiasm and persistence. At the same time travel may itself become addictive, as has sometimes been noted by my friends and family. So I add my great thanks herewith for the well-nigh endless patience shown by all of them, especially by my wife Christine who has a profoundly frontier-free imagination. In spite of all the travel, one of the lessons which may be learned in the course of a Buddhist pilgrimage is that, in the end, it is not really necessary to go round at all.

Michael Pye
Kyōto 2013

— Chapter One —

Introduction

Circulatory pilgrimages in Japan

Japan is a land of many religions. The Buddhist tradition has taken on a variety of forms with revered founder-figures, distinctive teachings and practice, and many notable temples in beautiful landscapes. Its strength arises partly from well-established functions in connection with cemeteries and reverence for ancestors, but this is by no means its only significance. As well as having a high cultural profile, Buddhism addresses the practical religious needs of a majority of the population. Well established Shintō shrines also form a nation-wide network, now separate from the state but still providing typically Japanese rites and customs throughout the year, in which millions participate. While Shintō and Buddhism can certainly be distinguished, they have been closely associated in many ways, and their divinities are sometimes referred to collectively as "gods and buddhas" (*shinbutsu* 神仏). As if this were not enough, modern times have seen the emergence of many new religious groups with charismatic leaders and special attractions of all kinds, some of which have attracted millions of followers. Because the religions of Japan have so many features in common and at the same time do present distinctive characteristics they offer a fascinating field of study. This holds good for the widespread activity of "pilgrimage," and particularly for the circulatory pilgrimages of Buddhism in Japan, which are the subject of the present work.

Pilgrimages in Japan, which in total attract millions of people each year, may be divided broadly into two kinds. Some of them, like pilgrimages all over the world, require travel to a single important religious centre. Well-known examples of this include leading Shintō shrines such as Ise Jingū or Izumo Taisha, the head temples of leading Buddhist denominations such as Mount Kōya (Shingon Buddhism) or Mount Minobu (Nichiren Buddhism), and the sacred sites of new religions such as Tenrikyō or Sekai Kyūsei Kyō. Other pilgrimages however are

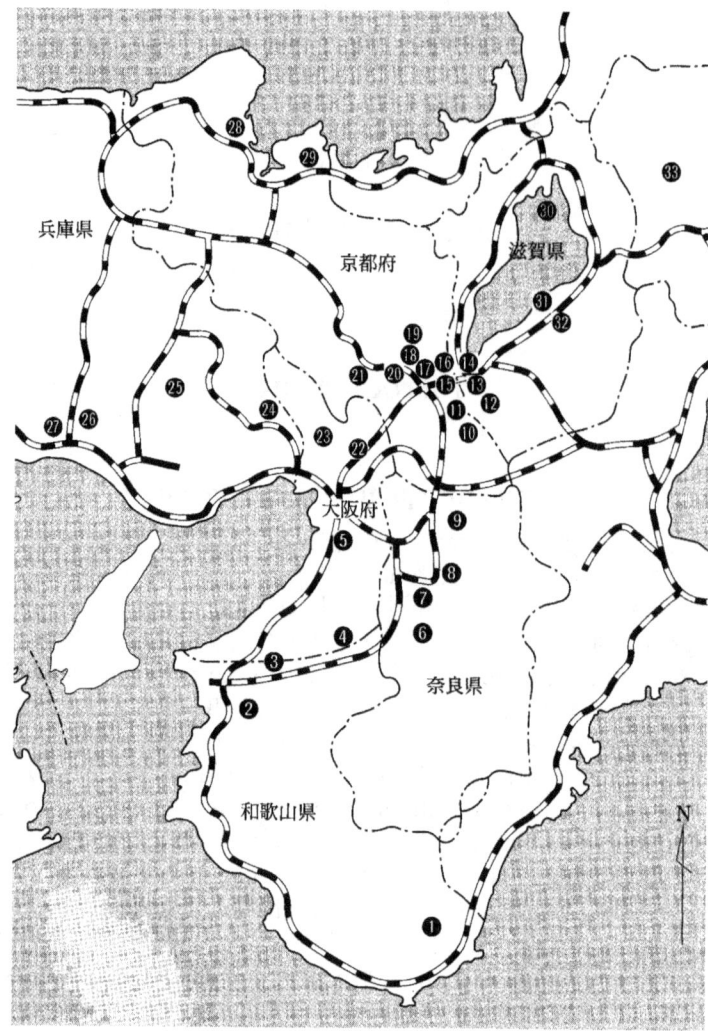

Figure 1.1 Simplified map of the Saikoku Kannon Pilgrimage.

based on the idea of visiting a considerable number of holy places *in sequence*, which seems to be particularly characteristic of Japanese Buddhism. They are referred to here, distinctively, as *circulatory* pilgrimages. The numerous circulatory pilgrimages of Japan are mainly, though not entirely, Buddhist in orientation. Two of them are overwhelmingly famous and provide the model for most of the others.

The first symbolically dominant model, the Saikoku Pilgrimage, is a chain of 33 temples dedicated to the compassionate Bodhisattva, Kannon-sama. These temples are located in western Japan, which explains the name of the pilgrimage, the *sai* 西 of *saikoku* 西国 meaning "west"

Introduction

and the *koku* 国 element meaning "country" or "land." The pronunciation Saigoku is also be found.[1] Much of Japan's early history was made in the area covered by this pilgrimage, and nine of the 33 temples are in the historic capital of Kyōto itself. The rest, on the other hand, are quite widely scattered, some being in remote and steep hills. Even in modern times, when some of the mountains are mastered by cable-cars, it is not particularly easy to visit them all.

The second very famous route is the Shikoku Pilgrimage, a chain of no less than 88 temples scattered across Japan's fourth largest island, Shikoku 四国. Note the difference in the rather similar first character here (四 not 西). This time the first character 四 means "four" and the *koku* are the four traditional lands or provinces of the island (now prefectures). These four lands, as will be seen, play a certain role in the conceptualization of the route. This pilgrimage is associated especially with Kūkai, the much revered founder of Japanese Shingon Buddhism. Kūkai, posthumously known as Kōbō Daishi, is believed to have visited the sites of all these temples in person. Today's pilgrim is therefore thought to be following in his footsteps, and indeed is encouraged to understand the journey as being made in the spiritual company of Kōbō Daishi, or Daishi-sama as he is more conveniently yet respectfully called. Until the development of modern transport, the island of Shikoku was relatively remote for most of the population of Japan. It was separated from the main centres by the Inland Sea (Setonaikai). No one could have imagined the impressive road and rail bridges of today. To travel to Shikoku from one of the larger urban centres such as Ōsaka, and then to succeed in going all the way round to visit the 88 temples, used to be a truly significant physical performance. For this reason the figure of a Shikoku pilgrim with his or her large protective hat, white garments and stick, is a traditional symbol both of the island of Shikoku and, in Japan, of the very idea of pilgrimage.

Most of the other pilgrimages in Japan are modelled on these two classic examples. The population of eastern Japan centred on Edo (now Tokyo[2]) has benefited for centuries from the Bandō 坂東 pilgrimage, this being their own alternative journey round 33 temples devoted to

---

1. The first consonant of the second element of a compound word is sometimes hardened, and sometimes not. Although Saikoku is sometimes hardened to Saigoku, and both forms can be found in dictionaries, we have retained the more common Saikoku here. The old character form 國 for 国, giving 西國 will also be found in some older, or nostalgic contexts. When the same characters are pronounced *seikoku* (*sei* being another reading for the first character) reference is being made to "western countries," that is, countries to the west of Japan.
2. The length of vowels is very important in Japanese, and the vowel-lengthening sign is therefore used regularly in this book where needed, e.g. in Kyōto and Ōsaka; an exception is made only for the conventionalized name of the capital city Tokyo, which ideally should be Tōkyō.

Kannon-sama. However, these 33 temples are also spread over a large and relatively inconvenient area. A third option was therefore devised, namely the much shorter pilgrimage centred on the city of Chichibu 秩父, located in the mountains not far from Edo. This pilgrimage can be completed in a few days, even on foot. The Chichibu pilgrimage is peculiar in that it includes not 33 but 34 temples; this means that a pilgrim who completes the three important traditional routes devoted to Kannon-sama, namely Saikoku, Bandō and Chichibu, would visit the round number of one hundred temples in all.

To these must be added other Buddhist pilgrimages with varying numbers of temples, a very large number devoted to the Seven Gods of Good Fortune and, more recently, some sequences of Shintō shrines. Taken together the various circulatory pilgrimage circuits in Japan may be regarded as falling into the following groups (cf. Pye 2005):

1. The three most famous Kannon-sama pilgrimages: i.e. the Saikoku 33 followed by the Bandō 33 and the Chichibu 34.
2. The Shikoku pilgrimage of 88 temples, with an additional goal at Mount Kōya, the traditional headquarters of Shingon Buddhism.
3. Regional and local imitations of the two main models referred to above, namely the Saikoku and Shikoku pilgrimages.
4. Routes based on devotion to Buddhist divinities such as Fudōson (36 temples) Yakushi Nyorai (49 temples) or Jizō-sama (e.g. six temples).
5. Routes based on devotion to Buddhist leaders or "saints" such as Hōnen or Dōgen, or following their tracks. The Shikoku pilgrimage falls partly into this category because of the reverence for Kōbō Daishi; each temple visit on this route includes a visit to the Daishi Hall.
6. Specialized routes taken by unusually qualified religious leaders such as the 1000 day pilgrimage of Tendai Buddhism (known as the Kaihōgyō).
7. Multiple sites for mountain ascetics (*yamabushi* 山伏) such as the ancient route from Yoshino to Kumano. The *yamabushi* are organized in various groups under the general heading of Shugendō.
8. Miniature versions of some of the famous pilgrimages mentioned above, which can be completed in a very short time.
9. Subjectively defined, modern journeys to numbers of temples chosen mainly on aesthetic or nostalgic grounds.
10. Religiously mixed circulatory pilgrimage, especially to the

Introduction

Seven Gods of Good Fortune (Shichifukujin), in which both Buddhist Temples and Shintō shrines may be included.
11. Circulatory pilgrimage round a series of Shintō shrines without any reference to Buddhism.

With types 10 and 11 the Buddhist meaning of the pilgrimage is reduced or displaced completely by other motivations and perspectives. Though still current, types 6 and 7 are especially important from a historical point of view, because the mediaeval tradition of outdoor ascetic practices provided a conceptual matrix for the development of circulatory pilgrimage in general. However this book is concerned less with historical studies than with the state of pilgrimage in contemporary Japan.

While the pages below provide details of all the main pilgrimage routes in popular use today, description alone is not enough, for there are also interesting questions of analysis and interpretation to be considered. This account is therefore divided into three main steps, using a well-tested scheme (Pye 1987, 2005).These steps may be summed up under the following keywords:

ROUTE
TRANSACTION
MEANING

First, under "route," essential information about the geographical pattern and physical form of Buddhist pilgrimages in Japan is provided. Second, under "transaction," the various "rites of transaction"[3] which are commonly performed in the context of pilgrimage are considered. Third, under "meaning," the dimension of Buddhist meaning is explored which, in varying degree, is appropriated by the pilgrims in the course of their journeys.

The detailed implications of these terms will become clear in due course, but the main point lies in a progressive interpretation which leads beyond geographically definable travel into ritualized activity and opens up potential realms of religious meaning and personal development for the participants. In other words, while the significance of the relation between pilgrimage and tourism or travel culture is certainly recognized here, it is also maintained that in many cases the physical business of "going round" is not necessarily just pleasure or fun, which it may be, but also has a more serious intention which goes beyond the immediate needs and interests of ordinary life. The transformations of meaning which are involved here can only be understood in the context of the wider dynamics of Japanese religious life and in the perspective of the dialectical tradition of Buddhist thought. In this perspective, very simple rituals may have a practical role in daily, this-worldly matters

---

3. For the introduction of this phrase see Pye 1996a and Pye and Triplett 2004.

but also open the way to a deeper interpretation of life.

The completion of a circulatory pilgrimage route, apart from the sheer going along or going around, includes the performance of specific ritual *transactions* with the celestial bodhisattvas or buddhas to whom devotion is paid, for example, Kannon-sama. These transactions are in many cases quite overtly related to benefits sought for this ordinary life, such as the healing of a chronic sickness or the assurance of one's family's welfare. Such benefits are generally known as "this-worldly benefits" (*genzeriyaku*). However, the transactional element in the overt ritual activities of individual pilgrims does not exhaust the meaning of these pilgrimages. While such transactions are a basic feature of the general pattern of Japanese religion, there is also a dimension of *Buddhist* meaning. This goes beyond the merely transactional. It represents a dimension of meaning into which the pilgrim may mature gradually, or indeed suddenly. The perception of this dimension of meaning by the pilgrim may amount to some kind of personal development or transformation, as will be considered further below.

These three organizing concepts, route, transaction and meaning, amount to an inductively derived model for the phenomenology of pilgrimage which arises out of a considerable number of examples in Japan. At the same time the model is thought to be relevant also to other cases of pilgrimage, in other parts of the world, whether they are circulatory or not. The corrective value of the view of pilgrimage developed in the Japanese context lies mainly in that it places less emphasis on the *goal* of pilgrimage and more emphasis on the *route*, a point which will be discussed further below.

Looking at pilgrimage in this way is an example of what is taken to be the prime task of the phenomenological approach to the study of religion, that is, the creation of reliable characterizations which are consistent with the self-understanding of the believers or participants themselves. Such characterizations may be drawn upon in comparative studies or used in explanatory theories of various kinds. Without such characterizations, which can be checked by others in the same or related fields,[4] theoretical explanations of religion as well as philosophical discussion on the subject are largely speculative and hence of little worth.

The principle of circulation

The special feature of the Japanese Buddhist pilgrimages described here is that they are *circulatory*. This is almost unique, though a few parallels will be mentioned later. This does not mean that the routes are circular,

---

4. Strictly speaking there is never any such thing as the *same* field in the study of human society and culture, for the field is always changing, but much is repeated and much is analogous, so that it is usually open to other researchers to check the value of observations and analysis by going to take another look.

Introduction

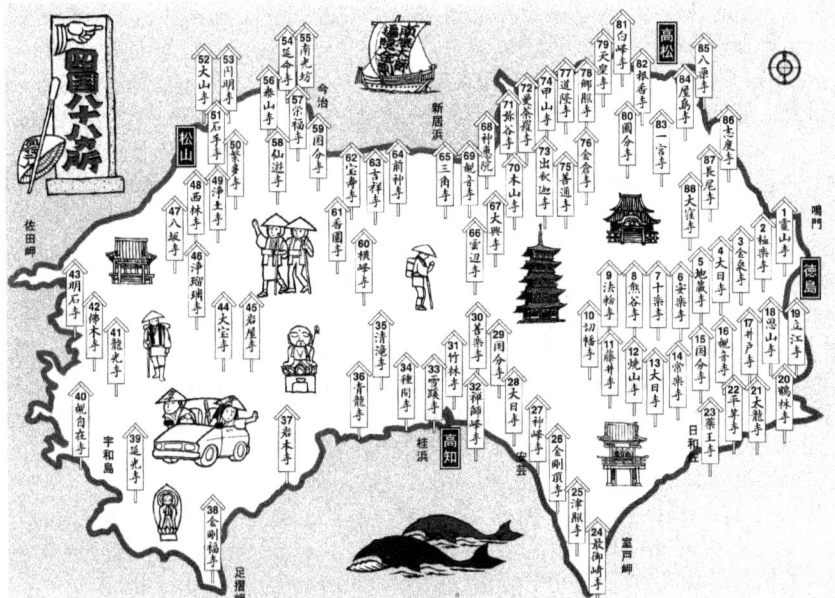

Figure 1.2 A popular map of the Shikoku Pilgrimage.

and the relationship between circumabulation and pilgrimage will also be briefly considered later. What it means is that the routes consist of a series of designated temples, for example 33, *all* of which have to be visited for the pilgrimage to be completed. In the case of the Shikoku Pilgrimage, all 88 temples are supposed to be visited. Hence the pilgrims circulate. This means that there is not one single goal, but many. Consequently the emphasis is laid not so much on any one of the various goals as a climax, but rather on the path or *route* which the pilgrim traverses. The aim of the pilgrim is the completion of his or her *route*.

This idea of completing the route as a whole sequence is encapsulated in the Japanese word *o-meguri*, which (with the respectful prefix *o-*) means quite literally "going round."[5] This is a verbal noun derived from the plain verb form *meguru*.[6] These are perfectly ordinary words in themselves, and yet their association with pilgrimage does lend the slightly special feeling that "going round" is something which is particularly well worth doing. In this sense it is sometimes picked up in other contexts. Tour operators frequently use it of going round famous places (*meisho*), itself a well-established concept since early modern

---

5. It is because the term *o-meguri* is so characteristic for Japanese pilgrimage that it was used as the title of the exhibition referred to in the Preface: *O-meguri. Pilgerfahrt in Japan* (Marburg 1987).

6. A close synonym is *mawaru*, both verbs meaning to "go round."

times. But the usage has become even wider in commercial contexts. For example, a mineral water supplier recently launched bottles of table water with the label *meisui meguri*, which means "going round famous waters." Within this spectrum of usage the idea of "going round" may be employed both religiously and yet more loosely, as in a recently published series of books whose title might be translated as "Journey round the Buddha images."[7] These books are made up in a format similar to pilgrims' guidebooks, with maps showing how to reach particular temples and an indication of what benefits may arise as a result of worshipping there. However they are based not on routes as such but on tourist regions. The selection of temples is more random. This looser usage may therefore be regarded as secondary. In such cases "going round" does not imply an imperative to complete a particular course of visits. On the other hand, in clearly defined pilgrimages the standard usage does imply completion of a specified sequence.

There is no doubt that the circulatory character of the pilgrimages is clearly present in the consciousness of the pilgrims. The same idea is included in two other important words for pilgrimage in Japanese, namely *junrei* 巡礼 and *junpai* 巡拝. In these words the element *jun-* implies circulation, and the character is the same as that used for the verb *meguru* or its verbal noun *meguri*. Although both *junrei* and *junpai* are usually translated into English as "pilgrimage" they literally mean "going round and worshipping." The single word *junrei* forms the title of a well-known work by Hoshino Eiki on pilgrimage (Hoshino 1981). He deals mainly with circulatory pilgrimages in Japan but, quite rightly, sets these in the wider context of pilgrimages which are not circulatory. We may infer from this that, when people refer to "pilgrimage" (*junrei*) in a Japanese context, they may also include reference to journeys made to one particular sacred place (for which the term *o-mairi* might otherwise be preferred), but they are more likely to think of people "going round and worshipping" at a sequence of places. When the terms are more strictly used, as they usually are, it means that a very clear emphasis is placed on the route, rather than on any one goal. This point is of great interest for the wider study of pilgrimage, as will be explored further below.

Single-goal pilgrimages in Japan

The emphasis on circulatory pilgrimage in this study should not at all be taken to suggest that uni-directional pilgrimage, that is, pilgrimage to one main goal, is of no importance in Japan.[8] On the contrary, it is a very

---

7. *Butsuzō meguri no tabi*. At the time of writing six titles had appeared in this series for the popular market dealing with Kamakura, Nara (two titles), Kyōto (two titles) and Shin'etsu/Hokuriku.

8. In the meantime (since the formulation of the main conceptions presented here),

prominent feature of almost all Japanese religions which have a call on the faith and loyalty of the people. The major Shintō shrines all invite pilgrimage on a national or regional basis. The head temples of many Buddhist denominations or sects are also pilgrimage centres. One thinks for example of the huge Shin Buddhist temples Higashi Honganji and Nishi Honganji. In modern times the headquarters of popular new religions such as Tenrikyō, Kurozumikyō, Ōmoto, or of lay Buddhist movements such as Reiyūkai, Risshō Kōseikai and Sōka Gakkai are also, each in their own way, pilgrimage centres with facilities for visits by believers from all over the country, and indeed from abroad. Of particular interest is the long and complex tradition of pilgrimage to mountain centres occupied by the devotional foci of both Shintō and the Buddhist-related practice of mountain asceticism known as Shugendō.[9] Famous examples of such mountains are Mount Ontake in central Japan, and the three linked mountains in Yamagata Prefecture, to the north-west of the country, known as Dewa Sanzan (i.e. Hagurosan, Yudonosan and Gassan) and Hikosan in Kyūshū (the ending -san or -zan means mountain).[10]

Historically, one of the most famous pilgrimages in Japan has been the "Ise-mairi," which means "going up to Ise," Ise Jingū being the grand shrine of greatest national importance in the Shintō consciousness.[11] The phrase "going up," as used here, is simply intended to be a graphic, literal translation for the word *o-mairi* (which usually carries the respect prefix as in *o-meguri*). Ise Jingū itself is situated in flat country, as are many Shintō shrines of overwhelming national importance such as Atsuta or Izumo. The significance of the expression lies therefore in the concept of humbly proceeding "up" to the shrine. The inner shrine building, where the divinity (*kami*) resides, is always raised architecturally. *O-mairi* is one of the fundamental forms of Japanese religious action. It means making a definite point of proceeding to the geographically identifiable point of worship, performing the appropriate actions, which usually include petitionary prayers, and then returning home. The "return" is part of it, completing the action and indicating that one went there, to that spot, to that focus of the sacred.

There is therefore a subtle, overlapping relationship between *o-mairi* and the idea of pilgrimage, not least with the idea of circulatory pilgrimage. Proceeding (or "going up") to the prescribed position before the shrine or temple may involve simply stopping briefly at the side of the road, or taking up a certain position in a room where there is a small shrine. Probably

---

a rather different account of the relations between circuits and "single-line" pilgrimages has been published by Hoshino Eiki (1997).

9. Cf. For example Kubota 1985.
10. These and other mountains have been ascended by the writer for observational purposes.
11. For further information see Nishigaki 1983 and Jingū Shichō (ed. authority) 1979.

most would not regard this as "pilgrimage," except in the case of miniature and abbreviated pilgrimages, but rather, much more straightforwardly as a simple religious action. However, o-mairi may also involve quite a long journey, perhaps taking a whole day or even several days, and this would immediately be recognized by observers as a pilgrimage. A visit to one major shrine or temple, or to the top of a particular sacred mountain, is a uni-directional pilgrimage. There is one goal. After the central goal has been visited, and the appropriate ritual actions carried out, the pilgrim retraces his or her steps to withdraw into the secular world and return home. Circulatory pilgrimages on the other hand include the repeated performance of o-mairi at a series of goals and hence are described as o-meguri, which implies going round. Each particular visit has its own conclusion, in that the pilgrim withdraws to the secular world to continue the journey to the next temple. But the overall journey has several, even many goals. Sometimes the visits to the numbered temples are performed in convenient batches, and so this provides an opportunity to interrupt the process of pilgrimage temporarily. During such an interruption, the pilgrim is not a pilgrim. However, he or she remains a pilgrim in the interstices when the pilgrimage is carried out in a continuous manner. Final completion, and the concluding return, is only effected after all of the visits.

There are some in-between cases, and hence the vocabulary in use may float by free association. Consider for example the fascinating Mount Hiko in northern Kyūshū, which has just been mentioned. At the base of the mountain is a large shrine complex which can be reached by rail and road. After passing through various symbolic gates (torii), the visitor or pilgrim proceeds up a steep path to the top. The central, highest peak has a Shintō shrine at the summit described as the "main shrine" (honsha). However, there are several peaks. On the lesser peaks, and at various points on the mountain paths, are other places where religious practice or devotion may be offered. Approached from afar, the mountain is most easily understood as having the character of a single-site, uni-directional pilgrimage. Even on arrival at the foot of the mountain, the main onward route is clear, though it may appear arduous. However the additional possibilities of this multiple mountain have been developed over the centuries so that it is easy to conceive of performing o-meguri around its various attractions. For this reason the title of a traditional guide map reads: Hikosan yama-meguri annai, that is, "Guide to the mountain meguri of Hikosan."[12] In all probability the idea of "going round" to various places on this mountain site arose because it was used by Shugendō adepts (yamabushi), who sought out difficult areas for their ascetic routines. The map contains some indications to this effect, even though it was published in 1941, at a time when the Shintō nature of religious sites was being emphasized. The basic distinc-

---

12. Author's collection.

Introduction

tion between uni-directional and multi-centred pilgrimage is nevertheless clear enough, as may be seen from the current existence of a sign-pole about half way up the mountain, near the main shrine and the Shugendō buildings, which advertises this site as Number One of a "Kyūshū Saikoku" pilgrimage, indicating a circulatory pilgrimage of thirty-three temples devoted to Kannon-sama on the model of the Saikoku pilgrimage. This sign leads away from Hikosan itself.

Sacred places, especially Buddhist ones, are referred to in Japan as *reijō* 霊場, a term which simply means "spiritual places," but implies places with spiritual power. Such places usually have their foundational story or *engi* 縁起. Literally, *engi* means "the origin of the connection" or "the origin of the affinity," just as an *ennichi* is an "affinity day," a specific date in each month on which a temple is especially to be visited. The *engi* may recount a story of salvation, the discovery of a miracle-working statue, or the appearance of a bodhisattva. However merely because a site is religiously special and is consequently provided with a temple or shrine, it does not automatically become part of a pilgrimage route. Nor does visiting such a place necessarily amount to a pilgrimage at all. It may after all lie in the immediate vicinity of most of those who visit it, in other words, it may be a part of their normal habitat. By contrast, as will be seen in a definition provided below, a pilgrimage takes one *out of* one's normal habitat.

Various theories of pilgrimage

Pilgrimage has been studied in various perspectives which cannot all be reviewed in detail. While the presentation below is based on personal experience in the field it is also quite impossible to be completely impervious to the effects of positions taken by others in various publications and specialized seminars. On the other hand the literature today is so vast, that any attempt to discuss it could easily lead into a work on the history of the subject, instead of what is intended. Let it suffice therefore to mention just a few well-known orientations in order to set off the approach which is taken here.

First, many have found the work of Victor and Edith Turner on pilgrimage in Christian contexts to be extremely stimulating, in which a central role is played by the concepts of "liminality" and "*communitas*" (Turner and Turner 1978). These are sociological concepts which both have a wider relevance than to pilgrimage alone. In fact, the concept of liminality was originally used by Arnold van Gennep (1960, first edition 1908) to refer to a temporary stage in any rituals which involve a change of social status, of which there are many. It may also be questioned whether the creation of a special sense of community or *communitas* shared by pilgrims who are somehow suspended from the strains of ordinary life is really so different from that shared by other groups of people who get excited by sporting events or rave gatherings. Even if similar, the sense of common identity in pilgrimage, at least in many cases and in modern times, is often weaker than in some such contexts. Admittedly in some cases it is very strong, as in the Muslim pilgrimage to Mecca. Japanese pilgrims often travel in groups, which strengthens their corporate identity, though conceptually there is also room for the individual pilgrim or for people travelling two by two. Creative of *communitas* is the distinctive clothing usually worn by pilgrims travelling in groups, but also often by individuals, of which more details will be given later. The temporary otherness of the pilgrims is recognized on Shikoku by the inhabitants of the island in the concept of *settai*, which means offering small gifts of provisions to pilgrims. *Settai* seems to have had a certain practical importance in earlier times, as recorded in Alfred Bohner's descriptions from the early twentieth century,[13] but nowadays it is little more than an occasional gesture to be enjoyed now and then, a symbol which shows recognition of the pilgrim's identity, and respect for it.

Compared with other activities which create *communitas*, pilgrimage is nowadays a relatively serious affair. It is costly. It takes up time in which one could have done something else. In some cases it may provide exercise, relaxation and even fun, but more important seems to be the reaping of the expected benefits, whether they are "this-worldly" ones, or whether they are seen in the perspective of some kind of personal spiritual development, even in the form of the attainment of heightened spiritual powers. A necessary corrective has therefore been provided by René Gothóni in his writings on pilgrimage in relation to Mount Athos in Greece which highlight the individual transformatory process or at least the possibility of such. Writing in a much wider comparative perspective, he concludes among other things that "the journey—the transformative phase between departure and return—provides a period of reflection, during which the pilgrim mirrors and reviews his life, perceives the discrepancy between precept and practice, and begins to long to bridge the gap."[14] This may not fit the case of Japanese pilgrims exactly, but the possibility of individual spiritual development or transformation is certainly an aspect to be taken seriously.

Second, considerable attention has been paid in recent years to the relation between pilgrimage and commercialized tourism.[15] This is of

---

13. Bohner, Alfred: *Wallfahrt zu Zweien*, Tokyo 1931.

14. Gothóni 2000, page 145. See also Gothóni 1994, especially the section entitled "Pilgrimage as a transformation journey" on pages 189ff.

15. Cf. Reader 1987, Hoffmann 2004, and many occasional journalistic references. The theme was documented by the present writer in an exhibition of relevant maps and posters at the University of Marburg, Germany in 2002 under the title "Religion and

Introduction

course a perfectly valid perception, although while this feature is ever-present in some sense, it is pertinent to ask *why* it is thought to be interesting. The reason may lie in a strong juxtaposition of images which in the popular mind apparently conflict. On the one hand there is the rather idealized view of pilgrims who wander around the mountains barefoot in special clothes which symbolize a temporary state of "death" and hence scorn public transport. On the other hand there is the recognition that people in ordinary life simply set about going on a pilgrimage much as they would set out on any other journey. If, as a Muslim, you want to go on the pilgrimage to Mecca, you have to get an appropriate flight ticket from your country, and it will probably be more economical and less complicated to go with a group. This is not to say that the preparatory devotions and meetings are not important. But some aspects of the enterprise are coterminous with the travel arrangements for other purposes. Exactly the same applies to pilgrimage in Japan. Why should a pilgrimage journey, in this age, be organized any differently than a journey to a series of cultural sites in Korea or China, or a trip round three or four European capitals to admire the buildings and do some shopping? Naturally the *intention* might be different, and one will not expect to find a Mitsukoshi department store at the top of every little mountain which has a Buddhist temple on it. The precise nature of the facilities in which one gets to clean one's teeth, to bathe, and to perform other bodily functions, will also be different in these various situations. On the other hand, while the practicalities are interesting, it is surely the *intentions* which are of central importance. So perhaps we should not be too carried away by the recognition that pilgrimages may be arranged for groups, and are widely marketed just like other travel. Pilgrimages have to be organized somehow from the practical point of view, and they therefore imply some kind of calculation about the time and money involved. These practical matters are important for most persons in ordinary life. Just because they are considered realistically it does not follow that the persons concerned are somehow not intending to go on a genuine pilgrimage, that is, a pilgrimage which is somehow meaningful for them.

A third important area is the way in which theoreticians have come to regard "sacred space." This has long been important in the older phenomenology of religion[16] and has recently been taken up again in connection with the concept of "locality."[17] It is also a matter of great

---

travel culture in Japan / Religion und Reisekultur." Similar items were provided for an exhibition in Berlin entitled *Japan Reiseland* (Pye 2000).

16. For a historic landmark, though the material is brief, see Mircea Eliade 1959 (previously in French and German).

17. Cf. Knott 2005.

general interest for the study of Japanese religions.[18] As has already been pointed out, there is a complex interplay, in Japan, between single goal and multiple goal pilgrimages. In addition there is the most interesting question of the way in which concepts of pilgrimage contribute to the development of regional identities and ultimately to an overall sense of location within the "Japanese archipelago" (*nippon rettō*). This latter concept is treated with great reverence by publishers and politicians alike and functions rather like a late equivalent to the pre-war notion of *kokutai* meaning "national entity" or if taken quite literally "national body," referring to the whole of Japan, physically.[19] A similar line of thought was advanced by Surinder Mohan Bhardwaj for India where, he argues, various pilgrimages conspire to create a greater symbolic whole, as suggested in the pilgrimage section of the *Mahābhārata*.[20] The pilgrimages considered here do not directly contribute to the *kokutai* concept, but they play an important role in structuring the sense of place to which most Japanese people feel they belong in regional and trans-regional terms.

In this perspective account may be taken of wider theoretical reflections on contemporary Japanese religion, and in particular of the way in which concepts of sacred space are built up in network-like patterns across the country. Two particular terms which sum up this process are *interlacement* and *superimposition.* "Interlacement" means first of all that both Buddhist temples and Shintō shrines may be associated in groups or chains across the country, often in a senior-junior denominational relationship. But there is more to it. In many specific cases one pilgrimage goal is also part of another series of goals. Thus a particular Buddhist route may add a major Shintō shrine such as Ise Jingū or Izumo Taisha to the beginning or the end, just as pilgrims around the Shikoku 88 like to add Mount Kōya to their journey as a spiritual home for Shingon Buddhism. Moreover some major Buddhist temples function as number so-and-so of more than one route, a dramatic case being the temple Shitennōji, in modern Ōsaka, which is often included because it is the place where Buddhism was first set up in Japan. "Superimposition" means that the reasons for proceeding to any particular place are multiple, for the simple reason that the dominant occupancy of a notable site has changed hands in the course of time. Many Buddhist temples are located on hills or mountains which were previously regarded as the residence of mysterious spirits, and at the level of popular faith

---

18. I have regularly explored the use of space as one of five key concepts in the general phenomenology of contemporary Japanese religions (e.g. 1996, 2004, 2009).
19. For a translation of the ideological work *Kokutai no hongi* see Gauntlett and Hall 1974.
20. Bhardwaj 1973.

Introduction

these are still regarded as powerful and deserving of occasional visitation. At the time of the ideologically enforced separation of Buddhism and Shintō in the nineteenth century new Shintō buildings appeared where previously Buddhist temples or image halls had stood. The small island of Chikubushima in Lake Biwa has seen a seesaw between Shintō and Buddhism for the claims of the goddess Benzaiten, famous also on other islands, while it is often visited because of the Kannon Hall which is at Temple Number 30 of the Saikoku Thirty-three.[21] The terms interlacement and superimposition are therefore commended as summary reminders of these complexities and in that sense as heuristically valuable theoretical terms.

The observations presented below are of course also supplemented by a certain amount of information drawn from secondary sources in Japanese and other languages. Particularly interesting, after I had already visited Shikoku myself, was the discovery of Alfred Bohner's fine, detailed account of the Shikoku Pilgrimage entitled *Wallfahrt zu Zweien* (i.e. "Two on a Pilgrimage"), published in Tokyo in 1931. The "two" who are here on pilgrimage together are the pilgrim at any one time and the religious leader Kōbō Daishi (774–835), who is thought by pilgrims to be present with them in spirit and is symbolized by their pilgrim's staff. Bohner's work provides a valuable historical perspective in view of the major political and social changes of the intervening decades. In fact, apart from the radical and still increasing motorization of the pilgrimage, it is remarkable how consistent its main features have remained. Students may find it instructive to compare Bohner's work with an anthropologically oriented, if rather personal account of the Shikoku pilgrimage by Ian Reader which has been published recently.[22] Excellent research has also been carried out on historical and textual materials relating to the Shikoku pilgrimage by Nathalie Kouamé.[23]

Most Japanese publications on pilgrimage turn out to be promotional guidebooks or the personal musings of journalists and general writers, of which there are very many. These may be regarded as part of the phenomenon itself, and the bibliography below includes a selection only. Independent contemporary documentation and valuable statistics are

---

21. Documented and analysed in "Buddhism and Shintō on one island" in: Pye, *Strategies in the Study of Religions, Volume Two: Religions in Relation and Motion* (de Gruyter, Berlin 2012).
22. *Making Pilgrimages. Meaning and Practice in Shikoku* Honolulu 2005. Reader has also explored various facets of the social organization of pilgrimage, relations between pilgrimage and travel, and so on in a series of articles, details of which can be found in his own bibliography.
23. E.g. Kouamé 1997, and in particular *Pèlerinage et société dans le Japon des Tokugawa: Le pèlerinage de Shikoku entre 1598 et 1868* (Paris 2001).

found above all in two recently published works by Satō Hisamitsu, one of which is sociological in orientation and one of which is fitted into the very strong Japanese tradition of "folklore" studies.[24] Valuable documentation is also prepared for occasional exhibitions on the subject in leading centres under such titles as "The thirty-three places of Saikoku –faith and beauty of the spiritual places of Kannon" or "Worshipping Kannon: Treasures from the Thirty-three Pilgrimage Sites of Western Japan."[25] In both of these cases particular attention was paid less to the pilgrimage as such than to statues, paintings and calligraphies of high artistic merit which cannot usually be seen by the pilgrims themselves when they are en route. The work by Hoshino mentioned above is a little unusual, for Japan, in encouraging consideration of Japanese pilgrimage in the context of pilgrimages worldwide. In general, questions for the comparative study of pilgrimage which arise because of the circulatory character of Japanese Buddhist pilgrimage have not yet been carefully discussed. It is most desirable that these be taken into account in the wider theory of pilgrimage.

In general, the present work is not intended to be read as falling into the category of ethnology, folk-lore or art history, or indeed of any particular discipline other than the study of religions. In this discipline, the appropriate methods are drawn together or clustered, and the theoretical terminology developed in accordance with its appropriateness to the subject matter.[26]

Defining and understanding pilgrimage

A general definition of pilgrimage may be formulated as follows:

Pilgrimage is the deliberate traversing of a route to a sacred place which lies outside one's normal habitat.

On this definition, the nature of pilgrimage, as distinct from simply visiting a special or holy place such as a local shrine or church, lies as much in the *way* as in the goal.[27] This is not always immediately obvious, for it is common when considering pilgrimage to emphasize the goal,

---

24. 2004 and 2006.

25. Tōbu Art Museum at Ikebukuro (Tokyo) and Kyōto Museum of Culture (see Tōbubijutsukan 1996); and at Nara National Museum and Nagoya City Museum (see Nara Kokuritsu Hakubutsukan 2008).

26. This underlying disciplinary orientation is set out in my article entitled "Methodological integration in the study of religions" (1999) republished in *Strategies in the Study of Religions, Volume One: Approaches and Positions* 2012.

27. This and the following general observations about the nature of pilgrimage are based on the dictionary entry (composed by the present writer) in the *Macmillan Dictionary of Religion* (London 1993).

Introduction

the sacred place of aspiration. We think of Mecca, Jerusalem, the Basilica of the Mexican Virgin of Guadalupe, Lourdes, Mount Kailash, Lhasa, and many other places which attract the religious traveller. The very names seem to sum it all up. Yet the destination is not itself the pilgrimage. The pilgrim *sets out* with an aspiration to reach a place, or indeed places, which is or are other than his or her starting point. For this reason pilgrims are often depicted, quite rightly, as being *en route*.

The importance of the *route* or the *way* may be judged from two of its effects on reflection about pilgrimage. The first is the use of the pilgrimage theme in literature, whether overtly religious or other. It is because of the significance of the way, rather than the destination, that pilgrimage can be used metaphorically for journeys which have no known geographical goal at their end, for journeys of intention and faith, or for the journey of life itself. The second is the attention which has been drawn to the separation of pilgrims from ordinary daily life through ritual preparations, special clothing and the choice of a prescribed route, and to a special relationship of equality which they enjoy, at least in principle, with fellow pilgrims. These two features correspond to the widely used terms "liminality" and "communitas" mentioned above. Thus both literature and sociological analysis have borne witness to the primacy of the way over the goal for an understanding of the phenomenology of pilgrimage. This in turn brings out further, secondary characteristics of pilgrimage. Three are particularly striking.

First the way is often difficult and in economic terms costly. For this reason merit, or to phrase it less doctrinally and more generally, value, is associated with its completion. In fact the way may be so arduous and dangerous that the pilgrim never returns. A compensatory religious value may be assigned to dying while on pilgrimage, as is frequently noted in the case of the Islamic *hajj* or the Hindu concept of pilgrimage to Benares. Yet paradoxically, precisely because it is difficult and should be completed if possible, a pilgrimage is often purposely made easier by the provision of roads, airports, special trains and other arrangements, and in many cases by the provision of alternative pilgrimages and abbreviated pilgrimages. *Abbreviation* is particularly common in the Japanese context as will be seen below. Even the standard route is improved, facilitated, quickened, shortened. Japanese Buddhist pilgrims are nowadays much more likely to travel at considerable expense by minibus or taxi than to go on foot. This all shows that the actual covering of the route is more important than its degree of difficulty. Difficulty and expense, which are weighed against each other, are secondary to the *de facto* traversing and completion of the pilgrim's way.

Second, although the way is important in itself, not every pilgrim goes the same way in detail. For example, there are several ways to Santiago de Compostela, and yet all of them are *the* way to Compostela. It depends on the starting point. Pilgrims from various countries follow routes appropriate to them until these are united in the landscape of northern Spain to form the one way which, ideally, they always were. The same is true of the Islamic *hajj*. Pilgrims come from every direction, from all over the world, and yet they are all travelling on the same way, namely the way to Mecca.²⁸ This is not just a casual transfer of meaning; for the direction of Mecca is indicated architecturally by the *mahrib* in every Muslim's local mosque. Looking at it more individually, every pilgrim sets out from a starting point in ordinary life, the "normal habitat" of the definition given above. This is different for each person, but while proceeding on the appointed journey he or she is drawn increasingly into a recognized form of the pilgrim's way. The practical reasons for this are rapidly overlaid with the increasing recognition, through the convergence of the ways, that his or her way is indeed *the* way which was intended from the start. There is a special variant on this feature in Japanese Buddhist pilgrimage in that the temples visited are normally supposed to be visited in a certain order, following the numbers 1–33 or 1–88, as shown on the maps and signposts. However, as later details will illustrate, it is acceptable to vary this order for practical reasons, or even to pursue it in reverse (*gyaku-mawari*). It still counts as the same pilgrimage.

Third, it is quite common for a pilgrimage to end with some sign or proof that it has in fact been carried out. Something which carries the power of the holy place may be brought back home for others, holy water to bring healing or an amulet for the protection of relatives. Similarly, the outside wall of Muslim houses in Egypt may be proudly painted with a picture of the Ka'aba housing the Black Stone, indicating that a family member has successfully completed the pilgrimage to Mecca. The Japanese Buddhist pilgrim returns with the calligraphically ornamented "seals" of all the temples visited. These are inked on to the pilgrim's shirt, into a folding booklet specially made for the purpose or, most expensively, on to a hanging scroll which can be displayed later. Naturally such symbols, in any particular religion, reflect the special nature or power of the sacred place visited. Yet equally they prove *completion* of the route itself. Consequently, returning, unless one dies *en route*, is part of the going. In unifocal pilgrimages, arriving at the goal is in one sense the climax of the journey as a whole, but the proofs brought back

---

28. This is important for Sunni and Shi'ite alike. For an informative and otherwise simply fabulous example of a pilgrimage narrative from Tehran to Mecca, and the return, see Mirzâ Moḥammad Ḥosayn Farâhâni's *Safarnâmeh* (translated by Farmayan and Daniel 1990). The author's dates are 1847–1912, his pilgrimage covered 1885 and 1886 and his narrative is filled with contemporary observations of all kinds.

Introduction

on the return journey show that this arrival is not quite the end. Rather, arrival at the special holy place provides a central symbolic focus for the overall, integrated pilgrim's journey, which still needs to be completed by the homeward journey to one's normal habitat, bringing the proofs.

The striking characteristic of the Japanese Buddhist pilgrimages is that they have multiple goals. In principle the pilgrimages are conceived as sequential. There is a recommended, numbered sequence, which is usually followed in broad outline. Yet there may be variations and, as noted already, even the possibility of going round in reverse order is entertained. Therefore, bearing in mind that the pilgrims are "going around" the route, possibly with variations in the sequence, the best terms to characterize these pilgrimages are "multifocal" and "circulatory." Comprehensive completion of the route is not only more important than visiting any one goal but is also more important than the recommended and preferred order. The aim is to visit each and every one of the prescribed temples.

This distinction may be illustrated by what may be the closest parallel to multi-focal pilgrimage outside Buddhism, namely the following of the Stations of the Cross as a Christian devotion. This is usually set up in a relatively limited space, either within a church building around the walls of the nave, or on a small hill dedicated to "a calvary" (in France, *un calvaire*). This brief, meditational pilgrimage is clearly sequential, for it follows the path of Christ's last journey to his crucifixion, the *via dolorosa*. Fourteen steps or "stations" are differentiated, following events in the Passion narrative and leading to Christ's death on the cross (12th station), his being taken down from the cross (13th station) and his entombment (14th station).[29] The stations are usually indicated by a picture, or a sculpted relief, before which devotions are carried out. In a particularly interesting case in Tlaxcala, Mexico, the "stations" are found at the sides of a road going up a steep hill which leads to the very impressive cathedral, providing an ascending sequence. In fact there are more than fourteen stations in this case because the stations of the cross are combined with devotions to the Virgin Mary. However, since the church at the top forms a final goal in its own right, the little Tlaxcala pilgrimage is not circulatory. The same applies generally to calvaries mounted on small hills, for these culminate in the crucifix at the top. If anything, the Stations of the Cross are closer to being "circulatory" when set up within a church building, for typically they lead first along one side of the nave

---

29. Sometimes a fifteenth station shows the resurrection, but this is secondary, because the stations of the cross are usually used in Holy Week and particularly on Good Friday, so that the appropriate end is in the entombment. There are also non-Catholic versions with less stations, designed in attempt to follow more closely the narratives of the New Testament.

and then back along the other side, not being focused at the main altar. These cases show that the development of a sequence can easily occur on the basis of a pattern which has been established in order to encourage individual or corporate devotions.

Another interesting parallel may be seen in an ecumenical initiative in Bavaria, Germany, at Scheidegg in the Allgäu region. In 2002 a Protestant minister and his wife, together with a Catholic priest in the neighboorhood, inspired like many others in recent years by the pilgrimage to Compostela,[30] decided to link together a number of chapels in a "path of reflection." The chapels each have their own story and appear to be of equal importance, so that this could be regarded as an example of circulatory pilgrimage. Moreover, the chapels can all be visited in a single day, and this was regarded as an advantage over distant pilgrimages which require much effort such as the road to Compostela. We can see from this example that religiosity which captures the imagination can easily lead to new initiatives and that circulatory pilgrimage is not intrinsically related to any one religious culture, though it is rare outside Japan.

The Oxford Diocese of the Church of England has recently promoted the idea of going on pilgrimage to fifteen different churches which all have historic associations of various kinds. The list begins with the church of St. Peter ad Vincula (St. Peter in chains) and concludes with Christ Church Cathedral and the University Church of St. Mary the Virgin. The Bishop of Oxford writes:

> People have always gone on journeys to enrich their spiritual lives. The desire seems to be deeply ingrained in human nature. Pilgrimages nurture and sustain our inner life, our 'sacred centre.' I hope you'll use this map to help you find your way to a handful of the many wonderful sacred places within our diocese.[31]

Though the various churches are numbered and also shown with these numbers on a map, there is no particular emphasis on the sequence as

---

30. A case is known to me where a non-Catholic woman in her later years simply walked from her home in Germany to Compostela and back, twice. Indeed, hiking to Compostela has become quite popular in recent years and is not at all restricted to Catholics. There is evidence, reported at an exhibition of the Ōsaka National Museum of Ethnology in 2007, that many who begin this journey as an interesting adventure eventually come to view it as a journey of personal discipline and self-discovery.

31. Bishop John Pritchard, quoted in a pamphlet about the fifteen churches available in 2012. He also provides a prayer for pilgrims which begins: "Pilgrim God, you are our origin and our destination. Travel with us, we pray, in every pilgrimage of faith, and every journey of the heart. Give us the courage to set off, the nourishment we need to travel well, and the welcome we long for at our journey's end. So may we grow in grace and love for you and in the service of others, through Jesus Christ our Lord, Amen."

Introduction

such and also no obvious way of recording the visits. As yet, in spite of occasional suggestions,[32] there is no explicitly linked pilgrimage to the various great cathedrals of England (Canterbury, Ely, Salisbury and so on), which could conceivably amount to a chain of growing spiritual experience, perhaps spread over considerable time. In general, pilgrimage in Christianity has in fact been of the single goal variety, as in such cases as Canterbury, Compostela, Marburg, Lourdes. and so on.

Another extremely interesting example of linked pilgrimage sites is found in the context of Islam, namely in the practice of performing "visits" (*ziarah*) to the tombs of the Nine Walis in Java, Indonesia. These *wali* are Muslim leaders who are revered for having introduced and established Islam in Java, thus being, in anthropological language, culture heroes. In the dominant understanding of Islam a distinction is made between the *hajj* to Mecca, for which the English word "pilgrimage" is often reserved, and devotional "visits" to other places, as in this case. The Nine Walis (known in Javanese as the Walisongo) are associated with different parts of the island of Java, but there is considerable interest in visiting all of their tombs for devotional purposes. No particular sequence is required, but in so far as the Nine Walis are regarded as a unit, we might see here a case of a multifocal pilgrimage rather than one which leads to a single goal. By considering these deeply rooted examples from Christian and Muslim contexts, the slightly different character of the circulatory pilgrimages in Japanese Buddhism comes out all the more clearly.

The altogether clearest example of the importance of the *way* or the *route* is to be found in the circulatory Buddhist pilgrimages of Japan, for here the task lies in completing the path to multiple goals, for example the 33 temples of the bodhisattva Kannon-sama. There is no single, central goal which lies somewhere beyond the way to be traversed. Rather, the goal is, so to speak, dispersed throughout the way.[33] This state of affairs leads imperceptibly on into the more mystical interpretations of Mahāyāna Buddhism, in which it is not necessary to distinguish between the way and the goal at all. Such paradoxical identifications are based on a dialectic between differentiated characteristics, in this case of "a way" and the view that phenomena are ultimately "empty" of such characteristics. This underlying thought, well known to students of the Mahāyāna (meaning "Great Vehicle") will reappear at various points below, especially in the concluding chapter. Interestingly enough, the profound collapse of this distinction between the way and the goal also occurs in the popular, convenient, miniature forms of Buddhist pilgrimage. When such a pilgrimage can be completed in one small area in an hour, or even

---

32. Made informally by the present writer.
33. Cf. *O-Meguri, Pilgerfahrt in Japan* (Pye 1987), where this was clearly set out.

in a few minutes, it seems fair to say that the goal has become identified with the way in practice, as well as in mystical comprehension!

Although the pilgrim's way is emphasized here, in order to bring out something of the structure of pilgrimage, the goals as conventionally perceived are of course also quite significant in the pilgrims' own consciousness. The point is that they tell us less about the general character of pilgrimage. This is, firstly, because they share characteristics, as sacred places, with many other religious foci which themselves are not really the object of pilgrimage in a precise sense. Many places which are visited or attended for religious reasons are in the immediate habitat of those concerned and thus do not require a journey with special characteristics. If I pay a short visit to a temple just down the road, for example to visit a cemetery, this does not really amount to a pilgrimage in a special sense. Secondly, the features of the goals of pilgrimage are more varied than some of the truly common features of pilgrimage. One need think only of the immense diversity presented by sacred cities such as Jerusalem, Lhasa, Tenri, or Auroville, by mausolea such as Konya, Sanchi or Westminster Abbey, by special objects such as the Black Stone at Mecca, or the innumerable places where visions and healings have been experienced such as Lourdes. As for Japanese pilgrimage destinations, these too have their many particular reasons for being what they are. Every Buddhist temple and every Shintō shrine has its *raison d'être*, usually summed up, as mentioned above, in a short traditional statement called an *engi*. Buddhist temples in the same circulatory pilgrimage route all have their own various reasons for being special. It would be tempting to attempt a systematic typology of the *goals* of pilgrimage, and no doubt this would have some interest. However the typology of sacred places as goals does not itself disclose the character of pilgrimage and therefore will not be pursued here in any detail.

Indirectly, and conversely, the diversity of the goals itself sheds further light on the importance of *the route* to the various sites. In not a few cases, one religion displaces an older tradition at the same sacred spot, as happened very notably at Mecca, and in other cases the sacred destinations have dual occupancy, e.g. Kataragama in Sri Lanka, Mount Kailash in the Himalayas, the hotly disputed Ayodhya in northern India, or Chalma in Mexico. People go to these places not only because of the goal, but partly because of the power of the route in the popular memory. At Chalma in Mexico, where there is nowadays a substantial Catholic church, I have witnessed the arrival into the nave of a surging procession of *campesino* pilgrims (i.e. from the indigenous rural population) who showed total disregard for the officiating priest. They had evidently been travelling for quite some time without washing facilities, so that many other visitors quickly left the church. The priest did his

Introduction

Figure 1.3 Notice showing combined approach to Nachi Shrine and Saikoku Temple No. 1.

best to continue with the liturgy, practically ignoring the sudden influx of pilgrims, but it seemed a hopeless task as two conflicting patterns of activity clashed on the same sacred spot.[34] This shows that the pressure to carry out pilgrimage, once this is learned behaviour in a particular region, can continue regardless of which religion is currently dominant in power terms. The drive to traverse the way remains a powerful force, regardless of what has happened to the goal.

Both dual occupancy and displacement can be documented at pilgrimage sites in Japan. The first temple in the great Saikoku Pilgrimage, Seigantoji, which is certainly and distinctly Buddhist, nestles right against the famous Shintō shrine near the waterfall of Nachi. The visitor who climbs the hill can proceed to either of these quite easily. It is only for the very last part of a lengthy climb that the temple and the shrine have their separate approach paths, one being marked by the *torii* typical of a Shintō shrine and the other having the more general character of steps up to a Buddhist temple. Having visited either one at the top of the hill, however, it is a simple matter to slip through a side gate to pay one's respects at the other place. Most visitors do this.

---

34. The dual occupancy is referred to by Turner and Turner (1978), but the contestation is not described. Another fascinating example of syncretistic tension in Latin American pilgrimage, this time in Peru, was described by Renate Stegerhoff (1990).

Such dual occupancy may seem natural to those familiar with the relative tolerance between religions for which Japan is known. Indeed it was considerably more common before the officially enforced separation of Shintō from Buddhism in the late nineteenth century. Displacement is by its very nature less obvious. This applies to cases where Buddhist pilgrimage temples on the main pilgrimage routes are located at the top of hills or small mountains which had previously been sacred sites in their own right. Thus the effective displacement of local divinities by Kannon-sama or other Buddhist divinities is not at all unknown, even though it may not fit the common stereotype of religious tolerance.

In sum, the circulatory Buddhist pilgrimages of Japan share many of the characteristics of pilgrimage as known elsewhere. However, because the way predominates over the goal, these characteristics can be seen with particular clarity.

Materials and methods

A few words may be added about the source materials and research methods underlying this presentation. Above all it is based on personal observation, and to a considerable extent on *participant* observation. This was a time-consuming activity which also included numerous conversations with pilgrims. Apart from carrying out selected pilgrimages, visits were made to innumerable Buddhist temples, Shintō shrines and other religious sites with a direct or indirect bearing on the subject, and in almost every case some form of religious activity was observed.

Before commenting further on these two obvious forms of approach, attention may be also drawn to a particularly important source of information, namely a fascinating range of ephemeral artefacts, many of which bear some kind of written indication of a pilgrim's provenance and intention.[35] These ephemera include route-maps and brochures which tell the pilgrims where to go, how to get there, how much it costs, and how long it will take. Of direct religious significance are the votive tablets and the pilgrims' slips (*o-fuda* お札) deposited at the temples, which may be examined in their thousands. This vast array of information cannot be studied on the spot comprehensively, not least because of the time factor, but on the other hand much of it is publicly visible and can be photographed. This material provides a mass of documentation on the attitudes and intentions of pilgrims. The particular impor-

---

35. As explained in "Philology and fieldwork in the study of Japanese religion" (Pye 1990) and "Philology, fieldwork and ephemera in the study of Japanese religions" in *Strategies* (Pye 2012). The study of ephemera requires philological expertise, and a division of studies of religion into philological studies and field-based studies is, except in particular contexts where the relevant materials and options are not available, completely artificial.

Introduction

tance of such ephemera in the study of contemporary Japanese religions is threefold. First, all of these varied ephemera are so numerous that they come to assume a quantitative value.[36] Second, they have a real function in particular situations, unlike the published books which, while apparently helpful to scholars, may not be widely read by others. Third, ephemera amount to an independent material source which is not disturbed as a source of information by the incidental characteristics of face-to-face encounters between observers and informants. In sum therefore, the methodological importance of ephemera in the study of Japanese religions, including pilgrimage, lies in the fact that they provide a quantitatively significant source which is not affected by the vagaries of personal interaction. An exhibition in Marburg in 1987 was largely based on such artefacts,[37] and it was during the development of that exhibition that the organizing concepts "route, transaction and meaning" emerged as a convenient framework of analysis and representation, as in the structure of this book. In other words, these most valuable ephemera provided the raw materials out of which it was possible to develop a very stable theoretical understanding.

This is not to say that hearing what the pilgrims have to say in person is not important. Of course it is. In spite of a confessed predilection for artefacts, the author has had many conversations (in Japanese) with pilgrims on the various pilgrimage routes. Typically, conversations were initiated with the simplest greeting or a very general, polite question, and then followed the preferred vocabulary of the pilgrims themselves. In other words, the first task was to get the pilgrims, who after all were in the middle of a tight schedule, to talk in their own terms about what they were doing. Systematic questioning is a little difficult in that the pilgrims are usually under pressure because of their shared transport arrangements. Again, when the pilgrims are in groups they may be reluctant to reveal private motivations in front of others, even when they know each other well. In spite of such difficulties it may be said that the overall picture gained is really quite stable. The questions addressed again and again to pilgrims were about their intentions and hopes in undertaking the pilgrimage. The answers received were not only consistent to the point of predictability, but corresponded clearly, convinc-

---

36. That is, ephemera provide a bridge not only between "philology" and fieldwork, but also between qualitative and quantitative research, which are often unnecessarily counterposed. Cf. the discussion in Pye and Triplett 2007, 169–177.
37. This is the exhibition referred to above under the title *O-Meguri, Pilgerfahrt in Japan* (1987). It included photographs, maps, guides, votive tablets and other artefacts. Many additional materials have been gathered, and a new temporary exhibition was opened in 2009 (in collaboration with Katja Triplett) which focused on the hanging scrolls used in pilgrimage (see *Pilgerfahrt Visuell*, Pye and Triplett 2011).

ingly and repeatedly to the range of intentions, aspirations or prayers evidenced on the pilgrims' slips, votive tablets and other ephemera.

In the field the researcher naturally wishes to go round the pilgrimage in person. It is easy to get into the mood. Going round a complete route or routes is certainly something which the researcher should experience, but there are also other considerations. It should be remembered that simply going round the route actually *reduces* the number of different pilgrims whom one is likely to meet, simply because in any one day it is likely that one will meet the same people at the next temple, and so on. This can of course be valuable in itself, in that personal acquaintanceships can be developed which may lead to more illuminating conversations. It is indeed interesting to speak with the same people at different stages of their journey. Moreover, by going round the pilgrimage from beginning to end, one gets a direct feel for the physical operation which is required. For this reason, in 1985 and 1987, I went round the Chichibu circuit of 34 stations. Admittedly this is a relatively short route, but in this case it was done on foot and by bicycle. On the other hand, when I visited the great route of 88 stations on the island of Shikoku in 1983, although I performed sections of the route sequentially, unlike normal pilgrims I elected to stay for several hours at fixed points. This made it possible to question a variety of pilgrims who passed by the same spot one after another. In the case of the Saikoku route I was able to complete it temple by temple by combining several opportunites, as is documented by the seals and calligraphy in my own pilgrim's book.

Such observations in the field certainly present a logistical challenge. It may sound odd to speak of logistical difficulties in a country like Japan with its highly developed infrastructure, including its splendid railway systems. However in order to go to all the sites in question it is necessary to follow a complex plan which can only be worked out in detail by taking into account local transport timetables and the limited opening hours of the temples. Buses can take quite a long time to manoeuvre up a series of hills as far as a remote temple, and the posted local timetables may be decorated with little additional symbols in the small print providing many a trap for the unwary. This planning would be made unnecessary by joining an organized pilgrimage group, which itself has some attractions from an investigatory point of view. However the cost of such tours is very high, and one's freedom to spend a longer time in a particular place, for example in interviewing a temple priest, is severely restricted.

Nowadays many Japanese pilgrims go round by car, taxi or minibus, but the main value of imitating this as an observer would lie in making an intensive study of a few individual companions. Experience of such a bus journey in 2010 showed that there is indeed little time left over

Introduction

to take in the mass of incidental material which is so interesting.[38] The sheer expense of pilgrimages done with commercialized transport also means that a very tight schedule has to be kept. Frequently the last walk up to each temple has to be done on foot in any case, and it is in these areas and in various resting places that conversations with or between the pilgrims usually take place.

Finally it may be emphasized that the detailed presentation of Japanese Buddhist pilgrimage below has arisen on the basis of long-term observations in the field. It is in no way an attempt to apply an arm-chair theory from elsewhere. This does not mean that there is no theory; the proper study of religions is always engaged in the development of theory. At the same time, the theoretical reflections proposed in this introduction and illustrated step by step in the chapters below have been informed and led by observations, and not the other way round.

---

38. This was a journey to Numbers 1–7 of the Shikoku route with which the agency hoped to interest pilgrims in making subsequent journeys to the other temples in batches, with a very substantial overall budget. It rained persistently all the time, but this had no influence whatever on the effective performance of the temple visits.

— Chapter Two —

Going Round to Visit Kannon-sama

Saikoku 33—the classic sequence

In this chapter we will take a closer look at some of the most well-known Buddhist circulatory pilgrimage routes in Japan, namely those which focus on the bodhisattva Kannon, or Kanzeon. This is the same celestial buddha-to-be who is widely known in China and among overseas Chinese as Guānyīn or Guānshìyīn, and who goes in the Sanskrit literature and Indian iconography of Buddhism by the name of Avalokiteśvara. The most famous of the Japanese pilgrimage routes devoted to this bodhisattva is that of the Saikoku Thirty-three Spiritual Sites (*Saikoku Sanjūsan Reijō*), and many others are modelled on this one. Some variations on the name of this and related pilgrimages will be found.[1] The Saikoku route has 33 "spiritual sites," i.e. places marked by temples, because according to *The Lotus Sūtra*, a key text of early Mahāyāna Buddhism, the bodhisattva Kanzeon appeared in 33 different forms to save living beings. In fact the iconography at the temples displays a smaller number of different forms, as will be detailed later. Kanzeon or Kannon Bodhisattva was originally conceived as a more or less male figure (as Avalokiteśvara in the Indian context), or a figure of indeterminate gender, but a feminine form developed in China and was carried over to Korea and Japan. She is now popularly known as Kannon-sama in Japan.[2]

The beginnings of the Saikoku pilgrimage are usually traced to two foundational legends, the precise historicity of which however remains

---

1. E.g. Saikoku (or Saigoku) Thirty-three Places (Saikoku Sanjūsankasho, or Saikoku Sanjūsansho), Saikoku Thirty-three Spiritual Sites of Kannon (Saikoku Sanjūsan Kannon Reijō), and so on.
2. For a general account of the early matrix of the Kanzeon faith, see Chapter 4 of *Skilful Means* (Pye 1978, 2003).

Figure 2.1 Modern map of the Saikoku Kannon Pilgrimage.

unclear.[3] Firstly it is said to go back to the activities of a monk named Tokudō Shōnin 徳道上人 (loosely translatable as Saint Tokudō, born 656) who began to pay particular reverence to the bodhisattva Kannon. The traditionally rehearsed narrative is that during an illness in which he was near to death, he encountered in a dream the king over the realm of the dead, Enma-Ō. With the injunction to visit thirty-three places sacred to Kannon-sama, he was released from the critical illness. In the year 718, therefore, he initiated the custom of visiting thirty-three such sites. Tokudō is also remembered as having been the founder of many temples throughout Japan including the well-known Hasedera ("Lotus Temple") in the province of Yamato, which is No. 8 in the series as now known. His mausoleum is located at a temple named Hokki-in 法起院 which he himself had founded in 726.[4] This temple, now administered by the Buzan branch of the Shingon denomination, is in present-day Sakurai City, Nara Prefecture, and is often visited by pilgrims as an extra-numerary (*bangai*) temple in addition to the 33 main sites.

---

3. For a brief assessment see Nara National Museum 2008 and for more detailed study see Hayami 1970, Chapter 3.

4. The above information is distributed by the temple authorities at Hokki-in.

Figure 2.2 Iconic depiction (*miei*)[5] of Tokudō Shōnin, reputed founder of the Saikoku Kannon Pilgrimage.

Tokudō Shōnin's practice apparently failed to establish itself as an uninterrupted tradition, and the practice of visiting multiple sites with their various transformations of Kannon-sama was taken up again by the young Emperor Kazan 花山 (968–1008, reigned 984–986), who for his piety also received the designation of "Dharma King" (*hōō* 法皇). Kazan is revered at a temple known as Gankeiji, located in the Yamashina district of Kyōto, which is also usually listed as one of the extra-numerary (*bangai*) temples for this circuit. Although the founding, or re-founding of the pilgrimage is ascribed to Emperor Kazan, there is no real certainty that he set it up in the precise form in which it later came to be known. Indeed, not all of the temples in question existed during his life time, Yoshiminedera (no. 20) having been founded in 1029, for example. On the other hand, by the Kamakura Period (late twelfth century onwards) the route was well established, even though the precise sequence was not always that of today. It is notable for example that at that period temple no.1 was none other than the Hasedera founded by Tokudō Shōnin. Nevertheless, Kazan's devotion to temples housing Kannon-sama may be said to have established the pilgrimage as something which the aristocratic class of ancient Japan could respectably perform, albeit with considerable effort and no doubt even some danger in the more far-flung areas. Because of this the Saikoku pilgrimage thereafter held

---

5. An "iconic depiction" (*miei* 御影, literally a "respected image") is printed on thin paper and acquired at the temple for commemorative purposes.

its place firmly in the elite Japanese Buddhist imagination, only later becoming democratized and popularized.

The closest and most important imitations of the Saikoku pilgrimage are known as the *Bandō Thirty-three Spiritual Sites* (Bandō Sanjūsan Reijō), which are a widely dispersed string of temples in eastern Japan, and the *Chichibu Thirty-four Spiritual Sites* (Chichibu Sanjūyon Reijō) which are located relatively close to each other in and around the city of Chichibu not far from Tokyo.[6] The literal meaning of the name "Bandō" 坂東 is "to the east of the hills," and in fact the first eight temples are located in what is now Kanagawa Prefecture to the east of Mounts Ashigara and Hakone (Ashigara-yama 足柄山 and Hakone-yama 箱根山), the remainder being located all over the Kantō area in six prefectures, with just one in metropolitan Tokyo. As previously noted, the Chichibu route has thirty-four sites, so that the combined number of temples in the three pilgrimages comes to the round number of one hundred. It is usually considered that the Saikoku Pilgrimage has been established since the Heian Period (794–1185), the Bandō Pilgrimage since the Kamakura Period (1185–1382) and the Chichibu Pilgrimage since the Muromachi Period (1392–1573). The oldest known reference to all three pilgrimages together is on a stone inscription dating from 1525.[7] However little is really known of the actual use of the pilgrimage routes during these older periods. The temples of the Saikoku and Bandō routes are geographically quite far-flung and it seems unlikely that they came into really popular use until the socio-political situation was auspicious and the necessary guide maps were available. As far as is known, the practice of circulatory Buddhist pilgrimage was therefore of limited importance before the Edo Period. It appears to have become a widely recognized religious form, with significant popular participation, in the seventeenth and eighteenth centuries. In the eighteenth century, which was a period of economic cohesion and consumption with relative lack of political strain, there certainly occurred the first major boom in pilgrimage. One author tells us that at Chichibu the number of pilgrims in 1750 far outstripped the local population at that time, possibly reaching some 50,000 in three months.[8] Moreover it was during the Edo Period that further pilgrimage routes were established in various parts of Japan, presumably to meet demand.

---

6. Or Bandō Sanjūsankasho, Chichibu Sanjūyokkasho, etc. The pronunciation Bantō may also be met with, the -tō being the same as that of Tokyo, "the eastern capital."
7. Information assembled by International Research Centre for Japanese Studies, Kyōto (web-site "Nihon Hyaku Kannon 2009).
8. Enbutsu 1990, 25. I have not been able to check these figures independently and the "archives" on which they are based are not identified precisely by the author. The period referred to is from New Year to March 21. The main pilgrimage season is nowadays usually held to run from spring till autumn.

Guide maps of the Saikoku 33 circuit have been preserved from the early eighteenth century, by which time Seigantoji, the Tendai Buddhist temple at Nachi, had established itself as No.1. Previously this position had been claimed not only by Hasedera (Hase Temple, now No. 8) but also by Mimuroto-ji (Mimuroto Temple, now No. 10). The earliest known guide maps of the Bandō 33 circuit cannot be dated before the beginning of the nineteenth century, though by this time printing was already sometimes in colour. However, similar maps of the Chichibu 34 circuit, which presupposes the existence of the Bandō circuit, date from before the middle of the eighteenth century. From these indications, together with the friendly, usable appearance of the maps, the conclusion may be drawn that the idea of going on a pilgrimage was a realistic and pleasurable as well as a religiously significant prospect for the urban population of the mid-Edo period, that is, from at least the eighteenth century onwards. As is often pointed out, it was one of the few reasons for which ordinary people could go on an interesting journey away from their home area.

As it became necessary to publish small guidebooks for the pilgrimages, some of them took the form of the folding book such as those used for sūtras and devotional texts, while others were bound with string at the spine as booklets. It seems likely that the non-folding booklets bound with string, forerunners of the modern guidebooks, were a secondary development. The distinctiveness of each temple, with its varying central object of reverence, was underscored by printing its set "song" (*go-eika*), which mentions some particular associations of the locality or the Buddhist divinity worshipped there. Thus the booklets had the dual purpose of providing this basic information needed at each temple as well as setting out where to go next in the sequence. The folding devotional booklets are still in use and in some cases continue to give similar basic information about each temple. However, any practical function which they once had as guides has now been totally supplanted by the bound versions. These observations apply equally to the Shikoku pilgrimage.

The guidebooks of today are more lavishly printed and increasingly depart from the traditional models. Typically they still include a list of the temples with basic information about them, now usually including a photograph, the song or *go-eika* which should be included in the devotions carried out at each temple, and a map to show its whereabouts in relation to the preceding one and the subsequent one. In addition to the practical guides there is also a genre of travel writing based on the pilgrim routes in which the author gives a narrative account of his or her journey, including personal impressions and reflections. Some may prefer a *manga* version, such as that by Nagatani Kunio (1991), while others are much fuller and more meditative as in Fukuda Tsuneo's *Chichibu junrei hitoritabi* (1981, "The Chichibu pilgrimage—a solitary journey").

Books of this kind provide something to read in advance, or in the evenings when the pilgrims usually have nothing else to do but stay in their lodgings and check the weather forecast. Pilgrimage routes are now also featuring occasionally in guidebooks for foreign tourists under such titles as *Chichibu, Japan's Hidden Treasure*.[9]

In general, with the emphasis shifting from rail to road, transport information has become more important in modern guidebooks. The indication of distances and times between the temples enables the pilgrims, often travelling in a group, to work out how many temples they can fit in within one day before darkness sets in and the temples are closed up. In the days when there were not even railways, the route was provided with small signposts here and there, some of which can still be seen. Even today the final part of the route to the temple, which often has to be traversed on foot, may be helpfully signposted. Sometimes a little "short-cut" is indicated on a wayside marker. These things are a reminder that today's pilgrims, for all the changes in infrastructure, are still following in the tracks of millions who have passed before them.

Before listing the names and other details of the individual temples which make up any particular pilgrimage routes, some general information may be useful about temple names, denominational affiliation, and the iconography of the bodhisattva Kannon-sama herself. This may be skipped by readers familiar with Japanese matters.

First, formally speaking, a Buddhist temple in Japan has two main names, the first ending in -*san* (literally "mountain") and the second ending in -*ji* or -*dera* (meaning "temple" as such). The first is rather like a surname and the second is more like a personal name. Usually it is the second one which is used to designate an individual temple for ordinary purposes, such as pointing out where it is located. The character for -*ji* or -*dera* is the same one: 寺. When pronounced as -*ji*, it corresponds to the Chinese -*sì* (earlier transcribed *ssu* or *szu*) or the Korean -*sa*. The Japanese variant reading -*dera* arises from *tera*, the first consonant being hardened when occuring in a name. The usual Japanese word for "a temple" is therefore *o-tera*, with the honorific prefix, while the colloquial expression for a temple priest is *o-tera-san*, the -*san* being simply the polite suffix used at the end of anybody's name. Within the temple grounds there may be more than one hall, and such halls are usually indicated with the ending -*dō*, as in Kannon-dō, Daishi-dō etc. In a few cases the name of a special sub-temple concludes

---

9. Enbutsu 1990. The book gives a little historical and legendary background on the temples of the Chichibu route with instructions on how to reach them in manageable groups for walkers. The general approach may be seen in the sentence "The use of a taxi or bus is recommended occasionally to eliminate overly long and less interesting hikes, *but the true charm and significance of the pilgrimage lies in walking*." (Page 26, emphasis added.)

Going Round to Visit Kannon-sama

with the term *-in* which conveys the nuance of a retreat, hermitage, or Buddhist home limited to particular persons. Since this suffix begins with a vowel, it is used here with a hyphen to separate it from any preceding vowel, simply for the reader's convenience. In the lists of temples linked in the pilgrimage routes, there is occasionally some variation in the names because of popular usage. This will be indicated when appropriate.

Second, in the lists given in this book the denominational affiliation given is that of contemporary times. There have been a number of changes of denominational affiliation or self-definition from time to time, but these are not of great significance for our present subject. Nevertheless the spread of denominational affiliation is of some interest. In general, as one might expect, the pilgrimages focused on Kannon-sama are relatively inter-denominational, while others relate to particular denominations and their founders. The Japanese terms for these affiliations are *-shū* (denomination, sometimes "sect") and *-ha* (sect, or sub-sect). These will simply be given as suffixes where they usually occur, and again a hyphen will be used for the reader's convenience. For example Tendai-shū means the Tendai denomination based on Mount Hiei in the north-east of Kyōto and Sōtō-shū means the school or denomination of Sōtō (Zen) Buddhism with its head temple at Eiheiji in Fukui Prefecture.

Third, the bodhisattva Kannon, who is the main object of reverence in the Kannon pilgrimages, is colloquially referred to as Kannon-sama. However in the formal iconographic designations used by the temples she is usually referred to as Kanzeon. The name Kanzeon repeats the form of the name found in Chapter 25 of the Lotus Sūtra, which is otherwise known in its own right as the Kannon Sūtra (*Kannongyō*). The simpler name Kannon may also be found in user-friendly guides. This is because, whatever the particular iconographic form, she is in the mind of the pilgrim or believer always just Kannon-sama. This may also be seen from the widely used expression *kannon shinkō*—faith in Kannon-sama. This focus on the bodhisattva goes some way to explaining the fact that not a few of the temples listed later have alternative names referring to Kannon-sama. This sometimes reflects the fact that Kannon-sama is herself in a special hall, the main hall of the temple having a different Buddhist divinity as the central object of reverence.

Table 2.1 The most frequent iconographic forms of Kannon-sama.

Shō Kanzeon	聖観世音	Holy Kanzeon
Jūichimen Kanzeon	十一面観世音	Eleven-faced Kanzeon
Nyoirin Kanzeon	如意輪観世音	Kanzeon with the Wheel of Wishes
Senju Kanzeon	千手観世音	Thousand-armed Kanzeon
Senjusengen Kanzeon	千手千眼観世音	Thousand-armed and thousand-eyed Kanzeon

Somewhat less frequent forms are:

Batō Kanzeon[9]	馬頭観世音	Horse-headed Kanzeon
Fukūkensaku Kanzeon	不空羂索観世音	Kanzeon of the Rope of Sure Deliverance
Juntei Kanzeon	准胝観世音	Kanzeon of Purity

Specialists may notice that this list departs slightly from conventional iconographic lists in which either six or seven forms are usually counted. This is because the list above reflects the forms which in fact occur in the temples of the Saikoku pilgrimage. When we look at the specific temples it will be seen that variations arise partly through combinations of the main forms. Indeed, in other temples around Japan there are yet further forms of Kannon-sama. When the iconographical forms of Kanzeon or Kannon are listed specifically as six without reference to pilgrimage, the following are usually named: Shō Kanzeon (or just Kannon), Jūichimen Kanzeon, Nyoirin Kanzeon, Senju Kanzeon, Batō Kanzeon and Juntei Kanzeon.

Fukūkensaku Kanzeon may be named as an alternative to Juntei Kanzeon, or added as a seventh form. The interest in enumerating six forms arose because of an association with six possible realms of rebirth, just as in the case of Jizō Bosatsu (cf. Chapter Four), but the connection runs with the number and not with any specific iconographical feature. The form of Kannon as "thousand-armed and thousand-eyed," named

Figure 2.3 Iconic depiction (*miei*) of Kannon Bosatsu (Nyoirin Kanzeon) from Saikoku No.14.

Figure 2.4 Iconic depiction (*miei*) of Shō Kannon from a pilgrim's book. Mitake-san Kōsanji (Chita Shin Shikoku No. 61 and a local Saikoku No. 12).

Figure 2.5 Iconic depiction (*miei*) of Jūichimen Kanzeon from Saikoku No. 33, Kegonji, here referred to by the "mountain name" Tanigumisan.

Figure 2.6 Iconic depiction (*miei*) of Senju Kanzeon from Saikoku No. 19 (Gyōganji).

above, does not occur in conventional lists, but may neverthless be met with quite frequently, so it is perhaps best seen as a variation of the "thousand-armed" Kannon. Indeed, the Shō Kannon or "Holy Kannon" is really the simplest form, of which all the others may be regarded as variations.

In the Kannon Sūtra (or Chapter 25 of *The Lotus Sūtra*)[10] there is reference to thirty-three forms which the bodhisattva adopted in order to adapt to the needs of the living beings. So Kannon-sama has many faces directed towards the living beings all around her, many eyes to see their existential situation and many arms or, more literally, hands with which to help them. However, although the idea of visiting 33 temples to revere Kannon-sama is said to be based on this, the number of different iconographic forms in use is in fact much smaller. The traditional concentration of the iconography on six, seven or eight main forms does not mean that an interest in 33 forms has died out altogether or that other representations will not be found. Some more details are given on such variations in Chapter Seven.

---

10. This refers to Chapter 25 in the Chinese version by Kumārajīva, which is regarded as the standard text in Japan. In Sanskrit editions and translations thereof it appears as Chapter 24.

Figure 2.7 Iconic depiction (*miei*) of Fukūkensaku Kanzeon from Saikoku No.9 (Kōfukuji, Nan'endō).

The somewhat mysterious designation Fukūkensaku Kanzeon, shown in the initial list as "Kanzeon of the Rope of Sure Deliverance," includes two elements. First, *fukū* means "not in vain," meaning that the assistance offered by Kannon-sama is assuredly reliable. Second, a *kensaku* (also read as *kenshaku* or *kenjaku*) is a rope used in fighting or hunting which here symbolizes the *determination* of Kannon-sama to persist in the deliverance of all living beings without exception. So it means that Kannon-sama will surely come to our aid against demons and other threats to eternal welfare. In this context therefore it is not so much a weapon as a symbol of sure deliverance.

The Horse-headed Kannon, Batō Kannon (also read as Mezu Kannon), is a fierce representation indicating the ability of the bodhisattva to crush all evils including both passions and disasters. Because of the horse's head, he—or she—was also expected to protect horses and cattle, and in Japan it was not long before this form of Kannon-sama took on a certain independence from the world of temples as an agricultural divinity.

The Kanzeon of Purity, Juntei Kannon, represents a call to leave the passions behind, and at the same time can provide benefits such as protection against disasters and conceiving unwanted children, long life and the avoidance of disease. In sum it is evident that Kannon-sama

Figure 2.8 Iconic depiction (*miei*) of Batō Kanzeon from Shikoku No. 70 (Motoyamaji).

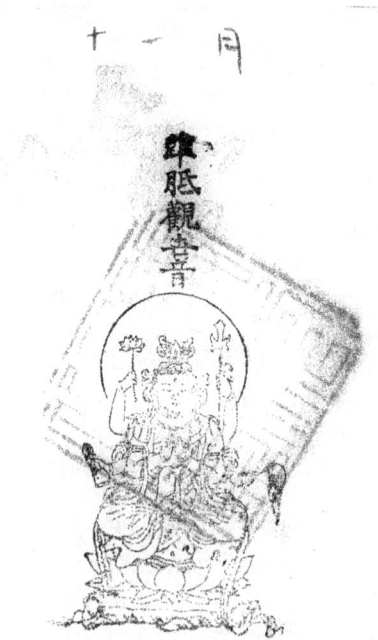

Figure 2.9 Iconic depiction (*miei*) of Juntei Kannon from a Chita pilgrim's commemoration booklet.

has something for everybody, and this is reflected in the range of initial motivations which pilgrims have when going round to visit her temples.

The main iconographic forms, usually in colour, are often found as centre-pieces in the pilgrims' scrolls which bear the seals and calligraphy of the temples visited (see further in Chapter Six). The same iconographic forms are found on small slips of paper, traditionally in black and white, and recently sometimes in colour, which are obtainable as devotional aids at each temple. These little pieces of paper, known as *mi-ei*, have the added value that they show the pilgrims which form of Kannon-sama they have been visiting, for in many cases the main image is hidden in a closed shrine at the back of the main hall, so that it can be worshipped but not seen.

On this background the list of the Saikoku Thirty-three Spiritual Sites of Kannon may now be presented. This is the normative model for all of the Kannon pilgrimages, but it has its own distinctive list of temples, images and affiliations. Alternative names or varying pronunciations of the same name are given in brackets where relevant, some of them being rare but some being popularly used. Various guidebooks have been compared for this purpose, some older and some newer. In the list in Table 2.2, the iconographical type of the Kannon-sama image is highlighted. For reasons of spacing, the denominational affiliation of the temples is found in Table 2.3 (further below).

The significance of the three *bangai* temples named here is as follows. Hokki-in[11] is the mausoleum of Tokudō Shōnin who, as already explained, was instrumental in the development of these pilgrimages. He was also the co-founder of the nearby temple Hasedera (No. 8), which at one time was the starting point of the circuit. The Emperor Kazan is revered at Gankeiji, because his image is installed in the main hall, and at Kazan-in Bodaiji because he spent his final years there (1003–1008).

In some guidebooks different temples are added on to the basic thirty-three. Frequently mentioned is the well known temple Zenkōji 善光寺 in Nagano Prefecture. Zenkōji is jointly managed by priests of the Tendai and the Jōdo (Pure Land) denominations and has historically been an important centre of pilgrimage in its own right. In other cases the spiritual home of Shingon Buddhism, Mount Kōya, is listed. This is in any case a standard addition to the Shikoku pilgrimage, but is also of interest to Shingon devotees who perform the Saikoku pilgrimage. A guidebook dating from Taishō 14 (1925), untypically for today, lists these two and also the major Kannon temple at Asakusa in Tokyo, naming it as Asakusadera 浅草寺, although its staff nowadays insist on the formal reading Sensōji (for the same characters). A recently published devotional fold-

---

11. Some Japanese guides give the pronunciation as Hōki-in, for the ease of modern readers.

Table 2.2 The Saikoku temples with the iconographical types of Kannon/Kanzeon.

	Name	(alternative)	Kannon type
1	Seigantoji 清岸渡寺	(Seigandoji)	Nyoirin Kanzeon
2	Kongōhōji 金剛法寺	(Kimiidera)[a]	Jūichimen Kanzeon
3	Kokawadera 紛河寺		Senjusengen Kanzeon
4	Sefukuji 施福寺	(Makinoodera)	Senjusengen Kanzeon
5	Fujiidera 葛井寺		Jūichimen Senjusengen Kanzeon[b]
6	Minami Hokkeji 南法華寺	(Tsubosakadera)	Senjusengen Kanzeon
7	Ryūgaiji 龍蓋寺	(Okadera)	Nyoirin Kanzeon[c]
8	Hasedera 長谷寺		Jūichimen Kanzeon
9	Nan'endō 南円堂		Fukūkenshaku Kanzeon
10	Mimurotoji 三室戸寺		Senju Kanzeon
11	Kamidaigoji 上醍醐寺		Juntei Kanzeon
12	Shōhōji 正法寺	(Iwamadera)	Senju Kanzeon
13	Ishiyamadera 石山寺		Nyoirin Kanzeon[d]
14	Onjōji 園城寺	(Miidera)	Nyoirin Kanzeon
15	Kannonji 観音寺	(Imakumano)	Jūichimen Kanzeon
16	Kiyomizudera 清水寺		Senju Kanzeon
17	Rokuharamitsuji 六波羅蜜寺		Jūichimen Kanzeon
18	Chōhōji 頂法寺	(Rokkakudō)	Nyoirin Kanzeon
19	Gyōganji 行願寺	(Kōdō Gyōganji)	Senju Kanzeon
20	Yoshiminedera 善峰寺		Senjusengen Kanzeon
21	Anaoji 穴太寺	(Bodaiji)	Shō Kanzeon
22	Sōjiji 総持寺		Senju Kanzeon
23	Katsuōji 勝尾寺	(Kachiodera)	Jūichimensenju Kanzeon
24	Nakayamadera 中山寺		Jūichimen Kanzeon
25	Kiyomizudera 清水寺		Jūichimensenju Kanzeon
26	Ichijōji 一乗寺		Shō Kanzeon
27	Engyōji 圓教寺		Nyoirin Kanzeon[e]
28	Nariaiji 成相寺		Shō Kanzeon
29	Matsunoodera 松尾寺		Batō Kanzeon
30	Hōgonji 法厳寺		Senjusengen Kanzeon
31	Chōmeiji 長命寺		Senjujūichimen Shō Kanzeon[f]
32	Kannonshōji 観音正寺		Senjusengen Kanzeon

33 Kegonji 華厳寺   Jūichimen Kanzeon

a) This arises from the formal *-san* name: Kimiisan 紀三井山.
b) This image is a "national treasure."
c) Also Nihi Nyoirin Kanzeon, referring to two ornaments (*hi* 臂) on the upper arms.
d) Also Nihi Nyoirin Kanzeon, cf. previous note.
e) Also Rokuhi Nyoirin Kanzeon, referring to six ornaments on the upper arms.
f) In full, Senjujūichimen Shō Kanzeon Sanzon Ittai: the additional phrase *sanzon ittai* 三尊一体 explains that these are "three objects of reverence in one image, or body."

Hokki-in 法起院[a]   Tokudō Shōnin 得道上人
Gankeiji 元慶寺[b]   Yakushi Nyorai 薬師如来
Kazan-in Bodaiji 花山院菩提寺[c]   Yakushirurikō Nyorai 薬師瑠璃光如来

a) Hokki-in is usually included between 8 and 9.
b) Gankeiji between 14 and 15.
c) Kazan-in Bodaiji between 24 and 25.

ing booklet (Heisei 12, 2000), oriented towards Pure Land Buddhism, announces that it includes the temple songs (*go-eika*) of the *bangai* temples. In fact it gives that for the Kazan-in at the beginning, with the story of how the young Emperor Kazan first visited the thirty-three places. After the thirty-three temples no less than nine other temple songs are listed, beginning with that of Zenkōji and ending with that of Mount Kōya. Near the end of the booklet we find a longer recitational song (a *wasan*) for Zenkōji, and at the very end there are the temple songs for Hokki-in, Gankeiji and Kazan-in.

Pilgrims often like to obtain the usual commemorative temple seal and calligraphy from these extra-numerary temples, and this explains why the pilgrim books and scrolls usually show more than thirty-three entries, and do not exactly match up with each other. More details on the collection of the seals and calligraphy, and the relevant artefacts, will be given in Chapter Six below. One scroll described there bears the seals and calligraphy of seven extra temples, the three usual ones plus the illustrious temples Shitennōji (designated "The first Buddha-dharma of Great Japan"), Zenkōji, Kōya-san and Sensōji, the latter being in Tokyo.

It can be seen from the main list above that the most frequent iconographical types of the Saikoku pilgrimage are Jūichimen Kanzeon (six cases) and Senjusengen Kanzeon (six cases) to which may be added the one case in which these are combined (Temple No. 5) and another case which combines them with Shō Kanzeon (Temple No. 31). Nyoirin Kanzeon occurs seven times when we include the two variations at Temples No. 13 and 27. Shō Kannon appears three times and in the combination already mentioned (No. 31). The other iconographical forms occur once each. This evidently unsystematic distribution reflects the fact that

Figure 2.10 A worn-out signpost on the Saikoku Pilgrimage pointing right to Kannonshōji (temple No. 32) and left to nearby railway stations and a bus stop.

the temples in question are ancient, and had their images of Kannon-sama for reasons independent of the invention of the pilgrimage. They fall severally into the generally recognized category of the respectworthy historic past of Buddhist Japan. Indeed one of them is a National Treasure, the Jūichimen Senjusengen Kanzeon of Fujiidera (Temple No. 5). The public respect accorded to such images gives status to the pilgrimage itself. At the same time it should be remembered that the images are not usually to be seen. They are hidden behind curtains and wooden doors. Only for a short time are they on view, usually briefly in the autumn, or on some other special occasions in the life of the individual temple. This accounts for the interest in exhibitions such as that held in Nara and at Nagoya City Museum in 2008 on the "treasures" of these temples, though even then the main images themselves were not on show.[12]

We turn now to the current denominational affiliation of the Saikoku temples, which is shown in Table 2.3 (opposite).

The significance and distribution of denominational affiliation will be discussed below when more temple circuits have been introduced. The

---

12. Catalogue: Nara National Museum 2008.

Table 2.3 Current denominational affiliation of the Saikoku temples.

1	Seigantoji 清岸渡寺	(Seigandoji)	Tendai-shū
2	Kongōhōji 金剛法寺	(Kimiidera)	Kyūsei Kannon-shū
3	Kokawadera 紛河寺		Kokawa Kannon-shū
4	Sefukuji 施福寺	(Makinoodera)	Tendai-shū
5	Fujiidera 葛井寺		Shingon-shū Mimuro-ha
6	Minami Hokkeji 南法華寺	(Tsubosakadera)	Shingon-shū Buzan-ha
7	Ryūgaiji 龍蓋寺	(Okadera)	Shingon-shū Buzan-ha
8	Hasedera 長谷寺		Shingon-shū Buzan-ha
9	Nan'endō 南円堂		Hossō-shū
10	Mimurotoji 三室戸寺		Honzan Shugen-shū
11	Kamidaigoji 上醍醐寺		Shingon-shū Daigo-ha
12	Shōhōji 正法寺	(Iwamadera)	Shingon-shū Daigo-ha
13	Ishiyamadera 石山寺		Shingon-shū Tōji-ha
14	Onjōji 園城寺	(Miidera)	Tendai Jimon-shū
15	Kannonji 観音寺	(Imakumano)	Shingon-shū Senryūji-ha
16	Kiyomizudera 清水寺		Kita-hossō-shū (independent)
17	Rokuharamitsuji 六波羅蜜寺		Shingon-shū Chizan-ha
18	Chōhōji 頂法寺	(Rokkakudō)	independent
19	Gyōganji 行願寺	(Kōdō Gyōganji)	Tendai-shū
20	Yoshiminedera 善峰寺		Tendai-shū
21	Anaoji 穴太寺	(Bodaiji)	Tendai-shū
22	Sōjiji 総持寺		Kōyasan Shingon-shū
23	Katsuōji 勝尾寺	(Kachiodera)	Kōyasan Shingon-shū
24	Nakayamadera 中山寺		Shingon-shū Nakayamadera-ha
25	Kiyomizudera 清水寺		Tendai-shū
26	Ichijōji 一乗寺		Tendai-shū
27	Engyōji 圓教寺		Tendai-shū
28	Nariaiji 成相寺		Kōyasan Shingon-shū
29	Matsunoodera 松尾寺		Shingon-shū Daigo-ha

30 Hōgonji 法厳寺	Shingon-shū Buzan-ha
31 Chōmeiji 長命寺	Tendai-shū (independent)
32 Kannonshōji 観音正寺	Tendai-shū (independent)
33 Kegonji 華厳寺	Tendai-shū
Hokki-in (between 8 and 9)[a]	Shingon-shū Buzan-ha
Gankeiji (between 14 and 15)[a]	Tendai-shū
Kazan-in Bodaiji (between 24 and 25)[a]	Shingon-shū Kazan-in-ha

a) Extra-numerary temple.

term "independent" means that a temple has become independent as a religious corporation, even though it may still have various kinds of affinity with a parent tradition. There are various reasons for such legal and financial independence; Kiyomizudera in Kyōto, for example, has a particular niche in the tourist industry. Generally speaking, denominational and sectarian divisions in Japanese Buddhism are extremely complicated and cannot be pursued in detail here.

Bandō 33 and Chichibu 34

While imitations of the famous Saikoku Pilgrimage are found in most regions of Japan, the Bandō and Chichibu Kannon-sama routes have to be regarded as the two most important exemplars. It is usually explained that the reason for their appearance was, long before the age of the train, to provide substitute pilgrimages for persons not able to make the long journey to western Japan. However, while this was without doubt the original reason, they have in the meantime come to be regarded as complementary additions to the Saikoku route. It will be recalled that the Bandō route has thirty-three temples but that the Chichibu route has thirty-four, thus making a total of 100 temples. This indicates that at least in the minds of Chichibu devotees these three routes belong together. At the same time it must be said that those who live in the Kansai region of Japan, the home of the Saikoku pilgrimage, are seldom familiar with this concept. The positive correlation can be seen in the design of a series of 101 wood-block prints from the late Edo Period which show all the temples with a text and an illustration for their foundational story (*engi*). In addition to the one hundred temples, one extra print gives a summary list of the names of them all.[13] The Chichibu pilgrimage undoubtedly owes its repute in part to association with the others, for this established its claim

---

13. These have been reprinted in various forms, even on telephone cards, but the most convenient reference point is now the web-site "Nihon Hyaku Kannon" of the International Research Centre for Japanese Studies (Nichibunken), (Kyōto, 2009).

Table 2.4 Temples of the Bandō pilgrimage.

#	Temple		
1	Sugimotoji 杉本寺	Sugimotodera	Sugimoto Kannon
2	Gandenji 岩殿寺		Iwadono Kannon
3	Anyō-in 安養院	Tashiro 田代観音	Tashiro Kannon
4	Hasedera 長谷寺		Hase Kannon
5	Shōfukuji 勝福寺	Iizumi Kannon 飯泉観音	Iizumi Kannon
6	Hasedera 長谷寺	Iiyama Kannon 飯山観音	Iiyama Kannon
7	Kōmyōji 光明寺	Kaname Kannon 金目観音	Kaname Kannon
8	Hoshigayaji 星谷寺	Shōkokuji	Hoshinoya Kannon[a]
9	Jikōdera 慈光寺	Jikōji	Jikōji Kannon
10	Shōhōji 正法時	Shōbōji	Iwadono Kannon[b]
11	Anrakuji 安楽時	Yoshimi Kannon 吉見観音	Yoshimi Kannon
12	Jionji 慈恩寺		Jionji Kannon
13	Sensōji 浅草寺	Asakusa Kannon 浅草観音[c]	Asakusa Kannon
14	Gumyōji 弘明寺		Gumyōji Kannon
15	Hasedera 長谷寺	Chōkokuji	
		Shiraiwa Kannon 白岩観音	Shiraiwa Kannon
16	Mizusawadera 水沢寺		Mizusawa kannon
17	Manganji 満願寺	Izuru Kannon 出流観音	Izuru Kannon
18	Chūzenji 中禅寺	Tachiki Kannon 立木観音	Tachiki Kannon
19	Ōyaji 大谷寺		Ōya Kannon
20	Saimyōji 西明寺	Mashiko Kannon 益子観音	Saimyōji
21	Nichirinji 日輪時	Yamizosan 八溝山	Yamizosan
22	Satakeji 佐竹時	Kitamuki Kannon 北向観音	Kitamuki Kannon
23	Shōfukuji 正福寺	Kanzeonji 観世音寺	
		Sashiro Kannon 佐白観音	Sashiro Kannon
24	Rakuhōji 楽法寺	Amabiki Kannon 雨引観音	Amabiki Kannon
25	Chisoku-in Chūzenji 知足院中禅寺	Ōmidō 大御堂	Ōmidō
26	Kiyotakiji 清滝寺	Kiyotaki Kannon 清滝観音	Kiyotakidera

27	Enpukuji 円福時	Iinuma Kannon 飯沼観音	Iinuma Kannon
28	Ryūshō-in 龍正院	Namekawa Kannon 滑河観音	Namegawa Kannon[d]
29	Chibadera 千葉寺	Senyōji	Chibadera
30	Takakuradera 高蔵寺	Kōzōji	Takakura Kannon
31	Kasamoridera 笠森寺	Kasamoriji	Kasamori Kannon
32	Kiyomizudera 清水寺		Kiyomizu Kannon
33	Nakoji 那古寺	Nagoji, Nakodera	Nako Kannon

a) Hoshinoya = Hoshigaya ("star valley").
b) This would be written in the same way as the alternative name for No. 2.
c) Note that in this classic case of an alternative name, the characters for Sensō and Asakusa are the same. Moreover, Kannon-sama is the central object of reverence in the main building. While the name Asakusa Kannon is widely known, the temple authorities lay great emphasis on the formal designation Sensōji.
d) The hardening of Namekawa to Namegawa is a variation in pronunciation only.

to being one of the big three in Japan. Other factors for its popularity are that it is easily accessible from Tokyo, though it would still have been quite hard to reach in the Edo Period when there were as yet no railways. Once in the area however, the pilgrimage is geographically compact and therefore attractively manageable, without being a mere miniature. Thus while benefiting from association by name with Saikoku and Bandō, the Chichibu route draws many pilgrims who never actually get around the two larger and more widely dispersed routes.

Temples of the Bandō pilgrimage are shown in Table 2.4. Variations will often be found for the names of the temples of the Bandō pilgrimage, and it is interesting to see the interplay, not only between alternative ways of reading the same characters, but also between formal and less formal designations. In Table 2.4 (above) four sources are used. The left-hand column shows what may be considered to be standard designations drawn from (i) a typical pilgrim's book (*nōkyōchō*) for the temple seals and calligraphy forming proof of visit. The second column shows variations given in the same source or found in (ii) a general catalogue of Japanese "spiritual sites"[14] or in (iii) other recent ephemeral sources.[15] When no characters are shown in the second column, it means that it is

---

14. Rekishi Tokuhon Series: *Nihon reichi-junrei sōkan* (1996).
15. Other ephemeral sources offer the same variants, but sometimes in slightly different combinations.

the same ones which are pronounced differently.

The right-hand column shows (iv) an oral rendition by an informant. This was given, very deliberately, by the wife of the temple priest of No. 28 (Namegawa Kannon) on July 8, 1993, after she had provided the usual seal and calligraphy for her own temple. It is notable that in this oral listing designations ending in "Kannon" are highly favoured. Such reference to the "Kannon" names indicates that people do not care to use the formal names of the temples; rather they have an affectionate relationship to the temples in question which is based on their devotion to Kannon-sama, who may be lodged in a sub-hall of her own.

Note that No. 26 is known here as Kiyotakiji or Kiyotakidera (meaning Pure Waterfall Temple), whereas the same characters in the name of a well-known temple in Kyōto are read Seiryūji. Note also the unusual reading Ōyaji 大谷寺 (i.e. Ōya, rather than Ōtani which is otherwise common in names). In so far as three different temples bear the name Hasedera, we can see that the popular differentiations of the names are quite useful.

The same Bandō list is given again in Table 2.5, showing the iconographical type of the Kannon image and the denomination of the temples. This shows that seventeen of the Bandō temples are Shingon oriented (including Sensōji), twelve are Tendai oriented, two are Jōdo-shū and two are Sōtō Zen Buddhist.

We turn now to the temples of the Chichibu pilgrimage, shown in Table 2.6 below. In this case alternative designations are rather numerous, sometimes arising because the Kannon hall itself, or the office for getting the seal and calligraphy, is located at a short distance from the formal temple seat. In the table below the left-hand column shows the names as given in the *nōkyōchō* used by the writer during his own pilgrimage. Alternatives are drawn from various ephemeral sources. When no characters are shown in the second column, it means that it is the same ones which are pronounced differently. Temples of the Chichibu pilgrimage are shown in Table 2.6.

The same Chichibu list is given again in Table 2.7, following the first designation only and showing the iconographical type of the Kannon image and the denomination of the temple. This shows that twenty of the Chichibu temples are Sōtō Zen Buddhist and eleven are Rinzai Zen Buddhist (mostly in the Nanzenji line). Only three are Shingon temples, and other denominations are not represented at all. Ever since Sōtō temples began to be built there has been a consistent predilection for hosting images of Kannon Bosatsu, so the strong representation of this denomination is not surprising in itself. Nevertheless the difference in denominational emphasis compared to that of the other major pilgrimages is quite marked. A synoptic table will be found later in this chapter.

Table 2.5 Bandō list showing the iconographical type of the Kannon image and the denomination of the temple.

	Name	Kannon type	Denomination
1	Sugimotoji	Jūichimen Kanzeon	Tendai-shū
2	Gandenji	Jūichimen Kanzeon	Sōtō-shū
3	Anyō-in	Senshu Kanzeon	Jōdo-shū
4	Hasedera	Jūichimen Kanzeon	Jōdo-shū
5	Shōfukuji	Jūichimen Kanzeon	Kogi Shingon-shū
6	Hasedera	Jūichimen Kanzeon	Kogi Shingon-shū
7	Kōmyōji	Shō Kanzeon	Tendai-shū
8	Hoshigayaji	Shō Kanzeon	Shingon-shū Daikakuji-ha
9	Jikōdera	Senju Kanzeon	Tendai-shū
10	Shōhōji	Senju Kanzeon	Shingon-shū Chizan-ha
11	Anrakuji	Shō Kanzeon	Shingon-shū Chizan-ha
12	Jionji	Senju Kanzeon	Tendai-shū
13	Sensōji	Shō Kanzeon	Shōkannon-shū
14	Gumyōji	Jūichimen Kanzeon	Shingon-shū Kōyasan-ha
15	Hasedera	Jūichimen Kanzeon	Tendai-shū Jimon-ha
16	Mizusawadera	Senju Kanzeon	Tendai-shū
17	Manganji	Senju Kanzeon	Shingon-shū Chizan-ha
18	Chūzenji	Senju Kanzeon	Tendai-shū
19	Ōyaji	Senju Kanzeon	Tendai-shū
20	Saimyōji	Jūichimen Kanzeon	Shingon-shū Buzan-ha
21	Nichirinji	Jūichimen Kanzeon	Tendai-shū
22	Satakeji	Jūichimen Kanzeon	Shingon-shū Buzan-ha
23	Shōfukuji	Senju Kanzeon	Sōtō-shū
24	Rakuhōji	Enmei Kanzeon	Shingon-shū Buzan-ha
25	Chisoku-in Chūzenji	Senju Kanzeon	Shingon-shū Buzan-ha
26	Kiyotakiji	Shō Kanzeon	Shingon-shū Buzan-ha
27	Enpukuji	Jūichimen Kanzeon	Shingon-shū Chizan-ha
28	Ryūshō-in	Jūichimen Kanzeon	Tendai-shū
29	Chibadera	Jūichimen Kanzeon	Shingon-shū Buzan-ha
30	Takakuradera	Shō Kanzeon	Shingon-shū Buzan-ha
31	Kasamoridera	Jūichimen Kanzeon	Tendai-shū
32	Kiyomizudera	Senju Kanzeon	Tendai-shū
33	Nakoji	Senju Kanzeon	Shingon-shū Chizan-ha

Going Round to Visit Kannon-sama

Table 2.6　Temples of the Chichibu pilgrimage.

	Name	Alternative designation
1	Shimabuji 四万部寺[a]	Myōonji 妙音時
2	Shinpukuji 真福寺	
3	Jōsenji 常泉寺	Iwamotoji 岩本寺[b]
4	Kinshōji 金昌寺	Arakidera 新木寺
5	Chōkōji 長興寺	Gokadō 語歌堂
6	Bokuunji 卜雲寺	Oginodō 荻ノ堂
7	Hōchōji 法長寺	Ushibusedō 牛伏堂
8	Saizenji 西善寺	
9	Akechiji 明智寺	Akechidera
10	Daijiji 大慈寺	
11	Jōrakuji 常楽寺	
12	Nosakaji 野坂寺	
13	Jigenji 慈眼寺	
14	Imamiyabō 今宮坊	
15	Shōrinji 少林寺	Kobayashidera
16	Saikōji 西光寺	
17	Jōrinji 定林時	
18	Gōdoji 神門寺	
19	Ryūsekiji 龍石寺	
20	Iwanouedō 岩上堂	
21	Kannonji 観音寺	Yanodō 矢之堂
22	Dōjidō 童子堂[c]	Eifukuji 永福寺[d]
23	Ongakuji 音楽時	
24	Hōsenji 法泉寺	Shirayama Kannon 白山観音
25	Kyūshōji 久昌寺	Otebanji (Otehandera) 御手版寺
26	Enyūji 円融寺	Iwaidō 岩井堂
27	Daienji 大淵寺[e]	Tsukikagedō 月影堂
28	Hashidatedō 橋立堂	Hashidateji 橋立寺[f]
29	Chōsen-in 長泉院	Ishifudadō 石札堂

30 Hōunji 法雲寺

31 Kannon-in 観音院 — Iwadono Kannon 岩殿観音

32 Hōshōji 法性寺 — Ofune Kannon お船観音

33 Kikusuiji 菊水寺

34 Suisenji 水潜寺 — Kechiganji 結願時[g]

a. Or in the old form: 四萬部寺.
b. This is derived from the -san name of the temple.
c. In this case the pilgrim's book as the name of the hall rather than the formal name of the temple.
d. Also found as 栄福寺.
e. Shown in the pilgrim's book with the non-standard form 大渕寺.
f. Though apparently more formal, this variant version of the temple name is probably secondary.
g. I.e. the temple of the completion of the vow (to perform the pilgrimage to the one hundred temples).

Table 2.7 Temples of the Chichibu pilgrimage showing the iconographical type of the Kannon image and the denomination of the temple.

	Name	Kannon type	Denomination
1	Shimabuji	Shō Kanzeon	Sōtō-shū
2	Shinpukuji	Shō Kanzeon	Sōtō-shū
3	Jōsenji	Shō Kanzeon	Sōtō-shū
4	Kinshōji	Jūichimen Kanzeon	Sōtō-shū
5	Chōkōji	Juntei Kanzeon	Rinzai-shū
6	Bokuunji	Shō Kanzeon	Sōtō-shū
7	Hōchōji	Jūichimen Kanzeon	Sōtō-shū
8	Saizenji	Jūichimen Kanzeon	Rinzai-shū
9	Akechiji	Nyoirin Kanzeon	Rinzai-shū
10	Daijiji	Shō Kanzeon	Sōtō-shū
11	Jōrakuji	Jūichimen Kanzeon	Sōtō-shū
12	Nosakaji	Shō Kanzeon	Rinzai-shū
13	Jigenji	Shō Kanzeon	Sōtō-shū
14	Imamiyabō	Shō Kanzeon	Rinzai-shū
15	Shōrinji	Jūichimen Kanzeon	Rinzai-shū
16	Saikōji	Senju Kanzeon	Shingon-shū

17	Jōrinji	Jūichimen Kanzeon	Sōtō-shū
18	Gōdoji	Shō Kanzeon	Sōtō-shū
19	Ryūsekiji	Senju Kanzeon	Sōtō-shū
20	Iwanouedō	Shō Kanzeon	Rinzai-shū
21	Kannonji	Shō Kanzeon	Shingon-shū
22	Dōjidō	Shō Kanzeon	Shingon-shū
23	Ongakuji	Shō Kanzeon	Rinzai-shū
24	Hōsenji	Shō Kanzeon	Rinzai-shū
25	Kyūshōji	Shō Kanzeon	Sōtō-shū
26	Enyūji	Shō Kanzeon	Rinzai-shū
27	Daienji	Shō Kanzeon	Sōtō-shū
28	Hashidatedō	Batō Kanzeon	Sōtō-shū
29	Chōsen-in	Shō Kanzeon	Sōtō-shū
30	Hōunji	Nyoirin Kanzeon	Rinzai-shū
31	Kannon-in	Shō Kanzeon	Sōtō-shū
32	Hōshōji	Shō Kanzeon	Sōtō-shū
33	Kikusuiji	Shō Kanzeon	Sōtō-shū
34	Suisenji	Senju Kanzeon	Sōtō-shū

Other Kannon-sama routes

While other Kannon-sama pilgrimages do not count towards the top group of one hundred temples, they are nevertheless highly regarded as alternatives for regional use. Visiting them saves much expense and hardship, or nowadays, stress. Interesting examples are found for Edo[16] (former Tokyo), at Kamakura just south of Tokyo, Sendai in the north, the Izumo region on the Japan Sea coast, and the "Enshū" region on the Pacific coast around the city of Hamamatsu, but there are many others. In Kyūshū, Japan's southernmost major island, a Kannon-sama pilgrimage begins at Mount Hiko, a mountain which since ancient times has attracted practitioners associated with Shintō, Buddhism and Shugendō alike. A significant correlation with Shintō is found on the Kunisaki Peninsula of northern Kyūshū where thirty-three Kannon temples are conceptually linked to the regionally dominant Usa Hachiman Jingū, regarded as the Hachiman shrine *par excellence* for all Japan.[17] This pilgrimage may be

---

16. See Yamada 1979.
17. See Watanabe 1990.

referred to in full as Kunisaki Rokugō Manzan Reijō Meguri. Some of these routes, like the Izumo circuit, are evidently well trodden, but others such as a circuit on the Izu Peninsula appear to be relatively little used.

Many of the regional pilgrimages for Kannon-sama are of old pedigree, and their names, ending in -*kuni*, show a relationship to the various ancient provinces (*kuni*) of Japan, which were replaced by "prefectures" (*ken*) in the nineteenth century. Thus the historic Ōmi Province around Lake Biwa has its own circuit of thirty-three temples, starting at the Tendai temple Jōrakuji and ending at the Rinzai temple Myōkanji. The regional pilgrimage of what was Echigo Province (now taken up into Niigata Prefecture) is another old pilgrimage of uncertain date, beginning at a temple named Iwayadō near Nadachi, and ending at a Shingon temple named Saimyōji.[18] The "Shinano Thirty-three" for its part links temples in Nagano Prefecture and apparently has a significant history. A commemorative board at the Kannon Hall of temple Number 27, Gofukuji 牛伏寺, dated at Tenna 2 (1682), refers to a person having completed 133 visits to Kannon-sama, that is, to Saikoku, Bandō and Chichibu, and in addition to the thirty-three Shinano sacred sites. This pilgrimage was made for the sake of the enlightenment of his parents, i.e. for their successful achievement of buddhahood, presumably after their death.[19]

However, the designation -*kuni* does not always imply genuine antiquity. The Settsukuni Thirty-three pilgrimage, for example, was set up in February of Shōwa 55 (1981).[20] This includes temples in the urban areas of Ōsaka and Kōbe. Here the name Settsu-kuni (*kuni* meaning land or country) harks back nostalgically to one of the ancient provinces. Such usage suggests that pilgrimage is an activity which lives in part by the re-creation of a pre-modern sense of being, even though the carrying out of the pilgrimage is nowadays almost always dependent on modern transport. It is rather like using the names of the old regions (*pays*) in France such as Quercy, or referring to Wessex in England. Incidentally, temple Number 1 of the Settsukuni Thirty-three is Nakayamadera, which is at the same time Number 24 of the main Saikoku pilgrimage. This illustrates a tendency for influential or active temples to draw visitors by networking the pilgrimage routes.

The city of Kyōto has older routes, for example the Rakuyō Thirty-three, which is purported to go back to an initiative of the Emperor Go-Shirakawa (reigned 1156–1558), who found the Saikoku Thirty-three too troublesome. In the early fifteenth century it was known to begin

---

18. Guidebook by Satō Takashi 1989.
19. Kakinoki and Seki 1991, 21.
20. So stated in the guidebook which has been current since 1982, entitled *Settsukuni Sanjūsankasho Reijō Annai Chizu*, published in Kōbe by the Settsukuni Sanjūsankasho Reijō Society.

at Gyōganji and to end at the Shintō shrine Kitano Tenmangū, but the sequence became disrupted during the Ōnin War (1467–1477). In the early Edo Period (1665) it was revived by imperial command, this time starting at the centrally located Rokkakudō and ending at the Buddhist temple Seiwa-in not far from Kitano Tenmangū. The temples are spread over the main parts of historic Kyōto. Another route, the Rakusai Pilgrimage, covering temples located in the western areas of the city of Kyōto, was in effect re-founded in Shōwa 53 (1978) to take advantage of the booming interest, as it says in a booklet, "not only among older people, but also among the young" (Rakusaikannonreijōkai 1987). The occasion for the reformulation of this route was the discovery of an old votive board which suggested that the pilgrimage had existed in the Edo or even the Muromachi Period, since which time some of the temples have been relocated or have disappeared altogether.

Some relatively new circuits overlap with areas which were really already provided for. A good example of this is the "New Saikoku Thirty-three" in western Japan (Kyōto Shinbunsha 1979). However the "new" Saikoku route has also been redesigned as "thirty-eight." This somehow loses touch with the thirty-three transformations of Kannon-sama in the *Lotus Sūtra*, but it allows more temples to participate! This series, beginning with the historic (but rebuilt) temple Shitennōji in Ōsaka, now has four temples in the Kyōto District (Kyōto-fu) as compared with 11 in the traditional Thirty-three, but includes twelve in Ōsaka District (Ōsaka-fu) compared with four previously, and 15 in Hyōgo Prefecture compared with only four previously. This all shows that it is intended above all to attract visitors, especially from the big conurbations of Ōsaka and Kōbe, in competition with the privileged temples of the ancient Saikoku route.[21] Another example is the Musashino Thirty-three which falls geographically into the general area of the Bandō circuit. Though Musashino is a traditional name for the northern part of the huge alluvial plain around Tokyo, which suggests an aura of relative antiquity, this route was in fact founded in Shōwa 33 (1958) and thus originated at or near the beginning of the post-war revival of interest in pilgrimage. Similar nostalgia, if secular, is generated by the use of the name Musashino in a major outer-urban railway line of relatively recent origin. Then again there are revisions and replacements such as the Shōwa Newly Selected Edo Pilgrimage which only partly parallels an older Edo Thirty-three, while maintaining the romantic name of "Edo" for old Tokyo.[22] There seem to have been various versions of an Edo Thirty-three, the oldest having been launched round about the year 1698.[23] However, strident

---

21. Information in a leaflet from Shitennōji at Ōsaka, early 1990s.
22. Edofudashokai 1993, 2000.
23. Yamada 1979, 10.

Japanese Buddhist Pilgrimage

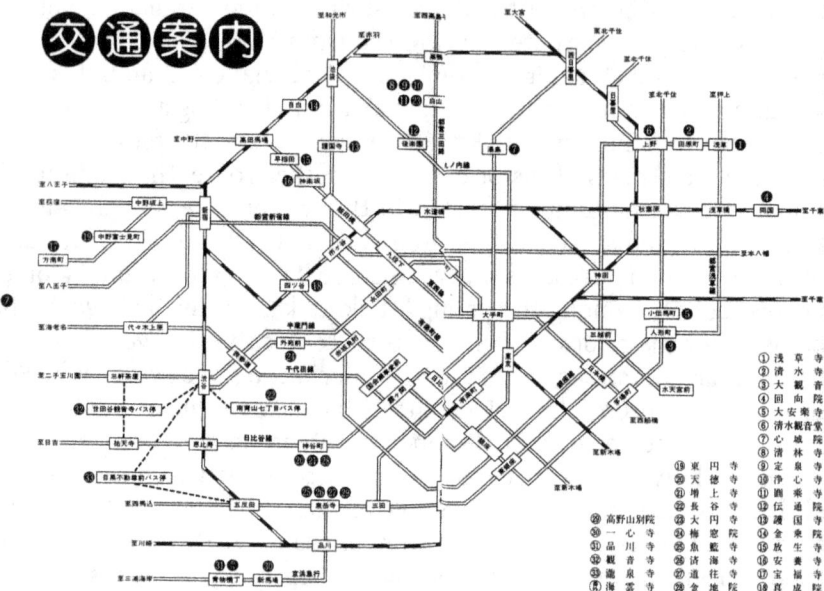

Figure 2.11 Diagram of a Kannon 33 pilgrimage route in Tokyo showing modern infrastructure.

policies of the Meiji government in the later nineteenth century led to the displacement of some of the temples and later revisions could therefore not be precisely authentic. On the other hand, the complex relationship between temple locations and the modern urban railway system, both underground and overground, is quite fascinating.

The total number of routes devoted to Kannon Bosatsu which link thirty-three temples cannot in fact be ascertained. But they are very numerous. A "hands-on" pilgrimage expert, Hirahata Ryōyū, working from his temple Manganji in Chōshi City, Chiba Prefecture, has not only recorded details of many pilgrimages but also reactivated them. In effect he has developed a huge publishing business over recent decades, producing guidebooks to all the major pilgrimages and not a few little known ones, mainly concentrating on the Kannon-sama routes but including Shikoku and some of its variations in his purview as well. For just a few of these titles, see the bibliography. As of 2008 he included the following Kannon routes in his series entitled "Pilgrimages to Old Temples Series" (*Koji Junrei Shiirizu*), the list betraying a certain conceptual priority:

Saikoku Kannon Junrei

Bandō Kannon Junrei

Chichibu Kannon Junrei

Musashino Kannon Junrei	
Saijō Kannon Junrei	(a circuit in the mountains of central north-eastern Japan, convenient for hot springs, but only in summer)
Tsugaru Kannon Junrei	(the northernmost circuit of Honshū, near the Tsugaru Straits dividing Honshū and Hokkaidō)
Saikoku Sanjūsankasho Doraibu Kannon Junrei	(the Saikoku route for drivers)
Kamakura Sanjūsankasho	
Rakusai Sanjūsankasho	(temples in the western part of Kyōto City)
Owari Kannon Junrei	(temples in an ancient province around Nagoya)
Okushū Kannon Junrei	(temples spread across Fukushima, Miyagi and Iwate Prefectures in northern Japan)

These "routes" are of varying length. The Owari circuit, for example, covers 336 kilometres according to Hirahata (1987), but of course, it depends somewhat on the choice of transport, interruptions in the journey, and so on.

In the same list we find a booklet for recitations at one hundred temples devoted to Kannon Bosatsu on the large island of Shikoku, which is of course mainly known for its characteristic circuit of 88 temples.[24] The one hundred include many of the Shikoku 88 but also some others, so a competitive effect is evident here. The series also includes four booklets on the Shikoku series and its imitations, which will be considered in the next chapter.

In addition Hirahata has a series of booklets on seven Kannon-sama circuits which are described as being revived or "resurrected." These are (2008):

Aizu Kannon Junrei
Izumo Kannon Junrei
Shinano Kannon Junrei
Izu Ōdō Kannon Junrei
Awa Kannon Junrei
Hokkaidō Kannon Junrei
Hokuriku Kannon Junrei

These are spread widely across Japan. Note that the Awa referred to above is not the ancient province name for part of Shikoku (the present-day Tokushima Prefecture) but an area between the sea and the mountains of southern Chiba Prefecture. This pilgrimage is listed as hav-

---

24. *Shikoku Junrei Hyaku Kannon, Junpai Gongyō Seiten.*

ing 34 sites to be visited, evidently in imitation of Chichibu. Circled in a map of the whole of Japan, the approximate locations of the above pilgrimages are shown together with two further Kannon routes, namely Echigo Sanjūsan Kannon and Chūgoku Sanjūsan Kannon.[25] The "revival" referred to here neither reliably implies, nor excludes serious antiquity, but any claims to antiquity which are evidently used to bolster the nostalgia effect require independent historical research which cannot be undertaken here. All who are familiar with Japanese religions in general will be used to the vaguely suggestive expression "it is said that" which occurs so often in apparently serious descriptions.

Other writers with temple connections are also active. Kurashige Ryōkai, for example, has published and republished his guide to the Echigo Thirty-three (Kurashige 1982, revised 1987), being himself the incumbent of Number 25, Shinjō-in 真城院. According to Kurashige, the Echigo route is 650 kilometres long, but can be covered in four days with three overnight stops by the use of "my-car," as Japanese refer to their private cars. Indeed, his books urge, such a journey combines the new with the old, and "calms the mind." Another colourful guide to the Echigo Thirty-three is by Satō Takashi who, born in 1939, has made ethnology his *raifuwaaku* (lifework), being accompanied for the Echigo pilgrimage guide by photographer Takahashi Yohei.[26] Without prejudice to any particular authors, it may be said that the edges between journalism, anthropology, photography (as done by what is known in Japan as a "cameraman"), travel and diary writing, religious promotion, and indeed general entrepreneurship, are often rather blurred. When we add to this all the various institutions from temples to printing houses which may be involved in "publishing," and an endless flurry of subtitles and contributing names, it will be seen both that the production of a "bibliography" in any typical sense is sure to be an imperfect art, and that the numbers of those somehow involved in the world of pilgrimage is very great. And in these remarks the pilgrims have not even been included.

Not even the indefatigable Hirahata has been able to write guides for all the Kannon pilgrimages which can be named. In a recent book devoted to the practice of copying out the verses of the Kannon Sūtra, both as a calligraphic and a merit-making exercise, no less than 82 different routes were listed with an administrative office (usually in a temple) and a telephone number.[27] These routes are spread over the prefectures of the whole country, except that none are given for Okinawa and only one for Hokkaidō. By simple multiplication the total number of temples involved here would come to 2706, although there are occasionally cases

---

25. Hirahata 1987, 92–93.
26. Satō 1989. The details about the author are in the publisher's page of the book.
27. Matsubara 2007.

of one temple functioning within more than one route. Given this huge number of pilgrimages devoted to Kannon Bosatsu, we will now take a closer look at just three selected instances, at Izumo and Kamakura and on the Izu Peninsula, to bring out some particular characteristics and issues. For easier reading below, the characters are given for particular temple names only in particular cases.

The Izumo, Kamakura and Izu Kannon routes

The Izumo Thirty-three Kannon route covers a fairly coherent area in south western Honshū (Japan's main island), and is said to have been inaugurated about 1300 years ago by the previously mentioned Buddhist monk Tokudō, who founded among others the Nara temple Chōkokuji. Temples number 1 and 8 of the Izumo circuit also bear the name Chōkokuji. A special feature of the Izumo pilgrimage is that it bears the same name as Izumo Grand Shrine, from the "land" (*kuni*) of Izumo, and that this leading, and very beautiful Shintō sanctuary is nowadays named as the first sacred place to be visited. Indeed, the shrine is so important in the religious geography of Japan that it would be almost unthinkable for a pilgrim travelling in this region, even though performing a Buddhist pilgrimage, not to visit it. After all, temple No. 1 (Chōkokuji) is approached from the seashore just behind the great Shintō sanctuary, while Number 2 is just across the roadway going down past the shrine to the coast. It would be practically impossible to go to these two temples while ignoring the great shrine. It is therefore listed in a recent pamphlet before temple Number One (Chōkokuji) as a "special number" (*tokuban* 特番),[28] short for *tokubetsu bangai* 特別番外).

This pamphlet was published by the "Office" of the Izumo Pilgrimage located at a famous temple named Ichibatadera, also lying on the route which pilgrims would take. Ichibatadera is not one of the thirty-three, but appears as an "extra-numerary" temple (*bangai*). The reason for this is not hard to find. Ichibata Temple, run by Rinzai Zen Buddhists, houses one of the more famous images of the "Medicine Buddha," Yakushi Nyorai. Yakushi-sama is particularly noted for the beneficial effects which he can bestow on persons with eyesight problems. Either he can improve one's eyesight or, as informants explain, he can prevent poor eyesight from getting worse.[29] Since the temple is so popular (for people with bad eyesight) it is a good place at which to inform a greater number of visitors about the Izumo pilgrimage and to encourage its performance. In sum, visiting the Yakushi image of Ichibatadera, whether listed or not, has also long been popular

---

28. While this literally means "special number" it probably arose as an abbreviation from *tokubetsu bangai* 特別番外 meaning "special extra-numerary."

29. This temple was briefly introduced in an article entitled "Suffering and health in Mahayana Buddhism" (Pye 1983).

Japanese Buddhist Pilgrimage

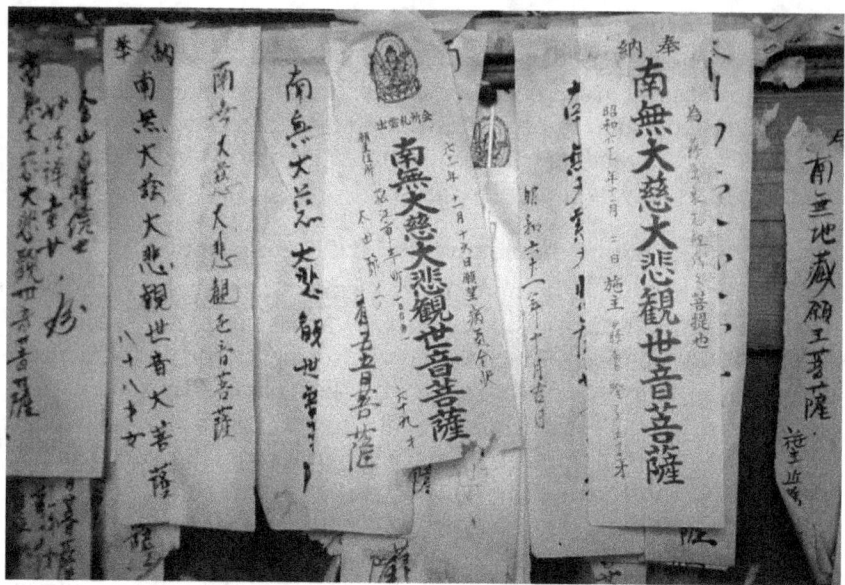

Figure 2.12 Pilgrims' slips (cf. Chapter Six) of the Izumo Kannon Pilgrimage.

with many visitors to the region, though rather more effort is required to reach it for those pursuing the circulatory pilgrimage route in itself.

Interestingly enough, neither Izumo Grand Shrine nor Ichibata Temple are listed in an older pamphlet which the writer obtained from the first temple of the pilgrimage, Chōkokuji, apparently dating from Taishō 2 (1913). The fact that Izumo Taisha is not listed here illustrates the official separation of Shintō from other religions, especially Buddhism, which was enforced during the period in question. The current situation represents something of a return to the much more intimate associations between Buddhism and Shintō characteristic of long periods before the Meiji Restoration of 1868.

The names and (simplified) denominations of the Izumo Thirty-three temples are given in Table 2.8.[30]

Note that more than a third of these are Zen temples. Three of them belong to the Rinzai Zen tradition, while another ten belong to the Sōtō Zen tradition. We can see from this, as we do from the Chichibu route, that the Zen tradition, sometimes regarded as meditationally austere and spiritually superior, is frequently connected with more widely current forms of religious practice.

The Kamakura sequence of thirty-three Kannon pilgrimage sites is a typical if little known local alternative to the far-flung Bandō series. It begins at Sugimoto-dera 杉本寺, which is also Number 1 of the Bandō thirty-three circuit, and ends at the celebrated Rinzai temple Engakuji 円覚

---

30. As given in Moriguchi 1977.

Table 2.8 The names and denominations of the Izumo Thirty Three temples (simplified).

1	Chōkokuji	Shingon-shū	
2	Yōmeiji	Shingon-shū	
3	Gakuenji	Tendai-shū	
4	Kannonji	Rinzai-shū	
5	Kandōji	Jōdo-shū	
6	Rendaiji	Shingon-shū	
7	Kōmyōji	Sōtō-shū	
8	Chōkokuji	Sōtō-shū	
9	Mineji	Shingon-shū	(also read as Minedera)
10	Zenjōji	Tendai-shū	
11	Entsūji	Tendai-shū	
12	Jufukuji	Sōtō-shū	
13	Manpukuji	Shingon-shū	
14	Rengeji	Sōtō-shū	
15	Kōanji	Sōtō-shū	
16	Fusaiji	Sōtō-shū	(also known as Jōeiji)
17	Hoshigamiji	Sōtō-shū	
18	Iwakuraji	Shingon-shū	
19	Kannonji	Shingon-shū	
20	Chōdaiji	Tendai-shū	
21	Kiyomizudera	Tendai-shū	(also read as Kiyomizuji)
22	Chōrakuji	Tendai-shū	
23	Gankōji	Sōtō-shū	
24	Jōonji	Shingon-shū	
25	Chōsuiji[a]	Sōtō-shū	(also known as Chōkeiji)
26	Senjuin	Shingon-shū	(also known as Oguraji)
27	Senkōji	Sōtō-shū	(also known as Chōfukuji)
28	Jōsōji	Shingon-shū	(also known as Fuonji)
29	Asahiji	Shingon-shū	
30	Kongōji	Rinzai-shū	

31	Manganji	Shingon-shū	
32	Zenkōji	Ji-shū	(also known as Fukuōji)
33	Seiganji	Rinzai-shū	(also known as Iwayaji)
	Bangai[b]	Ichibatadera	(also read as Ichibataji)
	Tokubetsu bangai[c]	Izumo Taisha	

a) Also read as Sunzuji.
b) Extra-numerary
c) Special extra-numerary

寺, or more precisely at a particular building within its large grounds, the Butsunichi-an 仏日庵. This building was originally erected for the shōgun Hōjō Tokimune and then used as a Buddhist retreat for members of the Hōjō family. The circuit had a precursor which enjoyed great popularity in the eighteenth century and which covered a wider area around Kamakura. However the reorganization of Buddhist temples during the Meiji Period, including closures and relocations, threw this circuit out of balance. It was therefore reorganized in the 1920's on a more limited geographical basis, keeping it within the confines of the city of Kamakura.[31]

As a result it is now possible to complete the pilgrimage in two days. For this purpose the recommended order departs somewhat from the formal sequence. According to Hirahata's popular guidebook the temples are even introduced in the preferred visiting order, with the remarkable result that each temple is given two numbers, as seen in Table 2.9.

It may be observed from the table that the sequence begins and ends correctly. The thirteen visits after No. 1 are in a miscellaneous order, but in the second half only No. 4 still requires to be taken into the otherwise regular sequence. Since almost all of the irregularities take place on the first of the two days envisaged for the pilgrimage, the practical rearrangement will hardly be reflected in date-stamps (if any) of the commemorative seal-book or scroll. Nevertheless the explicit recognition of the coexistence of the sequence as it should be (after having been redefined in the early twentieth century!) and the order as practically recommended at the present, shows that there is some tension between these two. It is recognized that a circuit pilgrimage should *normally* be done in the right sequence, or at least in a recommended alternative sequence, for otherwise it runs the risk of descending into miscellany and no longer being a sequence at all. The level of popularity of this circuit is far from clear. It is possible to visit both Sugimotodera and Engakuji without realising that these are regarded as the first and last temples respectively of a Kamakura Thirty-three Kan-

---

31. This historical information is given in a guidebook by Hirahata Yoshio entitled *Kamakura Sanjūsankasho*, Chōshi 1987.

Table 2.9 The Kamakura 33 Kannon showing alternative numerations.

Temple name	Visiting order	Formal number
Sugimoto-dera	1	1
Jōmyōji	2	9
Myōōin	3	8
Kōsokuji	4	7
Hōkokuji	5	10
Zuisenji	6	6
Raikōji	7	5
Hōkaiji	8	2
Kyōonji	9	12
Enmeiji	10	11
Betsuganji	11	13
Anyōin	12	3
Kōfukuji	13	15
Raikōji	14	14
Kuhonji	15	16
Budarakuji	16	17
Kōmyōji	17	18
Renjōin	18	19
Senjuin	19	20
Jōjuin	20	21
Gokurakuji	21	22
Hasedera	22	4
Kōtokuin	23	23
Jufukuji	24	24
Jōkōmyōji	25	25
Kaizōji	26	26
Myōkōin	27	27
Kenchōji	28	28
Ryūhōin	29	29

Meigetsuin	30	30
Jōchiji	31	31
Tōkeiji	32	32
Engakuji	33	33

non series. Sugimoto-dera presents itself rather as the beginning of the more illustrious Bandō pilgrimage, whereas Engakuji is a major centre of Rinzai Zen Buddhism, for which Kannon-related pilgrimage is of peripheral interest only. On the other hand this example illustrates very clearly the ups and downs in the fortunes of particular pilgrimage routes. This one flourished during the later Edo Period when the merchant population enjoyed prosperity and peace, and after the politically caused difficulties experienced by Buddhist temples during the Meiji Period it recovered in the 1920s. Following the Pacific war and the stringent post-war years, it was once again fostered as part of the pilgrimage boom. The "Pilgrimage Association" (Junrei no kai) inspired by author Hirahata, referred to above, has evidently been a driving force in this recovery, seeking to increase the number of journeys which pilgrims might be persuaded to make. The association is based at Manganji in Chōshi City, Chiba Prefecture, a temple which is not itself part of any pilgrimage circuit.

There seems to be no end to the number of new pilgrimage routes which can be designed on the basis of imitation. Yet even though the Kannon routes are in general very popular there does come a point where activity peters out for lack of enthusiasm. The following observations were made in March 1988. According to one of the many pilgrimage guides penned by Hirahata, there is a 33 Kannon pilgrimage route in the Izu peninsula, which is an extensive country and resort area southwest of Tokyo. However the starting point, the Number 1, of this route was not known to local people at Kawazu, where it was supposed to be situated. This suggests that enthusiasts, whether writers or readers, like to inflate the sheer number of possible pilgrimages beyond those which are really established by substantial tradition. A different series of 33 Kannon covering approximately the same area was known however at the travel information office (*annaisho*) at the station, where it was also possible to obtain, after some searching, a photocopied sheet (of uncertain derivation) bearing information about it. Two or three of this series are indeed at Kawazu, but not the "No. 1" of repute. On a visit to No. 15 of this series on the same day, being a temple named Tōdaiji (like the famous Tōdaiji at Nara) located up a small country road at the foot of a hill, there was no sign of life until a woman eventually emerged with some caution. Having adjusted to the sight of a foreigner she agreed that the temple was indeed "No. 15." There was little sign of this however, and apparently no expectation of pilgrims with

Going Round to Visit Kannon-sama

the imminent onset of the season. When asked what the pilgrims do when they come round she said that they just do *o-mairi* (i.e. they perform a visit for prayer). Asked if perhaps they do not come very often, for there is little sign of anything being left there, she replied that they do not leave anything at all. Normally of course the temples are festooned with pilgrims' visiting slips, votive tablets (*ema*), etc. So what about the seal (*shūin*) for the pilgrim's record book? These are done at a little building next to the Kannondō, which is itself the main building. Just inside the threshold of this office there stands a feeble wooden Kannon-sama placed slightly to one side. A photograph of this was allowed, but not one directly of the main altar where the main image would be. Originally there was a Horse-head Kannon (*batō-kannon*), my informant explained, but this had been replaced by an Eleven-faced Kannon (*jūichimen-kannon*). This was apparently done when the temple was refurbished, aligning it with a wider range of interests than the mainly agricultural reference of the horse-head Kannon. What is in fact visible, looking in towards the main altar, is a shrine-style mirror! The temple is affiliated to the Sōtō Zen Buddhist denomination.

In a case like this one can only conclude that those caring for the temple agreed to be entered on a list of 33 Kannon, since their main image was a Kannon-sama, and since they were asked. Personal enthusiasm was as lacking as any evidence of real pilgrims. Neither this series nor the other Izu series supposedly starting at Kawazu seem to enjoy any particular prominence in local consciousness. They seem to have come into existence for the benefit of hobby pilgrims from the major cities and those who cater for them with information booklets.

The Kannon routes are typically based on thirty-three temples, but other variations may be found. A sequence of eleven temples with images of Kannon has been devised around the rather extensive shores of Lake Biwa in western Japan, the first of them being at Miidera, which is at the same time No. 14 of the famous Saikoku pilgrimage. This route, provides an excellent way of combining Buddhist devotions with a manageable scenic journey.

Miniature Kannon-sama routes

The principle of imitation leads naturally on to those of *miniaturization* and *abbreviation*. In the wider field of Japanese religion these modes of religious adaptation are taken for granted as acceptable procedures in the provision of patterns for religious activity, although they have seldom been addressed theoretically.[32] Both abbreviation and miniaturiza-

---

32. Cf. Preface; the importance of miniaturization in Japanese religions was introduced in teaching from 1980 onwards and examples were given in *O-meguri*, Pye 1987. For miniaturization and replication with special reference to the Shikoku pilgrimage see Reader 1988 and Chapter Three below. As has later become evident, it is only on the basis of a theoretical perception of these matters that the relevance to new

tion are at work in the often cited example of votive tablets as "horse pictures" (*ema*), so called because historically they first came into use as a miniature substitute for the offering of a horse, on which a *kami* may ride. Thus live horses, still sometimes to be seen, were replaced by model horses and by large paintings of horses, then by small pictures of horses and finally by pictures of quite different things. Though *ema* now bear many motifs and are almost as common in Buddhist temples as in Shintō shrines, this derivation is still cherished in some *ema* which show a horse surmounted by a *gohei*, indicating the presence of a *kami*. At Buddhist temples, the *ema* usually bear Buddhist themes such as a depiction of the main buddha or bodhisattva revered at the temple, horses and *gohei* having been long forgotten. On the use of *ema* see further below in the context of the pilgrim's transaction (Chapter 6).

Similarly, when it comes to sacred places there is no difficulty, in the Japanese imagination, in imitating and miniaturizing these at one and the same time. This may be seen in the miniature imitations of Mount Fuji, which seem to be particularly popular in the Kantō region. There is a nice example next to Hakusan Shrine in Bunkyō-ku, Tokyo. Here is to be seen a small fenced-off mound which can be mounted in a few steps, so that the shrine at the summit may be visited with ease. This mound, with its little shrine at the top, is called Sengensha 浅間社, after the shrine on the peak of Mount Fuji itself. Another example may be found in the grounds of Shiki Shrine in Saitama Prefecture, where the artificial mound is also referred to as Sengensha. In other cases no more than a temporary cone of sand is used.

It has not often been remarked just how closely miniaturization and abbreviation are connected to each other. It is the attitude of being prepared to abbreviate a religious practice which makes the physically evident miniatures possible. As a result, the miniature pilgrimages of interest here are an intermediate form which combines the convenience of a concentrated location with the fiction of arduous circulation. It is rather easy to set up a tiny pilgrimage based on thirty-three images of Kannon-sama, or even just thirty-three stones, which may be "visited" in turn, in quick succession.

Some of the temples on the main routes have their own miniatures within their grounds, thus providing a pilgrimage within a pilgrimage. At the Bandō circuit's temple Rakuhōji, No 24, also known as Amabiki Kannon, thirty-three such stones are ranged towards and round behind the temple itself, each one bearing a relief of Kannon-sama. In 1980 these had been recently renewed, but the older stones were still stacked in one place as a group. At a temple in Sendai the thirty-three stones, engraved with the names and numbers of the temples of the far distant Saikoku

---

developments such as religion in the internet can be assessed, cf. Pye 2005.

route (not the Sendai route!) were set up in one place, with a large and friendly Jizō Bosatsu (see further in Chapter Four) standing guard at each end. In such cases there is no longer any need to "go round," since it is possible to perform *o-mairi* at all the "temples" in one single action which stands for an abbreviated "going round." The same is true before a well-used assemblage of thirty-three Kannon-sama images at one of the temples of the Saikoku route, namely the Rokkakudō of Chōhōji (No. 18). Since this temple is in central Kyōto near an underground railway stop hardly ten minutes distant from the main station, it is relatively easy to reach for anybody travelling in Japan. Any visitors there can participate symbolically in the whole of the Saikoku route without the trouble of going all the way round.

More remote but of considerable interest is the Temple No. 27 of the Saikoku route, Engyōji, where an interesting miniature series of contemporary Kannon statues leads up the small mountain pathway to the main hall. The variety of iconographical forms reflects those of the original temples, but here they are instructively open to immediate view. It is also interesting for students of religion because of the inscriptions on the base of the statues. The bases carry varied votive texts of the individual or corporate donors, most of them with a commercial background, providing evidence of their prayers and aspirations. The sequence is slightly interrupted in that No. 27 (being the main temple in this case) places its own miniature first, at the bottom of the hill. Later on there is therefore a jump from 26 to 28. The introductory statue introduces all the rest as a pilgrimage within the main pilgrimage which leads to the real No. 27 at the top of the up-hill climb. At No. 33 of this miniature a connection is made to the *Heart Sūtra*, a short text which begins with reference to Kanjizai, or Kannon-sama. More will be said below on the role of this *sūtra* in the pilgrimages, but we may note in anticipation a most significant point. Much Japanese religion, including the making of pilgrimages, is carried out at a transactional level. That is, votive offerings are made and merit-making activities are performed in the hope of recompense and benefits in this existence. However this level of understanding can also be transcended religiously, in a Buddhist sense, in that Kannon-sama is believed to free living beings from their sufferings. The bodhisattva can do this because he/she practices the perfection of insight, in terms of which the phenomena to which we may be attached are understood to be "empty." Thus devotion to Kannon-sama leads the practitioner into the possibility of a significant religious shift of consciousness. If anything, the *Heart Sūtra* is clearer in this regard than is the Kannon chapter of the *Lotus Sūtra* itself. We will return to this theme in Chapter Seven.

At the Yokawa complex of Mount Hiei near Kyōto, with its memorial temple for Ganzan Daishi and its training centre for young Tendai priests, there is a route of thirty-three small outdoor stopping points, one for each of the thirty-three real Saikoku temples, where prayers and offerings may be made before an appropriately inscribed stone. In this case some older stone markers have been joined by more recent, and more evident larger stones. The woodland path goes round between the above-mentioned institutions and some smaller Shintō-type shrines (with *torii*), including one to Benzaiten (see further in Chapter Five), and takes about three quarters of an hour to complete.

In a guidebook to Fukushima entitled *Fukushima kokutai gaidobukku* 福島国体ガイドブック we learn of thirty-three stone buddhas about 90cm in height, standing in Yabuki Machi 矢吹町 which are "said" to have been carved by Kōbō Daishi, though "this is uncertain." Such "uncertainty" of ascription is often obscured by phrases such as "it is said that" or "it is the tradition that." The politically nervous might like to know that *kokutai* here does not refer to the "national polity" of pre-war ideology but is an abbreviation for *kokumintaiiku* – "national (people's) physical (education)."

In the Aizu area, a local guidebook entitled "Fresh Pack Aizu" フレッシュパック会津 tells us that in the grounds of a temple known as Seiryūji 西隆寺 at Mishimamachi 三島町 "a young woman sculptor carved thirty-three Virgin Kannon" (*otome kannon* 乙女観音). Hidden behind this may be the imitative idea that if Mary the mother of Jesus is understood to be a virgin, so too can Kannon-sama. However that may be, there is plenty of room for invention and individual, local initiative.

If pilgrimages can be miniaturized it follows that more can be completed with less trouble. The city of Miura has miniature versions of the 100 Saikoku, Bandō and Chichibu Kannon-sama sites and also of the Shikoku 88. All of these, together with the seven gods of fortune (see below), can be visited in about three hours. More accessible for some travellers might be the temple Onjōji (or Miidera), Saikoku No. 14, at which there is a special hall for images of all one hundred, Saikoku in the middle and Bandō and Chichibu to right and left. Few pilgrims going the rounds in the usual way, and paying a full visit to Miidera, attractively located near Lake Biwa at Ōtsu near Kyōto, can resist paying devotions to all of them at once while they are there, after tossing in an appropriate coin. Further examples of miniature pilgrimages in the Shikoku tradition will be found in Chapter Three.

Denominational spread of Kannon-sama routes

As might be expected, most of the 66 temples in the Saikoku Pilgrimage and in the Bandō Pilgrimage are either Tendai or Shingon in their affiliation. However, these affiliations are not always predominant in other cases. It was already noted above that Zen temples form the over-

Going Round to Visit Kannon-sama

whelming majority in the Chichibu pilgrimage. The following table gives the denominational pattern of the 100 temples making up the Saikoku, Bandō and Chichibu Pilgrimages.

Table 2.10 Denominational spread of the leading Kannon-sama routes.

	Saikoku	Bandō	Chichibu	totals
Tendai	13	12	0	25
Shingon	15	16	3	34
Sōtō Zen	0	2	20	22
Rinzai Zen	0	0	11	11
Jōdo	0	2	0	2
other	5	1	0	6
totals	33	33	34	100

It is quite striking that, of the 34 temples of the Chichibu Pilgrimage, no less than 20 are Sōtō Zen Buddhist and 11 are Rinzai Zen Buddhist, while only three have a Shingon affiliation. There are no Tendai temples, although this is a major denomination. We have already seen that 13 temples of the Izumo circuit are Zen Buddhist in affiliation. While some perceptions of Zen Buddhism identify it in particular with meditation, the interactions with other aspects of Buddhist practice and piety should not be underestimated. In fact, quite apart from the practice of pilgrimage, many Zen Buddhist temples have statues of Kannon-sama as an important feature of their presentation to the general public, and indeed continue to acquire them. In 1973, for example, the Tokyo branch (Eiheiji Tōkyō Betsuin) of the leading Sōtō Zen temple Eiheiji raised a huge statue of Kannon-sama in its grounds, immediately opposite the printing house for denominational literature. An aesthetically pleasing figure of Kannon-sama also stands in the entrance area of the grounds of Eiheiji itself, the spiritual home of Sōtō Zen Buddhism. The participation of a large number of Zen temples in the Chichibu circuit is therefore not in itself especially curious.

Other, less known Kannon-sama pilgrimages display further variations in denominational spread. In the Sendai Pilgrimage for example, Sōtō Zen, Tendai and Jōdo (Pure Land) temples are prominent. The figures are Tendai 8, Shingon 3, Sōtō Zen 11, Rinzai Zen 1, Jōdo-shū 6, Ji-shū 1, Shin-shū 1, Shugen (Tendaikei) 2. If Jōdo-shū, Ji-shu and Shin-shū are taken together there are eight "Pure Land" Buddhist temples involved here, against none at all on the Saikoku route. The overall distribution in the Izumo pilgrimage is 13 Zen Buddhist temples (10 Sōtō and 3 Rinzai), 12 Shingon temples, 6 Tendai temples, 1 Jōdo temple and 1 Ji-shū temple. The Shōwa New Edo Thirty-three Circuit has a well-balanced spread, with 6 Tendai temples, 11

Jōdo temples, 9 Shingon temples (4 for the Kōyasan Shingonshū, 4 for the Shingonshū Buzanha and one for the Shingonshū Daigoha), 4 Zen temples (including both Sōtō and Rinzai Zen), 2 belonging to the Shōkannon-shū (a relatively small sect devoted to Kannon-sama) and one entirely independent temple called Kannon-ji.[33] The Ōmi route has 17 Tendai temples, 6 Shingon temples, 4 Rinzai temples, 2 Sōtō temples, 1 Ōbaku Zen temple, and 3 without any standardized denominational affiliation.[34] The Rakusai route in Kyōto is notable in that more than half of its temples are in the Pure Land tradition, mainly of the Seizan Jōdo denomination.

The denominational distribution of the Kamakura sequence listed earlier is also relevant here. It will not surprise the reader familiar with Kamakura that Rinzai Zen is well represented with twelve temples, and inevitably the Shingon and Tendai traditions also participate, with five and two temples respectively. The largest group is formed, however, by thirteen temples relating to Amida Buddha, of which seven are affiliated to Jōdo-shū and six are affiliated to Ji-shū. The remaining temple, bringing the total up to thirty-three, is Hasedera (also known as Hase Kannon), which is an independent temple institution. Casual visitors to Kamakura may be interested to know that while the famous Great Buddha (Daibutsu) of Kamakura is a representation of Amida Nyorai, it is situated in the grounds of Number 23 of the Kamakura series, the Kōtoku-in, whose Kannon-sama is in a quiet building to the rear.

It may be noted that there is no participation in these pilgrimages by Shin-shū temples for the simple reason that in Shin-shū doctrine merit-making practices, which on at least one level of interpretation pilgrimage is regarded to be, are regarded as useless and even misleading. This does not prevent Shinshū believers from journeying to historic sites which have a religious significance in India which have a connection with the historical Buddha,[35] whose birthday is also prominently observed in Shinshū temples. In disregard of official doctrine there is also certainly some participation in pilgrimage by members of families which are formally Shinshū by ancestral tradition. A taxi driver claiming quite definitely to be a Shinshū believer, and familiar with leading writings of his faith such as *Tannishō* and *Kyōgyōshinshō*, had accompanied

---

33. Under "other" we find six different religious corporations, namely: Kyūseikannon-shū 救世観音宗, Kokawakannon-shū 粉河観音宗, Hossō-shū 法相宗, Kitahossō-shū 北法相宗, Honzanshugen-shū 本山修驗宗 and Shōkannon-shū 正観音宗.

34. These details are drawn from guidebooks published by the Edo Fudasho Kai (Edo Pilgrimage Society) in 1993 and 2000 entitled *Shōwa Shinsen Edo Sanjūsan Fudasho Annai*. These booklets also provide five older variants at the back, and yet others are mentioned in the preface. Compare also Yamada 1979. It seems therefore that adjustments have been made over many years, reflecting various pressures and interests.

35. On Japanese pilgrimages to India see further in Chapter Seven.

his father-in-law on a pilgrimage to most of the temples of the Saikoku route. Moreover his interest in mountains also gives him the excuse to visit the Shingon temple Kami-Daigoji, near Kyōto, five or six times a year. This is a strenuous uphill walk which just happens to culminate in a visit to Number 11 of the famous Saikoku Kannon-sama route. Some interesting variations on pilgrimage in the Shin Buddhist tradition will also be noted in Chapter Four.

The distribution of the temples of the various Buddhist denominations in Japan is in itself due to the most varied historical and political reasons. Since these reasons are not usually inherently connected with the decision to install a statue of Kannon-sama, the pilgrimage routes cut across the denominational patterns to a considerable extent. An interesting case is Number 14 of the Saikoku route, Miidera, which was established as a result of a split between the followers of Enchin and the followers of Ennin, leading figures in the Tendai elaboration of Esoteric Buddhism (Tendai Mikkyō) which was a response to the powerful attraction exercised by Shingon Mikkyō in mediaeval times. While Ennin's followers remained on Mount Hiei near Kyōto, Enchin's followers established the Tendai Jimon Sect with its headquarters at Miidera (the formal name of the temple being Onjōji), near the shore of Lake Biwa. During the civil wars of the period Ennin's followers sided with the Heike while Enchin's followers sided with the Genji, with the result that the temple was burned to the ground.

This was once explained to me as a matter of some importance (which historically, of course, it is) by an attendant collecting entrance fees[36] at one of the gates. This attendant, though working at a Tendai temple, was himself a Shinshū believer, largely out of family tradition. He explained this carefully by use of the term *senzodaidai* 先祖代々, i.e. ancestors from generation to generation, and by drawing an analogy with my own membership in the Church of England, which he elicited through skilful questioning of his interviewer! It seemed quite natural for him to be serving a temple of a different denomination, admittedly for reward, in spite of the relatively strict teaching of his own.

The denominational distribution of temples lends a certain flavour to the various routes. However it is clear that there is no one dominant denominational base for the practice of circulatory pilgrimage as a whole. Moreover the picture is complicated by the extremely diverse and almost unchartable denominational allegiance of the pilgrims themselves. Nor do members of any one denomination restrict themselves strictly to particular pilgrimages, although some of those to be

---

36. The vast majority of Buddhist temples in Japan do not charge an admission fee but a number in the Kyōto and Nara area do so because of their extreme importance to tourists as cultural sites.

considered later attract some pilgrims rather than others. All of this means that the practice of circulatory pilgrimage to the sacred sites of Kannon-sama has an unstoppable religious legitimacy of its own in the consciousness of the innumerable pilgrims who seek her out. The meanings of the pilgrimage for them are only to a limited extent influenced by the teachings of particular schools.

Completing the pilgrimage routes

The various routes and the numeration of the temples to be visited along the way builds up into a fascinating picture in which the pilgrims have to orientate themselves. Every single number locates a temple somewhere in a specific landscape, making it part of a wider region which thus hangs notionally together. Yet the numbering is not entirely stable. As has been noted, revisions have often been undertaken for various reasons from time to time. Then there are the additional or "extra-numerary" (*bangai*) temples. Even Shintō shrines can be added to Buddhist routes. Just as the Izumo route cannot really ignore Izumo Taisha, so no performance of the Shikoku route (to be considered next) would be really complete without a visit to the great Konpira Shrine. Very recently there has been a trend to bring the nationally significant Shintō shrine Ise Jingū into the picture for the Kansai region.

Nor are the pilgrimages necessarily pursued in the formal order of the numbers, though this is certainly the most common approach. In the case of the Saikoku and Bandō Pilgrimages the precise order is not very important since the temples are geographically rather scattered and do not relate easily to the rail and road arrangements of modern times. Individual pilgrims may have their own reasons for starting with a particular group of temples. At Chichibu it is common to visit Number 4 first of all, simply because it happens to be on the way from the station to Number 1. Why fail to save precious minutes when there is a complex schedule ahead? Moreover, since the possibility of going round a pilgrimage circuit in reverse order (*gyakumawari*) is also quite well established, this too is regarded as acceptable if the transport connections from one's place of normal residence make it more convenenient and hence more effective. Though the procedure is not particularly common, and nowadays makes even less difference to the practicality than in earlier times, the very idea of going round in reverse order implies a combination of respect for the real order and recognition of the practical needs of particular pilgrims.

These indications show that a literalistic view of the route as numbered is not considered essential, even though the prescribed sequence is followed where possible or reasonable. The pilgrims' books and scrolls are usually set up in such a way that the temple calligraphy and seals

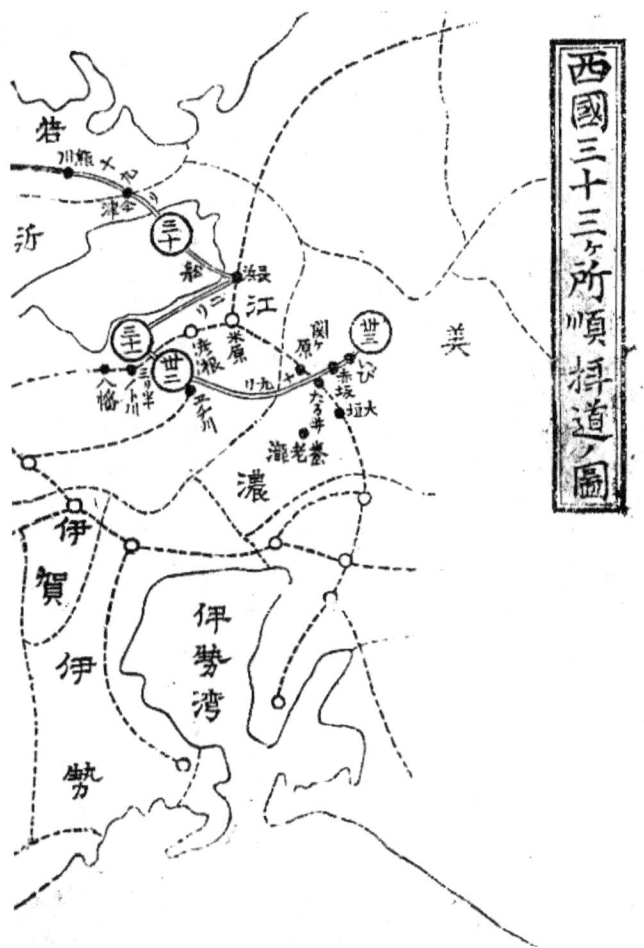

Figure 2.13 Traditional map of the Saikoku Kannon Pilgrimage, probably nineteenth century: detail showing the last few temples.

which record each visit are to be entered in a predetermined position. Of course, the prescribed sequence is also followed as far as possible, but since the seals have to be inserted during the journey, they are acquired in the *de facto* order of visiting. A large hanging scroll which is as yet incomplete may therefore very well show entries in miscellaneous boxes rather than sequential places. From these practical variations we can see therefore that the key lies not so much in the sequence as such as in visiting *all* of the temples, so that the circulation is *completed*. This completion lies in carrying out every one of the individual temple visits, each of which itself follows a prescribed ritual structure. There is a transaction to be performed at each of these temporary goals (on which see further in Chapter Six). So the pilgrim's way consists of a series of goals, each of which has its own significance. The final temple of any one pilgrimage is in a limited sense the goal of the whole route, but it is not necessarily a more outstanding holy place than the intermediate goals. On the contrary, its importance lies in symbolizing the *completion* of the whole way. This idea has a particular definiteness at number 34 of the Chichibu Pilgrimage, since it also counts as number 100 of the Saikoku, Bandō and Chichibu routes taken together. Yet the final temple of any one circulatory route is significant. On reaching it, the pilgrims often leave their special pilgrim hats and sticks behind. They have finished their circulation.

What the pilgrims keep with them are not the *means* for achieving the circulation but the *proofs* that they have done so. From the final temple, they therefore wend their way home by whatever route and mode of transport is convenient and economical. Back in their normal habitat they are able to report, to their families and to their ancestors, that they have travelled to the pilgrimage region, completed the circulation for the sake of their avowed intentions, and have now safely returned.

— Chapter Three —

The Shikoku Pilgrimage

Introducing the Shikoku pilgrimage

The second major pilgrimage route of Japan to be considered is the chain of eighty-eight temples spread through the four prefectures of Shikoku, the fourth largest island of the whole country. Although the Saikoku pilgrimage has a greater claim to antiquity, many people, and not only devotees of the Shingon Buddhist sects, would regard the Shikoku route as the most prominent symbol of all Buddhist pilgrimage in Japan. The Shikoku route has 88 temples which were reputedly designated by Kūkai (Kōbō Daishi), the founder of Japanese Shingon Buddhism. It is widely known as the "Shikoku Eighty-eight Spiritual Sites" (Shikoku Hachijūhachi Reijō) though variations of this such as "Shikoku Eighty-eight Places" (Shikoku Hachijūhakkasho) will be found. In this chapter some imitations and abbreviations of the Shikoku Eighty-eight will also be briefly introduced.

It is the Shikoku pilgrimage which has most captured the imagination of foreign writers so far and, without seeking to review their works in detail, a few words about their various approaches may be helpful. The first to write about it was the German Alfred Bohner in his *Wallfahrt zu Zweien. Die 88 heiligen Stätten von Shikoku* (1931), whose detailed documentation and descriptions are of great value, both in themselves and also when used in comparison with more recent and contemporary observations.[1] One of the dramatic differences between Bohner's times and today is the development of the transport infrastructure, which forces us to pose the question as to whether the meaning of the Shikoku pilgrimage has changed as a result. The brief answer, in the present writer's estimation, is that it has not significantly changed, but of course a more complex answer will depend on where significance is really seen

---

1. These were considered in the context of the exhibition "O-meguri" (cf. Pye 1987) and more systematically in a section entitled "Alfred Bohner's 'Wallfahrt zu Zweien': ein Vergleich im Rückblick" in Pye 2005.

(cf. Chapter Seven below). In English the first book length account was that by the American Oliver Statler entitled *Japanese Pilgrimage* (1983).[2] This book is in effect a vivid travel diary based on going the rounds of the Shikoku temples personally, with a Japanese travel companion, and it includes various snippets of information about Japanese Buddhism and other matters of greater or less relevance. Although there is no limiting sub-title, Statler's book is in fact restricted to the Shikoku pilgrimage. Ian Reader's more recent work *Making Pilgrimages* (2005) is similarly focused on the Shikoku Pilgrimage, as its sub-title *Meaning and Practice in Shikoku* indicates. This work is also something of a travelogue, though with a broadly anthropological orientation and backed up by good linguistic knowledge. The author explores various organizational aspects of contemporary Japanese pilgrimage, such as the role of group leaders (*sendatsu* 先達) and the relationship between pilgrimage and the travel industry,[3] and his circumstantial descriptions of meetings and exchanges with pilgrims are of particular value. It is unfortunate that he makes no reference at all to Bohner's work, for *Making Pilgrimages* is in a sense its successor book for our times on the Shikoku route.[4] Fourth, attention may be drawn to a quite different work in French, namely Nathalie Kouamé's *Initiation á la Paléographie Japonaise, à travers les manuscrits du pèlerinage de Shikoku* 2000. For those interested in pilgrimage this is much more than an introduction to the intricacies of Japanese palaeography, for the sources examined and translated in this most attractive work give direct evidence for the organizational prescriptions regulating pilgrimage in early modern times, that is, during the Edo Period. In addition, reproductions and translations of older pilgrims' slips left behind at temples as proof of their visit enable us to get a sense of the continuity and consistency of this practice from early modern times onwards.

In all significant respects, the main information given below will be found to match that found in these books, and indeed with other shorter accounts of the Shikoku pilgrimage.[5] However since it is independently drawn from the field and from Japanese guidebooks and ephemeral pil-

2. The bibliography gives the British edition of 1984.
3. Reader has explored such topics in various articles over the years. On *sendatsu*, for example, see Reader 1993, and for more, cf. his own bibliography in *Making Pilgrimages*.
4. Interestingly, Statler, who was dependent on advisers and translators for his substantial information, did refer to Bohner at a few points. According to his Postscript (p. 339) he made use of an unpublished English translation by Katharine Merrill Skog (1941). The present writer has had no opportunity to assess the completeness or adequacy of this translation, and it must be said that its impact on Statler seems to have been quite incidental.
5. E.g. Hoshino 1997, Hoffmann 2004. I was also privileged to have access to the typescript pilgrimage diary of Richard K. Payne (University of California).

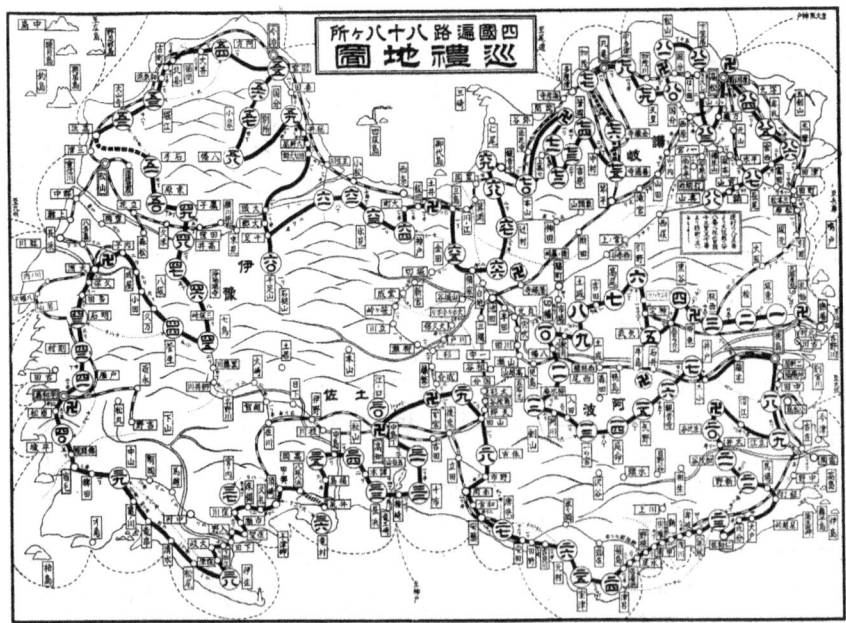

Figure 3.1 Traditional map of the Shikoku Pilgrimage with railways (reduced).

grimage documentation, no attempt is made to correlate it here point by point with the works mentioned. As a general comment however, a note of caution may be made about the *perception* of Japanese Buddhist pilgrimage generated by this widespread attention to the Shikoku route. Recent years have seen considerably increased sensitivity to the way in which "fields" of study are viewed and indeed constructed by those who study them. With this in mind, we should take care not to be led astray by the "purple passages" of some of the writing on Shikoku, or by the subliminal romanticism and conceptual adventurism which is occasionally prevalent. Moreover we should not allow our view of "pilgrimage" in Japan to be distorted by undue attention to this one leading case, significant though it is, without taking account of the wider phenomenon in all its diversity.

It is in connection with the Shikoku route that the term *henro* 遍路 is most widely used. Literally this means a "broad road" or a "widely [laid out] road," and a *henro-san* is a pilgrim in that he or she seeks the broad path or open road which links the many destinations in question all over the island of Shikoku. The term *henro* is transferred to the imitations of the Shikoku route as well, and sometimes, if less aptly, to the Kannon routes. Sometimes *henro* is translated as "pilgrimage." This may sometimes be appropriate, but we should remember that understood literally it refers to the route itself, rather than to the activity of pilgrimage, and that in Japanese it is most frequently used in connection with the Shikoku pilgrimage. The English term "pilgrimage" is therefore a much more general one, to which the nearest equally general Japanese term is *junrei*.[6]

We have seen that on the Saikoku route and its relatives it is the Kannon Hall (the Kannondō) of each temple which is above all to be visited, even when the object of reverence in the main temple is a different buddha or bodhisattva. There are other Buddhist pilgrim routes with one particular buddha or bodhisattva as the focus of attention, and different numbers of temples, but these will be considered in a subsequent chapter. On the Shikoku route the main buddhas and bodhisattvas revered in each temple are quite varied, and the connecting thread is provided by an additional visit to the hall where Kōbō Daishi is himself revered. Such a "hall" is known as the Daishidō. This feature makes the assessment of the historical development of the Shikoku pilgrimage particularly difficult, because it is inextricably entangled with the cult of Kōbō Daishi himself, who is regarded by Shingon-oriented devotees as a saviour figure in his own right. Indeed he is regarded by most Japanese of any religious orientation, or none, as a figure of symbolic significance comparable to Prince Shōtoku, the general father-figure of Japanese Buddhism. Both of these are the subject of hagiographical presentations of all genres including picture books and *manga*. At the most general level it may be said that the main focus of the Saikoku pilgrimage, Kannon-sama, is a mythological figure who is treated more or less as a real person, while the main focus of the Shikoku pilgrimage, Daishi-sama, is (i.e. was) a real person who is invested with a mythological aura. It must be added that questions about whether particular figures "existed" or not, or whether particular events of a miraculous character "took place" or not, are of little interest to the great majority of Japanese Buddhist pilgrims.

Another distinctive feature of the Shikoku route and its derivatives is that it is sometimes set out conceptually in four stages which are identified with the four ancient provinces of Shikoku respectively:

Awa province, now Tokushima Prefecture 1–23 (23 temples)
Tosa province, now Kōchi Prefecture 24–39 (16 temples)
Iyo province, now Ehime Prefecture 40–65 (26 temples)
Sanuki province, Kagawa Prefecture 66–88 (23 temples)

These stages, mentioned in guidebooks and sometimes shown on maps (for an example see Figure 7.2 on page 228 below) are also linked to four important Buddhist concepts:

---

6. As explained before this already includes the association of "going round" (*jun*) rather than going to a place. For further discussion of definitional problems see Hoshino 1997, 276ff.

Awa: *hosshin* 発心 giving rise to the mind (of enlightenment)
Tosa: *shugyō* 修行 discipline
Iyo: *bodai* 菩提 enlightenment (*bodai* = Sanskrit *bodhi*)
Sanuki: *nehan* 涅槃 nirvana

The four concepts named here are typical of Mahāyāna (Great Vehicle) Buddhism. In fact they represent the major stages in the development of a living being towards becoming a buddha. A person who "gives rise to the mind" of enlightenment thereby sets out on the path of bodhisattvahood. This in turn implies discipline. After the first flush of enthusiasm the pilgrim has to settle down into the routine of travel, coping with all the various difficulties of each day, moving forward physically, thinking not only of the temples already visited but of the far greater number which still lie ahead. Enlightenment and nirvana are of course two fundamental concepts identified with the historical Buddha himself. After attaining enlightenment the Buddha travelled widely until his last days when, at the end, he achieved the peace of nirvana without residue.

This does not mean, of course, that the pilgrims are expected to enter nirvana, or die, on reaching the final temple of the pilgrimage circuit. By no means. Although they have completed the circuit of eighty-eight temples, they are encouraged to visit the great Shingon Buddhist mountain, Kōya-san, where the mausoleum of the founder Kūkai (Kōbō Daishi) is to be found, and then to return to their own homes to report on their accomplishments. In so doing they will complete their pilgrimage in the broader sense outlined in the Introduction.

Previous treatments of Japanese pilgrimage have given the four stages of the spiritual journey some prominence. They appear for example in Alfred Bohner's work mentioned above.[7] However it is no longer possible to be sure whether they really played a strong role in the pilgrim's mind at that time, and their importance for the majority of pilgrims today is also not quite clear.[8] On the other hand, since the four concepts are each linked to a number of the temples successively, they do suggest a progressive process in the consciousness in the mind of some of the pilgrims, and this will be considered further in Chapter Seven below when we appraise the "meaning" of these pilgrimages. If anything, the four stages have come to be mentioned more frequently in recent years, and their being mentioned in pilgrims' guidebooks means at least that

---

7. Bohner 1931, 39.
8. Reader casts doubt on the influence of the concept on real pilgrims, while paradoxically emphasizing the idealist construction of the whole of Shikoku under the suggestive sub-heading "Symbolic structures, maps of enlightenment" as "a sacred terrain, a mandala" (Reader 2005, 54–55).

pilgrims think about them in the usually quiet evenings when there is nothing to do but to retire for nourishment, ablutions and rest.

Most of the time however, it is the detailed route itself which is more prominent. The Shikoku pilgrimage is the longest in sheer distance from temple to temple, from Number 1 to Number 88, and so it is quite understandable that its promoters and guides like to break it up into more manageable sections. It is usually reckoned to be about 1400 kilometres, but of course the precise length depends on the mode of transport, and decisions about short cuts (*chikamichi*), which may only work for those who abandon the convenience of some other mode of transport. The name Shikoku 四国 itself literally means "four countries" or in this case "four provinces," because the word *kuni* which is also attached to the character for *koku* used to mean country or region in the sense of a sub-region or province within Japan. In pre-modern times, without today's traffic infrastructure, the four provinces of Shikoku covered a rather wide area in practical terms, so the staging of the pilgrimage was a helpful form of orientation. In particular, the temples in the second stage are far apart, and rumour even had it that the local inhabitants were not so helpful as elsewhere. This proverbial inhospitality is the main point which was picked up by Statler from Bohner's treatment. However it is not at all borne out by the present writer's experience. Nevertheless going around to the temples of the second section really was, and to some extent remains a major effort, so that this section is appropriately designated as *shugyō* (again, see further in Chapter Seven).

The Shikoku pilgrimage is usually regarded as completed when all eighty-eight temples have been visited, but Shingon Buddhists usually reconfirm this completion with a supplementary visit to Mount Kōya, the traditional headquarters of Shingon Buddhism, itself founded by Kōbō Daishi. This is rather carefully phrased because Mount Kōya is located not on Shikoku but fairly close by in Wakayama Prefecture, on Japan's largest island, Honshū. So it is not precisely a part of the circuit, and nor does the circuit lead to it. Nevertheless it is usually regarded as an important additional confirmation that the Shikoku pilgrimage has been completed. Another supplementary destination, to which many pilgrims pay a visit in the general context of their pilgrimage, is the Shintō shrine Konpira (or Kotohira), the largest Shintō shrine on Shikoku and itself a powerful symbol for the whole island.

The origins of the Shikoku Pilgrimage are not clearly documented. The legend has it that it links together all the places where the great leader Kōbō Daishi stayed, and where consequently temples were established. It has been suggested that the term *henro* 遍路 as a designation for the pilgrims themselves somehow indicates a more general origin with practitioners of Shugendō, especially in connection with their wanderings and ascetic exercises, whether in Shikoku or in the mountains of Kumano (cf. Sakai 1960). However this may be, the Ōsaka entrepreneur Shinnen-bō 信念房 began to spread news of the Shikoku pilgrimage by means of publications during the Genroku Period (1688–1703), one of these being a work by the Kōyasan monk Jakuhon 寂本, entitled Shikoku Henro Reijōki 四国遍礼霊場記, i.e. *An Account of the journey round the spiritual sites of Shikoku* (1689).[9] This work is indeed a temple by temple account of the 88 temples, with a line drawing of the layout of each one being provided. It is not clear how far publications of this kind were popularizing a practice which was in principle already known, but there is no doubt that the pilgrimage goes back at least to his time in something similar to its present form. According to Bohner, The oldest known map of the Shikoku pilgrimage dates from 1747.[10]

The overall direction of the pilgrimage is in an approximately clockwise direction around Shikoku starting at an easterly point and ending in the north-east, although this is not, incidentally, a circumambulation in the true sense of the word, because there is nothing in the centre. Moreover the *de facto* starting point depends to some extent on where people cross over from the main island, Honshū. Those who cross over from the Hiroshima region on southern Honshū are quite likely to begin in the middle with temples numbers 47 to 53 near Matsuyama. To insist on starting at number 1, on the other side of Shikoku, ending at number 88 in the north-east and then returning to Matsuyama for the journey home, would lengthen the total distance by about 50%. Those crossing from Okayama to Takamatsu on the other hand do well to begin with number 88 and traverse the route in descending order. This is an example of the previously mentioned principle of "reverse circulation," known in Japanese as *gyakumawari*, which is in principle regarded as acceptable. The nearest crossings for pilgrims from eastern Honshū are from Wakayama Prefecture, and these lead over a shorter distance to number 1 than to any important alternatives. Nowadays however the older ferry and rail links are less convenient than going by Shinkansen to Okayama (from anywhere in Japan) and then across to Takamatsu. This trend was accentuated in that the first modern road bridge also led to Takamatsu. Seeking to counter non-standard sequences, Temple No. 1, Ryōzenji, urges in its pamphlet that people should start there and return again after finishing "to show gratitude," which incidentally means that the temple would collect double offerings. As can be seen on the map, after going right around Shikoku it is not so very far from No. 88 back to No. 1 again, but in practice much depends on transport decisions.

---

9. Available in a modern translation by Murakami Mamoru (1987). The different characters used for *henro* here (遍礼 where we would now expect 遍路) are correct in this title.

10. Bohner 1931, 74.

The massive development of road travel is generally popular with pilgrims. This is probably the biggest single factor underlying the overall growth in the numbers of pilgrims over recent decades. In 1984 the number of pilgrims reached nearly 50,000 and in 1992 the number was assessed at about 67,000. Even after the onset of economic unease the numbers remained clearly above 50,000, and they then surged again to over 80,000 at the beginning of the twenty-first century.[11] While there have been peaks and troughs in the statistical development, it seems clear that transport developments and associated commercialization have led to a steady overall increase in the number of pilgrims. This has led to a widening of the range of persons able to participate and consequently to adjustments in the general style of participation, in particular to the ways in which touristic provision and sales are linked to pilgrimage journeys.

The temples of the Shikoku eighty-eight spiritual places

The list below shows the names and the central objects of reverence (*gohonzon*), i.e. the buddhas and bodhisattvas, of the eighty-eight temples or "spiritual places" (*reijō* 霊場) of the Shikoku pilgrimage. As will be recalled, a Japanese temple name has two components, the "mountain" or *-san* name, and the usual temple name ending in *-ji* or *-tera*, or sometimes *-in*. For simplicity's sake however, only these latter names of the temples are given here, as is frequently done in Japan. If the *-san* name for any temple is required, recourse should be had to a Japanese guidebook with full details. It should be noted that the characters used in Buddhist contexts such as temple names are frequently pronounced in special ways. For example, the *rei* of *reijō* 霊場 referred to immediately above is pronounced as *ryō* in the name of the first temple, Ryōzenji, and the second character of the same name, *zen* 山 (the consonant being hardened from *sen*), is more commonly read as *san*, being that for "mountain," and consequently occurring regularly in the *-san* names of temples. Sometimes the characters for the names can be, or are, mistakenly read in slightly divergent ways, or there is simply a nickname. Any variants of this kind are given in brackets. Since the *gohonzon* are more varied than in the case of the Saikoku pilgrimage, they will be discussed immediately below the list of temples. On the other hand the temples are almost all of the Shingon school, so denominations are not shown in this table. The five exceptions are:

Numbers 11 and 33	Rinzai Zen
Number 15	Sōtō Zen
Number 43	Tendai-shū
Number 78	Ji-shū (Ji-shū being a denomination in the Pure Land tradition)

---

11. Figures following Satō 2004, 162.

The Shikoku Pilgrimage

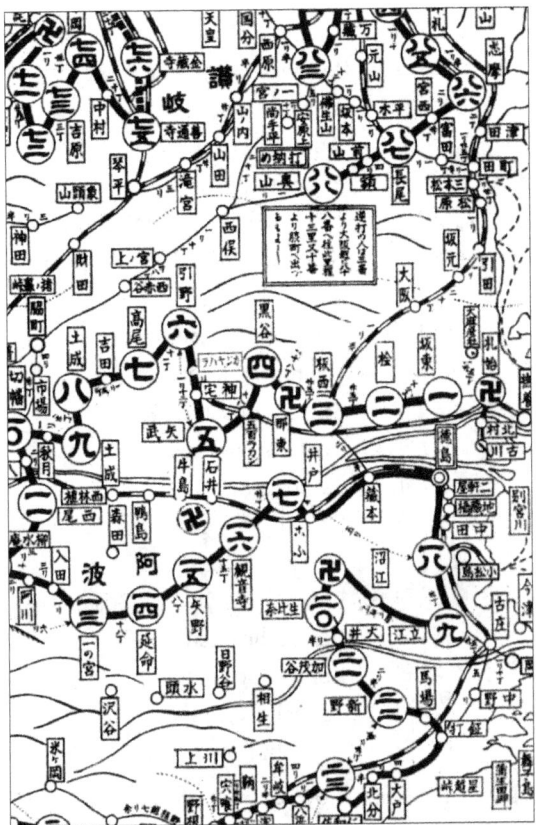

Figure 3.2 Traditional map of the Shikoku Pilgrimage with railways: detail showing the beginning and the end (temples 1–23 and 71–88).

As discussed above, it is customary to divide the list of temples into four sections headed "resolve," "discipline," "enlightenment" and "nirvana," and to refer to the ancient province names within Shikoku, giving the pilgrimage an aura of romantic antiquity. This helps to give some shape to what is otherwise a very long list, and so without prejudice to further interpretation, that framework is adopted here.

Table 3.1 The eighty-eight temples of the Shikoku pilgrimage with their main objects of reverence.

The 23 temples of Awa Province (now Tokushima Prefecture)

1	Ryōzenji	霊山寺	Shaka Nyorai
2	Gokurakuji	極楽寺	Amida Nyorai
3	Konsenji	金泉寺	Shaka Nyorai

4	Dainichiji	大日寺	Dainichi Nyorai
5	Jizōji	地蔵寺	Enmei (Enmyō) Jizō Son
6	Anrakuji	安楽寺	Yakushi Nyorai
7	Jūrakuji	十楽寺	Amida Nyorai
8	Kumadaniji	熊谷寺	Senju Kannon
9	Hōrinji	法輪寺	Nehan Shaka Nyorai
10	Kirihataji	切幡寺	Senju Kanzeon Bosatsu
11	Fujiidera	藤井寺	Yakushi Nyorai
12	Shōzanji	焼山寺	Kokūzō Bosatsu
13	Dainichiji	大日寺	Jūichimen Kanzeon
14	Jōrakuji	常楽寺	Miroku Bosatsu
15	Kokubunji	国分寺	Yakushi Nyorai
16	Kan'onji[a]	観音寺	Senju Kannon
17	Idoji	井戸時	Shichibutsu Yakushi Nyorai
18	Onzanji	恩山寺	Yakushi Nyorai
19	Tatsueji	立江寺	Enmei (Enmyō) Jizō Bosatsu
20	Kakurinji	鶴林寺	Jizō Daibosatsu
21	Tairyūji	太龍寺	Kokūzō Bosatsu
22	Byōdōji	平等時	Yakushi Nyorai
23	Yakuōji	薬王寺	Yakushi Nyorai

The 16 temples of Tosa Province (now Kōchi Prefecture):

24	Hotsumisakiji	最御崎寺	Kokūzō Bosatsu
25	Shinshōji	津照寺	Enmei (Enmyō) Jizō Bosatsu
26	Kongōchōji	金剛頂寺	Yakushi Nyorai
27	Kōnomineji	神峯寺	Jūichimen Kanzeon Bosatsu (also read as Kōmineji)
28	Dainichiji	大日寺	Dainichi Nyorai
29	Kokubunji	国分寺	Senju Kanzeon Bosatsu
30	Zenrakuji	善楽寺	Amida Nyorai
31	Chikurinji	竹林寺	Monju Daibosatsu
32	Zenjibuji	禅師峰寺	Jūichimen Kanzeon Bosatsu
33	Sekkeiji	雪蹊寺	Yakushi Nyorai
34	Tanemaji	種間寺	Yakushi Nyorai
35	Kiyotakiji	清滝寺	Yakuyoke Yakushi Nyorai
36	Shōryūji	青龍寺	Namikiri Fudō Myōō
37	Iwamotoji	岩本寺	Amida Nyorai (and others, see below)
38	Kongōfukuji	金剛福寺	Sanmen Senju Kanzeon Bosatsu
39	Enkōji	延光寺	Yakushi Nyorai

The Shikoku Pilgrimage

The 26 temples of Iyo Province (now Ehime Prefecture):

40	Kanjizaiji	観自在寺	Yakushi Nyorai
41	Ryūkōji	龍光寺	Jūichimen Kanzeon
42	Butsumokuji	仏目寺	Dainichi Nyorai
43	Meisekiji	明石寺	Senju Kanzeon Bosatsu
44	Taihōji	大宝寺	Jūichimen Kanzeon Bosatsu
45	Iwayaji	岩屋寺	Fudō Myōō
46	Jōruriji	浄瑠璃寺	Yakushi Nyorai
47	Yasakaji	八坂寺	Amida Nyorai
48	Sairinji	西林寺	Jūichimen Kanzeon Bosatsu
49	Jōdoji	浄土寺	Shaka Nyorai
50	Hantaji	繁多寺	Yakushi Nyorai
51	Ishiteji	石手寺	Yakushi Nyorai
52	Taisanji	太山寺	Jūichimen Kanzeon Bosatsu (also Taizanji)
53	Enmyōji	円明寺	Amida Nyorai
54	Enmeiji	延命寺	Fudō Myōō
55	Nankōbo[b]	南光坊	Daitsūchishō Nyorai
56	Taizanji	泰山寺	Jizō Bosatsu
57	Eifukuji	栄福寺	Amida Nyorai
58	Senyūji	仙遊寺	Senju Kanzeon Bosatsu
59	Kokubunji	国分寺	Yakushi Nyorai
60	Yokomineji	横峰寺	Dainichi Nyorai
61	Kōonji	香園寺	Dainichi Nyorai (also read as Kōenji)
62	Hōjuji	宝寿寺	Jūichimen Kanzeon Bosatsu
63	Kichijōji	吉祥寺	Bishamonten (also read as Kitsushōji, Kisshōji)
64	Maegamiji	前神寺	Amida Nyorai
65	Sankakuji	三角寺	Jūichimen Kanzeon Bosatsu

The 23 temples of Sanuki Province (now Kagawa Prefecture):

66	Unbenji	雲弁寺	Senju Kanzeon Bosatsu
67	Daikōji	大興寺	Yakushi Nyorai
68	Jinnein[c]	神恵院	Amida Nyorai (i.e. Jinne-in)
69	Kannonji	観音寺	Shō Kanzeon Bosatsu
70	Motoyamaji	本山寺	Batō Kanzeon Bosatsu
71	Iyadaniji	弥谷寺	Senju Kanzeon Bosatsu
72	Mandaraji	曼荼羅寺	Dainichi Nyorai
73	Shusshakaji	出釈迦寺	Shaka Nyorai

74 Kōyamaji	甲山寺	Yakushi Nyorai
75 Zentsūji	善通寺	Yakushi Nyorai
76 Konzōji	金倉寺	Yakushi Nyorai (also read as Kinzōji)
77 Dōryūji	道隆寺	Yakushi Nyorai
78 Gōshōji	郷照寺	Amida Nyorai
79 Kōshōin	高照院	Jūichimen Kanzeon Bosatsu (also Tennōji 天王寺)
80 Kokubunji	国分寺	Senju Kanzeon Bosatsu
81 Shiromineji	白峰寺	Senju Kanzeon Bosatsu (also read as Shiramineji)
82 Negoroji	根香寺	Senju Kanzeon Bosatsu
83 Ichinomiyaji	一宮寺	Shō Kanzeon Bosatsu
84 Yashimaji	屋島寺	Jūichimen Senju Kanzeon Bosatsu
85 Yakuriji	八栗寺	Shō Kanzeon Bosatsu
86 Shidoji	志度寺	Jūichimen Kanzeon Bosatsu
87 Nagaoji	長尾寺	Shō Kanzeon Bosatsu
88 Ōkuboji	大窪寺	Yakushi Nyorai

a) The name of No. 16 is usually given as Kan'onji, not Kannonji (as in No. 69).
b) The ending -bō refers to monks' quarters. It is rare as the name of an individual temple, as here, and more common as a designation for sub-institutions within a larger temple.
c) The only temple in the series with an -in name, more commonly found in secondary or private institutions.

As noted previously, when the circuit has been completed it is quite common to pay a visit to Mount Kōya, the eminently symbolic central monument of all Shingon Buddhism.

We now provide a brief commentary on the central objects of reverence (*gohonzon*) at the 88 temples including an explanation of their titles. These include buddhas, bodhisattvas and other celestial buddhist beings of various kinds.

In the first instance we find buddhas bearing the title Nyorai 如来, which means "Thus Come." Nyorai is a synonym for a Buddha who comes, or goes, in a state of perfect "suchness." The term corresponds to the Sanskrit *tathāgata*, which precisely speaking would mean "thus gone," i.e. into the state of nirvana, but the Chinese term *rú lài* 如来 (Japanese *nyorai*) highlights the nuance of "thus come." For a perfect Buddha there is thought to be no difference between going and coming. The *nyorai* found here are:

Shaka Nyorai (5 occurrences including the Nehan Shaka Nyorai, see again below)
Amida Nyorai (9 occurrences)

Dainichi Nyorai (6 occurrences)
Yakushi Nyorai (23 occurrences including the variants)

Daitsūchishō Nyorai (1 occurrence only, at No. 55). This seldom mentioned *tathāgata* is one of the *buddhas* who, mythologically speaking, appeared prior to the historical Buddha Śākyamuni. He plays a role in Chapter 7 of the *Lotus Sūtra*, which is a mythical flashback to a distant time when buddhas such as Śākyamuni (Japanese: Shaka) and Amida were his followers.

As variants we may note:

Nehan Shaka Nyorai: at no. 9. This is a variant on Shaka Nyorai, whose image in this case is lying in the nirvana position, i.e. the *nehan* position.

Shichibutsu Yakushi Nyorai: at no. 17. The *shichi* refers to *seven* buddha images (*butsu*) of Yakushi Nyorai to be revered conjointly, and this number is associated with the "immediate extinction of seven calamities" and the "immediate arising of seven happinesses."

Yakuyoke Yakushi Nyorai: at no. 35. This is a gloss on Yakushi Nyorai, emphasizing his ability to avert malfortune.

Below the *nyorai*, in formal status, come the great bodhisattvas, the compassionate buddhas-to-be who care for living beings in innumerable ways. The one who appears most frequently is Kannon-sama who takes various forms similar to those of the Saikoku pilgrimage, as introduced earlier. The forms found in the Shikoku pilgrimage are:

Senju Kannon, or Senju Kanzeon Bosatsu
Jūichimen Kanzeon, or Jūichimen Kanzeon Bosatsu
Sanmen Senju Kanzeon Bosatsu (No. 38)
Jūichimen Senju Kanzeon Bosatsu (No. 84)
Shō Kanzeon Bosatsu
Batō Kanzeon Bosatsu

It can be seen from this list that the title Bosatsu may be included in these names, or not. The formal designation is usually Kanzeon, but the more popularly used Kannon (as in Kannon-sama) is also found. The total number of Kannon or Kanzeon figures as central objects of reverence (*gohonzon*) in the Shikoku pilgrimage is 29, so that he/she occurs at more than one in four of the total. The sub-distribution of the Kanzeon iconographical types is more or less similar to that of the Saikoku pilgrimage, Jūichimen Kanzeon (Eleven-faced Kannon) and Senju Kanzeon (Thousand-armed Kannon) being the most frequent. The relative frequency of these forms of Kannon Bosatsu in Buddhist temples in general may be explained by the fact that they most fulsomely express the multiplicity of the ways in which her compassion is directed towards living beings and made available to them.

Another important bodhisattva is Jizō Bosatsu who appears very widely in Japan and who will have to be discussed in more detail when pilgrimages to his own sites are discussed in Chapter Four. Briefly, he is known for his great compassion in going right down into the most terrible hells to pull people out of them. He is here designated variously as:

Enmei Jizō Bosatsu (also Enmyō Jizō)
Enmei Jizō Son
Jizō Daibosatsu

The designation Enmei 延命 (also read as Enmyō) refers to longevity. Daibosatsu means "great bodhisattva," but of course all of the bodhisattvas mentioned here are "great" bodhisattvas. The title "Son" means respectworthy or venerable, and suggests a certain closeness to ordinary human beings; that is, it implies just another being to whom one looks up, rather than a transcendent being who is compassionately looking down. There are five occurrences of Jizō Bosatsu altogether.

Three other bodhisattvas may be found, namely:

Miroku Bosatsu 弥勒菩薩 (1 occurrence)
Monju Daibosatsu 文殊大菩薩 (1 occurrence)
Kokūzō Bosatsu 虚空蔵菩薩 (3 occurrences)

These three are not the objects of particularly popular cults in Japan, on the scale of Kannon and Jizō. Rather, they are regarded as particularly respectworthy (*erai*) buddha-figures. Though included vaguely in the class of beings referred to as *butsu*, the portmanteau term for buddhas and bodhisattvas, precisely speaking all three are bodhisattvas. Indeed they are all equally "great bodhisattvas," although the prefix *dai-* is just added when the temple authorities think fit. Miroku Bosatsu is expected to be the next future Buddha, the name being equivalent to Chinese Mílèfó and Sanskrit Maitreya, but in spite of this special position the bodhisattva has not become the focus of an anticipatory cult in Japan, as he has in some other countries of Asia.

Monju, or in full Monjushiri, is known for his wisdom, and is often found in Zen temples in other parts of the country, somehow standing guard at the meditation hall. He is also known for his impressive intervention in *The Teaching of Vimalakīrti* (*Yuimakyō*), being the only disciple of the Buddha who was able convincingly to discuss emptiness and nonduality. The name Monjushiri is equivalent to Wénshūshīlì in Chinese and derives from Mañjuśrī in Sanskrit.

The most mysterious bodhisattva for temple visitors is probably Kokūzō Bosatsu, whose name means literally "Storehouse of Emptiness." This "storehouse" is the underlying consciousness which, according to one major strand in Mahāyāna Buddhist thought, is the location of all apparently but not really external phenomena, which even in the

The Shikoku Pilgrimage

Figure 3.3 Iconic depictions (miei) from the Shikoku pilgrimage, showing nos. 1–6.

Figure 3.4 Iconic depiction (*miei*) of Dainichi Nyorai from Shikoku No 4.

Figure 3.5 Iconic depiction (*miei*) of Yakushi Nyorai from Shikoku No 6.

Figure 3.6 Iconic depiction (*miei*) of Amida Nyorai from Shikoku No 7.

storehouse have the character of emptiness. Perhaps it is not surprising that for most people this bodhisattva commands respect rather than personal affection and devotion.

In the wider class of celestial beings (*myōō* or *ten*) who are formally speaking neither buddhas nor bodhisattvas we find above all Fudō Myōō, i.e. Bright King Fudō. The name Fudō means "immovable" and corresponds to the Sanskrit Ācāla. Fudō bears a sword with which he cuts through the flames of passion, often shown raging behind him. An interesting variant is Namikiri Fudō Myōō at no. 36. Namikiri is Fudō Myōō who "cuts the waves," that is, stills the waters. The story is that when Kūkai was sailing to Tang China aged 31, in search of more and better Buddhism, there was a storm at sea, but Fudō, the immovable bright king, "cut" the waves and thereby stilled the storm. This is reflected in the very distinctive iconic portrayal (*miei*) of Fudō at this temple. There are four occurrences of Fudō Myōō altogether.

Bishamonten is the only *gohonzon* in the pilgrimage with the designation *ten* (meaning a resident of "heaven," cf. Chinese *tiān*). This divinity occurs once only, at no. 63. He is nowadays widely known as one of the Seven Gods of Good Fortune (Shichifukujin), but the Shikoku pilgrimage predates the emergence of these as a popular group. Here Bishamonten was basically a divinity supportive of Buddhism. Nevertheless the pilgrims know him as one of the Shichifukujin, and in the grounds of the temple a minor hall has been set up for the other six.

Temple number 37, Iwamotoji, is peculiar in having multiple *gohonzon*. These are: Amida Nyorai, Yakushi Nyorai, Fudō Myōō, Jizō Bosatsu and Kanzeon Bosatsu. The little printed paper (*miei*) shows all five, with Amida Nyorai in the centre. This is certainly unusual in that the very concept of a *gohonzon* implies that it, whatever it is, is the central or basic object of reverence. Sometimes, depending on the presentation, Fudō Myōō may be given as the *gohonzon*. Most temples have other buddhas and bodhisattvas in supporting roles. In the case of temple No. 17 (Idoji) there are seven statues of Yakushi Nyorai, but these are regarded as one *gohonzon*. In the case of temple No. 13 (Dainichiji), the Dainichi Nyorai was displaced as *gohonzon* by a statue of Jūichimen Kanzeon as a consequence of the enforced separation of Shintō and Buddhism in the Meiji Period. At a time when many reorganizations were taking place an honourable new home simply had to be found for the Kannon-sama, who had previously been in a Shintō shrine. Dainichi Nyorai was then presented as an attendant (*kyōji* 脇侍 to Kanzeon.[12] Similarly, at Kichijōji (No. 63), the divinity who might be thought to be the main resident,

---

12. Reader refers to them as two *gohonzon*, but this is apparently not quite accurate (Reader 2005, 273). The only temple which has a multiple *gohonzon* of *different* buddhas etc. is Number 37.

Kichijōten, is presented as an attendant to Bishamonten.

A summary head-count of the various central objects of worship (*gohonzon*) in the Shikoku pilgrimage gives the following (counting No. 37 as an Amida Nyorai, and showing a figure in brackets to take account of the multiple *gohonzon* at that temple).

Table 3.2 Statistics of central objects of reverence in the 88 Shikoku temples.

Buddhas:	
Amida Nyorai	10
Dainichi Nyorai	6
Daitsūchishō Nyorai	1
Shaka Nyorai	5
Yakushi Nyorai	23 (24)
Bodhisattvas:	
Kanzeon Bosatsu	29 (30)
Kokūzō Bosatsu	3
Jizō Bosatsu	5 (6)
Miroku Bosatsu	1
Monju Bosatsu	1
Other Buddhist divinities:	
Bishamon-ten	1
Fudō Myōō	3 (4)
Total:	88 (92)

Imitations of the Shikoku route

The great Shikoku route of 88 temples also has numerous imitations. This is not surprising if we recall that the original is estimated to be up to 1400 kilometres long. Instead of six to eight weeks on foot or about eight days by taxi, a miniature version can be covered in one day, one afternoon or even one hour. Some of these alternatives are quite famous and even ancient. Since the original pilgrimage covers almost the whole of the island of Shikoku, most imitations are to some degree abbreviations. In other words there is a whole spectrum of imitative substitution, miniaturization and abbreviation. All of these variations have in common that they offer the opportunity of visiting 88 temples associated with Kōbō Daishi over a smaller area and hence in a shorter length of time. The smallest of all are simply groups of eighty-eight statues, or stones, which are symbolic abbreviations of the original in Shikoku. These do not really have independent validity. The heart and mind of the devotee in such cases is in Shikoku itself. This is fully in keeping with the general principle of abbreviation so characteristic of Japanese religion, as already explained in the chapter on the Kannon-sama pilgrimages. Since there are in-between cases where it is not easy to decide if a route is an independent alternative pilgrimage or an abbreviated symbol of the original, one may conclude that these two aspects are not necessarily mutually exclusive. The relative importance of various alternative "Shikoku" pilgrimages seems to be a function of the imagination of the participant pilgrims. At the first temple of the Chita Peninsula (Chita Hantō) pilgrimage I was told very definitely that there were three "important" ones which carry the designation "New Shikoku" (*Shin Shikoku*), namely the Chita Hantō one itself, another at Sasaguri in Fukuoka Prefecture, northern Kyūshū, and a third at Shōdoshima, an island off the coast of Wakayama Prefecture

Let us take a look first at the quite well-known example of Shōdoshima 小豆島,[13] a small island set in the Inland Sea (Setonaikai), about twenty kilometres across each way as the crow flies. The Shōdoshima pilgrimage does link eighty-eight separate temples, but it is so evidently a miniature version of the original Shikoku route that it could be regarded as standing in for it symbolically, rather than having any separate identity as a pilgrimage route. It is thought to have become clearly established by the mid-eighteenth century.[14] It is in any case a very clear example of a pilgrimage with high tourist attraction. It can easily be reached from the large conurbations of western Japan, it can be covered in the space of a short excursion or holiday, and the temples may all be found clearly marked on an ordinary tourist map of the island along with other features of interest.[15] For example, it takes about one week to go around in the buses which come over from the mainland from March onwards. The pilgrims enjoy the outing, as was amply documented in a television programme in 2008 (March 16th) which dwelled on their favourite menus, especially *udon* (the thicker kind of noodle consumed in Japan), and on how they write charming thank-you letters to the landlords and landladies of their lodgings. It is in such ways that "pilgrimage," especially the Shikoku model, impinges constantly on the popular imagination.

The Sasaguri Eighty-eight route mentioned above is to be found in Fukuoka Prefecture in the northern part of Kyūshū, Japan's fourth largest island. This route includes a number of temples in the usual manner, but rather more small structures to make up the number. The total distance is between forty and fifty kilometres and it can be walked in two or three days. It is of particular interest for residents of Kyūshū. Pilgrims are recommended to start their journey at Hōmyō-in, near the railway

---

13. The second character in this name is read with a short vowel in this instance, irregularly. The first vowel is long.
14. Cf. Reader 1988, 54.
15. E.g. a tourist map entitled Kankō Shōdoshima published by Shobunsha in 1993.

station, even though this is number thirty-three. It is apparently usual to conclude the pilgrimage at number seventy-nine, also not far from the station and hence convenient for those whose journey has brought them from another part of the country.

Also relatively well-known are the 88 temples located in the Chita Peninsula south of Nagoya, which is quite far from the original Shikoku.[16] These are known collectively as the Chita Shikoku Hachijūhakkasho, as in the title of a guidebook by Mano Yukie[17] and are also described as a "New Shikoku" (*Shin Shikoku*) route. According to leaflets of the relevant pilgrimage association, the route was conceived in 1809 by Ryōzan 亮山, a monk of what is now Temple No.79 (Myōrakuji 妙楽寺). It is in this year that Ryōzan is said to have received instructions in a dream from Kōbō Daishi, so that this is regarded as the foundation of the pilgrimage (celebrating its 200th anniversary in 2009). The route was organized in detail some time later, in 1824, by the 44th incumbent of Temple No. 1 (Sōgenji 曹源寺) who went around the original Shikoku pilgrimage and collected from each temple small portions of sand, referred to respectfully as *o-suna*, and placed these in the hills behind the temples of the new pilgrimage. Going round this symbolic miniature version is said to bring the same merits as going around the original one. Of the 88 places, six situated in the southern part of the peninsula are designated as places where Kōbō Daishi himself had performed ascetic exercises in the year 814. Visiting these particular six places, which are Numbers 2-6 and Number 88 of the whole route, is referred to as the Kōbō-mairi, that is "going up to pay respects to Kōbō." While some information refers to ten extra-numerary temples (*bangai*), other sources refer to thirteen, so that while the route is not long in terms of sheer distance, the pilgrims have plenty to keep them occupied. Recent pamphlets urge that the pilgrimage can be started at any time, and at any one of the temples. It is recommended that one should perform this particular pilgrimage as often as possible. And indeed, a pilgrim's book from this route (thought to date from 1933) shows from the number of red seals in it that someone had gone around several times, using the same book.[18] Going round many times is also highlighted by the different colours of the pilgrims' slips left behind at each temple to show that one has been there. In this case six different colours are proposed to show how many times one has been round so far, ranging from white for the first nine times to a decorative brocade for any number of times from 100 upwards. More widely, these colours and their interpretation vary however, and for more information on them see the general account of these pilgrims'

---

16. Thanks are due to Clarke Chilson for giving me my first information about these.
17. Mano Yukie 真野 由季江 1993.
18. Catalogue item no. 7 in Pye and Triplett 2011, 23.

slips in Chapter Six below.

In spite of the supposed pre-eminence of the pilgrimages just mentioned, a relatively large Shikoku imitation, perhaps the largest, is that known as the Settsukuni Eighty-eight. This is certainly intended to be a pilgrimage in its own right, an alternative for those who cannot get across to Shikoku, or an additional pilgrimage for those who have already been there. The Settsukuni Eighty-eight Pilgrimage dates from the middle of the Edo period, when it was founded by Gekkai Shōnin, the resident priest at Temple No. 16, Kannonji. The eighty-eight are located geographically in Ōsaka City, in what is now the greater Ōsaka administrative area known as Ōsaka-fu, and on the coastline and mountainous hinterland running on down to Kōbe City. The first 41 temples are in Ōsaka City itself, Nos. 42–59 are in Ōsaka-fu, and Numbers 60–88 are in Hyōgo Prefecture. The southernmost is No. 88, Sumadera, not far from Suma JR railway station. The region, Settsu-kuni, was already referred to above in the context of the Settsukuni Thirty-three Pilgrimage. Temple No. 1 of the latter, Nakayamadera, also figures here as Nos. 69, 70 and 71. Almost all are Shingon temples of various denomination, but three belong to the Wa-shū sect of Buddhism, two are Jōdo-shū and one is Risshū. Many of the temples, being in an urban or semi-urban location, were destroyed during the Pacific War. The pilgrimage therefore fell into disuse. It was revived deliberately by the instigation of the incumbent of Temple No.14, Rokudaiin, in Shōwa 55 (1981), during one of the apparently recurrent pilgrimage booms.[19] Although this pilgrimage is relatively compact compared with the Shikoku Pilgrimage itself, it would still require considerable effort and expense to get round to visit all eighty-eight of these temples. It may be regarded therefore as a genuine alternative for those who prefer to remain in their own mainly urban area.

Another example of a "new Shikoku" pilgrimage is the Okutama Reijō Hajijūhachi Fudasho, which is described in a guidebook by Sakurazawa Takahira 桜沢孝平. Judging from its detail and informal photographs, the guidebook seems to have been written from inside knowledge of a local area rather than as a standard tourism-oriented guide to something which is well known. The route was founded in 1934 by a religious group known as the Tōkyō Zenshin-Kō 東京善心講.[20] The Okutama area lies to the northwest of Tokyo, taking its name from the upper reaches of the Tama River. Although the 88 are all named as "temples" (-ji) most of them are very small. In fact they amount to little more than local shrines to Kōbō Daishi who is protected by the simplest of huts or is even to be

---

19. This information is drawn from a guide published in 1987, edited by the Settsukuni Eighty-eight Temple Association, entitled *Settsukuni 88-sho Junrei*.

20. Sakurazawa 1978, 106.

seen standing outside on a stone pedestal. With such additions, it seems that the number of "new Shikoku" pilgrimages has no particular limits.

Similar huts are found on an island known as Ikinashima 生名島, at the northernmost tip of Ehime Prefecture. While being in close proximity to Shikoku, it is in fact easier to reach from Honshū. Here the eighty-eight points of call are simply dedicated to Daishi-sama himself. He is seated there in the huts, wearing a red apron just like a Jizō Bosatsu, and awaits his offerings of rice, citrus fruit, etc. The hut typically consists of a six-mat *tatami* room, where Daishi-sama's devotees can gather for a cup of tea and a social chat. What is their relationship with Kōbō Daishi? It is basically twofold: he is believed to protect them benevolently, so that anything good in life is "due to Daishi-sama" (*Daishi-sama no o-kage de*), and second he is therefore explicitly thanked for all this (*Daishi-sama arigatō*). Kōbō Daishi has here become a straightforward protective divinity, quite typical of the primal religious culture of Japan. The connection to Shingon Buddhism, or to any Buddhism, is tenuous indeed.

Miniature Shikoku pilgrimages

As with the Kannon pilgrimages, abbreviated and miniature versions of the Shikoku Eighty-eight are also well known and can be found both in Shikoku itself and elsewhere. Romantics who go for walking or relative hardship might regard the completion of the Shikoku pilgrimage by car in about ten days, as advised by Hirahata in his *Shikoku Henro, Meguriyasui Hachijūhakkasho* as a kind of mechanized indulgence. But in view of the widespread availability of miniature versions all over the country, this might seem to be a hard judgement. The motivations are apparently in conflict. On the one hand, an element of personal discipline and effort is required, but on the other hand the achievement lies in the completion of the route. Even those who walk the whole of the Shikoku route, taking about eight weeks, might be tempted by one of those little signposts on an uphill path which says "short-cut" (*chikamichi*). The miniature pilgrimages provide an opportunity for many who cannot go on the famous route to participate with their minds and intentions, if not in any serious way with their bodies. The line between "imitations" and "miniatures" is hard to draw, but here "a miniature" is thought of as an extreme abbreviation of the pilgrimage which can be carried out as a religious routine in about one hour, or even much less, without any serious walking at all.

In a rather glossy guidebook dating from 2006 a selection of precisely twenty of the Shikoku temples is presented with very clear indications of how to get there by car. The very title of this guide declares it to be "a journey for the extinction of the 108 passions—the path of Daishi-sama." The same guidebook advertises other journeys, both for the whole route of eighty-eight and also for 1000 "shrines and temples" of Shikoku.

The Shikoku Pilgrimage

In addition it prominently urges people to visit the "Shikoku Thirty-six Spiritual Sites of Fudō," and names these temples, so it suggests quite a lot of flexibility over how to go on pilgrimage in Shikoku. Returning to the selected twenty, the guidebook proposes collecting a bead from each temple to make a well-decorated rosary as a memento.

Better established are the real miniature versions of all 88 temples. Some miniature versions are hosted by individual temples of the major circuit, thus giving a pilgrimage within the pilgrimage. Temple Number 22 of the main Shikoku Pilgrimage has its own miniature version which is 1500 metres long, in a pleasant natural environment. This is cheerfully advertised as a *minihan* eighty-eight, *mini-han* meaning "miniature edition."[21] The eighty-eight outdoor points of devotion are called at in turn, and the pilgrimage thus amounts to a clockwise circumambulation of the small mountain or hill on which they are located. This is not spelled out as such but is illustrated on a large signboard which shows where the route goes. Temple Number 19 has a similar miniature route which covers some four kilometres, this time however in a roughly anti-clockwise direction which has no particular significance.[22] Others are not precisely linked to a particular temple, but visitors to Number 51 (Ishiteji) at Matsuyama might make an additional trip to Tōbe 砥部, well known as a pottery centre, and here they will find a miniature sequence of eighty-eight small, sheltered shrines dispersed across the area. The relative informality of these shrines and the signposting which guides the visitors towards them brings this route very close to the people. The simple structures do not amount to being temples in a full sense, and are referred to here as "shrines" only in the general sense of foci of devotion (and without any reference to the shrines of Shintō). They are referred to in Japanese simply as *fudasho* 札所, i.e. places where the pilgrims should deposit the little pieces of paper or "pilgrims' slips" (see further below) which document that they have absolved their visit.

At a place called Omuro, located just behind the well-known Shingon temple Ninnaji, in Kyōto, there is a similar miniature version of the Shikoku Eighty-eight which can be walked conveniently and pleasantly in two or three hours, giving nice views across the city below. This was set up in 1827 by the then abbot on the grounds that it was difficult for everybody to get to Shikoku, as indeed it then was. He performed the full Shikoku pilgrimage himself, and brought home a portion of "sand" (*suna*, i.e. soil) from each temple, which was then placed at eighty-eight spots around the low hills behind Ninnaji. Over each portion of sand, a small shrine was built for the worship of Kōbō Daishi.[23] This general idea

---
21. See illustration in *O-meguri*, 40.
22. *O-meguri*, 41–42.
23. For a more detailed presentation and a map, see Pye 2002.

has been repeated in many parts of Japan, for example in the grounds of the temple Nichirinji 日輪寺 at Tsukuba in eastern Japan, and in northern locations as far as Hokkaidō.

At the Shingon Buddhist temple complex on Mount Takao (near Hachiōji on the Central Line to the east of Tokyo) there is a miniature route called Takao Sannai Hachijūhachi Daishi Meguri, the name showing that Kōbō Daishi himself has become the object of devotion. This was founded in Meiji 16 (1903) by the twenty-sixth abbot, Shiga Shōrin, who similarly performed the Shikoku pilgrimage bringing back with him a little bit of soil from each of the eighty-eight temples. This he placed at various points on Mount Takao where statues of Kōbō Daishi were also set up. A guide map shows that these can be visited conveniently on a day trip, and it also divides the spots to be visited into the four stages mentioned earlier.

All of the miniature pilgrimages mentioned so far still involve walking some distance, but we turn now to miniatures which are entirely located just in once place and so require hardly any walking at all. Such "pilgrimages" require no more effort than a simple act of devotion to be repeated eighty-eight times.

A popular way of focusing the eighty-eight acts of devotion is, again, by means of a bit of soil or sand (*suna*) collected from the original temples. The procedure provides the suggestive hint that one was really there at the original spiritual sites (*reijō*). A good example is to be found at Temple No. 51 of the Shikoku route itself (Ishiteji), where the "sand" is kept in small bags arranged around the foot of the temple's pagoda, accompanied by a small print of the buddha or bodhisattva worshipped at each temple. This arrangement is sometimes referred to as *sunafumi* which means "treading the sand," and in many cases the sands are located on the ground where one can place one's foot on them. It is possible that this was the original form of such miniatures. Conveniently abbreviated religious practices of this kind are very popular, while somehow not being regarded as up-market. By contrast the three-tiered pagoda of Ishiteji is categorized as an "important cultural property" (*jūyōbunkazai*). Formal photographic presentations of it show it without the sandbags, which are evidently removed for serious representational purposes.

A well-known miniature pilgrimage is that found at the great temple complex located between Tokyo and Yokohama and generally known as Kawasaki Daishi. This temple, properly known as Heikenji 平間寺, attracts millions of visitors a year. The miniature "pilgrimage" in the grounds consists of eighty-eight slim rectangular stone pillars of about chest height standing very close to each other on three sides of a square. At the base of each stone, it is said, are buried a few grains of sand from the corresponding temple of the great Shikoku Pilgrimage. According to the temple's own published history of itself these grains were received by the abbot (*kansu*) of the temple during a threefold pilgrimage in Shikoku between April 1972 and April 1973.[24] The grains of sand are said to have the meaning of inviting the *gohonzon* of each of the Shikoku temples to be present at the stone in question. On the fourth side, which forms the entrance to the area, is a large bronze statue of Kōbō Daishi himself in pilgrim attire (and hence known here as Henro Daishi). Straw sandals hang down about him to emphasize the meaning. The devotees enter the area and sprinkle some water over Kōbō Daishi, or at any rate over the lower part of the statue which can be reached. They then proceed around the other three sides of the rectangle, stroking each stone down one side and placing a small coin on the top. According to the commemorative history the believers are requested to pay a formal visit (*sanpai*) in the form of *o-sunafumi*, or "treading the sand." This completes the pilgrimage in a few minutes. Simple though this method of performing the pilgrimage may seem, it should not be imagined that the devotees regard it as of little importance. On the contrary, they understand themselves to be performing in the Kantō region what would otherwise have to be done at great expense in Shikoku itself. When the site was opened on May 1st 1973, celebrating Kōbō Daishi's birthday, it was described (like the pilgrimage near Nagoya mentioned above) as the "New Shikoku Eighty-eight Spiritual Places" (*Shin Shikoku Hachijūhakkasho Reijō*) and declared to be "Protective Daishi's Number One Spiritual Place in the Kantō." It is notable that representatives of the Kawasaki Daishi Tourism Association were present at the "eye-opening" ceremony for the statue, a ceremony which implies the status of a salvific bodhisattva for Kōbō Daishi.[25]

Another example in the Kantō region is at the temple Kongōji 金剛寺 in Hino City on the Keiō railway line from Shinjuku station in Tokyo. The station is called Takahata Fudō, which is also the popular name for the temple. The temple is well known as one of the three leading temples dedicated to Fudō Myōō in the Kantō region, the other two being at Ōyama in Kanagawa Prefecture and the famous Narita-san in Chiba Prefecture. However, the miniature pilgrimage at Kongōji is not specifically dedicated to Fudō-sama (for whom see the following chapter), although it is well frequented on his affinity day (*ennichi*) which falls on the twenty-eighth of the month. It is a miniature sequence of eighty-eight, corresponding to the Shikoku model, which can be completed in one hour, including the eighty-eight acts of devotion, in other words at a rate of more than one "temple" per minute.

In the Kansai area two rather differently conceived miniatures may be mentioned, both at the city of Kōrien 香里園 not far from Ōsaka. One is a

---

24. Takizawa *et al.*, *Kawasaki Daishi Fukkō Sanjūnen no Ayumi*, Kawasaki 1973.
25. The details of the opening ceremony are also recorded in the temple's own history mentioned above.

side attraction of the Narita-san temple located here, which is extremely active in various respects, especially in the blessing or purification of motor vehicles to ensure their safety. To the left of the main hall, which is devoted to Fudō-son, there is a long, slightly curving line of small shrines, each raised on a single square pole. Each shrine represents one of the eighty-eight temples of the Shikoku pilgrimage. The word "shrine" is used advisedly, in its general sense, because although there is no Shintō connection, what we see is a box like structure, open to the front, which also hardly has the attributes of a temple. It is simply a place before which to render devotion. Inside there is a paper image of the relevant Buddhist divinity, a tiny box for offerings, and a small bowl-like gong on its little cushion which can be struck with a wooden hammer. The whole string of shrines covers about one hundred metres, there being just a little space between each one. A second miniature arrangement at Kōrien is even shorter, consisting of a series of Buddha-images around the front and side wall of a temple named Jizōji i.e. the temple of Jizō Bosatsu. Since these images are open to the street, any devotions can only be of the simplest kind. The particular feature is that for the temples in the Shikoku series of which the main object of worship is Jizō Bosatsu, the relevant image here is highlighted in a different colour. This miniature pilgrimage or series of statues therefore provides a kind of cross reference between Shikoku and the widespread cult of Jizō Bosatsu. More information on Jizō Bosatsu will be found in the following chapter on other Buddhist routes.

   A different theme is highlighted in a miniature version of the Shikoku pilgrimage near Fukuchiyama City in western Japan, namely "stone buddhas" (*ishibotoke* 石仏). The point about stone buddhas is that they can be left standing for very long periods on hillsides without coming to any harm, and they therefore become a point of attraction for walkers or hikers. Eighty-eight stone "buddhas" are placed around the hilly district known as Yakuno Kōgen 夜久野高原, i.e. Yakuno Heights, and without Shikoku even being mentioned, the name of the walk to visit them all is simply Hachijūhakkasho ishibotoke meguri 八十八ヶ所石仏めぐり i.e. "pilgrimage around the eighty-eight stone buddhas." This was found advertised on a plastic railway card. Since there are no temple offices in these isolated places, the emphasis is thrown back on the pilgrim to make an effort in which he or she finds finds satisfaction.

   It is not surprising to discover all these miniatures if we recall that the original Shikoku pilgrimage is some 1400 kilometres long. Instead of eight weeks on foot or about eight days by taxi, a miniature version can be covered in one day, one afternoon or even one hour. The miniaturized pilgrimages first make it easy for people who want to do a less arduous pilgrimage, and then again they make it easy for people who want to do more pilgrimages altogether.

The Shikoku Pilgrimage

Concluding the Shikoku route

In this chapter we have mainly been concerned with identifying the route of the Shikoku pilgrimage and its derivatives, and less with the meaning which it has or can have for pilgrims. This will be raised more directly in Chapter Seven below. Before leaving the Shikoku pilgrimages for the time being however, a few words may be added on the driving motivation which takes people around such long distances, or which makes people repeat the shorter pilgrimages many times, or which leads people to be happy if they can even complete a miniature, symbolic version of the pilgrimage. Whatever the physical length of the pilgrimage which is selected from case to case, the emphasis lies on the idea of completion.

As with the Kannon pilgrimages, there is a fascinating relationship between the various "Shikoku" routes and the landscapes within which they are set. The pilgrims are intrigued by the numeration of the temples, the varied distances between them and the relation of the numeration to the maps. In a few cases, two temples are almost next door to each other and can be shown on the same local map. In other cases, notably in the second stage of the main Shikoku route, in Kōchi Prefecture, the distances are rather great. Thus, however the pilgrimage is performed, a certain degree of effort and financial investment is involved. This in turn means that the pilgrims are under constraint to draw the matter to a successful conclusion with reasonable economic efficiency.

As with the other pilgrimages the route is not necessarily pursued in the formal order of the numbers, though this is certainly regarded as normative. Much more important is the concept of completion itself. Completion means visiting each one of the temples and getting this recorded appropriately. But how does one know when one has really finished? In the Shikoku route there are three ways of insisting that one has really completed everything. It is of course important to visit Number 88, the last one. But it seems good also to visit Konpira Shrine. Even though this shrine has nothing to do with Buddhism, it is very significant in the consciousness of "Shikoku." So to "do" the Shikoku pilgrimage regularly includes a visit to it. Finally, if not necessarily immediately, the Shikoku pilgrims are widely expected to pay a visit to Mount Kōya, in Wakayama Prefecture, which lies across the Inland Sea from Shikoku and cannot be easily reached from there. This mountain, opened by Kōbō Daishi, remains a spiritual centre for all Shingon Buddhists regardless of the internal denominational patterns within this tradition, which are themselves not insignificant. However, Mount Kōya is not the *central* goal of the Shikoku pilgrimage, which is conceived as a circuit. Of course, people may simply pay a visit to Mount Kōya as a religious (or somewhat touristic) journey in its own right, and in such cases they would be performing a single-goal pilgrimage. But as an addition to the Shikoku pilgrimage route, the visit to Mount Kōya is more like a coda, reasserting that the whole route has been completed. Indeed it is the first report that what was to be done, has been done.

— Chapter Four —

More Buddhist Routes

More Buddhas and more pilgrimages

A large number of circulatory Buddhist pilgrimage routes can be found in Japan which clearly follow the basic concept of the two main models but are associated with other buddhas, bodhisattvas and holy places. The number of variations is seemingly endless, though certain patterns are discernible. While the Saikoku route is specifically focused on Kannon-sama, it has already been seen that the Shikoku route only has an incidental relationship to this bodhisattva. In Shikoku it is the reverence for the Shingon founder Kōbō Daishi, in his Daishi Hall, which provides the consistent thread, while the main objects of reverence (*go-honzon*), i.e. the central buddhas and bodhisattvas of the eighty-eight temples, are diverse. In yet other pilgrimage routes, prominent Buddhist divinities (to use this convenient collective term) include Fudō Myōō, with thirty-six stations to visit, Yakushi Nyorai, with forty-nine stations to visit, and Jizō Bosatsu with six temples, or more simply six images in the grounds of a temple. Moreover, among human beings, Kōbō Daishi, or Daishi-sama, is not the only founding patriarch to be honoured with a pilgrimage. Buddhist leaders and teachers such as En no Gyōja, Hōnen and Dōgen are also featured at their own special, enumerated sites. All of these varied pilgrimages raise interesting further questions. For example, visits to the "Thirteen Buddhas" (details below) raise the question of the relationship between pilgrimage and the veneration of ancestors, while devotion to Jizō Bosatsu, affectionately known as Jizō-sama, raises with particular clarity the question of the relationship between enumeration and circulation.

The term "Buddhist divinities" has been used for convenience, and it corresponds to the rather vague Japanese term *butsu* which strictly speaking should mean "buddha" but in practice also refers to other buddha-like beings, in particular the bodhisattvas which are so prominent in Mahāyāna Buddhism. Simply put, a bodhisattva is a buddha-to-be. However the presumed achievements and great spiritual power of some of the well-known bodhisattva figures effectively leads to their being regarded as divinities with many possibilities of helping human beings in their need. Most bodhisattvas are mythical projections which belong in the same complex cosmology which permitted the endless replication of buddhas, and they have no basis in historical persons. However a small number of historical religious figures have retrospectively been designated by their enthusiastic followers as bodhisattvas, notably Shōtoku Taishi, En no Gyōja, Kūkai and Nichiren. In addition to buddhas and bodhisattvas we find references to the class of beings known as "bright kings" (*myōō* 明王), of which Fudō Myōō and Aizen Myōō are perhaps the most prominent examples. The pilgrimage circuits for Fudō Myōō will be introduced below. Junior to these is the class of "heavenly beings" corresponding to the status of the Indian devas. In Japanese, the names of these are graced with the Chinese-derived suffix *ten* 天, well-known examples being Bishamonten and Benzaiten who figure among the Seven Gods of Good Fortune.

What, for the pilgrim, is the relation between these various buddhas and bodhisattvas? When he or she enters the grounds of a temple there is a variety of actions to be performed, with reasonable speed, and several beings both human and supernatural to consider. In the main hall (*hondō*) of any one temple there is a "central object of reverence," known in Japanese as the *gohonzon*, which is most often an image of a buddha or bodhisattva. In addition there are usually secondary "halls" (*dō*), often quite small, in which other buddhas and bodhisattvas are housed. These symbolic figures are the main foci of the pilgrim's devotion and are therefore worthy of some attention. At the same time, Japanese Buddhist pilgrimage can to a great extent be understood without reference to particular buddhas and bodhisattvas, especially the lesser known ones. It is quite common for people passing through a temple area to pray briefly to such beings without knowing exactly who they are. At the same time those who are a little older, and a little more definite in their intention to seek assistance or express their gratitude, are quite well informed and to some extent can read the iconography as it stands. They no longer need the help of the wooden plaques which are conveniently placed to give names to the buddhas and bodhisattvas for those who are uncertain. Here we anticipate Chapter Seven slightly, but if we wish to follow through the *meaning* which is found in pilgrimage it is necessary to some extent to consider the foci of devotion at the temples themselves.

In the normal course of Japanese religious activity there is in effect not much difference between a buddha and a bodhisattva, and this may cause initial puzzlement to those not familiar with East Asian religious culture. Japanese Buddhism is almost entirely set within the tradition of Mahāyāna (that is, Great Vehicle) Buddhism. In this tradition the historical Buddha, Śākyamuni, is understood to be no more and no less than one among the many buddhas who are thought to have appeared in different quarters and time-spans of the universe, and who are expected to appear in future. Each of these buddhas will have spent previous existences as a bodhisattva leading up to the position or state of buddhahood. A bodhisattva is therefore one who aspires to buddhahood and of whom future buddhahood has already been authoritatively predicted by a buddha. On this basis a bodhisattva continues to practise the ten "perfections" (*pāramitā*) of which the "insight" (*prajñā*) mentioned in the *Heart Sūtra* is one. Another "perfection" is compassion (*karuṇā*), and this virtue implies that a bodhisattva is directed at one and the same time towards the attainment of supreme enlightenment and towards the assistance and salvation of all living beings. From the point of view of an ordinary person therefore there is little difference between a mighty bodhisattva and a being who has already realized ultimate buddhahood. In the widely used portmanteau expression *shinbutsu* "gods and buddhas," the "buddhas" also include bodhisattvas, and this is the bottom line in ordinary Japanese consciousness of the matter.

We have seen that the pilgrimage routes take devotees to the temples of various bodhisattvas and buddhas. In the case of a route linking, for example, temples for Fudō Myōō, or more popularly Fudō-son, this advanced buddhist being (not even being classed as a "bodhisattva") is the main object of reverence in each temple visited. On the Kannon routes however it is quite common for the object of reverence in the main hall to be, not Kannon-sama, but a perfected buddha. For example it could be Yakushi Nyorai, who specializes in healing poor eyesight and other afflictions. In such a case there will be a special hall for the reverence of Kannon-sama herself, and the devotee will expect to make a special point of visiting that one. But if the pilgrim is in a hurry the main hall may be omitted altogether. The hall in which the image of Kannon-sama is housed is usually called the Kannon Hall (*kannon-dō*), if it is not the main hall. In the Shikoku pilgrimage the standard practice, as already mentioned, is to pray before the main temple which houses a major buddha or bodhisattva and then to proceed to the Daishi-dō, the hall which contains an image of Kōbō Daishi. Kōbō Daishi is, so to speak, the hero of the pilgrimage, a Japanese bodhisattva, while also being the pilgrim's spiritual companion. Nevertheless the Daishidō is usually smaller than the main temple hall, and devotions at the latter are expected to bring specific benefits which may depend on which divinity is being addressed. There is a general feeling that all of the celestial buddhas and bodhisattvas are more or less equally powerful in religious matters, even though their specific competence is differentiated. In ordinary Japanese they may all be thought of as *butsu*, that is, as buddhas. Most might be thought of as a *hotoke-sama*, in which *hotoke* is another pronunciation for the character for writing *butsu*. They all have power to assist, and to point the way to a beyond with which they are familiar. In this sense, while residing in the imagination of the believers, as well as in their temple halls, they are understood to be transcendent beings.

The Japanese titles for the various buddhist divinities are as follows, and will usually be shown like this below:

-butsu 仏（佛）	= Sanskrit *buddha*
-nyorai 如来	"thus gone" = Sanskrit *tathāgata*
-bosatsu 菩薩	= Sanskrit *bodhisattva*
-myōō 妙王	"bright king" = Sanskrit *vidyārāja*
-son 尊	"venerable one" = Sanskrit *bhagavant* (for various respected beings)

Since the number of routes pertaining to these various buddhist figures is so great, no attempt has been made to catalogue them all in this book. In particular, sequences which in principle do little more than repeat another sequence are not listed in detail. However, the total number of temples linked by these circuitous routes is so large that in effect the whole country is criss-crossed with interconnected religious sites, even though this may not be immediately obvious to casual travellers. Only two or three exemplary lists are given below, as anyone who wishes to find complete information about a pilgrimage in a particular part of Japan can probably do so on the spot.

Visiting the Thirteen Buddhas

The easy association of different kinds of buddhist divinities is found notably in the list of the "thirteen buddhas" (*jūsanbutsu*) found in devotional books, especially in the context of Shingon Buddhism. This is because at any one temple a pilgrim might wish to chant the mantra (*shingon*) of the buddha or bodhisattva in question. The devotional books sometimes include line drawings next to the mantras in a standard iconographical style.

The thirteen include buddhas and bodhisattvas indiscriminately, though the names themselves usually include a title which indicates which they are. Whether in the context of Shingon Buddhism, Nichirenite Buddhism or elsewhere, these "thirteen buddhas" are frequently named on temporary funeral structures erected over urns which have been recently placed in a cemetery. In such a context they all have more or less equal status. There is no doubt however that some are far more pervasive than others in the popular imagination which reaches beyond the range of any one denomination.

Apart from having their names written on slivers of wood in cemeteries, the thirteen buddhas have been grouped in strings of temples which can be visited in sequence, the whole enterprise being called, for example, Kyōto Jūsanbutsu Mairi, i.e. "Kyōto Visits to the Thirteen Buddhas," Ōsaka Jūsanbutsu Mairi, Nara Jūsanbutsu Mairi and so on.[1] The sequential "Kyōto Visits to the Thirteen Buddhas" was set up in 1981, apparently in imitation of the similar sequence in Ōsaka.[2] A particular feature of such sequences is that they can be linked to the commemoration days which mark the gradual attenuation of mourning in Buddhist funeral arrangements, starting with the "first seventh day" after the person's death and ending on the thirty-third anniversary. In other regions of Japan, the counting may begin from the last day of the person's life, i.e. the day before death, or from the day of the funeral. However, these variations are not of great consequence, since "seventh day" is understood as meaning "up to" the seventh day, "up to" the fourteenth day ("the second seventh day") and so on. After the forty-ninth day (the "seventh seventh day") there is a space until the one hundredth day, and thereafter the visits are spread in an annual sequence.

Here is the list of temples for the Kyōto version, based on a leaflet distributed by the Kyōto Jūsanbutsu Reijō Kai, showing the varied denominational affiliation of the temples.

Table 4.1 Thirteen Buddhas and mourning anniversaries.

1. First seventh day: Fudō Myōō
   Chishaku-in, Shingon-shū (Chizan-ha, Sōhonzan)

2. Second seventh day: Shaka Nyorai
   Seikyōji (Shakadō), Jōdo-shū

3. Third seventh day: Monju Bosatsu
   Reiun-in, Rinzai-shū (Tōfukuji-ha)

4. Fourth seventh day: Fugen Bosatsu
   Daikōmyōji, Rinzai-shū (Shōkokuji-ha)

5. Fifth seventh day: Jizō Bosatsu
   Daizenji, Jōdo-shū

6. Sixth seventh day: Miroku Bosatsu
   Sennyūji, Shingon-shu (Sennyūji-ha, Sōhonzan)

7. Seventh seventh day: Yakushi Nyorai
   Byōdōji, Shingon-shū (Chizan-ha)

---

1. This should not be confused with the idea of *jūsanmairi* ("visit at age thirteen"), which refers to visits by girls aged thirteen years to a temple named Hōrinji in the Arashiyama area of Kyōto to pray for their health and further welfare.
2. Tanaka 1990, 88.

8. One hundredth day: Kannon Bosatsu
   Daihōonji, Shingon-shū (Chizan-ha)
9. First anniversary: Seishi Bosatsu
   Ninnaji, Shingon-shū (Omuro-ha, Sōhonzan)
10. Third anniversary: Amida Nyorai
    Hōkongō-in, Risshū[3]
11. Seventh anniversary: Ashuku Nyorai
    Hōkanji, Rinzai-shū (Kenninji-ha)
12. Thirteenth anniversary: Dainichi Nyorai
    Kyōōgokokuji (Tōji), Tōji Shingon-shū (Sōhonzan)
13. Thirty-third anniversary: Kokūzō Bosatsu
    Hōrinji, Shingon-shū (Gochi Kyōdan)

As the table shows, the first eight places are to be visited in the first hundred days, but after that the visits are spaced out over the first, third, seventh, thirteenth and thirty-third anniversaries. This attenuation means that visits become less frequent, except in so far as there are further deaths in the family. At the same time the number of possible visits to the temples is increased by the idea, which devotees are encouraged to entertain, that it is in any case a good thing to visit all thirteen "Buddhas" at least once a year. One understanding is that these are the powers which will eventually lead us ourselves into the Pure Land Paradise (Gokuraku Jōdo) and thence into Buddha-hood. It is also possible to link the astrological year of birth of the deceased with a specific buddha or bodhisattva and to make a point of getting a talisman from the relevant temple. This form of devotional pilgrimage therefore links the departed and the living in a chain of devotions. The meaning is complex. Not only can the bereaved mark and manage their grief literally step by step, but the process is also understood as one in which they are able to settle down their deceased relative and assist him or her into buddha-hood. This may include an element of pacification in the interest of the living, for it is widely assumed that a spirit which is dissatisfied for some reason might cause some kind of mischief. It will just be better, so it is thought, if the deceased becomes a *hotoke*, the usual expression for a buddha in these cases. That the practice belongs firmly in the field of pilgrimages can be seen from the fact that the supporting information specifies the cost of materials such as scrolls and booklets for stamping, and encourages people to go round once a year regardless of the death anniversaries. The initial visits after a death may trigger an interest in the custom of pilgrimage more generally.

---

3. I.e. Ritsu-shū (Vinaya Sect), but the usual elision to Risshū means that a hyphen cannot be used.

Among the "thirteen buddhas" the most prominent in popular devotion is Kanzeon Bosatsu, or Kannon-sama. Also highly visible is Jizō Bosatsu, who nowadays is of tremendous importance in the cult of remorse in respect of failed or terminated pregnancies, a subject which has attracted much attention of late. It should be noted however that his role in the ritual management of abortions by no means exhausts the meaning of Jizō Bosatsu, for he also stands at the entrance to many a cemetery for the guidance and salvation of all the departed. More information about Jizō Bosatsu and visits to his temples and locations will be found later in this chapter. As to the termination of pregnancies, recourse is also had in many cases to Kannon-sama. Thus there is some overlapping between these two very popular bodhisattvas. Among the others of "the thirteen buddhas," Monju Bosatsu has a symbolic function in Zen Buddhism as the bodhisattva most competent in insight (or "wisdom," Japanese: *hannya*, Sanskrit: *prajñā*), while Amida Nyorai took on particular importance as the central Buddha of Pure Land Buddhism (Jōdo-shū) and of True Pure Land Buddhism (Jōdo Shin-shū).

Returning to the context of Shingon Buddhism in general, a more recently formulated pilgrimage takes the pilgrim to a total of eighteen buddhas, or more precisely "basic objects of reverence" (*gohonzon*). This grouping took place on the basis of an alliance between a number of leading Shingon temples which in other respects are rather powerfully independent of each other and are therefore regarded as *honzan* 本山. The name of this pilgrimage, which seems to be more of a collection of places to visit than a significant sequence, is therefore Shingon Jūhachi-honzan. This reflects the strong interest among followers of Shingon Buddhism, often referred to loosely as *mikkyō* or esoteric Buddhism, in the practice of pilgrimage as representing *an effort*. For them the invention of new tasks appears to be quite a plausible matter. Value is laid on disciplinary effort, for in this view it is through effort that merit can be built up, various spiritual and material benefits acquired and supernormal powers developed, while ultimately even the goal of achieving buddhahood in one's own body (*sokushin jōbutsu* 即身成仏) might come into view. Of the eighteen temples, all well-known and worth a visit on general grounds, eight are located in the city of Kyōto, while the other ten are widely dispersed around Kagawa, Nara, Wakayama and Hyōgo Prefectures. Number eighteen is Mount Kōya itself.

Thirty-six Fudō Myōō and Forty-nine Yakushi Nyorai

Two figures who cross various denominational boundaries and whose own pilgrimages will now be briefly introduced are Yakushi Nyorai, the Buddha of Medicine and Fudō Myōō, the Immovable Bright King. Fudō Myōō, also known as Fudō-son, has long been important in those cults on the fringes of denominationally organized Buddhism where supernormal powers are sought through ascetic exercises.[4] In so far as this intention plays a part in pilgrimage, especially repeated pilgrimage, he takes on a certain prominence. Indeed, after Kannon-sama, he is one of the most prominent foci of pilgrimage routes in Japan.

Fudō Myōō is usually depicted as one who stands before a sea of flaming passions through which he can cut with his powerful sword. So he appears in paintings which have been made over many centuries, and so also he appears as a free-standing statue. He may often be seen standing unprotected in the open, for example at the head of a waterfall which is used for ascetic practices. There is frequently a link with temples in the Shingon tradition, with Tendai a close second, but he is also revered by ordinary pilgrims over a wide denominational range. Fudō is highly favoured in the mountain ascetic tradition of Shugendō (see further under En no Gyōja below) because of the connection with strenuous religious practice of a physical kind. When it is proposed that thirty-six Fudō Myōō should be visited, it does not mean that these thirty-six are iconographically varied to any significant degree. The point is simply that they are to be visited in sequence, just like the thirty-three Kannon-sama, in order to develop Buddhist devotion. We may recall that the name Fudō itself means, quite literally, "immovable," and it was acquired by this "bright king" (*myōō*) because he is believed to have achieved a state of spiritual unshakeability. In this sense he represents an ideal for Buddhist followers who aspire to make spiritual progress through their own efforts (not an approach taken in all denominations) and who would like to be assured that they have got somewhere with the help of all their ascetic exercises and arduous practice. Here we concentrate on the temple sequences.

In western Japan the main route focused on Fudō Myōō is called Kinki Sanjūroku Fudōson, i.e. Thirty-six Fudō of the Kinki Region.[5] As in the New Saikoku Kannon route referred to earlier the first temple is the famous Shitennōji in Ōsaka. Six others are in Ōsaka, while Kōbe, Kyōto, Ōtsu and Yoshino are also represented. The last two temples, numbers 35 and 36, are high up on Mount Kōya, the spiritual centre of Shingon Buddhism. The name Kinki, from Kinki Region, indicates that the temples to be visited are distributed over an area somewhat smaller than that of the Saikoku Kannon route, with which it overlaps geographically. Nevertheless the range includes the Ōsaka and Kyōto regions plus Nara, Wakayama, Hyōgo and Saga Prefectures.

---

4. Cf. my description of a waterfall cult at Manganji, in Tochigi Prefecture, which is at the same time No. 17 of the Bandō Kannon pilgrimage route (Pye 1997).

5. For detailed information see Kinki Sanjūroku Fudōson Reijōkai 1986 and Koji Kenshōkai (i.e. Old Temples Appreciation Society) 1979, 1992 (text by Shimoyasuba Yoshiharu).

Figure 4.1 Iconic depiction of Fudō Myōō from No. 4 of the Kinki Fudō Circuit.

Figure 4.2 Iconic depiction of Fudō Myōō from No. 11 of the Kinki Fudō Circuit.

Table 4.2 Temples of the Thirty-six Fudō of the Kinki Region.

No. 1	Shitennōji	四天王寺
No. 2	Kiyomizudera	清水寺
No 3.	Hōrakuji	法楽寺
No 4.	Kyōzenji	京善寺
No. 5	Hōon-in	報恩院
No. 6	Taiyūji	太融寺
No. 7	Kokubunji	国分寺
No. 8	Fudōji	不動寺
No. 9	Tairyūji	大龍寺
No. 10	Mudōji	無動寺
No. 11	Kaburaiji	鏑射寺
No. 12	Ankōji	安岡寺
No. 13	Daikakuji (Monzeki)[a]	大覚寺 (門跡)
No. 14	Ninnaji	仁和寺
No. 15	Rengeji	蓮華寺
No. 16	Jitsusō-in (or Jissō-in, but changed to Sanzen-in)[b]	実相寺 (三千院)
No. 17	Manshu-in (Monzeki)	曼殊院 (門跡)
No. 18	Shōgo-in (Monzeki)	聖護院 (門跡)
No. 19	Shōren-in (Monzeki)	青蓮院 (門跡)
No. 20	Chishaku-in	智積院
No. 21	Dōshū-in (but changed to Nakayamadera)	同聚院 (中山寺)
No. 22	Kitamukizan Fudō-in	北向山不動院
No. 23	Kamidaigoji	上醍醐寺
No. 24	Iwayaji (Sōtō-shū, Eiheiji-ha)	岩屋寺
No. 25	Enman-in (Monzeki)	圓滿院 (門跡) (also found as 円満院)
No. 26	Mudōji Myōōdō	無動時明王堂
No. 27	Katsurakawa Sokushōmyōō-in	葛川息障明王院
No. 28	Naritasan Ōsakabetsuin Myōō-in	成田山大阪別院明王院
No. 29	Hōzanji	宝山寺
No. 30	Nyoirinji	如意輪時
No. 31	Ryūsenji	龍泉寺
No. 32	Takidani Fudōmyōōji	瀧谷不動明王寺
No. 33	Shippōryuji	七宝滝寺
No. 34	Negoroji	根来寺

More Buddhist Routes

No. 35　Myōō-in (on Mount Kōya)　　明王院（高野山）
No. 36　Nan-in (on Mount Kōya)　　南院（高野山）

a) The designation *monzeki* implies that the head monks of a particular temple are in the direct line of a succession of teaching, or that it has been used by a member of the imperial family or higher aristocracy for Buddhist retirement. Though it was first used in the latter sense when Uda Tennō (reigned 887–897) took monastic ordination and resided at Ninnaji in Kyōto, the semi-incorporation into a limited number of temple names began from about the fifteenth century (Muromachi Period).

b) The changes for Numbers 16 and 21 occurred some time between 1992 and 2009.

Most of these temples have a Shingon or Tendai affiliation, but note the following others. Numbers 1 and 2 belong to a denomination known as Wa-shū, No 1 being the head temple Shitennōji, with Kiyomizudera (Number 2) being not far distant in southern Ōsaka. This Kiyomizudera should not be confused with others of the same name, such as the famous tourist attraction in Kyōto. Wa-shū is based on the teaching of Prince Shōtoku, renowned for the introduction of Buddhism into Japan. Number 18 is the head temple of the leading *shugendō* group, Honzan Shugen-shū. Number 21 was, as Dōshū-in, affiliated to the Zen Buddhist Rinzai denomination's Tōfukuji-ha, but it has been replaced by Nakayamadera in Hyōgo Prefecture. This leaves Number 24, Iwayaji, as the only Zen Buddhist temple in this sequence, it being affiliated to Sōtō-shū (the Eiheiji-ha). Number 30, Nyoirinji, is affiliated to Jōdo-shū.

In south central Japan a similar circuit of thirty-six temples dedicated to Fudō-son is called the Tōkai Thirty-six Fudō.[6] These are distributed rather widely in three prefectures: Aichi Prefecture, Mie Prefecture and Gifu Prefecture, with Nagoya City being a central focus from the point of view of transport. Temple Number 1 of this route, Daishōji 大聖寺, at historic Inuyama City in Aichi Prefecture, is affiliated to the well known Narita-san temple Shinshōji, not far from Narita International Airport in eastern Japan. Similarly, there are circuits linking thirty-six temples with a statue of Fudō Myōō in most parts of Japan: Hokkaidō, Tōhoku, Kantō, Shikoku and so on, thus establishing a symbolic network right across the country. For this reason, when editing a guidebook to the Thirty-six Fudō of the Kinki Region, Shimoyasuba Yoshiharu used no less than 47 pages to give a long list of major temples in all prefectures which have a statue of Fudō Myōō, either as their main object of reverence or in a special hall.[7] Narita-san (Shinshōji) itself functions as the concluding Number 36 of the Kantō Thirty-six Spiritual Sites of Fudō, of

---

6. Tōkai Sanjūroku Fudōson Reijōkai 1986.
7. Shimoyasuba 1979, 274–321. Shimoyasuba's first enthusiastic guide seems to have been superseded by the relevant book, Kinki Sanjūroku Fudōson Reijōkai 1991, in a series in which he played a major part in the provision of guide texts.

which the temples are spread all around the Tokyo geographical region.[8]

Yakushi Nyorai was mentioned above among the "Thirteen Buddhas" as the Buddha who is a Master of Medicine (literally a *yaku-shi*, that is, a "medicine master") and therefore of healing. A series of forty-nine Yakushi Buddhas in the Saikoku region was founded by mutual agreement of the participating temples in the first year of the Heisei Era (1989) and a guide describing them was written by Shimoyasuba Yoshiharu in the same year.[9] Since this is a relatively newly established series of temples it it is too soon to say whether it will become firmly established as a real "pilgrimage." A temple assistant at Kōfukuji in Nara (No.4) said in 1996 that "quite a few" people passed through there because of it, but since the whole list includes forty-nine temples in seven different prefectures it seems likely that only partial visits would be achieved by many devotees, even if they consider the idea of completing all of them. Kōfukuji itself is of course visited in any case by numerous tourists, being one of the most famous historic temples of Japan, as also are Yakushiji (No. 1) and Shinyakushiji (No. 6), both of which are also in Nara. Other well-known temples are included in this list, for example Shitennōji in Ōsaka (No. 16), Miidera (No. 48, and at the same time No. 14 of the Saikoku Kannon route) and the concluding temple No. 49, which is no less than Enryakuji on Mount Hiei. The fact that the name of the pilgrimage includes the famously suggestive designation "Saikoku" is not unreasonable because the area covered is similar to that of the ancient Saikoku pilgrimage. The temples are more or less grouped so that they can be visited in short bursts of activity, and that may be the basis for its long term persistence after surviving for its first two decades. An early leaflet proposed a program for "going round quickly" (*hayamawari*) in ten days/five nights in a "pilgrimage bus" for 140.000 Yen, still the best part of a monthly salary, and this program involved a dramatic scrambling of the numbers. In the first day, for example, Numbers 3, 37, 6, 14, 13, 15, 11 and 10 would be visited, and after an overnight stop Numbers 12, 9 and 7 would be covered during the following morning. For more details on this whole series of temples, of various denominations, see information available at the major temples already mentioned or Shimoyasuba's guide (1989). His text is of interest for its inclusion of short texts by various temple incumbents. The chief monk of Daigoji 醍醐寺 for example (Number 39), gives a brief account of "the five virtues of harmony," while a representative of Onsenji 温泉寺 (Number 29) appropriately explores the relationship between Yakushi Nyorai and hot springs (*onsen*).

---

8. Kantō Sanjūroku Fudōson Reijōkai 1999.

9. Saikoku Yakushi Reijōkai 1989.

More Buddhist Routes

Linked visits to Jizō Bosatsu

The bodhisattva Jizō, known in Japanese formally as Jizō Bosatsu and popularly as Jizō-sama, is particularly close to the people and is represented in a myriad statues all over the country. His main function is to guide all those who might otherwise lose their way after death and to protect them from the terrors of an unfavourable rebirth in one of the "six realms" (*rokudō*). For this reason he is often seen keeping watch at the entrance to a Buddhist cemetery. In many places in the Kansai area, each local community is likely to have its own Jizō, who serves in this case as a tutelary deity. It is unclear how this originally arose, but it is connected with a wider role in protecting the crossroads and entry points to villages or small towns. Indeed, more widely across Japan, Jizō Bosatsu is commonly found as a wayside divinity, simply guarding human pathways. This may have arisen in part because the character which is used in *rokudō* to mean "realm," in the sense of a potential region of rebirth, also very clearly means "way" or "road." So in an autumn *haiku* by Shiki (died 1902) we read:

The rice stacked up beside him
Jizō looks forlorn
At the side of the road[10]

On this, Blyth comments that Jizō looks forlorn by the roadside because the fields are bare and desolate after the harvest, but it also suggests a slight melancholy on Jizō's part in that he has to stay there by himself while the villagers have gone back home after their work of stacking up the rice. The roadside function is shared in the Japanese context with a male-female pair of fertility divinities called Dōsojin, and also with the horseheaded version of Kannon-sama who protects agricultural animals. All three, Jizō, Dōsojin and Batō-Kannon are often little more than rough-hewn stones with the barest indication of their identity. Exposed to the weather, they certainly look forlorn when the greenery has died away.

As to Jizō-sama in particular, in recent decades there has been a remarkable boom in his popularity as a guardian of aborted foetuses. These are regarded as living beings in need of care when no longer carried by their potential mothers. Abortions have been very numerous in Japan because the contraceptive pill was not legalized until 1999. Millions upon millions of Jizō statues have therefore been purchased for donation in memory of the lost children, as a way of somehow making up for a decision taken because of the pressure of social and economic circumstances. Some of these are just tiny figurines which can be enshrined in their thousands in halls specially built for the purpose. Others are larger statues, more expensive, though mass produced, and standing in serried ranks in temple

---

10. Adapted from Blyth 1952, 15. The Japanese text is *Ine tsunde, Jizō wabishiya, michi no hata*.

grounds. In some cases great hillsides have been terraced to make room for the apparently endless supply of these votive offerings.

Because of its visibility and social importance, this particular subject has aroused the interest of many observers, but since it does not bear directly on circulatory pilgrimage it need not detain us further here.

Just as Kannon-sama is believed to have appeared in 33 different forms to save living beings, so too was Jizō-sama believed to have appeared in six different ways corresponding to the six possible lower states of rebirth. Whether one is reborn as a *deva* (a peaceful celestial being), as a human being, as a warring celestial being, as a beast, as a hungry ghost, or in one of the terrible hells, there is always a Jizō-sama holding out the possibility of assistance. Thus many Buddhist temples offer, somewhere in their grounds, six standing figures of Jizō Bosatsu, often garlanded with necklaces of paper cranes symbolizing longevity, or wearing multiple aprons, because children need bibs when eating. Sometimes they are sheltered under a light roof, and sometimes they are exposed to the weather. Since one cannot tell in advance in which state one will be reborn, it is felt that it makes sense to pay reverence to the Six Jizō in advance. This can also be done on behalf of others. While the Six Jizō are usually set up together in one place, and may be prayed to during a single temple visit, they are also sometimes the focus of a circulatory pilgrimage.

The idea of Six Jizō seems to have emerged in Japan itself during the Heian Period and was at first popular among the aristocracy. According to Hayami Tasuku there are no examples of Six Jizō in Central Asia or China.[11] However there may be a connection with the idea that six forms of Kannon Bosatsu could be related to the needs of beings in the six lower realms of potential rebirth. It is suggestive that one of the ancient temples in Kyōto, the Senbon Shakadō 千本釈迦堂, has six statues of Kannon corresponding to the six potential realms of rebirth and collectively referred to as the Rokudō Kannon.[12] Nowadays, several famous temples in Kyōto make a special point of attracting visitors to revere Jizō-sama during the *o-bon* season in August, generously defined. The above mentioned Senbon Shakadō and another temple named Rokudō Chinnōji organize a *rokudō-mairi* just before the middle of August. The term *-mairi* used in these cases indicates a single visit to the temple in question, during which believers pray to Jizō-sama in one place as the bodhisattva responsible for all six realms. Other Kyōto temples which highlight Jizō Bosatsu, such as Rokuharamitsuji and Mibudera, have iconographic displays centred on Enma-ō,[13] who presides

---

11. Hayami 1975.

12. This in turn may have a basis in the Móhēzhǐguān (Japanese *Makashikan*), a key text of Tendai Buddhism composed by the Chinese patriarch Zhìyǐ (538–597).

13. From the Sanskrit King Yama via Chinese. The transcription Emma-ō will also be found.

like a Chinese official over the judgmental realms entered by the dead.

The most widely remarked observance of Jizō-bon, notably in the Kansai region, is that of extremely local neighbourhood communities who celebrate with little parties in front of the small covered roadside shrines of Jizō. This local Jizō-bon is sometimes said to be "for the children," and the children are indeed treated to entertainment, but at the same time it is an important and more or less obligatory neighbourhood event, however relaxed. While it is a fascinating subject in its own right, it should be distinguished from visits to the Six Jizō in Kyōto which take place about the same time. The dates for the latter are stated in temple pamphlets as the 22nd and 23rd, but in practice the 24th August gets to be included since the 24th of each month is Jizō's "affinity day." The historical evidence surrounding the emergence of these six is complex, but the main point of interest here is that the intentions evidently changed over time. In 1157 six statues of Jizō-sama housed at Daizenji 大善寺 at Fushimi in the south of Kyōto were distributed to various entry points of the city as guardians, leaving just one at Daizenji itself. Of the other five, one was set up in the grounds of the Shintō shrine Kamigamo Jinja, in the north of the city, but was later removed again because of the policy of "separation of gods and buddhas" (*shinbutsu bunri* 神仏分離). Its new location was a temple at the northern end of Teramachi 寺町 (a long north-south street with many temples, hence the name) called Jōzenji 上善寺. This temple, because of its location, is popularly known as Kuramaguchi Jizō 鞍馬口地蔵.[14]

Table 4.3 Temples of the Six Jizō in Kyōto.

Daizenji 大善寺	(Roku Jizō,[a] in modern Fushimi-ku)
Tokurin-an 徳林庵	(Yamashina Jizō, in modern Yamashina-ku)
Jōzenji 浄禅寺	(Toba Jizō, in modern Minami-ku)
Katsura Jizōji 桂地蔵寺	(Katsura Jizō, in modern Nishi-ku)
Jōban-in 常磐院	(Jōban Jizō, in modern Sagyō-ku)
Jōzenji 上善寺	(Kuramaguchi Jizō, in modern Kita-ku)

a) "Rokujizō," as one word, has become the name of an underground railway station, but here the parallelism with the other names is maintained.

At each of the six temples a paper banner bearing an image of Jizō can be purchased. However, the guarding of Kyōto has become very generalized. The benefits expected at each temple vary from childbirth to longevity, just as Jizō-sama assumed six forms in connection with six varied realms of possible rebirth. However the greatest overall coverage of benefits is thought to be achieved if all six are visited. Not surprisingly this practice of going round to all of them is described as a *Jizō-meguri*, literally a "Jizō-circulation" or as we might say more elegantly, a "Jizō pilgrimage."

---

14. For a brief introduction see Takemura 1994 and for more detail see Hayami 1975.

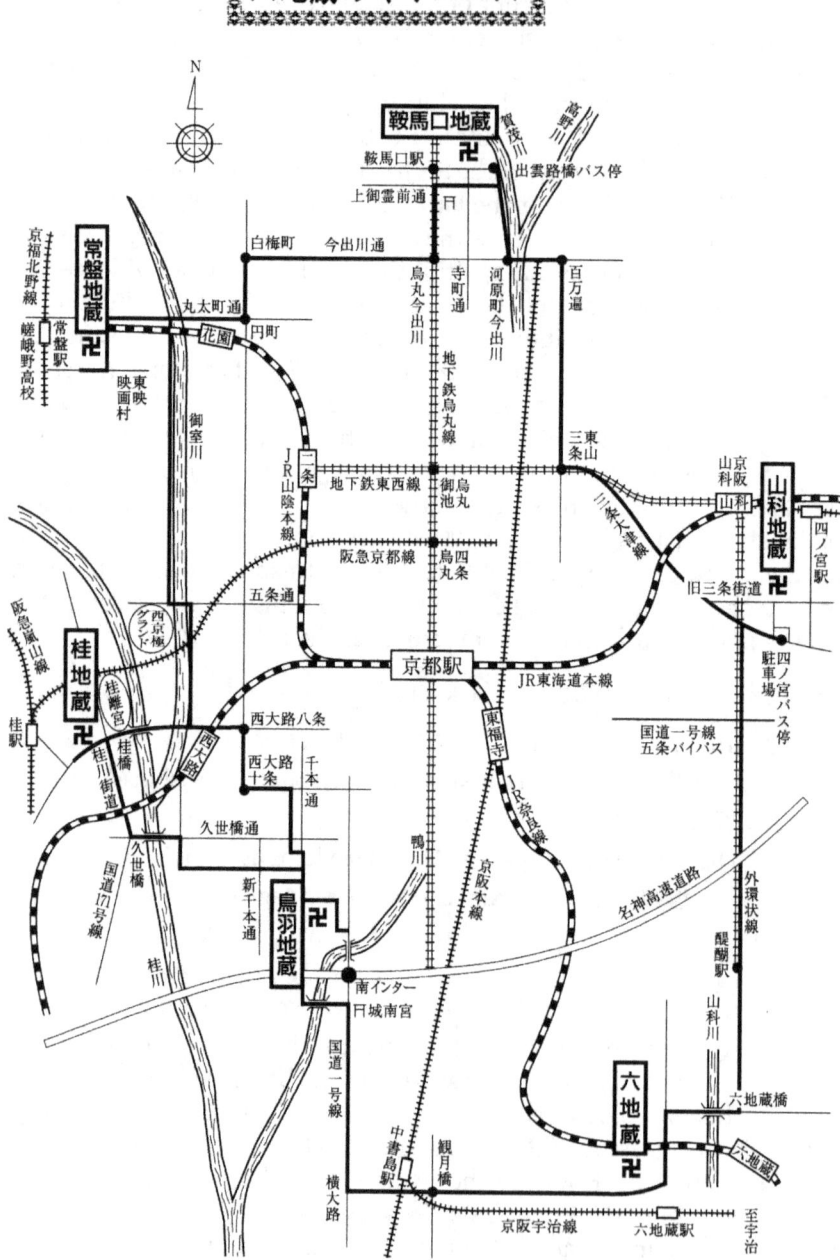

Figure 4.3 Map for visits to the Six Jizō in modern Kyōto with public transport.

The roots of this practice evidently go back to the late Heian Period, and its introduction is credited to the devout Emperor Goshirakawa 後白河 who in 1157 ordered Taira no Kiyomori 平清盛 to set up the statues at the city's entrances. Kiyomori for his part delegated the religious aspect of the task to the poet-priest Saikō 西光 (1118–1190), who duly carried it out. So it is recorded in the *Rokujizō Engi* of 1665, held in the storehouse of Daizenji. Note however that simply to set up the statues at the entrances to a city does not in itself imply the establishment of a popular circulatory pilgrimage, especially if all six Jizō can be worshipped at any one of these sites. The original intention was the symbolic protection of the capital city, and visits by politically powerful persons will have been intended to reinforce this, just as in the case of the Ten Shrines of Tokyo introduced below in Chapter Five. The development of a popular trail around all six is likely to have been a secondary phenomenon, whatever its earliest date. By the time of the Edo Period the value of the temples as a political statement was superseded by popular interest in the religious needs of the family and the individual.

The concept of a Jizō pilgrimage was later imitated in other places, for example in Kōbe. An English language leaflet about this sums up the themes simply as follows (slightly abbreviated):

> Jizō-sama, is a buddha who with his kindly face is particularly close to human beings. According to the teaching of Śākyamuni (Buddha) living beings can normally be reborn in six different places: the hells and the realms of hungry ghosts, animals, warring spirits, humans or divinities. After Śākyamuni's entry into nirvana it is Jizō who can save the living beings wandering in these realms. He is also "the buddha of children." If our faith is deep, we can receive this-worldly benefits of safety for our families as well as long life, so Jizō can save us from suffering not only in future worlds but also in this one. We recommend performing the pilgrimage to the Six Jizō by visiting these spiritual sites which all have deep karmic connections, for the sake of our ancestors, the continued happiness of our parents, the care of the recently deceased, for water babies (*mizuko*) who died without receiving sufficient care, and for safety in the home, the flourishing of family fortunes and health in mind and body.

The term *mizuko* (literally "water babies") is a euphemism for aborted foetuses. It is noticeable that Jizō is referred to here simply as "a buddha," though formally speaking he is of course a bodhisattva. He is a buddha for the here and now who meets the basic concerns of family life and responsibility.

While the number six remains in the imagination because of the six realms of rebirth, there are larger groups of temples which include Jizō among their attractions. In Kamakura for example, reference will be found to Kamakura Nijūyon Jizō 鎌倉二十四地蔵, i.e. "Twenty-four Jizō of Kamakura." Takemura Toshinori writes of no less than 48 Jizō temples or images inside the city of Kyōto being counted from the late seventeenth century, for which the Emperor Reigen composed short songs (*go-eika*).[15] These 48 temples or Jizō images were additional to the well known six, who guarded the city, and presumably were imagined to correspond to 48 vows which the bodhisattva made for the benefit of living beings. However there is no immediate evidence that this sequence, or linkage, was ever used as a connected route to be completed in its totality. Moreover many of those listed can no longer be identified with currently existing temples. To make up for this, Takemura fills his book on the Jizō figures of Kyōto (or Kyō, as he calls the city with pointed elegance in the title of the book) with no less than 80 examples of Jizō-sama with their various photographs and city bus connections. This is particularly useful for residents over seventy, who qualify for an inexpensive bus pass with unlimited travel on all the inner bus routes.

While devotion to the six Kannon of the realms of rebirth (*rokudō Kannon*) was largely overtaken in the popular imagination by the more elaborate circulatory pilgrimages, the Six Jizō are still very popular as a standing *group* for popular devotion, especially in the Kansai region. Thus a structural overlap may be observed here. On the one hand the six Jizō-sama may have contributed, if to a secondary degree, to the very invention of circulatory pilgrimage. On the other hand a parallel may be seen between reverence to all six of them lined up together on one spot for the purpose, and the performance of abbreviated pilgrimage before Thirty-three Kannon standing in a group in one place (as described in Chapter Two). The believer, or pilgrim, sees no contradiction between going round a series of places supposedly dedicated to the various forms taken by a bodhisattva, and finding all of these forms, or just six identical Jizō figures, standing together side by side in one place.

In the tracks of saintly founders

One of the distinctions between the leading Saikoku and Shikoku pilgrimages is that, while both are circulatory, in the latter the common thread is provided by a visit to the Daishidō at each temple, that is, to the hall where the founder Kōbō Daishi is himself revered. He is revered there because he is thought to have been there. In Japanese Buddhism in general it has become commonplace to make special visits to the various places connected with the founders of particular practices or teachings. The idea of following in their footsteps is one of the formative principles of Buddhist pilgrimage in Japan. Viewed more widely it is similar to the concept of visiting the sacred sites of the historical Buddha himself: notably those of his birth, enlightenment, first preaching and nirvana or decease. The sequential *enumeration* of sites on the other hand seems to

---

15. Takemura 1994, 196.

have been first undertaken in connection with Kannon Bosatsu because of the thirty-three forms which this bodhisattva can adopt according to the *Lotus Sūtra*. So when it comes to pilgrimages associated with saintly Buddhist patriarchs of Japan we find that the two principles are fused. The sites are connected with their lives and work, but in so far as they are multiple sites they also tend to be specifically enumerated.

One of the earliest figures in Japanese religious history to have become the focus of multiple-goal pilgrimage is En no Gyōja 円の行者 (634–701). In historical references, the name En no Ozuno will also be found, but he is most commonly referred to as En no Gyōja, *gyōja* meaning "practitioner," because it is above all for his arduous and pioneering "practice" in the mountains that he is remembered and admired. Retrospectively, En no Gyōja is also referred to as Shinpen Daibosatsu 神変大菩薩, a name which subtly suggests that he was not only a "great bodhisattva" (*daibosatsu*) but represented the "transformation of a divinity" (*shinpen*) in the more usual Japanese sense of a *kami*. He was a pioneer in the literal "opening" of mountains, where he was thought to harness the supernatural powers of the divinities who reside there for the greater promotion of the Buddhist Dharma. In a guidebook entitled *En no Gyōja Reiseki Fudasho Junrei*[16] 36 pilgrimage stations are listed of which the majority are in Nara Prefecture and the Ōsaka administrative region. The first is Kinpusenji, in the mountains behind Yoshino in western Japan. Through these mountains passes a difficult route to Kumano which is pursued by the mountain ascetics (*yamabushi*) to this day. In addition, covering the whole of Japan except for the large northern island of Hokkaidō, no less than forty-eight mountains are listed which all have some claim to an association with En no Gyōja. No matter what the other attractions are, it is the statues of this great pioneer ascetic which are particularly revered, even though many of them are relatively small.

We can see from the cases of both Kūkai and En no Gyōja that devotion to the founder and the places connected with him on the one hand turns these founders into more or less divine persons, and on the other hand assists in the creation of a denominational tradition, in these cases, Esoteric Buddhism (Shingon) and Shugendō. Without such key figures these two streams of religious practice and teaching would be inconceivable, at least for almost all of their Japanese adherents.

A further such case is that of the tradition of Nichirenite Buddhism, where there is also a complex relation between the founder figure and pilgrimage. A major family of Buddhist denominations in Japan goes back to the teaching of Nichiren Shōnin 日蓮聖人 (1222–1282) and indeed, being in a significant sense a movement of religious reform, it has thrown up a variety of related denominations and sects, ranging

---

16. Edited by a relevant association, the En no Gyōja Reiseki Fudasho Kai, 2002.

from the larger priestly or "monastic" temple systems such as Nichiren-shū and Hokke-shū right up to lay movements founded in the twentieth century such as Reiyūkai, Risshō Kōsei-kai and Sōka Gakkai. In this "family" there are both close relationships and sharply diverging opinions and fierce rivalries, and these cannot all be explained here. One important connection with Japanese Buddhist pilgrimage in general lies in the central focus on the *Lotus Sūtra*, which as one its chapters contains what is otherwise known as the *Kannon Sūtra*. This means that members of Nichirenite denominations or movements in general may easily develop an affectionate relationship with Kannon and feel quite at ease with the performance of pilgrimages devoted to this bodhisattva.

At the same time a major attraction is Mount Minobu, managed by the leading denomination Nichiren-shū. Nichiren spent the closing part of his life here and it therefore became a major focus of pilgrimage for his followers. This is what we have denoted in the Introduction as a single-goal pilgrimage, and is not part of a circuit. An associated goal is another mountain not far from Minobu-san, known as Shichimenzan, where a divinity is revered who is believed to support those who revere the *Lotus Sūtra*. Yet another significant single pilgrimage goal for Nichirenite Buddhists is the temple Kiyozumi-dera 清澄寺[17] in Chiba Prefecture. This is where Nichiren was first ordained as a buddhist monk, and where he later first announced the importance of reciting the title of the *Lotus Sūtra* with the formula: Namu Myōhō Renge Kyō. This use of the title, the *daimoku*, standing for the quintessence of the teaching of the *Lotus Sūtra*, became a leading and shared trademark of all the denominations, sects and lay movements which were inspired by Nichiren.

When it comes to the linkage of Nichirenite temples for pilgrimage purposes, we may look once again in particular to the city of Kyōto. Here leading denominations in the Nichirenite traditions encourage the practice of visiting the "sixteen head temples" (*jūroku honzan* 十六本山). The temples are numbered from one to sixteen but can in practice be visited in any order. A map showing all sixteen "head temples" also shows some others which have a special connection with Nichiren. An important example of an additional one is Jōkō-in 定光院 in the Yokawa area of Mount Hiei to the north-east of the city. Here Nichiren spent about twelve years of his life as a base for studying Buddhism before mounting his own personal mission. Number 16 among the "head temples" is Honkokuji 本圀寺; this was originally a temple in Kamakura where Nichiren had resided, but which was later "moved" from Kamakura to Kyōto.[18] Getting the visits recorded in a pilgrim's book is not required, though some people apparently do it.

---

17. Also pronounced Kiyosumi-dera.

18. For more information on this temple see Beatrice Lane Suzuki, *Buddhist Temples of Kyōto and Kamakura* (2013).

Table 4.4 Sixteen head temples of Nichirenite Buddhism in Kyōto.

1. Myōganji 妙願時
2. Myōkakuji 妙覚寺
3. Honpōji 本法寺
4. Myōkenji 妙顕寺
5. Myōrenji 妙蓮寺[a]
6. Honryūji 本隆寺
7. Honmanji 本満寺
8. Honzenji 本禅寺
9. Yūseiji 宥清寺
10. Ryūhonji 立本寺
11. Myōdenji 妙傳寺[b]
12. Chōmyōji 頂妙寺
13. Jakkōji 寂光寺
14. Yōhōji 要法寺
15. Honnōji 本能寺
16. Honkokuji 本圀寺

a) The head temple of the Hokke Denomination (Honmon Hokke-shū), founded in 1295 by Nichizō Shōnin, and thus one of the older variants of the Nichirenite tradition.
b) The simplified form of characters would be 妙伝寺.

Nichirenite temples are not averse to being part of connected series of temples with other foci of devotion. The Nichiren-shū temple Honmanji 本満時, for example, participates in a series of twelve holy sites for Myōken Bosatsu 妙見菩薩. This temple is Number 7 in the above mentioned series and is located in the upper part of Teramachi Street in Kyōto. Since Myōken was originally worshipped as the divinity of the North Pole Star, he is regarded both as a bodhisattva (*bosatsu*) and a Shintō divinity (*kami*), and his shrines may be fronted, as at Honmanji, by a Shintō-style symbolic entrance (*torii*). In Nichirenite Buddhism there is in general a strong interest in astrological connections and the "opening" of one's good fortune. The underlying idea is that through religious devotions one can encourage the blossoming of auspicious aspects of destiny. To manage this for the best, the current astrological calendar is consulted and special editions of these are usually on sale in Nichirenite temples. The religious culture involved here is one shared with many other Buddhist temples (but not all) and with Shintō shrines.[19] The series of temples

---

19. Cf. Pye and Triplett 2007.

giving hospitality to Myōken is known as "Rakuyō Jūnishi Myōken 洛陽十二支妙見, in which Rakuyō is a traditional regional designation within the city of Kyōto and *jūnishi* refers to the twelve astrological "branches."

Another religious figure who was not only important in his own day but became a rallying point for all later followers is Dōgen Zenji (1200–1253). While the Sōtō Zen associated with Dōgen is well known for its emphasis on *zazen* alone as the key practice for Buddhists who have a serious personal interest in the matter, we have already seen that a number of Zen Buddhist temples, Sōtō as well as Rinzai, lend their temples to the Kannon circuits. In addition, any Sōtō followers who develop a keen interest in Dōgen Zenji may find it valuable to visit a number of sites associated with his life, and this is quite in tune with what we have otherwise learned about circulatory pilgrimage.

There is a definite place for pilgrimage in Pure Land Buddhism, or Jōdo-shū, a denomination which in Japan goes back to the teaching and work of its founding patriarch Hōnen Shōnin 法然上人 (1133–1212), also known posthumously as Genkū 源空 and as Enkō 圓光. Accordingly the most widely visited series of temples is called the "Twenty-five Holy Places of Saint Hōnen." In a general sense "pure land" Buddhism may be found in all the countries of East Asia, being promoted in the context of various denominations according to developments in each country. There were also many who had earlier taught the value of calling on the name of Amida Buddha (Amitābha) with a view to being reborn in his Buddha-land in the west, the "Pure Land" (Japanese: *jōdo*). However Hōnen's contribution lay in selecting this practice for exclusive use, reciting the brief formula known as the *nenbutsu*, thus relying on the power of Amida Buddha alone for salvation. The English expression "Pure land Buddhism" should be used with care, because it may refer to all such religious orientations in general or it may mean quite specifically, as here, Jōdo-shū, i.e.the *shū* or denomination of Jōdo, the Pure Land. Of course there are sub-denominations or "sects" as well, and a few well-known temples have simply turned themselves into independent institutions. Note in particular that Jōdo Shin-shū (i.e. Shin Buddhism, on which see further below), should be carefully distinguished from Jōdo-shū.

While the main point of Jōdo-shū is dependence on the "other power" of Amida Buddha, its present-day temples encourage quite a wide range of religious activities which evidently entail some kind of input by the believers themselves, in expectation of a result. For example, the use of votive tablets (*ema*, see Chapter Six below) is not excluded. Although often associated with merit-making, pilgrimage is also not excluded, and in particular the practice of visiting twenty-five places associated with Hōnen is quite well established. These visits, often made by organized groups, may be recorded in the usual kind of pilgrim's book, or on a fine

Figure 4.4 Map of twenty-five spiritual places connected with Hōnen Shōnin.

hanging scroll (cf. Chapter Six below). The explanation given by temple informants is that this heightens devotion to the founder and therefore to the faith, but at the same time the alignment with the general practice of circulatory Buddhist pilgrimage, in which an achievement is intended, is quite evident. Since some Jōdo temples are to be found in the other circuits too, the possibility of transferring the practice may be thought to have easily occurred to temple authorities. However, as far as is known, this pilgrimage is an early modern development which can be traced back to a promotion by the Jōdo priest Reitaku 霊沢 in 1762 immediately following the 500th anniversary of Hōnen's death.[20] The purpose of it was to encourage followers to call to mind the places connected with Hōnen's life, work and death. In other words, the original intention was not so much to make merit as to heighten devotion.

---

20. Tōdō 1988.

Japanese Buddhist Pilgrimage

The commemorative scrolls usually show the six characters for the *nenbutsu* with a portrait of Hōnen beneath, holding a rosary for counting off the *nenbutsu* as recited. The fields for the seals and calligraphy may number two or three more than the basic twenty-five. This is because at the end visits may also be paid for example to Seiryūji, at the Tendai centre on Mount Hiei, or to the very scenic Jōdo temple known as Eikandō in Kyōto, noted for its spring flowers and autumn colours as well as one of the most exclusive kindergartens in the country. The temple names are shown on a leaflet as the "members" of the "Twenty-five Spiritual Places of Hōnen Shōnin." The list only gives the immediate temple names, without the *-san* designations, which illustrates that these are often not really necessary for identification.

Table 4.5 Twenty-five Spiritual Places of Hōnen Shōnin.

1.	Tanjōji	Okayama Prefecture (Kurube)
2.	Hōnenji	Kagawa Prefecture (Takamatsu)
3.	Jūrinji	Hyōgo Prefecture
4.	Nyorai-in	Hyōgo Prefecture
5.	Katsuoji Nikaidō	Ōsaka-fu (a *-fu* is equivalent to a prefecture)
6.	Shitennōji Rokujidō	Ōsaka City
7.	Isshinji	Ōsaka City
8.	Hōonkōji	Wakayama City
9.	Taimadera Oku-in	Nara Prefecture
10.	Hōnenji	Nara Prefecture
11.	Tōdaiji Shizudō	Nara City
12	Gonjōji	Ise City
13.	Kiyomizudera Amidadō	Kyōto City
14.	Seirinji	Kyōto City
15.	Genkūji	Kyōto City
16.	Kōmyōji	Kyōto City
17.	Nison-in	Kyōto City
18.	Tsukinowadera	Kyōto City
19.	Hōnenji	Kyōto City
20.	Seiganji	Kyōto City
21.	Shōrin-in	Kyōto City (This is in the grounds of No. 23)
22.	Daihonzan Hyakuman-ben Chionji	Kyōto City
23.	Daihonzan Shōjōke-in	Kyōto City
24.	Daihonzan Kurodani Konkaikōmyōji	Kyōto City

25.	Sōhonzan Chion-in	Kyōto City
	Special spiritual site	Hieizan Kurotani Seiryūji, Ōtsu City

In this list of temples denominational affiliation is not shown because most are of the Jōdo tradition. However No. 5 is a Shingon temple which is also No. 23 of the Saikoku pilgrimage, but occurs here on account of one special hall, the Nikaidō, i.e. the "two storey hall," associated with Hōnen. Similarly Shitennōji nowadays heads up its own denomination (Wa-shū), but includes the Rokujidō, otherwise known as the Nenbutsudō, among its buildings. As mentioned before the "special spiritual site" Seiryūji is part of the Tendai complex at Mount Hiei. From the general indications of their whereabouts, it will be seen that these temples are all in western Japan, just over half being in Kyōto, but with others ranging from Ise to Kurube in Okayama and the second one even being on Shikoku.

Tracking the denominational developments of Pure Land Buddhism, we come to a series of sixteen temples, with five "guest temples," which are referred to as "spiritual sites with traces of Seizan Kokushi." Seizan Shōnin 西山上人, here designated with the title of *kokushi* 国師, "National Teacher," was a Buddhist priest in the successor generation to Hōnen himself. After him are named a number of sects, notably the Seizan-ha with its head temple at Kōmyōji, at Nagaokakyō, and the Seizan Fukakusa-ha with its head temple at Seiganji in Kyōto.

Finally, a circuit of forty-eight temples marking the forty-eight vows made by Amida Buddha is also relevant to Pure Land Buddhism. These are the vows which Amida (Amitābha) made for the benefit of all living beings, when he was still a bodhisattva, as set out in one of the canonical texts of Pure Land Buddhism.

Pilgrimage in Shin Buddhism

The largest Buddhist denominations to follow on from the Pure Land Buddhism of Hōnen can be referred to collectively as Shin Buddhism. There are several sub-denominations, the two largest ones being the Honganji-ha with its headquarters at Nishi Honganji, and the Ōtani-ha with its headquarters at Higashi Honganji. All of them go back to the teaching of one of Hōnen's disciples, Shinran (1173–1262). The latter is greatly revered by the followers of Shin Buddhism, but the doctrinal tradition is very cautious about the concept of pilgrimage. Shinran himself radicalized the teaching of reliance on nothing but the "other power" (*tariki*) of Amida Buddha to such an extent that in the formal teaching of Shin Buddhism any kind of pilgrimage is regarded as inappropriate. After all, it could lead to the idea that one might achieve some kind of merit by one's own efforts or one's own power (*jiriki*). At the same time certain sites related to the movements of Shinran and his own followers are treated with honour and may certainly be visited. Maps showing their location even make use of the term *meguri*, and such maps have been seen prominently displayed in a resting room for the believers at Higashi Honganji, the main temple of the Ōtani branch of Shin Buddhism, and are also available for free distribution. Of course, it may be argued that this is not so much evidence for a deviation from Shin Buddhist teaching as simply an example of the widespread and rather general use of the term *meguri*.

On the other hand, the pilgrimage industry has taken it up with the publication of guidebooks. In one case a guidebook edited by Hosokawa Gyōshin (1983) provides plenty of information for would-be travellers with a Shin Buddhist orientation, and also includes an appendix on Rennyo's journeys (see also below). The many temples presented, with maps and edifying photographs, are however *not* numbered. This careful approach was no doubt welcome to the publishing house, Hōzōkan, which has a big programme relating to Shin Buddhism and would not wish to depart too far from orthodox positions. Another work displaying no such compunctions, authored by Niizuma Hisao (Niizuma 1996), appeared from the Ōsaka publishing house Toki Shobō which is responsible for many works on pilgrimage and has no close connections with Shin Buddhism. In this book the temples *are* numbered, just as in any other circulatory pilgrimage. The author was born in 1932 in Manchuria, studied politics at Waseda University, and worked at the Japan Atomic Energy Research Institute for more than thirty years. After retirement in 1991 he received ordination in the Honganji Branch of Jōdo Shin-shū,[21] but this book may be regarded as a slight departure from the doctrinal orthodoxy of the Honganji Branch regarding pilgrimage.

With all respect for the doctrinal severity, or clarity, of Shin Buddhism, there are three main groups of sites to visit, one in an area around the Japan Sea coast (Echigo Province) where Shinran spent some time in exile, another in Eastern Japan, all over the Kantō plain but mainly in what are now Tochigi and Ibaragi Prefectures, and a group in and around Kyōto where Shinran had important experiences and where his life also ended. Hosokawa presents all of these. Among them, the most well-known group is that in eastern Japan where Shinran spent many years with loyal companions, preaching the *nenbutsu*. His associates

---

21. This major denomination, the Honganji-ha, is based on the western head temple, Nishi Honganji, and is distinguished from its sister denomination, the Ōtani-ha, less by any doctrinal difference than by the massive institutional networks and social arrangements, many hereditary, which characterize each of them. The spelling Hongwanji is often found, representing an outdated romanization system which has become the conventional norm in American branch "churches," as they are referred to there.

are known as the "twenty-four companions" (*nijūyohai* 二十四輩)[22] and the places to visit are therefore known summarily as Shinran Shōnin Nijūyohai 親鸞聖人二十四輩. Niizuma's guide is restricted to this group.

Hanging scrolls may be seen which show the *nenbutsu* ("Namu Amida Butsu") in the centre with an ink drawing of Shinran beneath it, and left and right the names of the temples and their individual songs (*go-eika*). It is significant that the temples are numbered from one to twenty-four, while at the bottom of the scroll six additional ones are shown which are also of special significance in the tradition. This arrangement allows for the practice of getting the red seals of the temples stamped on the relevant places of the scroll. In the case of a similar scroll acquired by the writer, some fifty percent of the space at the top, being originally blank, is filled with the twenty-four temple seals, which were apparently collected in sequence. Below these is a painting of Shinran with two followers in a landscape which takes up a little more than a quarter of the scroll and is contained within a light ink frame. This leaves a further space below, clearly available for the additional seals, of which four of the possible six were in fact entered.[23] Since pilgrimage is not actively encouraged in the case of Shin Buddhism it is left up to the visitors to enter the seals for themselves, if they wish, and no money is collected. This is a significant difference from the standard Buddhist pilgrimages in Japan. Because of this informality it is rather difficult to assess how frequently it is in fact done.

Another very important figure in the development of Shin Buddhism was Rennyo Shōnin (1415–1499). Rennyo journeyed from Kyōto to Yoshizaki (at present day Awara City in Fukui Prefecture) and the route which he is said to have traversed attracts a pilgrimage in his memory. Thus on April 17th 2008 some thirty believers set off to walk the 240 kilometer long route, starting from the head temple of the Ōtani school, Higashi Honganji. The departure was preceded by a ceremony (*gogekōshiki* 御下向式) in the Amida Hall (the main hall, the Goeidō, was undergoing repairs at the time). After services at the Yoshizaki temple (Yoshizaki Betsuin 吉崎別院) they returned to the head temple in Kyōto during the early days of May. They took with them a painting of Rennyo, or Rennyo Shōnin as he is usually more fully and reverently called, which is moved in a portable shrine. The formal term for the portrait is *miei* 御影, which implies that it is an extremely respected sacred image. The meaning is that they are not merely retracing the route, but they are traversing the route together with Rennyo Shōnin.

---

22. Also sometimes pronounced more formally as *nijūshihai* (but the pronunciation *shi*, for four, is often avoided because it is a homophone for "death").
23. Illustrated in Pye and Triplett 2011, 34 (catalogue number 18).

Temples within temples

The concept of "going round" is sometimes harnessed to encourage visits to a number of halls within one major temple complex. Important examples here are of course Mount Hiei, Kyōto's centre of Tendai Buddhism, and Mount Kōya, the ultimate home of Shingon Buddhism. On Mount Kōya, with its various places of devotion and discipline, the route ultimately leads one to the mausoleum of Kōbō Daishi at the Oku no In, the "further temple," so that it is not exactly a circulatory journey. On Mount Hiei, the concept is a little more fitting. The whole area at the top of the mountain is known collectively as Enryakuji, but there are three main complexes known as the Eastern "Pagoda" (Tōdō 東塔), the Western "Pagoda" (Saitō 西塔) and Yokawa 横川[24] respectively. While many visitors hardly get beyond the first of these, the temple authorities encourage going round to visit all the halls (*shodō meguri*). So too do the providers of auxiliary transport, for whom it provides a livelihood. For many visitors the village of Sakamoto, at the foot of Mount Hiei on the Lake Biwa side, is more or less part of the same sacred area. It includes the important Shintō shrine Hiyoshi Taisha 日吉大社, as well as the temple Shōgenji 生源寺, the reputed site of the birth of Dengyō Daishi (Saichō), the initiator of Japan's Tendai Buddhism.

Enryakuji on Mount Hiei also forms a crossroads for five wider pilgrimages, namely:

i   Saikoku Kannon Reijō
ii Saikoku Yakushi Reijō
iii Tōkai Yakushi Reijō
iv Shinsaikoku Kannon Reijō
v   Ōmi Saikoku Reijō

Enryakuji's main hall, the Konponchūdō, a particularly beautiful building with an impressive, dimly lit, sunken gallery of buddha images, has a particular position in four of the pilgrimages mentioned here. For (i) it is an extra-numerary, for (ii) it is Number 19, for (iii) it is a "special fuda place" and for (iv) it is Number 18. Regarding (v), a Kannon pilgrimage in the nearby Ōmi area, attention is drawn to Shōgenji 生源寺, a related temple at Sakamoto, at the bottom of the mountain.

Another case of this kind is the well known temple Shitennōji (near Tennōji station), a major draw for visitors in Ōsaka which prides itself on having been the first substantial Buddhist temple to have been founded in Japan, in the year 593. This was the work of Prince Shōtoku (Shōtoku Taishi, 574–622) who was the regent of Japan under Empress Suiko, and under whose direction Buddhism was set up as a leading ideological

---

24. The place-name reading Yokawa is correct, though Yokogawa might be expected.

orientation for the emerging Japanese state. His approach reputedly combined an emphasis on the role of the laity and the combination of Buddhism itself with the Confucian value of harmony (*wa* 和) between the various levels of social organization. As previously mentioned, Shitennōji is currently the head temple (*sōhonzan*) of its own denomination, Wa-shū, while at the same time it is a nodal point in various networks which it encourages. The temple authorities like to remind us that all the major founders of the various denominations in the country revered Prince Shōtoku and were influenced by his approach to religious matters. Eight denominations are named which are called upon to see one of their homes here: Tendai-shū, Shingon-shū, Jōdo-shū, Jōdo-Shinshū, Nichiren-shū, Rinzai-shū, Sōtō-shū and Ji-shū. This is not the place to describe or appraise these relationships in detail, but there are many associations with them in the precincts of the temple. Not satisfied with this, the temple authorities encourage the practice of going around 33 places within (or very close to) the precincts and recording these in a commemorative book. These places include various halls for Amida Buddha, Kōbō Daishi, Shōtoku Taishi himself, Jizō Bosatsu, Benzaiten, Hoteison, and others. They also include a Kenshin-dō, so named in honour of Shinran Shōnin, posthumously named Kenshin Daishi, whose tall statue stands just outside. This is, at least on some occasions, surrounded by banners announcing this-worldly benefits, even though petitions for such things are abhorred in the doctrine of Shin Buddhism as such. This shows how doctrinal clarity can be quickly obscured when a different denomination takes control.

Shitennōji also prides itself on being a crossroads for a number of different pilgrimages, listing no less than fifteen. This large number arises because several of them list Shitennōji as an extra-numerary temple. There is a comfortable centre for pilgrims following quite different routes to get their books, their scrolls or their traditional pilgrims' shirts. On the writer's last visit no less than three staff members were waiting helpfully behind generously opened counter windows, rather like clerks in a railway station.

A temple does not need to be of such overwhelming national importance to be a cross-roads for various pilgrimages. The Pure Land temple Seiganji in Kyōto lists six circuits, shown here in abbreviated form with Seiganji's own place in the respective circuit in brackets:

Hōnen 25 Reijō (No.20)
Rakuyō Kannon Reijō (No. 2)
Shinsaikoku Kannon Reijō (No.15)
Kyōto 6 Amida (No.6)
Seizan Kokushi Reijō (No. 9)
Jishō Daishi 25 Reijō (No. 6).

The last named pilgrimage was inaugurated by Shinzei Shōnin (here referred to by his posthumous name Jishō Daishi 慈摂大師), the founding patriarch of Tendai Shinzei-shū 天台真盛宗. So we see here a working collaboration between two sub-groups of the Tendai and Pure Land traditions respectively.

Returning to the theme of "temples within temples" we should not overlook a famous site in Yamagata Prefecture in the Tōhoku (north-eastern) region of Japan. Here a temple known as Ryūshakuji 立石寺 was founded in 860 by Jikaku Daishi (Ennin) as a regional version of Mount Hiei. The main hall bears the same name as that of Mt. Hiei, namely Konponchūdō, the "fundamental central hall," but since there are numerous sub-temples all over the mountain, the whole area came to be known as Yamadera 山寺. Here one can circulate as the stone stepways dictate, though without numeration. Some will visit it less for Buddhist reasons than because the poet Matsuo Bashō was there in 1689. Here he wrote a famous *haiku* which runs:

Stillness
Piercing the stones
The hum of the cicadas[25]

But what this example also shows is that we have here left the phenomenon of circulatory pilgrimage and entered the realm of Japanese religious mountains, a fascinating area of study in its own right which would take us beyond the range of the present volume.

One of the most dramatic forms of pilgrimage in Japan, known as the Kaihōgyō 回峰行, is reserved for specialist monks and their entourage. It was based in the first instance on Mt. Hiei, but at some time in its long history was extended to take in the city of Kyōto, thus bringing it down to the people. Unfortunately there is no evidence of this development prior to the burning of the temple complex of Enryakuji in 1571, on the orders of warlord Oda Nobunaga, when any relevant documents will have been lost.[26] However it has been known as a "one thousand day" practice since that time, whereas earlier it only lasted for seven hundred days. The full name nowadays is Sennichi Kaihōgyō 千日回峰行, which includes the expression "one thousand days" (*sennichi*). The expression *kaihōgyō* means literally "practice of going round the peaks," i.e. various spots on the mountain, where in particular devotion is directed to Fudō Myōō, the special inspiration of those performing seri-

---

25. *Shizukasaya/iwa ni shimiiru/semi no koe* 閑さや岩にしみ入蝉の声.

26. Cf. Rhodes 1987, 185–202 for a careful factual introduction. The main information is brought out regularly in popular works and in other media presentations. For an excellent photographic presentation of the achievement of a recent adept, Utsumi Shunshō, see Hayashi and Murakami 1983, and for a general account of the practice centred on the *ajari* Sakai Yusai see Shima 1984.

ously demanding physical "practice" (*gyō*). The repeated circulation of all these places is extremely arduous, and because there are so many places, all with accompanying rituals, it has to be done in a hurry, even to fit it all into one thousand days. Since the practitioner is rather like a long-distance runner covering many kilometres every day, recent performers have attracted much media interest and a well-known work by John Stevens bears the suggestive title *The Marathon Monks of Mount Hiei* (Boston 1988). In fact it amounts to 1000 marathons, totalling a distance significantly more than 30,000 kilometres. The run around 270 sacred sites on the mountain peaks begins at 2.00 a.m. each day and is concluded at 7.30 with a *goma* ritual (offering the prayer sticks of believers through burning them). Most of the achievement is therefore invisible to the public, but keen interest is aroused when the practitioner comes down from the mountain and passes through famous Kyōto temples such as Shinnyodō, Kiyomizudera and Rokuharamitsuji, devotees kneeling to receive a blessing as he passes through the sometimes narrow streets. The route around Kyōto also takes in well known Shintō shrines such as Heian Jingū, Yasaka Jinja, Kitano Tenmangū, Kamigoryō Jinja and Shimogamo Jinja. At the end of the first seven hundred days, the adept enters a special hall named Myōōdō 明王堂 where he spends nine days in ritual activity without any sleep or sustenance, emerging in a state of complete physical exhaustion and presumed spiritual mastery. How can he survive at all? Since some water is needed for survival, the adept emerges at night to collect it from a spring guarded by Fudō Myōō. While it is said that he does not actually drink the water, it is also said that the night mist assists in the reduction of dehydration. This errand to the spring takes longer and longer as the body loses about a quarter of its previous weight and becomes weaker and weaker. Most aptly, the name of the temple in whose grounds the hall of immurement is situated is Mudōji 無動寺, with the literal meaning of "temple of not moving." On completion the practitioner is described as an *ajari* 阿闍梨, one who is able to transmit spiritual teaching and benefits to others, and in recent years there have been just a few *ajari* alive at any one time. The immurement was apparently the conclusion in the early days, being an expression of the practitioner's own spiritual development, but the additional circulation around parts of the wider world of Kyōto was added to bring benefits to others. Of great interest are also the activities and attitudes of a well organized devotional support group, who in part go around with the main practitioner and thus participate in what must be the most arduous circulatory pilgrimage of them all.[27] Such pilgrims

---

27. Information on this support group may be found in a valuable detailed study by Catherine Ludvik (2006). It is presumably participation of this kind which Carmen Blacker meant when she referred to "permission to perform the *kaihōgyō* in 1961"

More enumeration and circulation

Returning to the activities of the wider population, it seems that there is a strong appetite for ever more varied suggestions about potential pilgrimages. Buddhist temple authorities have therefore begun to cater quite readily for those who do not have a strong devotional attachment to any one buddha, bodhisattva or religious leader. Thus in 1984 a group known as the "Society for Familiar Temples"[28] came into existence in order to promote visits to a collection of forty temples in Kyōto. These are not numbered in a sequence, but they are located in the regions of the city named after the four cardinal points of the compass and the centre, thus creating a spatial identity.[29] These temples can be reached by local public transport. A small guidebooklet describes visiting these temples as a *meguri* and as a *junpai*, terms which were introduced above, and its cover shows a cheerful cartoon picture of a pilgrim complete with the traditional outfit. However, it is only in a derived sense that this really amounts to a pilgrimage.

In the same manner, another group of scenic temples known for their wonderful flowers seeks to attract visitors. These are much more widely spread in various prefectures of western Japan and can be reached typically by car. The concept therefore provides an excellent excuse for weekend tourism without very specific obligations.

The invention of such groups of temples complements from an institutional perspective the long-standing practice by which individuals make up their own personal list of temples visited, recording them with the appropriate seals and calligraphy in a pilgrim's book which is not designed for any specific pilgrimage. More details on these pilgrims' books will be found in Chapter Six.

Apart from historic or scenic temples, there is a certain interest in iconographic monuments as artistic or cultural attractions. In the former province of Iyo (now Ehime Prefecture, Shikoku) one is invited to visit thirteen "stone buddhas." Stone buddhas (*ishibotoke*) are simply buddhas or bodhisattvas carved in stone and most frequently standing

---

(Blacker 1975, 10).

28. Tsūshōji no kai 通称寺の会. The pilgrimage is known as Tsūshōji Meguri 通称寺めぐり. *Tsūshōji* means, more literally, "temples with popular names," i.e. as well as their formal names, which may not be widely known. Information is drawn from a booklet entitled *Tsūshōji junpai no shiori* which was issued by the above-named association without further publication details or date, though available in 2006.

29. Special terms are used for this in Kyōto: Rakuchū, Rakutō, Rakuhoku, Rakusai and Rakunan.

outside in all weathers. Some people take a particular interest in this tradition of Buddhist iconography, and find it rewarding to go on walking tours which lead them to the stone buddhas of a particular area. In a guidebook entitled *Iyo jūsanshibotoke* ("Thirteen stone buddhas of Iyo") it says at the end that one may visit them in any order –or a few at a time. Usually however there is no particular enumeration at all. The literature on "stone buddhas" is immense, sometimes offering local information and sometimes ranging over large regions of Japan. Since they are all visible, and not hidden behind doors and curtains as in many temples, their visitors can take delight in the iconographical variations. At the same time part of the attraction seems to lie in the fact that the buddhas show signs of having been out in all weathers, but are still waiting there when the human beings feel like going for a walk.

We have seen that the "Six Jizō" amount to an *enumeration* of six related forms, but these are most frequently revered all at once, without circulation. Another theme is "Six Kannon," but as there are various Kannon routes anyway, these are not made into a pilgrimage as such. Yet the number "six" does not go away, simply because of the importance of the six ordinary realms of rebirth (leaving aside the more elevated ones).[30] So we find that there is a linked sequence of "Six Amidas" in the city of Kyōto. The temples include some famous ones.

Table 4.6 Six linked Amida temples in Kyōto.

No. 1	Shinnyodō	真如堂	
No. 2	Zenrinji (Eikandō)	禅林時	永観堂
No. 3	Kiyomizudera (Amidadō)	清水寺	阿弥陀堂
No. 4	Mokujikidera (Anshōin)	木食寺	安祥院
No. 5	Anyōji	安養寺	
No. 6	Seiganji	誓願寺	

Enumeration as such is not restricted to specifically Buddhist temples or statues. An important female divinity on the margins between "Buddhist" and "Shintō" culture is Benzaiten, and very well known are "the three great shrines of Benzaiten," all on islands, namely Chikubushima, Enoshima and Itsukushima. This enumeration tends to make people want to visit all three, but the fufilment of such an aspiration does not really amount to a circulatory pilgrimage. Benzaiten will appear again among the Seven Gods of Good Fortune in Chapter Five below.

---

30. The likely realms of rebirth for most living beings are: celestial beings (devas), warring spirits (asuras), humans, animals, hungry ghosts, and the hells of karmic retribution. The more elevated realms are those of worthy monks, bodhisattvas, pratyekabuddhas (who achieve Buddha-hood in glorious isolation) and buddhas.

Also supposedly on the margins between Buddhism and Shintō is a recently founded rosary pilgrimage (*juzu junrei* 数珠巡礼), which presents itself as a collection of "shrines and temples" (*shaji* 社寺) spread widely in Kyōto and the surrounding region. Information about this is disseminated by an association named Juzu Junrei Kai.[31] In fact the listed places to visit are almost entirely Buddhist and there are no specifically Shintō shrines. Three of the Seven Gods of Good Fortune, Daikokuten, Bishamonten and Benzaiten, figure at just one place. The rosary-like string of beads, well known in Buddhist contexts, can be assembled by collecting them up from the temples visited, for a small charge, each bead bearing the name of the temple in question. The resultant rosary is described as a "rosary of happiness." It is emphasized that no particular sequence is prescribed for the visits and that denominational affiliations are transcended.

There is apparently no end to the inventive ability of temple authorities. A recently devised pilgrimage in western Japan is known as the "Senility Prevention Kinki Ten Happy Kannon Spiritual Places" (Bokefūji Kinki Jūrakukannon Reijō ぼけ封じ近畿十楽観音霊場). A similar pilgrimage is located in the Tōkai region. In the Kinki region these temples are quite wide-spread, with two in Kyōto City, one in Kyōto District (*fu*), two in Shiga Prefecture, one in Ōsaka District (*fu*), one in Ōsaka City, one in Kōbe City and two in Hyōgo Prefecture. All ten temples are of the Shingon tradition, the first being Imakumano Kannonji 今熊野観音寺 in Kyōto. Though they are not particularly close to each other, they can be reached quite conveniently with the complex railway infrastructure of the region. The concept may encourage people to get out and about for significant journeys, perhaps combining them with a visit to relatives. The perceived need for this particular blessing by Kannon-sama evidently goes hand in hand with the steady demographic trend towards an ageing population at the present time. In a promotional leaflet we read:

Living joy,
Life that gives us life,
To the Kannon-sama of the ten temples,
Let us pray for the prevention of senility.[32]

The visitors or pilgrims are invited to make use of a pilgrim's record book for the temple seals and calligraphies, and also to recite the Kannon Sūtra in Ten Lines (see Chapter Seven).

Pilgrimage and circumambulation

The practice of circumambulation is widely current in various religions of the world and involves walking respectfully around a particular

---

31. 数珠巡礼会, apparently a very recent foundation: pamphlet obtained in 2011.
32. Leaflet from 2005, author's translation.

focus. While the English term derives from Latin (*circum+ambulare*), the practice in Japan is ultimately derived from ancient India, where it was known as *pradakṣiṇa*, meaning to circulate around a person or an object of veneration while keeping one's right shoulder and side pointing to that person or object. The right hand side is pure and the left hand side is impure and hence disrespectful. As a result circumambulation usually takes place in a clockwise direction.

Circumambulation occurs in many different contexts in Japanese Buddhism to this day. For example there is a practice known as *kaidan-meguri* 戒壇めぐり which is practised at Zenkōji and at Temple Number 33 of the Saikoku pilgrimage route, Kegonji. This involves descending beneath the main floor of the temple and proceeding in a clockwise direction, in pitch darkness, around the base of the central object of reverence. It is also possible to do this at a derivative temple of Zenkōji in Kyōto known as Tokujōmyō-in 得浄明院. The term *kaidan* literally refers to the "ordination platform" or the place from which the rules of discipline are made known and the ordination of monks takes place. In the cases mentioned here it refers in practice metaphorically to the base of the central statue, to the buddha from whom good practice flows. The emphasis is placed on the extinction of sin and the origination of good (*metsuzai shōzen* 滅罪生善) on the part of believers, thanks to the merit of the Tathāgata who is up above.

Although the term *kaidan-meguri* is used here, the element *-meguri* is being adopted for what is in fact an example of circumambulation. It is therefore fair to ask whether the circulatory pilgrimages of Japan have anything to do with circumambulation. As the maps show, the routes of circulatory pilgrimages are not distinctly circular. The large number of sites involved and the particularities of the landscape in which the temples are set precludes this. The most that can be said is that a broadly clockwise direction is usually maintained. This is especially evident in miniature pilgrimages where the points to be called at are set in limited, manageable terrain. It might be thought that this alone means that such pilgrimage is akin to the practice of circumambulation, which is widespread in many parts of the world, including Japan, and is usually performed clockwise. This tempting association may be misleading, however, for the circulatory pilgrimages have *no centre* which could itself be an object of reverence. The purpose of circumambulation on the other hand is to revere the object or symbol, typically a relic or a statue, which is at the centre.

Moroever circumambulation is often directly invited by the architectural structure. In northern Kyūshū there is a large statue of the Buddhist reformer Nichiren around which believers in his teaching (in the tradition, specifically, of the denomination known as Nichiren-shū) hurry in a clockwise direction. The statue is surrounded by a circular walkway enclosed by a stone wall, so that any visitor will naturally circumambulate the statue anyway, even if only once. For the believer who repeats this walk again and again the focus of devotion is massively evident at the centre.

A parallel case in Korea, in which the architecture more or less *invites* the practice of circumambulation, may be found in a statue of the Venerable Sot'aesan, the founder of Won Buddhism. The statue, sculpted in the form of a Buddha who has attained enlightenment, is set in a generously sized hall in the grounds of the headquarters of Won Buddhism at Iksan City. The statue itself once had a base with a circular rim at about hand height, with the result that visitors could touch it lightly with their hand, usually their right hand as most people are right-handed, and move round, usually clockwise because of stretching out their right hand and then moving forwards. It must be noted that any idea that this is itself some kind of religious practice is expressly denied by representatives of Won Buddhism, and it is even doubtful whether it was actually intended by sculptor or architect. Yet, as seen shortly after the opening, believers were in fact carrying out a reverent circumambulation of their founder, sculpted as a Buddha. They were implicitly led into doing this by the position of the statue and by the nature of the hall which housed it.[33] Apart from being a fascinating case of a religious practice coming into being before one's very eyes, even if only to be rejected on doctrinal grounds, this also illustrates the importance of the central symbol and the constructed space around it for circumambulation. This aspect is not present in the pilgrimages which link a number of sacred, but geographically scattered spots, so that it would not really be accurate simply to identify circumambulation with circulatory pilgrimage.

There is however another way in which the practice of circumambulation may be psychologically close to circulatory pilgrimage. This lies in the tendency to enumerate. When a devotee goes round and round the statue of Nichiren for example, as mentioned above, it is the number of times, namely one hundred, which matters. In Japanese this practice is known as *hyakudo-mairi*, meaning "one hundred reverences"; it involves hurrying round a central object of reverence one hundred times. On the one hand there is no particular relation between "one hundred times" and the numbers of the various circulatory pilgrimages studied in this book, thirty-three, eighty-eight, and so on. There is however a similar importance in completing the set number. The number provides a target.

The variations in actual practice are quite fascinating. If the lay-out does not permit going completely round the object of reverence the practice is adjusted to going to and fro between the place of reverence

---

33. For a contemporary documentation of this phenomenon, also with a doctrinal disclaimer, see Pye 2002b.

and a special marker stone set nearby, one hundred times. This may be called modified circumambulation. It is performed for example at the Shingon temple Shinnyodō in Kyōto, where the marker stone is dedicated to "Kannon the Mother of Compassion." Another excellent example is at the mausoleum of Kōbō Daishi on Mount Kōya which attracts pilgrims as a single site pilgrimage goal in its own right. In this case the devotee worships before the mausoleum itself, which is set in a wooded hill, and then hurries to the right. Having passed round a marker stone, he or she returns to the mausoleum for the next act of devotion, and so on. The shape traversed on the ground is simply there and back, round the marker stone. It therefore appears to be linear; however *it stands for* circumambulation.

Other modifications are also possible. Thus the one hundred circumambulations do not have to be done in one day, but may be spread over a longer period. When I observed a similar practice at Temple Number 8 (Hasedera) of the Saikoku pilgrimage I was told that performing, say, twenty circuits on five different days would be all right. It would even be all right to do only ten on each day for ten different days. This information was given by an attendant at the entrance who also pointed out that spreading out one hundred circumambulations over ten days would multiply the entrance fee for the temple from 400 Yen (per day) to 4000 Yen in all. Why do people perform these practices? In this case at least it was a straightforward reinforcement of the prayers brought before the Kannon-sama in the main hall of the temple, prayers (the informant said) for cure of illness, for success in examinations, or of gratitude for wishes fulfilled. It may be noted that one priest of this Shingon temple flatly refused to make any comment at all about the practice, except to say that it was not promoted as such by the temple, even though the very earnest practitioners were hurrying past right under his nose. He did admit however that the temple, Hasedera, supported the practice of pilgrimage round the thirty-three temples of Kannon-sama.[34]

It is assumed here that circumambulation as known in Japan is a practice which derived originally from India. All the more interestingly, it has also spread over into the context of Shintō. Various Shintō shrines have a marker post with the very words *hyakudo-mairi* chiselled on it; the practitioner goes round the post, which is somewhere to one side of the main approach path to the shrine, and goes up to the front of the shrine to pray, one hundred times. A small shrine specialising in students' prayers next to Fushimi Inari Taisha in southern Kyōto is an example.

---

34. The positive information was reinforced with faultless consistency by two other attendants. The concerned urgency of the practitioners themselves does not really allow of interruption without serious rudeness, and this should be avoided when studying religions.

One Shintō priest consulted about the marker stone at his own shrine was surprised at the idea that this might originally have been a practice deriving from Buddhism.

Another case of numbers being linked to one single sacred spot is the so-called "stone staircase marathon" (*ishidan marason*) of the Shintō shrine Konpira-san in Shikoku. "Marathon" is of course a word which has recently been introduced into Japanese, and refers to marathon races and hence to the completion of an arduous course, whether competitively or not. In recent years a Konpira-san festival held on October 8th is introduced by a marathon which culminates in the ascent of the stone steps of the shrine. Participants (in men's and women's sections) come from all over the country, for Konpira-san is widely popular, especially among those whose families derive from Shikoku. They begin by submitting to purification (*o-harae*) by a Shintō priest. The event in its present form appears to be a transformation of the practice of climbing the 1368 steps of the shrine 100 times. At the top of the steps there is a stone marker to step round, so that the achievement of the devotion is defined.

Following these examples from a Shintō context we pass over next to a more detailed consideration of the ways in which circulatory pilgrimage has been transposed into the wider culture of religious activity in Japan.

— Chapter Five —

Going Round to other Divinities

Buddhist pilgrimage and the wider field of Japanese religion

Buddhism does not just exist by itself in Japan. The various denominations, temples and other structures, including the patterns of pilgrimage already described, are rooted in many ways in a wider field of religious concepts and activity which is generally understood by practically the whole population of the country. Indeed it is fascinating to see how the diverse interpretations of Buddhism lend support to, or distance themselves from this field of "primal religion" as the present writer usually denotes it.[1] For example, while most Buddhist temples which participate in the provision of pilgrimage routes actively encourage prayers for traffic safety, the welfare of the family, healing, good health, and so on, Shin Buddhists reject the concept of this-worldly benefits. But whichever tendency is adopted, some positioning is unavoidable in this respect. There has also been a long tradition of the "fusion of gods and buddhas" (shinbutsu shūgō),[2] only for this to have been forcibly broken up in the nineteenth century, during the Meiji Period, in the interests of setting up a purer form of Shintō. This policy of separation was not entirely successful. In the second half of the twentieth century the previously enforced differences were already being renegotiated to a limited extent, and the process is continuing. The association of major Shintō shrines with Buddhist pilgrimages has already been noted in some cases, e.g. Izumo Shrine with the local Kannon-sama pilgrimage and Konpira Shrine as a "must" for pilgrims going round Shikoku. In the many mountains of Japan which attract religious activity this process of readjustment has also been pushed along by particular groups such

---

1. See various sections of *Strategies in the Study of Religions* (2013).
2. Recent scholarly treatments of this subject, concentrating on pre-modern aspects, are found in the multi-authored work entitled *Buddhas and Kami in Japan, Honji Suijaku as a Contemporary Paradigm*, Teeuwen and Rambelli 2003.

as the *yamabushi*, the mountain ascetics of the Shugendō tradition, who have traditionally operated at the borders of Buddhism and Shintō.

The institutions sometimes get drawn into a tug-of-war over divinities of diverse origin such as the Seven Gods of Good Fortune to be discussed shortly. Very complex, for example, is the goddess Benzaiten (or Benten for short; the ending *-ten* means "divinity," usually implying a divinity of non-Japanese origin). On the small island in the middle of Lake Biwa in Shiga Prefecture known as Chikubushima, this goddess was at one time revered in a Shintō shrine from which she was however expelled during the nineteenth-century drive for the purification of Shintō. She was then lodged in a new hall on the same island, administered by Shingon Buddhists. When Shintō was disestablished after the end of the Pacific War the state-driven ideological pressure for separation lost its force. As a result, although the Buddhist hall for Benzaiten remains, there has recently been a tendency to try to get her back into the Shintō area by reduplicating her, as can be seen from the installation of a new image to one side of the main Shintō shrine near the shore of the lake.[3] On the other hand, the well-known Buddhist temple Ryōanji, a Rinzai Zen temple in Kyōto which is justly famous for its superbly meditative rock garden, does not fail to have its shrine to Benzaiten on an island in its scenic lake. This is entered through a small Shintō-style *torii*. A similar example may be found in the grounds of the Jōdo (Pure Land) Buddhist temple Eikandō in Kyōto. Near Demachi Bridge in Kyōto the goddess, here known as Myōon Benzaiten, has her own shrine with a *torii*. But her main festival includes not only live *biwa* (lute) performances but also a ritualized visit by monks from the Rinzai temple Shōkokuji, while in the elegant grounds of the temple, a short walk away, there is a small shrine to Benzaiten with a stone *torii* to the front of it.[4] Thus Benzaiten somehow manages to be herself, between Shintō and Buddhism.

Another divinity with an ambiguous identity is Daikoku (or Daikokuten), who on the one hand has Indian origins, coming to Japan via Buddhism, and on the other hand is identified with the Shintō *kami* Ōkuninushi (see further below). Daikoku appears among the Seven Gods of Good Fortune. However, among the many famous Buddhist temples of the city of Kyōto are to be found six where Daikoku may be visited some-

---

3. See the article "Buddhism and Shintō on one island" in my *Strategies in the Study of Religions* Vol. II (2013b); Pye 2013, vol. 2.

4. The visit by the Rinzai monks involves bringing to the shrine an Edo Period scroll depicting the goddess which is normally kept at the temple for safe-keeping, and returning it afterwards. The ritual consists mainly of reciting the great *Hannya Sūtra* (*Daihannyakyō*) in many folded volumes, which is achieved by applying the *tendoku* system of shouting out the beginnings and ends of each volume while fanning them out through the air.

Figure 5.1 Iconic depiction (*miei*) of Myōon Benzaiten at Demachi, Kyōto.

where in the grounds. In other words, there is a series specializing in Daikokuten. The series of temples with a place of worship for Daikoku is as follows: 1 Hōji, 2 Daitokuji, 3 Shōhōji, 4 Henshōji, 5 Byōdōji and 6 Daikokuji (at Fushimi). Note that the second in the sequence is the famous Rinzai Zen temple Daitokuji, which is evidently not shy of hosting this popular wealth-bringing divinity. The group is described as a "circuit for benefits" (*goriyaku meguri*), each temple being responsible for a particular aspect of human welfare.

Of the above temples, that specifically devoted to Daikokuten, i.e. Daikokuji in the Fushimi area of Kyōto is also part of a series of five stations known as the Fushimi Gofuku Meguri 伏見五福めぐり, or "Fushimi Circuit of Five Happinesses." Fushimi is known for the great Shintō shrine Fushimi Inari Taisha, which regularly attracts about two million visitors in the first three days of the New Year. Those who want more than just the New Year's visit can visit the following shrines and temples which each provide their own specific benefit:

Nogi Jinja	乃木神社	benefit: success in studies
Chōkenji	長建寺	benefit: opening of fortune, flourishing of business, success in the arts
Fuji no mori Jinja	藤森神社	benefit: success in scholarship
Daikokuji	大黒寺	benefit: career, opening of fortune, prosperity
Gokō no Miya (Jinja)	御香宮(神社)	benefit: safe childbirth, opening of fortune, averting ill-fortune

It can be seen from this list that three of the five are Shintō shrines (*jinja* or *jingū*). Of the two Buddhist temples (the names ending in *-ji*) Chōkenji has a shrine to the goddess Benzaiten while the main object of reverence in Daikokuji is Daikoku himself. For the combined group the well established term *shaji* is used, meaning literally "shrines and temples" (just as *shinbutsu* means "gods and buddhas"). Those who visit all five are invited to assemble the seal of each institution on a commemorative card indicating the benefits of each and bearing a picture of the calendrical animal for the year. The total cost of the card and inscriptions corresponds approximately to the cost of two or three good talismans (*o-fuda*) of the type otherwise acquired at shrines and many temples. In a newspaper description it is said that the shrines and temples can be visited in any order.[5] In traditional Chinese lore the five happinesses are: long life, wealth, good health, love of virtue and leading life in accordance with the decrees of heaven.[6] The benefits at Fushimi could therefore be regarded as more clearly geared to personal success and welfare than to morality.

In general, the widespread interest in this-worldly benefits plays an important role in the mixing of religious sites, because the people may go first to one divinity and later to another, regardless of doctrinal niceties, if indeed these can be identified at all. This leads to a steady market for books setting out the benefits of numerous shrines and temples scattered through a particular city or area. At the same time, the popularity of the practice of circulatory pilgrimage itself contributes to the blurring of the edges. Not only are the Seven Gods of Good Fortune, who cannot really be assigned definitively to either Buddhism or Shintō, immensely popular, but quite apart from them there has also recently been a definite transfer of the model of circulatory pilgrimage from the Buddhist to the Shintō context. This is undoubtedly in response to popular demand.

---

5. Information on this group was presented in the local page of the *Asahi Shinbun* for 13 January 2006. A similar report appeared on the "Kyōto page" on 6 December of the same year, with the argument that one could prepare for the new year by visiting these places well in advance!

6. See standard reference works such as the Japanese dictionary *Kōjien* under *gofuku*.

The very existence of this complex phenomenon may help us to see more clearly, especially in the last chapter of this book, just where the distinctive meaning of the Buddhist pilgrimages is to be found.

A close link between Buddhism and Shintō is maintained at the Tendai Buddhist headquarters on Mount Hiei, where a special hall is devoted to "thirty deities" (*sanjūbanjin*) who protect those who believe in the teaching of the *Lotus Sūtra*. The idea is based on the "Chapter on the Merits of Teachers" (i.e. of the *sūtra*), but in this case the divinities are not Indian but Japanese. This is explained in a leaflet from the temple as being based on the transformation bodies of Fudō Myōō and Kannon-sama, whose compassionate forms derive from the activity of Dainichi Nyorai (Vairocana Buddha) and then find further expression in the divinities of any particular country. The hall is said to be always open, day and night, although in practice visitors cannot usually visit Mount Hiei at night time. In the centre of the hall is an arrangement with images of Kannon-sama and the denominational founders of Tendai Buddhism, namely Tendai Daishi (in China) and Dengyō Daishi (in Japan). Plaques are mounted round the polygonal interior wall to indicate the names of the thirty divinities. Each of these divinities, Atsuta Daimyōjin, Suwa Daimyōjin, etc. (the ending *-jin* being the equivalent of *kami* as in the name of Shintō divinities), stands at the same time for a well-known buddha or a bodhisattva. In a printed overview of all these correspondences[7] the Buddhist figures are described as the *honjibutsu*, following the mediaeval terminology with which the Shintō divinities used to be explained as being "originally" or "essentially" Buddhist figures in a provisional form. Thus Atsuta Daimyōjin (No. 1) is "essentially" Dainichi Nyorai, Tenshō Kōtaijin (Amaterasu, No. 10) is "essentially" Dainichi Nyorai, Hachiman Daimyōjin (No. 11) is "essentially" Shaka Nyorai, Inari Daimyōjin (No. 22) is "essentially" Nyoirin Kannon Bosatsu, and so on. This interpretative tradition lives on therefore, if a little tenuously, in spite of the enforced separation of Buddhism and Shintō during the Meiji Period. There are even occasional indications that these associations are still remembered from the Shintō side, for example at Kumano and at some of the sacred mountains such as the three mountains of Dewa Sanzan which were once famous for them. The main point to notice here however, right at the centre of the Mount Hiei complex, is that by circling round the hall and revering the thirty Japanese divinities, one is at the same time revering buddha figures. By proceeding around the divinities on the outer wall, step by step, one also circumambulates the buddha figures which are at the centre of the hall.

In 2008 a major new initiative was taken by the Tendai Buddhist authorities of Mount Hiei and the Shintō authorities of Ise Jingū to reconnect their

---

7. Pamphlet from 2006, and identical earlier versions.

traditions by means of circulatory pilgrimage. A new circuit was launched which begins at Ise Jingū and ends at the temple complex on Mount Hiei, known collectively as Enryakuji. The two main shrines at Ise, the Kōtai Jingū (the Naikū) and the Toyouke Daijingū (the Gekū) are highlighted for receiving a "special visit" before the long, enumerated sequence begins with Kumano Hayatama Taisha 熊野速玉大社 as Number 1 and the Buddhist Seigantoji 青岸渡寺 as Number 2. It may be recalled that Seigantoji is Number 1 of the Saikoku Kannon Pilgrimage. After the Ise shrines no less than 150 further shrines and temples are included, ranging over seven prefectures (*ken* or *fu*): Mie, Wakayama, Nara, Ōsaka, Hyōgo, Kyōto and Shiga. Visiting all of these represents a considerable task even for those who love nothing better than driving around all over the country in their cars, and so it may be questioned whether it has really been completed by many individuals so far. The most likely scenario is that when pilgrims are visiting particular temples or shrines for other reasons, they will slowly assemble the record of their visits to these at the same time. The list is a very subtle balance of Shintō shrines and Buddhist temples, and the further development of this pattern will repay further study in future. The pilgrimage is known as Shinbutsu Reijō Junpai no Michi 神仏霊場巡拝の道, i.e. Pilgrim Path of the Spiritual Places of Gods and Buddhas. The combination of "gods and buddhas" in the expression *shinbutsu* is significant. This expression can also be spelled out, as in the title of a guidebook published in 2008 which runs *Kami to hotoke no michi wo aruku*[8] Although this literally means "walking the path of the *kami* and the buddhas," there really would be very little sense in trying to walk physically all round these shrines and temples, criss-crossing numerous built-up areas to do so. Each one of the shrines and temples is provided with a somewhat dreamy illustration, either photographic or drawn, which adds to the nostalgia, as befits a "network of the heart which is old and yet new." These are paradoxical connections, explicitly seeking to go back 140 years (counting from 2008) to return to a pre-Meiji association of shrines and temples. Yet we should not oversimplify the intervening separation of Shintō and Buddhism. In Taishō 12 (1923) a handy pilgrim's guidebook was published which first set out visits to the mausolea of 121 generations of emperors, to be visited in 25 clusters based on locality, and then the 33 temples of the Saikoku Kannon pilgrimage, in the same book. Moreover, on page 83, where the Kannon pilgrimage is introduced, the pilgrim is urged to begin this new journey, which after all is a Buddhist pilgrimage, by first performing *sanpai* to "the two shrines of Ise" i.e. the Naikū and the Gekū mentioned above. After that, one should proceed to the Buddhist temple Seigantoji to launch the visits to the 33 temples of Kannon-sama.

---

8. Shinbutsureijōkai 2008. Note that the editorial society, Shinbutsureijōkai 神仏霊場会, specifically incorporates the traditional term *shinbutsu* in its name.

Betwixt and between Shintō and Buddhism, there are also rather more general religious or spiritual concepts today. Of apparently recent construction is a set of links between 108 "spiritual places" (*reijō* 霊場) around Lake Biwa. It seems that any "spiritual places" will do. Particularly popular in recent times is the idea of paying visits to "power spots." With such ideas we see a new commercialization of spirituality which is easily understood in the context of contemporary mass culture. Everybody "knows" what a power spot is, although further explanations are hard to come by. It is no more and no less than a place, hallowed by time and layers of historic fame, from which one can draw personal spiritual energy or "power" (*pawaa*). Needless to say, many major shrines and temples present themselves as "power spots" and recently guidebooks are devoted to them without any specific reference to the orthodoxies of one religion or another. The purpose of such guidebooks seems to be partly to give suggestions on the particular benefits (*genzeriyaku*) of various "spots," apart from the sheer "power," and partly to advise on how to get there and in particular what specialities to eat in the vicinity (illustrated).

The Seven Gods of Good Fortune

We turn now to a more traditional but still extremely popular subject. The Seven Gods of Good Fortune (*shichifukujin*) are among the most accessible of all the divinities in Japan, and that is a strong statement, for in general the divinities of Japan are certainly accessible rather than remote. Their individual shrines, usually of relatively modest size, are places at which visitors perform a simple devotional visit (*o-mairi*) which is considered likely to bring benefit. Any of them may be found in a particular shrine which is not itself linked to any pilgrimage, such shrines being found in the grounds of larger institutions. As mentioned the Zen temple Shōkokuji in Kyōto has a small shrine for Benzaiten (the individual divinities will be explained immediately below), while the Tendai temple Miidera, near the shores of Lake Biwa, has a shrine for Bishamonten, in a distinctive Chinese style. The Shintō-style shrines for Ebisu, a god of commerce, are flourishing independent institutions in their own right. However, in the imagination the seven gods are frequently linked, and this is the point of interest here because they therefore share in the principle of circulatory pilgrimage. Indeed, as has been explained on earlier occasions, they provide an important link between Buddhist pilgrimages and Shintō pilgrimages.[9]

The name Shichifukujin arises from the following elements: *shichi* meaning seven, *fuku* meaning good fortune and *-jin* meaning "gods." In the last

---

9. These pages draw in part on an earlier presentation (2004); the circulatory pilgrimage aspect was highlighted but the contextual information provided was not comprehensive.

element the consonant is hardened from *shin*, and the same character is also read as *kami*, which means "god/s" in general and especially in the context of Shintō. Since these gods (including one goddess) are considered to be so beneficial from a practical point of view, it is in everybody's interest that the route should not be particularly arduous. So it is usually assumed that it should be possible to do the rounds in one day. This is a strong reason for having local versions which can be reached easily in a single excursion. Since going round to see the divinities is particularly popular at new year, the routes in one's neighbourhood are advertised appropriately. Thus the Hankyū railway company based in Ōsaka publishes a leaflet giving details of the "Saikoku" Seven Gods of Good Fortune, which just happen to be reached conveniently by using the company's Takarazuka Line, and which are gratuitously provided with the elite connotations of "Saikoku" in pilgrimage matters. In 1990 the *Asahi Shinbun* (a leading daily newspaper) set out five different routes in Tokyo and a further twenty in surrounding prefectures and nearby cities such as Chichibu, Ogose, Irima and Hannō, thus advertising a mixture of 175 Shintō shrines and Buddhist temples altogether.[10] Even so, well-known routes in Kawagoe and Kamakura were not even mentioned. One book lists no less than 62 different circuits with details of the participating temples and shrines (Satō and Kaneko 1989, 1996), but this is by no means exhaustive. In other words, they will be found in practically every area where there are active temples and shrines in relative proximity to each other, and every visitor or resident in Japan comes across their own local version. We can conclude that there are not just dozens of circuits for the Seven Gods of Good Fortune, but hundreds. The practice of visiting them is therefore widespread and easily followed through even when people are outside their normal home area. Even though the arrangements do not fall under the responsibility of any one religious organization, they are easily recognizable to all.

Seven itself is regarded as a lucky number, in Japan as in many other places. However the seven gods are not quite seven of the same. Their origin is diverse. Some of them have a tenuous connection with Buddhism, but some have no such connection. The seven appear to have been linked with each other as early as the Muromachi Period, but they came into great popularity during the Edo Period (Edo being the name of present Tokyo until the Meiji Restoration). According to local information in the city of Kawagoe it was the Buddhist priest Tenkai (1536–1643) of the well-known temple Kita-in, who first designated the seven as a group to be visited in turn. Kawagoe is not far from Tokyo and because of its traditional features is sometimes referred to as "little Edo." At Kawagoe, the Seven Gods of Good Fortune are all housed in Buddhist temples. Tenkai's intention was to pray for the peaceful governance of the land (*tenka taihei*) under the *shōgun*

---

10. *Asahi Shinbun* December 27th 1990.

Tokugawa Ieyasu. It is also known that the seven were familiar to Ieyasu, who patronized them—and they perhaps him!

One of the most well-known examples of a pilgrimage round the Seven Gods of Good Fortune is that in the Asakusa area of downtown Tokyo, one which dates from the Edo Period. Such pilgrimages are a typical product of popular Japanese religion as this developed during the time of urban expansion and prosperity. Indeed it is conceivable that the linkage of the Seven Gods of Good Fortune with each other was initially a contribution of the Kantō region of Japan. One version in Kyōto known as Kyōto Shichifukujin Meguri was launched in 1936, while a variation named Kyō no Shichifukujin Meguri was formed in its present grouping in 1979 but may have older roots. It may be supposed, in view of the overlapping between the various Kyōto routes, that there have been other variations in the past, and that various changes in institutional arrangements and relationships have given rise to the combinations which happen to be promoted nowadays.

In the Edo Period, as now, the Seven Gods of Good Fortune promised above all success and well-being, and are therefore particularly popular at the New Year period, when hopes are high. Many find it easy to fit in such visits in addition to making their first shrine visit of the year (*hatsumōde*) or their first visit to a Buddhist temple with which they feel a special affinity. The number seven being itself auspicious, so too is the wide-spread idea that these gods should be visited above all during the first seven days of the year.[11] In Kyōto the Miyako Shichifukujin Mairi is covered by special buses during the whole month of January. The organizers clearly do not wish to lose visitors by being restrictive. Moreover, as a pamphlet points out, the seventh of any month is a particularly good day for the Seven Gods of Good Fortune, and indeed the commemorative booklet can be stamped on any day between nine o'clock in the morning and four o'clock in the afternoon.

It is typical of the Seven Gods of Good Fortune that they link Buddhist and Shintō institutions in a single circuit, although the Buddhist temples seem to preponderate. Some of the gods such as Daikokuten and Ebisu are much more likely to be in Shintō shrines. We have seen that Benzaiten is more likely to enjoy Buddhist patronage, having come into Japan in the train of Indo-Buddhist culture, but that she is often housed in a Shintō-style shrine, with the characteristic symbolic *torii* in front of it. The previously mentioned shrine in the grounds of the Rinzai Zen temple Shōkokuji is a clear example of this, as is the often overlooked

---

11. This is a little different from, though reminiscent of the Mongolian idea that prayers should be offered to the "seven old men" on the seventh day of the intercalary month (Heissig 1980, *The Religions of Mongolia*, 82). The seven old men are not the same as the *shichifukujin*, for one of the latter is female, but "white old man" may be identifiable with Jurōjin (see further below).

shrine for Benzaiten in the grounds of Ryōanji, also in Kyōto and otherwise known for what is probably the most famous Zen garden of all. In view of the very close relations between Buddhism and Shintō at Nachi in Wakayama Prefecture, known for the Kumano shrine complex and Temple No. 1 of the Saikoku Kannon pilgrimage, it is not surprising that the Seven Gods of Good Fortune can be visited there too. The various versions of the Shichifukujin in the great metropolis of Tokyo include a series in Shinjuku Ward which is based on two Shintō shrines and five Buddhist temples. Number 1 is the shrine to Ebisu (see below) near the Seibu Shinjuku station. Others may find it more convenient to start at the Nichirenite Buddhist temple Number 6, Zenkokuji 善国寺, near Ichigaya, where Bishamonten will be found.

The Seven Gods of Good Fortune have in common that they all offer a positive contribution to a happy life of well-being. While the Seven Gods of Good Fortune are remarkably diverse in origin and characteristics, it is notable that they are frequently depicted and sculptured in readily recognizable forms. Their common characteristic is that they all look very cheerful indeed. Often they are shown standing together as a group in a ship of good fortune (*takarabune*), a ship which is often carved in wood and may also be used for a celebratory serving of *o-sushi*.

The seven divinities in question, whose derivations can only be very briefly indicated here, are as follows:

Daikoku-ten 大黒天

Daikoku-ten is of Indian origin, as can be seen from the ending *-ten* which is usually translating *deva* (via Chinese). In Indian form, Mahākāla was originally a wrathful deity who was pressed into service to guard Buddhist monasteries, taking on the care of virtue and thereby also of happiness. The name Daikoku is written with two characters meaning "great" and "black" (corresponding to *mahā* and *kāla*) but because the characters used to write Ōkuni "great" 大 + "country" 国 can also be read as Daikoku, an identification took place with the Shintō *kami* Ōkuninushi. For this reason Daikoku carries the heavy wooden hammer associated with Ōkuninushi, who in Shintō legend played an important role in the construction of the country and is revered at the great shrine of Izumo on the Japan Sea coast. As one of the Seven Gods of Good Fortune, Daikokuten's particular function is to give wealth, for which reason he also carries a sack of fortune. He may also carry or sit on top of a bale of rice. One should remember in this connection that during the lengthy Edo Period serious wealth was counted in terms of *koku* of rice, even though coinage was in use, just as in other cultures one might count wealth in heads of cattle or barrels of oil. Daikoku is usually shown as a rather plump and jolly figure, rather like Ebisu with whom he is often linked and who will be considered next.

Going Round to other Divinities

Ebisu 恵比寿

Ebisu, a *kami* of mysterious derivation, is the only one of the Seven Gods of Good Fortune who is originally Japanese. Even so, the name Ebisu is thought originally to have meant "foreigner," so that as a divinity, Ebisu may have originated as a stranger who brings good fortune. Sometimes designated Ebisu-ten, the ending *-ten* seems to hint at an Indian derivation by analogy to the names of other gods containing this element, but no specific identification can be made in this direction. In Shintō shrines however he is usually referred to as Ebisu Daijin 恵比寿大神. Traditionally responsible for success in fishing, Ebisu's functions have been extended to provide safety at sea and prosperity in business. In this connection he came to be an extremely popular figure in the commercial art of the Meiji Period, being shown on advertising handbills (*hikifuda*), for example, with a giant sea-bream (*tai*), carp or lobster. This tradition continues today, though less prominently due to the sheer proliferation of other symbols in contemporary commercial art. A recent marketing campaign by the Chiyoda Kasai Ebisu Seimei Hoken Kabushiki Kaisha (Chiyoda Fire and Ebisu Life Insurance Company) used a poster showing the ship of riches (*takarabune*) sailed by the Seven Gods of Good Fortune with Ebisu to the fore. The ship bears the name Ebisu-maru. (Japanese ships all bear names ending with *-maru*.) Ebisu is highly revered in the great commercial city of Ōsaka at the Imamiya Ebisu Shrine, the 10th of each month being deemed to be a particularly auspicious day for paying him a visit. The 10th of January is the great annual day for it. A similar, ancient shrine is to be found in Kyōto, also focussing above all on the 10th of January. Ebisu's largest shrine of all however is the ancient Nishinomiya Jinja 西宮神社, in the area of the great port of Kōbe, a very suitable location for a divinity who is so often portrayed holding a weighty fish.

Bishamon-ten 毘沙門天

Bishamonten, also known as Tamonten, is a god of Indian derivation (Vaiśravaṇa) who was carried along with Buddhism into East Asia as a protector god. For this reason he is shown wearing armour. The spear in his right hand shows that he can destroy demons. At the same time the stūpa of endless riches carried in the left hand shows that he is helpful in bringing wealth.

Benzai-ten 弁才天 (or 弁財天)

Benzaiten, also known popularly as Benten-sama, is a transposition of the Indian goddess Sarasvatī who was introduced to East Asia in the context of Buddhism. In India she is the goddess of the wonderful sounds of the Sarasvatī river, and therefore a goddess of music and eloquence.

Even in Japan she may therefore still be described as Myōonbenzaiten ("goddess of wonderful sounds"), as at the previously mentioned shrine at Demachi in Kyōto. Carried along in the context of Buddhism, she also stands for wisdom. She is the only female divinity among the Seven Gods of Good Fortune (except when Kichijōten is included). Through a play on the characters used to write her name, in that zai can be written with a character which means wealth as well as one which means ability (弁財天 for 弁才天), she is thought to add a financial advantage as well. Benzaiten is the focus of considerable cultic activity at particular centres, of which three are particularly famous: the small island of Enoshima near Kamakura, the previously mentioned island of Chikubushima in Lake Biwa, and the famous scenic spot known as Itsukushima, an island in the Inland Sea well-known for the red symbolic gates of the Shintō shrine standing in the water. Note that the word shima in these place names means island. Indeed Benzaiten is frequently identified with islands, that is, small islands recognizable as such to the naked eye. A well known lake with an island for Benzaiten is to be found in Ueno Park in Tokyo, not far from Ueno Station and a popular place for people out for a stroll.

Reference may be found to "The Five Benzaiten of Japan," that is, to five sites where Benzaiten is revered as a "great divinity" (ōkami) in five different provinces (kuni) of old Japan. These are:

Aki no kuni: Itsukushima Ō-kami
Yamato no kuni: Tenkawa Ō-kami
Ōmi no kuni: Chikubushima Ō-kami
Sagami no kuni: Enoshima Ō-kami
Rikuzen no kuni: Koganeyama Ō-kami

However these locations are quite far-flung and do not amount to a sequential pilgrimage.

Because of the connection with water Benzaiten has a complex mythological relationship with a water spirit named Ugajin 宇賀神, represented either as a dragon (i.e. Ryūjin 竜神 the "Dragon God") or as a white snake.[12] At her shrines may be seen votive tablets depicting the

---

12. These endless ramifications cannot be pursued here because they would lead far away from our subject. One of them is the legend of Matsura Sayohime. The key elements in this legend, studied in detail by Katja Triplett (2004), are as follows. On the one hand there is the filial piety of a girl who sells herself to an unknown man in order to finance the rites which will enable her deceased father to attain buddhahood. The purchaser, on the other hand, is acting in order to fulfil his own duty in providing a sacrifice to a huge water-snake in a distant part of the country, where this responsibility is presumed to fall to various families in turn. The girl is placed on a sacrificial stand in the middle of a lake, in order to be eaten, but when she reads from a copy of the Lotus Sūtra which was given to her by her mother as a protective memento, the dragon-like water-snake is deeply moved and attains buddhahood. The sacrifice is thereupon abandoned, the water-snake is revealed

snake, although the snake is admittedly not always white, at least nowadays. At the Rinzai Zen temple Shōkokuji in Kyōto the small Benzaiten shrine has some old votive tablets of this kind, one showing a white snake coiled around her lute. The main point is that the snake, or the dragon, is tamed by Benzaiten. When we realize that in the grounds of Ryōanji, the Rinzai Zen temple in Kyōto with its famous stone garden, there is also a large artificial lake with an island on which there is a small Shintō-style shrine to Benzaiten, we can understand why the name of this temple means the place where the dragon comes to rest.[13] There is a chapter on Benzaiten in the *Sūtra of Brilliant Golden Light*, but while this *sūtra* was important when Buddhism was newly imported into Japan it now plays no particular role in popular devotions.

Fukurokuju 福禄寿

Fukurokuju is a god of Chinese origin who is regarded as the northern personification of the south pole star. He offers three blessings: happiness, material good fortune and long life. In some, possibly older variations of the Seven Gods of Good Fortune Fukurokuju does not appear. In such versions there was still room for Kichijōten, whom he seems to have largely supplanted in most modern versions. Why did this happen? This may be because the blessings which he offers, even though also provided by other divinities, were particularly geared to the needs or wishes of the people. There are also occasional indications that he is confused with Jurōjin (see next), or that the two somehow belong together.

Jurōjin 寿老人

Jurōjin, the old man of long life, is usually regarded as deriving from China and is also known in Korea. With his elongated forehead he is remarkably similar to the "white old man" of Mongolia. In his book *The Religions of Mongolia*, Walther Heissig indicates various central and East Asian parallels to "white old man" who rules "the length and shortness of men's lives," and an illustration shows a strong similarity to the Japanese Jurōjin.[14] However there seems to be a complex problem here, for

---

to be the bodhisattva Kannon-sama, waiting to reward the pious, and the girl herself to be the goddess Benzaiten of Chikubushima. Quite apart from the theme of human sacrifice, the legend is interesting for the way in which a dramatic, and apparently tragic story highlighting filial piety turns out to lead into a Buddhist revelation. At the same time the cult of Benzaiten is given a strong legitimation through these identifications. In quite another direction the snake god Ugajin has also been identified with the harvest deity of the Inari shrines, Uka no Mitama (c.f. Duquenne 1994, Exhibit 18. ad loc.). Recently a most valuable study of the Indian origins of Benzaiten was published by Catherine Ludvik (2007).

13. Note the unusual reading *ryō-* in place of the *ryū* of Ryūjin.
14. Heissig 1980, 76–81.

sometimes Fukurokuju, who is also good for long life, has been identified with Jurōjin, bringing in the connection with the stars which is prominent among the Mongolian "seven old men." When this identification is made, Fukurokuju can be replaced by Kichijōten, thus maintaining the number of divinities at seven.

Hotei-son 布袋尊

Hotei-son, or The Venerable Hotei, is the legendary tenth century Chinese monk Bùdài, revered in the Chinese Zen (Chan) tradition. While reputed to have achieved detachment from this world, he is shown carrying a cloth sack thought to be full of good things. Since this is the meaning of his name he could be called in English "the Venerable Cloth Sack." Depictions of Hotei-son also show him with a substantial stomach, looking rather like the widespread Chinese representations of the future Buddha Miroku (Chinese Mílèfó, Sanskrit Maitreya), who will, it is believed, usher in a new period of prosperity. On the other hand, a number of particularly famous statues of Miroku Bosatsu in Japan, categorized as "national treasures," are of extreme beauty and grace, and in these cases the stomach is iconographically insignificant. Consequently, a Japanese person seeing a Chinese Mílèfó sometimes thinks that it is none other than Hotei-son. In either case the substantial stomach has traditionally indicated prosperity or other forms of success for the believer, so there seems to have been an iconographic association at some point.

As already noted, The Seven Gods of Good Fortune are sometimes to be found in Buddhist temples and sometimes in Shintō shrines, and there seems to be no strongly defined pattern in this regard. In the case of the Asakusa group, three are in temples and the rest are in shrines. In fact this amounts to six shrines, because two of the gods, Fukurokuju and Jurōjin, appear twice in different shrines which are all listed as valuable to visit. This amounts to nine in all, justified in a pamphlet on various grounds, namely that nine is "the highest number," that the character for one 一 can easily be converted into that for seven 七, which in turn can easily be converted into that for nine 九, and that the character for nine is used with that for bird to write "dove" 鳩 (hato) which symbolizes atsumaru meaning to collect together and hence completion. The pamphlet also says that one should appreciate the culture of Edo, with Kannon-sama (housed at the temple Sensōji) at its centre.

In the Sumida River sequence, also in Tokyo, the seven are housed in six places only, three temples, two shrines, and a flower-park belonging to the City of Tokyo which otherwise boasts the flowers of "the four seasons," itself an auspicious concept. The recommended starting point is Mii Shrine, where both Ebisu and Daikoku can be venerated. According to a commemorative booklet available at the sites and used for collecting the imprints which are proof of the journey, the total route amounts to a distance of 3250 metres.[15] In the city of Miura there is a sequence in which seven of eight named places are Buddhist temples, and of these only one is a Shintō shrine. In Kyōto the already mentioned "Kyō Shichifukujin Mairi" links just one Shintō shrine with six Buddhist temples. A pamphlet issued from an office in Kyōto's Ebisu Jinja calls the seventh of each month the *ennichi* (affinity day) of the Seven Gods of Good Fortune. Thereby a Shintō shrine is aligning itself with a concept (*ennichi*) of Buddhist origin.

Sometimes all seven are to be found in Buddhist temples. This holds good in the city of Chichibu in Saitama Prefecture, for example, where they can all be visited in one day. According to a local pamphlet they offer the following benefits: unlocking of fortune, bringing good luck, long life, healing of disease, success in business, wealth and wisdom. With this in mind it is beneficial, according to the pamphlet, to visit them in each of the four seasons of the year.[16]

Mention was already made of the Seven Gods of Good Fortune in the city of Kawagoe, which are also to be found exclusively in Buddhist temples there. A local pamphlet emphasizes that these may be visited to advantage not only during the first seven days of January, which amounts to an extended New Year, but also on the first day of each month which is described as the day of causal affinity (*ennichi*). The total route is some six kilometres and follows a recommended order from one to seven, the starting and returning at points being within reach of the railway stations which serve the city. The order of the seven in this case is as follows:

1. Bishamonten
2. Jurōjin
3. Daikokuten
4. Ebisuten
5. Fukurokuju
6. Hoteison
7. Benzaiten

Further afield, there is a Shichifukujin Meguri in Hawaii, on Oahu Island, referred to in English as "The route of the Shichifuku-jin (Seven Good Luck Gods)," and based on seven Buddhist temples of various denominations. Number One (Hawaii Shichifukujin Ichiban) is located at the Waipahu Soto Zen Temple, where Fukurokuju may be revered, although the main focus of worship (*gohonzon*) in the temple is Śākyamuni Buddha.[17] This is but one

---

15. *O-meguri* 20.4 and 20.5.
16. This information has been publicized since 1976 in a leaflet from the Chichibu Tourism Association, which of course also publicises the 34 Kannon-sama sites. (*O-meguri* 20.3)
17. This information is drawn from a bilingual leaflet available at the temple. C.f. Pye 1987.

small aspect of the complex and fascinating transplantation of Japanese religion, especially Japanese forms of Buddhism, to Hawaii.[18]

In Kyōto, the well-known Rinzai Zen Buddhist temple Tenryūji 天竜寺 has its own *shichifukujin meguri*, each divinity being located in one of the sub-temples within the extensive grounds. The temple itself was founded in 1339, during the Ashikaga shogunate and, being known for having one of the earliest and most splendid "Zen" gardens, using natural features and borrowed scenery (*shakkei* 借景), is a much frequented tourist attraction in western Kyōto. The Seven Gods of Good Fortune by contrast are a recent grouping housed in sub-temples located in the approach area, with its car park and lotus ponds, which can be visited without charge. They are completely ignored in the temple's own leaflet. Here the list of divinities is distinctly non-standard, running: Daibokuten, Bishamonten, Benzaiten, Fukurokuju, Ebisugami, Fudō Myōō, Hōtoku Inari. Lacking here are Jurōjin and Hoteison. Number six is the Buddhist figure Fudō Myōō, while number seven is the Shintō *kami* Inari-sama. Ebisu is also denoted with the specifically Shintō term *kami* (here *-gami*) rather than *-ten*, which is more usual. Why are there such variations? Historical explanations are not available, but we see here an attempt to tap the popularity of two extra figures who usually do not appear among the Seven Gods of Good Fortune. First, the Inari shrines are in any case among the most popular forms of Shintō, but the name Inari here bears the prefix *hōtoku* meaning "wealthy in nature." This is appropriate for the wealth-giving divinity Inari, but it also picks up one of the era names of the emperor Go-Hanazono (reigned 1429–1464), this particular "era" lasting from 1449 to 1451. Second, Fudō Myōō is a standard and very popular figure in the Shingon Buddhism which has such an extensive presence all over Japan. This is the same Buddhist divinity who is otherwise known as Fudō-son and whose own pilgrimage routes circulating thirty-six temples were noted in Chapter Four. Fudō Myōō is a distinctly Buddhist figure, more so than any of the other Gods of Fortune, and almost imperceptibly shifts the focus towards Buddhist devotions. This series therefore shows up the range of variations in the meanings which may be ascribed to such groups of divinities.

A list of fifteen "shrines and temples," using the joint term *shaji*, is promoted in the Kawachi area to the east of Ōsaka. This sequence of *o-mairi* begins at the Shintō shrine Sumiyoshi Taisha 住吉大社, proceeds to the mausoleum of Ōjin Tennō at the Honda Hachimangū 誉田八幡宮, and then leads on to Shitennōji for the hall of Hotei-son. It is of interest here because seven of the temples have halls for the Seven Gods of Good

---

18. See Yanagawa and Morioka 1979 and 1981, for wide-ranging surveys, and Pye 1987 for brief descriptive information relating to the subject of this-worldly benefits in Japanese religions in Hawaii.

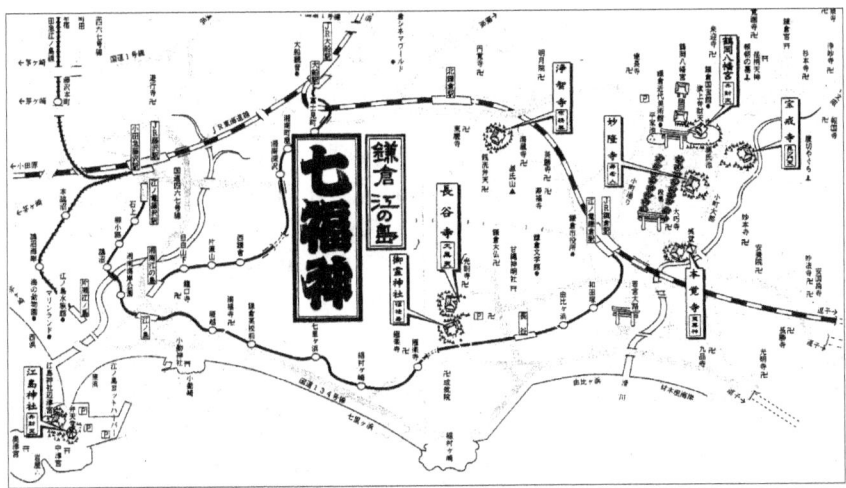

Figure 5.2 Map of Kamakura Enoshima Shichifukujin circuit.

Fortune, while others are listed for their particular buddha or bodhisattva. In this case therefore the seven are fully integrated into a complex group of places to visit which also correlates Buddhism and Shintō.

In some cases, the number of places to visit for the Seven Gods of Good Fortune is not stable, or there is a duplication. This can arise when the authorities of a particular shrine or temple wish to get their own institution on to the circuit, to attract visitors, and manage to achieve a compromise with the rest. However it is not possible to see at once which are the "extra" ones, for they are not designated as *bangai* ("outside the numeration"), as they would be in a route of 33 Kannon-sama temples. The reduplication as such can be seen clearly enough in that there are no extra gods. When one of them features twice there is simply an extra shrine or temple. However the visitor has no way of knowing which of the two has been added in later, and indeed this could only be established, if at all, by turning over buried or half-buried local rivalries. Nor is it just that a Buddhist temple and a Shintō shrine both claim to revere one and the same divinity. In the case of the Asakusa Shichifukujin circuit, the two reduplicated divinities are Jurōjin and Fukurokuju. Each of these is venerated in two quite separate Shintō shrines lying rather far apart from each other.

In another case, a Shichifukujin route in Kamakura and Enoshima, it is the goddess Benzaiten who figures twice. As a result there are eight places to visit, five Buddhist temples and three Shintō shrines.[19] These can all be visited on a day trip from Tokyo. Of course Benzaiten is very important on the island of Enoshima, where her hall or chapel is in the grounds of the main Shintō shrine, Enoshima Jinja. Here there are two impressive statues

---

19. Information sheet published by the Enoden Ensen Shinbunsha, an information service publicising leisure activities along the Enoshima railway line. (*O-meguri* 20.2)

of the goddess. In one image deriving from the middle of the Kamakura Period she is strumming a lute (*biwa*) and is, unusually, completely naked. She is designated here as Myōon Benzaiten (Benzaiten of Exquisite Sound). The other image is from the early Kamakura Period and much more traditional. It shows the goddess with "eight elbows," i.e. eight arms, holding various symbolic implements, and is classified as an "important cultural property." These images can be seen easily, unlike some which are concealed behind shrine doors, but although the walk is worth it perhaps not everybody visiting Kamakura has time to get to Enoshima as well.

There is usually no standard order in which these gods themselves are to be visited. It is largely a matter of geography, infrastructure and personal convenience. Though the temples and shrines are sometimes numbered in sequence, as in the case of those at Kawagoe City, the model of the Buddhist pilgrimages is often not followed in this regard. A curiously ambivalent example is the Asakusa Shichifukujin sequence, mentioned above. In this case a leaflet first lists the sites with addresses and bus stops, and then shows them as sectors in a circle, in the same order. A more substantial booklet lists the sites by number and also shows the circle.[20] The circle shows the distance which it takes to walk between them on foot. The first in the list is the temple Sensōji, but this does not appear as the uppermost sector in the circle. The implication is that one can begin anywhere in the circle and the sequence will give a total walking time of two hours and twenty-two minutes "not counting time needed for devotions"[21] If the direction taken through the circle follows the sequence shown in the vertically ordered list, starting with the temple Sensōji and then going to Asakusa Shrine, and so on, the visits would take place in an *anti*-clockwise direction. If travelling on foot, this would also occur in reality, though it would be a rather approximate circle. In practice however, the features of urban landscape prevent any consciousness of circularity arising. Moreover nothing is encircled.

Thus both the sequence and the direction may be regarded as largely incidental, with some emphasis being given to a dominant temple, such as Sensōji in the example just considered. The important number is the number of the gods, namely seven, not the number or the sequence of the sites at which they are housed. By contrast the numbered Buddhist pilgrimages number the sites, while the specific forms of the celestial beings, Kannon-sama or other, display a random distribution through the numbered temples. Notwithstanding this difference the Shichifukujin devotions certainly belong to the class of circulatory pilgrimage for various reasons.

---

20. The title of the booklet, which offers considerable information about each station in the sequence, can be translated "Visiting the Seven Gods of Good Fortune of the Famous Places of Asakusa" (see Asakusa Nadokoro Shichifukujin Kai 1979—N.B. *nadokoro* is the prescribed reading here for what would normally be *meisho*).

21. Devotions: here *sankei*, a synonym for *o-mairi*.

In particular the idea of completing the linked route of several stations is itself quite firm. In Japanese consciousness, visiting the Seven Gods of Good Fortune is considered to be a particular type of *o-meguri* (circulation). The routes are usually so designated in tourist guides, on local leaflets and when signposted on the spot. Moreover the forms of religious transaction, which will be considered below, have the same general character as those of the Buddhist circulatory pilgrimages, and reinforce in the same way the value set on the completion of a sequence.

Shintō circulatory pilgrimages

We now turn to the phenomenon of circulatory pilgrimages made to a specific number of Shintō shrines, which has hitherto attracted little attention from observers.[22] Historically, this appears to have developed in three main streams. First, there has long been a certain interest, at latest since the Edo Period, in visiting certain small groups of shrines associated with each other. Three shrines in eastern Japan provide an example of this, namely Katori Jingū 香取神宮, Kashima Jingū 鹿島神宮 and Ikisu Jinja 息栖神社, the divinities of which were all entrusted with taking care of the region since ancient times. According to a substantial guidebook, this practice dates from the middle of the Edo period, and it was customary to visit them by boat.[23] However it may be noted that, viewed precisely, the purpose was to perform *o-mairi* to three associated shrines, which does not really amount to a circulatory pilgrimage in the full sense. Second, the political espousal of Shintō in the late nineteenth and early twentieth century created an interest among patriotic citizens in visiting leading Shintō shrines and special sites connected with the imperial family. Such visits were documented in booklets and scrolls just as were the Buddhist pilgrimage circuits upon which they were evidently modelled. Indeed, personal commemorative booklets from the period often combine Buddhist temples and important Shintō shrines. Third, there has been a

---

22. As far as I know, the first presentation of materials on this theme in any detail was in my essay *The Structure of Religious Systems in Contemporary Japan: Shintō Variations on Buddhist Pilgrimage* (2004), from which some of the text below is drawn. However, the historical complexity of this development was not fully worked out there. Sakai Usaku included a short section on Shintō pilgrimages in his article of 1960 (pp, 356-358), but he focuses on the uni-focal pilgrimages to Ise and to Mount Fuji. He also refers, in two sentences, to the practice of visiting one hundred shrines (*hyaku-sha-mairi*), in any sequence, in order to paste up one's *o-fuda* in a high place, and interprets this as "une sorte de jeu," reaching his general conclusion, widely imitated, that pilgrimage in Japan has gradually lost its religious content and become a journey of pleasure and a form of tourism. There is some truth in this, but it is not the whole story.

23. *Nihon hyakkei to miyageshina (II). Jishamōde tabi annai* (no editor named) Tokyo 1980 (Heibonsha), 52.

stronger interest in the second half of the twentieth century and beyond, i.e. in the post-war period, in developing short, easily manageable "good fortune" circuits comparable to those of the Seven Gods of Good Fortune. Indeed, at the time of writing, it appears that the idea of visiting a number of Shintō shrines and collecting the "seal" or "stamp" of each one is becoming more and more popular. We have already seen that among the many variations on the Seven Gods of Good Fortune either Buddhist locations or Shintō locations may predominate. This meant that it was particularly easy for the idea of circulatory pilgrimage to be transferred from Buddhism to Shintō. While all of these practices are clearly modelled on the much older Buddhist pilgrimages, it is possible to see two main kinds of influence, one being direct imitation, and one being mediated by the combination with the Seven Gods of Good Fortune in a large number of shared local circuits.

Making a journey to a single, specific Shintō shrine is of course a basic, recognizable and even important feature of Shintō. As explained in the Introduction, such a journey is known as an o-mairi, a "humbly going up to." An act of o-mairi may be very long and arduous or it may be extremely short. Historically the most dramatic example of o-mairi, which certainly qualifies to be considered in the general context of pilgrimage, is the journey to the great Ise Shrine, known in its heyday in the Edo Period as o-Ise-mairi[24] and often featured in woodblock prints of the time. Considering the importance of single-goal pilgrimage in Shintō, we may regard circuit pilgrimage linking several Shintō shrines as more of a secondary phenomenon, though an interesting one. Nevertheless the significance of the fact that millions of such pilgrimages have in fact been enacted should not be underestimated.

In the groups now to be considered there are only Shintō shrines, no Buddhist temples, and this leads to a recognizable emphasis on the Shintō view of the world. If the Shichifukujin remain almost entirely in the realm of the transactions of what I call "primal religion," except for some very distant associations with Buddhism, the Shintō linkages seem to lead into a slightly more specialized religious consciousness. In the main, an appeal is nevertheless made to the idea that one can somehow maximize benefit by visiting more than one shrine, indeed several. Thus the transactional pattern remains similar and the visit to each Shintō shrine will usually be linked to a request for supernatural assistance in some matter or other. That the visit was made will usually also be documented by the acquisition of a red seal, either in a booklet for that purpose or on a hanging scroll. This practice may be said to lie somewhere in between the Buddhist documentation of temple visits in the pilgrim's book (nōkyōchō) and the stamping of a souvenir book with the rubber

---

24. For a standard modern account see Nishigaki 1983.

stamp of historic or remote railway stations. In the case of the Buddhist *nōkyōchō* the significance lies in the idea that the seals are a receipt for having symbolically sponsored the copying of a *sūtra*. They are therefore issued on the authority of the temple in exchange for a fee. In railway stations, the rubber stamps with inkpads are usually just available somewhere in the waiting room or entrance hall, and their use costs nothing. At Shintō shrines there is usually a small fee to pay, and this means that it should be understood as part of a religious transaction, however lighthearted the mental connections may be. However since in Shintō contexts it does not imply sponsoring a *sūtra* the pilgrims' books are known as *shūinchō* 集印帳 meaning, quite straightforwardly, a booklet for collecting seals. The point is that the pilgrim's visit is authoritatively documented. This is an example of the way in which the Buddhist and Shintō meanings of similar practices can be seen to diverge, a matter which will be pursued in more detail in Chapter Seven.

Naturally, the practice of "going round" to Shintō shrines is also driven by commercial interests, in particular those of the transport industry, especially local railways. Such pilgrimage therefore has an intimate relation to the transport infrastructure.[25] Here one example for the case of Shintō will suffice. Visitors to Kyōto may have used the light railway known as Keifukuden or more recently as Randen, which is regarded by the local population with much affection. In its older name, the element "kei" refers to the *kyō* of Kyōto, and "fuku" means happiness as in the name of the Shichifukujin, while in the new name "Randen" 嵐電 the element *ran* is there to honour the railway's destination at Arashiyama 嵐山, the first character being the same. During the New Year period the Randen offers a special, low-cost ticket which can be used for multiple short journeys during any one day up to January 15th.[26] The ticket is issued with a little talisman in the form of the astrological animal of the year and a leaflet which suggests paying a visit to no less than thirteen Shintō shrines. The average walking distance from the relevant station to each shrine is just under seven minutes, a path which has to be retraced, while the travelling time between stops (after the train has arrived) is two to three minutes. Thus if all thirteen shrines are visited about three hours would be spent in movement. There is no strong pressure necessarily to visit all thirteen, but the invitation to do

---

25. It was explored by the author from various points of view in an exhibition of maps, posters, etc. entitled "Religion and travel culture in Japan / Religion und Reisekultur in Japan" (Marburg 2002), for which a brief catalogue was prepared.
26. Information as of the year Heisei 18 (2006). The ticket can be used for multiple journeys between any of the stations on two linked lines between central Kyōto (Shijō Ōmiya), Arashiyama and Kitano Hakubaichō, and costs 600 Yen, while one journey would normally cost 200 Yen.

so is clear. This specialized focus on Shintō shrines is interesting not least because the Keifuku railway also takes passengers to some very well known, touristically attractive Buddhist temples in Kyōto such as Kōryūji, Tenryūji, Myōshinji, Ninnaji and Ryōanji. The pamphlet is illustrated with talismans (*o-fuda*) and *ema* and expressly states that one should go with the railway to get "benefits" (*riyaku*). This is short for the longer expression "this-worldly benefits" (*genzeriyaku*), however since Shintō, unlike Buddhism, is mainly about the present world anyway, a full designation is not necessary. The most famous of the shrines is Kitano Tenmangū, known to all the inhabitants of Kyōto and far beyond, for here is enshrined the famous Sugawara no Michizane, god of calligraphy and scholarship. Among the other shrines may be noted in particular Kishima Jinja, the "silkworm shrine," important for the textile industry traditional to Kyōto. Another interesting one is the more recently founded Dendengū, a small shrine tucked away in the grounds of a temple named Hōrinji, just over the famous bridge at Arashiyama; the double *den* refers to *denki* (electricity) and *denpa* (radio waves), and a particular festival is held to honour the pioneers of applied science in this field on May 23rd each year.

It is common for the various railway companies to highlight what famous places, shrines, temples and so on can be visited conveniently by using their facilities. In this case the company publishes a pamphlet which briefly describes thirteen Shintō shrines and specifies the benefits which prayers at these shrines will bring, the whole being illustrated with an assortment of amulets and votive tablets. While this is not really a coherent pilgrimage with one single overriding conception, we can see from this example how commerce and religion collaborate to produce linked journeys to various sites. Again, while the word *meguri* is not used, almost surprisingly, the differentiation of the various benefits makes it seem as though it would be a good idea to visit all the shrines, or most of them, in order to get good coverage of an average family's needs.

Patriotic shrine pilgrimages

Though the motivation has waned to a considerable extent, the transfer of the idea of circulatory pilgrimage to Shintō shrines during the period of high patriotism should not go unrecorded. Nowadays this can be documented most directly by reference to the commemorative scrolls of which some still exist. A hanging scroll in the writer's possession, dating from 1940, carries the red seals of 34 shrines overwritten in black ink with their names. There is no picture of any divinity, but the uppermost, central shrine named is Tenshō Kōdai (or Kōtai) Jingū, a synonym for the shrine of Amaterasu Ōmikami, i.e. Ise Shrine. This name is given in huge calligraphy. Prominently to the right and left of this appear Ishiki-yomizu Hachimangū and Kasuga Jinja respectively. The highlighting of these three shrines or in effect, divinities, places this scroll firmly into the genre of scrolls known as *sanja takusen* 三社託宣 presented by Brian Bocking (2001) which had undergone an increasing process of political ideologization. The difference from all of the examples treated in his work however is that 31 other shrines are recorded on a single scroll and that they were all visited as a feat of pilgrimage. The inside of the scroll's box carries an inscription stating that the pilgrimage was completed on February 10th (1940) in commemoration of 2600 years of the imperial succession. The performer of the pilgrimage is described as a *sanpaisha* 参拝者, that is, as a person who paid "visits" (*o-mairi*) to the shrines in question. Buddhist words for pilgrims (*junreisha, henro*) are not used. Nevertheless it is clear that the pilgrim, a Mr. Yoshida, completed visits to all of the shrines. He did this just in time to be able to hang up his complete scroll in the appropriate place in his home on February 11th, that is, Kigensetsu, the date when the age of the imperial line is supposed to have been inaugurated. As a group, the shrines for which the seals (*shūin*) were collected are referred to on the box as the Kanpei Taisha 官幣大社. This term, which no longer has any legal validity,[27] refers to a number of shrines at which the imperial household is held in particular reverence. Following the order of priority illustrated on the scroll, starting with the main ones already mentioned and then proceeding from top right to bottom left, from the point of view of the beholder, the shrines are as follows.

Table 5.1 Kanpei Taisha appearing on a pilgrim's scroll

Amaterasu Kōdai Jingū	天照皇太神宮
Iwashimizu Hachimangū	石清水八幡宮
Kasuga Jinja	春日神社
Kashihara Jingū	橿原神宮
Kamo Wake Ikazuchi Jinja	賀茂別雷神社
Kamo Mioya Jinja	賀茂御祖神社
Meiji Jingū	明治神宮
Izumo Ōyashiro	出雲大社
Atsuta Jingū	熱田神宮
Heian Jingū	平安神宮
Isonokami Jingū	石上神宮

---

27. The more common expression is *kanpeisha* 官幣社. The term is also taken up in the more comprehensive expression *kankokuheisha* 官國幣社. This combines *kanpeisha* and *kokuheisha* in a list totalling 205 shrines, in various categories, which in pre-war times had an officially privileged status and function (*Shintō Daijiten* 1937). Since the abolition of State Shintō these categories no longer have any legal status.

Yoshino Jinja	吉野神社
Taga Jinja	多賀神社
Matsuo (or Matsunoo) Jinja	松尾神社
Inari Jinja	稲荷神社
Ōshima Jinja	大島神社
Izanagi Jinja	伊弉諾神社
Ōmiwa Jinja	大神神社
Tatsuta Jinja	龍田神社
Hinokumo/Kunikakasu Jinja	日前国懸神社
Sumiyoshi Jinja	住吉神社
Ikukunitama Jinja	生國魂神社
Hirota Jinja	廣田神社
Hirose Jinja	廣瀬神社
Ōyamato Jinja	大和神社
Hirano Jinja	平野神社
Hiyoshi Jinja	日吉神社
Kameyama Jinja	龜山神社
Makioka Jinja	牧岡神社
Yasaka Jinja	八坂神社
Niu Kawakami Jinja	丹生川上神社
Takebe Jinja	建部神社

The current (post-war) names or designations (*jinja, taisha* etc.) of these shrines may vary from those shown here and the transliterations of the characters reflect the usage of the period.[28] This particular selection of the *kanpeisha* includes many shrines which are important nationally, but otherwise shows a certain bias towards those located in the Kansai area of Japan.

Also well known in modern, if mainly pre-war times, was the practice of visiting sites relating to the imperial family, in particular their tombs. These may also be found listed on large hanging scrolls. Unlike scrolls for

---

28. Amaterasu Kōdai Jingū is usually known today as Amaterasu Kōtai Jingū, though "Kōdai" seems to have been in wider use at the time of the scroll. This refers to the Naikū of Ise Shrine, i.e. Ise Jingū, or often just Jingū. The term Taisha has now come into more common use. Thus Kasuga Jinja (as on the scroll) is known as Kasuga Taisha ("grand shrine"), Taga Jinja as Taga Taisha and Takebe Jinja as Takebe Taisha. It is likely that the name of the great shrine of Izumo was read as Izumo Ōyashiro at the time, whereas Izumo Taisha (same characters) is now normal. Hinokumo/Kunikakasu Jinja refers to two shrines at the same address which are also known summarily as Nichizengū. The reading Ōyamato (Shrine) diverges from the usual reading of 大和 as Yamato; the "Ō" emphasizing the literal meaning of the first of the two characters. Many shrines bear the name Inari Jinja, but in this case the major shrine at Fushimi, Kyōto, is presumably intended.

the *kanpeisha* these can theoretically still be purchased today, if the advertisements of the hanging scroll shops are to be believed. However, while many of the carefully preserved locations are in or near Kyōto, the imperial residence for hundreds of years, I have seen no evidence of pilgrimage taking place. Nor are there any places nearby where the red seals could be acquired. Indeed, information drawn carefully from older persons tells us that while there used to be such places, they were all removed after the end of World War II. The sites themselves themselves are managed by the Imperial Household Agency (Kunaisho), and under the new constitutional arrangements it would not be possible for this agency to engage directly in activities which could be construed as religious in the wider public domain. So though the sites themselves are well preserved, the residents of Kyōto pass by them daily while paying little attention. Enquiries at the Gyoen in Kyōto, the large park containing the former imperial palace, led to the response that there are just six key places around the country where the seals can be acquired, namely the mausolea department of the Imperial Household Agency in Chiyoda-ku (Chiyoda 1-1) in Tokyo, and regional offices at Hachiōji, Kyōto (two), Kashiwara City in Nara Prefecture, and Habikino City in the Ōsaka administrative region.

In general it is fair to say that a strongly patriotic perspective has had a relatively low profile in Japan in post-war times, but it is of course promoted in various ways at Shintō shrines, at some more than others depending on the predilections of the responsible priests. Devotion to the Imperial Family is one of the themes which can be highlighted in various ways, for example with banners expressing congratulations on birthdays, and a complementary theme, because of the connections to the Imperial Family, is support for Ise Jingū, especially in the run-up to its ritualized reconstruction every twenty years. It is well known that there have been disputes over Yasukuni Shrine as a focus of the nationalistic memory, over the procedures for the enthronement ceremonies, and other matters. However, these are all matters which, though they need to be thought about carefully, would lead away from our present theme. Just a hint of a connection with "circulation" is found in reference to the 25 shrines of Amaterasu, set out in all brevity in a booklet from Moto Ise Kono Jinja, or Tanba no Yosa no Miya, which is situated near the famous scenic spot Amahashidate, at the foot of the hill to Nariaiji, Temple Number No. 28 of the Saikoku Kannon pilgrimage. In the shrine's booklet we find a reference to twenty-five places associated with Amaterasu, numbered, and ending with Ise Shrine itself.

Interestingly enough, an older patriotic perspective has resurfaced, after a certain manner, in the *Tōkyō jussha meguri*, or "Tokyo Ten Shrines Pilgrimage." Although this pilgrimage (note the term *meguri*) is not particularly well known, it is interesting not only in that it parallels Buddhist circulatory pilgrimages, but also because it accentuates a certain form of Shintō interpretation. It also has a slight, if recently constructed claim to a pedigree of its own. The following information is based on a combination of visits and interviews at the shrines and information from leaflets issued there.

The pilgrimage was founded in 1975 (Shōwa 50) as an act of conscious construction, on the occasion of the fiftieth anniversary of the commencement of the reign of the Emperor Hirohito. However, the principle linking these particular ten shrines is that on November 8th 1868 the Emperor Meiji, having relocated the imperial residence in the eastern capital, Tokyo (renamed from Edo), sent messengers to selected shrines to pray for the pacification of the city and the safety of its people. This was an act of demonstrative rule to emphasize the power of the "Restoration" which had overthrown the Tokugawa shogunate. Promoting a pilgrimage to each of these same ten shrines in 1975 was no doubt in part due to recognition of the general popularity of circulatory pilgrimage. Shrine priests will certainly have noted the popularity of the Seven Gods of Fortune and the effectiveness of linkage in attracting visitors. At the same time the circuit clearly celebrates not only the nineteenth century Restoration of imperial power but also its twentieth century endurance. It also celebrates "our Tokyo" as "the political, economic and cultural centre of the nation's life"[29] Prayers are meant to be offered both for the brilliance of the state (*kokka no ryūshō* 国家の隆昌) and for the flourishing of family fortune (*go-kaun no han'ei* 御家運の繁栄), thus combining nationalism with self-interest.

The participating shrines include some which are very well known for other reasons, for example Kanda Shrine, commonly known as Kanda Myōjin. In the following list the city wards (-ku) are also shown.

Table 5.2 The Tokyo Ten Shrines Pilgrimage and locations in city wards.

Nezu Jinja[a]	根津神社	Bunkyō-ku
Kanda Jinja[b]	神田神社	Chiyoda-ku
Kameido Tenjinsha[c]	亀戸天神社	Etō-ku
Hakusan Jinja[d]	白山神社	Bunkyō-ku
Ōji Jinja[e]	王子神社	Kita-ku
Shiba Daijingū[f]	芝大神宮	Minato-ku
Hie Jinja[g]	日枝神社	Chiyoda-ku
Shinagawa Jinja	品川神社	Shinagawa-ku
Tomioka Hachimangū	富岡八幡宮	Etō-ku
Hikawa Jinja	氷川神社	Minato-ku

---

29. Pamphlet dating from 1988.

a) Also known as Nezu Gongen. The term *gongen* 権現 (*avatar*) reflects an earlier association with the Buddhist theme of the appearance of bodhisattvas in the form of local divinities.
b) Popularly known as Kanda Myōjin.
c) Also known as Kameido Tenmangū.
d) Named after the mountain Hakusan in western Japan.
e) Popularly known as Ōji Gongen. C.f. note on Nezu Gongen above.
f) Popularly known as Shiba Jinmyō-sama.
g) Also known as Sannō-sama, providing an association with the Sannō Shintō which historically was involved in a syncretistic relationship with Buddhism.

The above order is that given on the leaflets, but the shrines are not specifically numbered. The sequence in which they are visited is said by shrine officials to be unimportant. However there is currently no information about the way in which visitors to the shrines themselves regard this, or indeed about the degree of interest in performing the pilgrimage. One leaflet, from Hakusan Jinja, says that special days for these visits are between the 1st and 10th October, but no reason is given for this. During observations at Kanda Shrine on an ordinary day[30] a couple requested calligraphy for an undefined pilgrimage book, but proved to be unaware of the Tokyo Ten Shrines Pilgrimage. They were simply visiting shrines of their choice, but still expected the shrine office to provide calligraphy, which was duly delivered by a female attendant. Thus it appears that lay people simply make up their own pilgrimages!

Although this shrine circuit was constituted as a *meguri* in 1975, on the initiative of the head priest of one of the shrines, Shinagawa Shrine, the promotional leaflet reprints a map which has all the appearance of being considerably older, giving the impression that it might date from the Meiji Period. The whereabouts of the original is unfortunately unknown, even at Shinagawa Shrine, so there is no way of assessing its real age or its authenticity. However the map is extremely interesting in various respects. In the centre is a circle symbolizing the Imperial Palace, containing the characters *kin ri*, meaning that it is a taboo area for the common people. Next to the circle are indicated the four cardinal points of the compass, and further out, in their approximate, asymmetrical geographical locations, are shown the ten shrines. These are joined with lines which suggest at once both a route and a protective enclosure around the centre. The order in which they here appear geographically, wherever one were to start, is not the order in which they are otherwise listed. However distances are shown, in the traditional measurements of *ri* and *chō*.[31] Since the map is said to date from the Meiji Period (according to the priest serving Shinagawa Shrine in 1988) it implies that the

---

30. March 21, 1988.

31. There are 36 *chō* in one *ri*, and one *ri* equals 3.9 kilometres. Visits today, however, would be made by local railway or by car, so that a calculation of these distances is much less relevant than a knowledge of the traffic system.

practice of going from one shrine to the next, presumably following the route of the imperial messenger, was not unknown at that time. A short text on the map suggests this and also lists the *kami* which are revered at each of the ten shrines. According to a priest serving at one of the other shrines however, Shiba Daijingū, the idea of ordinary people going round to visit these shrines is recent, simply picking up the Meiji connection in retrospect.

As with the Buddhist circulatory pilgrimages and the Shichifukujin routes, there is an expectation that one will record one's visits to these shrines in some way. One possibility is for the leaflet giving information about each of the shrines to be covered with their commemorative red seals. Alternatively a blank book for collecting these stamps or seals, such as is used when visiting Buddhist temples, may be carried. A distinctive form of record is to make a collection of one miniature votive tablet (*ema*) from each shrine, and to mount these jointly on a larger piece of wood cut in the same general style. A leaflet from Kanda Shrine illustrates these miniatures and calls them "commemorative *ema*." Normally the function of an *ema* is to symbolize the offering of a specific prayer, and for this reason it is usually *left behind* at the shrine or temple. Simply to take them home, as in this case, is a less common practice, but is also not unknown. The same method of collecting miniature *ema* to mount on a board is used for the Seven Gods of Good Fortune in Ōsaka.

In spite of notice boards set up to advertise this linkage of ten shrines, it does not seem to have become particularly popular. Starting from New Year 2004 therefore a new initiative was taken at Shinagawa Jinja to encourage visits to shrines in Shinagawa Ward, listing sixteen shrines as "Shinagawa-ku o-Miya-Meguri." A map of the area is provided for stamping, on which a further fifteen smaller shrines are marked which have no resident priest. The priest at Shinagawa Jinja explains that the idea is to encourage worship of one's local *kami* (*ujigami*) and indeed this message is prominently displayed on a notice board at the entrance. Gratitude should be shown to the *ujigami* at least once a month. There might seem to be an illogicality in emphasizing the local *kami* while urging people to visit sixteen different shrines, however it seems that they are all regarded as belonging to the same local area. And of course the priests are aware that the people visit different shrines in accordance with what they want. It is too early to say whether this linkage of sixteen shrines in Shinagawa Ward will become popular, but it seems in any case to be addressed to local people rather than a wider public.

In sum, the revival of linked visits to these ten shrines in the form of the "Tokyo Ten Shrines Pilgrimage" is evidently an attempt to imitate the popular appeal of the Shichifukujin routes, combining a patriotism focused on the Emperor with an understandable attempt to attract visitors.

Various Shintō shrine circuits

A much more straightforward example of a pilgrimage in Tokyo round linked Shintō shrines is known as *Hassha Fukumairi* or, literally, Good Fortune Visit to Eight Shrines. A fuller name is Good Fortune Visit to Eight Shrines in Downtown Tokyo.[32] Significantly, another variation is *Shitamachi Hachifukujin Meguri*. In this designation *hachifukujin* means "eight gods of good fortune," so that an association with the traditional Seven Gods of Fortune is created, although none of them is identical with these. Various leaflet-sized maps are provided for this circuit, showing convenient underground railway stations and in one case linking the shrines with an arrowed route. There is no numeration or any obligatory order for visiting, but the eight shrines, with their specified benefits, are usually listed as follows.

Table 5.3 Eight shrines of good fortune.

Ōtori Jinja	大鳥神社	*shōbai hanjō* (prosperity in business)
Imado Jinja	今戸神社	*enmusubi* (knotting a partnership)
Dairokuten Sakaki Jinja	第六天榊神社	*kenkō chōju* (health and long life)
Shitaya Jinja	下谷神社	*enman wagō* (wealth and harmony)
Onoterusaki Jinja	小野照崎神社	*gakumon geinō* (scholarship and arts)
Suitengū	水天宮	*anzan kouke* (safe delivery and conception)[42]
Koami Jinja	小網神社	*kyōun yakuyoke* (strengthening destiny and averting bad luck)
Sumiyoshi Jinja	住吉神社	*kōtsū anzen* (safety in traffic)

There is no evidence for any antiquity in the linkage of these shrines, although some of them individually go back to mediaeval times. Rather, the linkage would seem to be a recent arrangement promoted by the "Downtown Tokyo Shrines Association." This name is in fact the only reference to a specifically Shintō-related interest. Various ephemeral indications do not seem to lead into any particular area of interpretation which would go beyond the level of rites of transaction as well known elsewhere.

This impression is reinforced by observations of a promotion by the Takashimaya Department Store, which in the New Year season of 1991 set aside an exhibition area for this purpose. The area was entered through a temporary symbolic shrine gate (*torii*) and there was a focal point at the far end with an offerings box. Thus it was possible to perform *o-mairi* on the spot, in the department store. It was also possible to have a commemorative card stamped as an indication that the pilgrimage had been performed. This was part of the "service" of the Department Store, *saavisu* in Japanese meaning a free gift in the context of a commercial transac-

---

32. Tokyo Shitamachi Hassha Fukumairi.

tion. The card bore the names of the eight shrines, with figurative symbols and the benefits which accrue, at the bottom the name of the department store, and in the centre a variant on the name of the journey round the shrines, namely Tokyo Downtown Eight Shrines First Visit of the Year. Also given out was a cost-free fortune-telling slip (*o-mikuji*).[33]

A related perspective current in Tokyo, building on the collector mentality but without quite forming a series to be completed as a pilgrimage, is offered by the grouping of five Shintō shrines in Bunkyō Ward, Tokyo. A pamphlet put out by Hakusan Jinja refers us to "the five great flower festivals of Bunkyō Ward." These are, in calendrical sequence:

February	*ume-matsuri* (plum blossom festival)	Yushima Jinja
April	*tsutsuji-matsuri* (camellia festival)	Nezu Jinja
April	*sakura-matsuri* (cherry blossom festival)	Bunkyō Sakura Dōri
June	*ajisai-matsuri* (hydrangea festival)	Hakusan Jinja
November	*kiku-matsuri* (chrysanthemum festival)	Yushima Jinja

This presentation links locality and calendricity very neatly, and keeps interest in shrine visits alive after the excitement of the New Year season. Four of the localities are shrines (*jinja*) while the fifth, for April, is a religiously neutral avenue of cherry trees.

Shrines in Kyōto have also taken the initiative themselves in creating linkages. One circuit which takes people around much of the city is known as "Kyōto Sixteen Shrines Seal Pilgrimage." For this pilgrimage, or round tour, a large paper is provided on which the seals of the various shrines can be stamped, thus encouraging visits to all of the shrines. The sequence was earlier known as "Kyōto Fourteen Shrines Seal Pilgrimage," but starting from 1997, two further shrines were added, making sixteen in all. The newly added shrines were Goryō Jinja (i.e. Kami Goryō Jinja)[34] and Imamiya Jinja. A reason for adding these two shrines was cited at Imamiya Jinja as being that one of them was to the east and one of them to the west of a major road in Kyōto known as Horikawa, which runs from south to north. This is supposed to give a feeling of comprehensiveness or inclusiveness. However, neither of the added shrines stands in any particular relationship to that road, and Goryō Jinja even lies to the east of another major road, Karasuma-dōri. Evidently, with similar reasoning, almost any shrines could be added to any pilgrimage series. The underlying reason was undoubtedly that the authorities of these two well-known shrines

---

33. The fortune is told, in part, under specific headings. The slip which I drew informed me under the heading "learning" that danger threatened and that my fullest efforts were required.

34. There is also a Shimo Goryō Jinja (Lower Goryō Shrine), in a more southerly position in the city.

Going Round to other Divinities

Figure 5.3 Notice for sixteen shrines in Kyōto as a New Year's pilgrimage.

also wished to participate in the business, especially at New Year. We see here therefore a combination of competition and cooperation between the shrines. In the main, an appeal is made to the idea that one can somehow maximize benefit by visiting more than one shrine, indeed several. At the same time, there are only Shintō shrines in these groups, and this leads to a gentle emphasis on the Shintō view of the world. By contrast the Shichifukujin remain entirely in the realm of the transactions of primal religion. The Shintō linkages seem to lead into a slightly more specialized consciousness.

The paper on which the seals are to be stamped is provided in a large envelope, which bears the following text (here translated):

Kyōto Sixteen Shrines Seal Pilgrimage
New Year Shrine Visit
Opening of Fortune

In the refreshing spirit with which we meet the New Year, taking this paper for the seals with us as we go round to worship at the sixteen shrines, we pray that we may receive the virtues of each one of the great *kami* for body and soul alike.

When this paper for the seals of the pilgrimage to the sixteen shrines is completed it will serve as a protection for everybody for the whole year, so please pay reverence to it carefully.

The implication of this is that the completed paper should be kept in a respected place at home, e.g. on the house-altar (*kamidana*), so that prayers may be said. For each shrine the special benefits which may be obtained are indicated. The sixteen shrines are not numbered sequentially, but on a poster (2006), they were listed from top right to bottom left as follows.

Table 5.4 Sixteen linked shrines in Kyōto.

Nyakuōji Jinja[a]	若王子神社
Kumano Jinja[b]	熊野神社
Imakumano Jinja	新熊野神社
Kisshōin Tenmangū	吉祥院天満宮
(Kami) Goryō Jinja	(上) 御霊神社
Gokō no Miya	五香宮
Awata Jinja	粟田神社
(Sai-in) Kasuga Jinja	(西院) 春日神社
Okazaki Jinja[c]	岡崎神社
Toyokuni Jinja	豊国神社
Ichihime Jinja	一比賣神社
Waraten Jingū	わら天神宮
Rokuson no Ō Jinja	六孫王神社
Fuji no mori Jinja	藤森神社
Nagaoka Tenmangū	長岡天満宮
Imamiya Jinja	今宮神社

a) In full, Kumano Nyakuōji Jinja.
b) I.e. Kyōto Kumano Jinja.
c) In full, Higashi Tennō Okazaki Jinja.

The sequence shown varies on other promotional materials, but the grouping as a whole appears to be stable.

A smaller group of shrines, focused on central Kyōto, is known collectively as Kyōraku Hassha 京洛八社, i.e. eight shrines in the central Kyōto area west of the river (Kamogawa), and visitors are encouraged to visit all of these, in any order, while collecting their seals on a specially prepared card.

Table 5.5 Kyōraku Hassha: Eight Shrines of Central Kyōto.

Ayako Tenmangū	文子天満宮
Kandaijin Jinja	管大臣神社
Shimo Goryō Jinja	下御霊神社
Sugawara-in Tenmangū Jinja	菅原院天満宮神社
Goō Jinja	護王神社
Goryō Jinja[a]	御霊神社
Shiramine Jingū	白峯神宮

Suika Tenmangū	水化天満宮

a) I.e. Kami Goryō Jinja.

These shrines all have a long history, but it is not clear when this unnumbered list was first assembled, and the assumption must be that it is quite recent.

A different starting part for the encouragement of sequential acts of *o-mairi* may be observed at the well known shrine known as Imamiya Jinja 今宮神社, which has within its grounds a whole series of sub-shrines which are listed (with the ending *-sha*).

Table 5.6 Sub-shrines of Imamiya Jinja.

Eyamisha	疫社
Orihimesha	織姫社
Hassha	八社
Hachimansha	八幡社
Taishōgunsha	大将軍社
Hiyoshisha	日吉社
Inarisha	稲荷社
Wakamiyasha	若宮社
Jinushisha (also Jishuinarisha)	地主社 (also 地主稲荷社)
Tsukiyomisha	月読社
Munakatasha	宗像社

Visitors are encouraged to stop and pray before all of them. In commemoration they may purchase a large sheet of paper bearing the names of these shrines with a different seal for each. In the centre is a *takara no fune* meaning "boat of riches" and reminiscent of the *takarabune* in which the Shichifukujin are often shown to be sitting. In this case no divinities are shown, but the name of the main shrine, Imamiya, is written on the sail. The boat is surrounded by an elevating text, which runs as follows (here translated):

> By having a sincere heart, bright and pure thanks to the light of the very first day at the beginning of the year, you will find happiness at the eleven shrines in these grounds both now and throughout the year. Whosoever prays whole-heartedly will receive this wealth bestowing ship as the august token of the high, most revered great *kami*.[35]

The "eleven" shrines (of which the third in the list itself consists of eight minor shrines) have complex associations in Kyōto and in some cases were removed here altogether from other parts of the city due to reorganiza-

---

35. Thanks are gratefully recorded to Katja Triplett for assistance in clarifying this rather stylized text, both calligraphically and in terms of its meaning.

tions of various kinds. Imamiya Shrine provided them with a new home in its grounds, and as a result it became possible to perform a "visit" (o-mairi) to several shrines in one place. The conceptualization and marketing of this remarkable assembly of divinities was initiated, according to a shrine attendant, in the early 1990s.

One of the features of the famous Gion Festival in Kyōto is the practice of strolling around to see the floats (yamaboko)[36] which will later be dragged through the streets in procession. There are thirty-two[37] of these floats in all, and a little book is offered for sale in which a rubber stamp can be impressed on the appropriate page for each area represented. This encourages people, including young ladies clad in their rarely worn *kimono*, to go around taking a look at all of them, no doubt spending pocket money on the way. At the same time there is so much going on at the Gion Festival that this practice, or invitation to a practice, is hardly noticeable except to the keen observer. It simply illustrates how natural it is, in Japanese religious culture, for anything which is numerable to be turned into a challenge for completion.

A similar development occurred at Kasuga Grand Shrine (Kasuga Taisha) in Nara, where a group of twelve sub-shrines was organized in the grounds, for "going round," at the very end of the twentieth century just after the regular rebuilding of the shrine in 1999. Kasuga Taisha, dating back to 768 CE, is one of the most illustrious shrines of all Japan, being famous as the family shrine of the extensive Fujiwara family or clan, which effectively ruled Japan during the Heian Period when the capital was in Kyōto, partly by holding high offices and partly by providing marriage partners for the various branches of the imperial family. In modern times it became a pleasant sightseeing spot to visit in the deer park at Nara and emphasized the function of prayers for marriage arrangements (*enmusubi*). Near the impressive buildings of the main shrine, with their bold red paint, is a sub-shrine named Wakamiya which has been functionalized as Number One of the recently devised sequence of twelve. Other smaller shrines around it have been added, or at least in some cases rebuilt on the basis of previous points of worship for miscellaneous divinities. Number Twelve, now the concluding place of devotion, is a shrine named Meoto Daikokusha which is dedicated, as the name implies, to Daikoku (as in the Seven Gods of Good Fortune), but as a husband and wife pair. The husband is Ōkuninushi no mikoto while the wife is Suseri hime no mikoto. (Ōkuni and Daikoku, as mentioned earlier, are alternative pronunciations for the same characters. *Meoto* is a special reading for two characters which are normally read as *fūfu*, meaning husband and wife.) The divinities of this shrine, said to be the "only" shrine for "hus-

---

36. Some are called *yama* (mountain) and some are called *hoko* (halberd).
37. From 2014 the number was increased to thirty-three.

band and wife" in the country, are especially competent in providing a completely satisfactory marriage (*fūfu enman*), good partnerships (*ryōen*) and happy fortune and protection (*fukuun shugo*). Several of the other shrines, but not all, are connected with aspects of family life such as the welfare of children. Although it is only necessary to walk a few hundred metres altogether, after a longer walk up to the main shrine complex to start with, the practice of visiting all twelve shrines is held together by the instructions. The visitor goes first to Number Twelve to collect a bundle of *tamagushi* (small leaved twigs) to offer at each of the shrines, secondly a brief purification is performed, thirdly the twigs are offered with a sincere heart, and finally, back at Number Twelve, a concluding purification is carried out using as a symbol the chunky wooden hammer for which Ōkuninushi is well-known, being the constructor of the country. When this is all completed, an amulet is received together with the seals for the twelve shrines. The fee for this was 1000 Yen (in 2006).

In Tochigi Prefecture there is a group of eight shrines which may be visited in sequence, the practice being known as Shimozuke Hassha Mairi. Shimozuke is the traditional province name of the area in which the shrines are situated. Four of the shrines are in Utsunomiya City and the others are in the surrounding region, all in the modern Tochigi Prefecture. The starting point is a shrine named Yakushiji Hachimangū, which may be reached from Jichiidai station. The name of this shrine combines those of the Buddhist figure Yakushi Nyorai and the Shintō divinity Hachiman who for centuries doubled as a bodhisattva. Yakushi Nyorai is a Buddha thought to be particularly competent in medicinal matters, while Hachiman has traditionally been a god of war. The combination of a Buddhist and a Shintō divinity in the name of one single shrine (sometimes in the shorter form Yakushi-Hachimangū) is very unusual and reflects the fact that this area was of great importance in the early history of Buddhism in eastern Japan, although now there are fewer temples left here. The trip around the eight shrines was set up in the year Heisei 10 (1998) with the formation of a Shimozuke Hassha Mairi Association. According to local tradition[38] the sequence is older, having been known during the Meiji Period as Hachiman Hassha Mairi. However there is no documentary evidence available to support this assertion. Each shrine is advertised as bringing a particular benefit or benefits, and visiting all eight shrines is said to multiply the benefit for one's family by eight times and is therefore particularly meritorious. This principle of expanding benefit is known as *suehirogari* 末広がり meaning literally "broadening out towards the end." Visitors are encouraged to collect the calligraphy and seal at each shrine office for a fee of three hundred yen at each shrine (in 2003), and to assemble these on a special paper or a hanging scroll as a proof (*shirushi*) of the visits.

---

38. This information was offered by the chief priest (*gūji*) of Yakushi Hachimangū in 2003.

Table 5.7 Shimozuke Eight Shrines and their benefits.

Yakushiji Hachimangū 薬師寺八幡宮
  seichō kenzen (growth and health)
  byōki heiyu (recovery from sickness)
Shirasagi Jinja 白鷺神社
  kōtsū anzen (safety in traffic)
  kanai anzen (safety for the home)
Utsunomiya Futaarayama Jinja 宇都宮二荒山神社
  kanai anzen (safety for the home)
  shōbai hanjō (prosperity in business)
Tochigiken Gokoku Jinja 栃木県護国神社
  gōkaku tassei (success in obtaining qualifications)
  hisshō kigan (prayer for certain victory)
Imaizumi Yasaka Jinja 今泉八坂神社
  kanai anzen (safety for the home)
  yakuyoke (averting bad luck)
  katatagaeyoke (averting a threatening direction[a])
Hiraide Raiden Jinja[b] 平出雷電神社
  kaminariyoke (averting lightning)
  sainanyoke (averting disaster)
Yasuzumi Jinja 安住神社
  kouke (conception)
  anzan (safe delivery)
Ōsaki Jinja 大崎神社
  kaiun chōfuku (opening destiny and inviting fortune)
  enmusubi (knotting a partnership)[c]

a) I.e. averting a potentially harmful influence from a quarter such as the northeast, when the *fūsui* (Chinese *fēngshui*) cannot be avoided naturally because of economic weakness or urban congestion.
b) Also known either as Hiraide Jinja, from the place name Hiraide, or as Raiden Jinja, Shrine of Thunder and Lightning.
c) I.e. usually with a view to eventual marriage.

It is apparently soon time to take a trip to "The Dream Gods of Happiness," for in the same area a sequence known as Yumefukujin Meguri is announced. Unfortunately, apart from the evident association with the Seven Gods of Good Fortune (*shichifukujin*), no further details of the dream gods of happiness are immediately available.

Shintō pilgrimage considered

It is possible to have varied opinions about what should count as "Shintō." As already noted above, modern times have seen a politicization of Shintō which is reflected in some of the arrangements relating to pilgrimage, both pre-war and post-war. At the same time, travellers in Japan will come across innumerable places where a short act of devotion can or could be carried out, many of which have only a tenuous relation to organized Shintō, if any.

Very widespread, for example, are the wayside divinities known as Dōsojin 道祖神, which most commonly appear as a stone carving of a male and female figure in a gentle embrace. Thus they are thought to stand for fertility. In addition, since they are frequently seen where paths cross, or at the approach to a village, they are thought to have a guardian function, rather like the Buddhist-derived Jizō Bosatsu who in various ways has taken on a life of his own. It is not really appropriate to assign the Dōsojin to Shintō as such, or to any specific religion. Traditionally, they have been regarded as an expression of "popular religion," and though this term is very often used without precision it has a certain appropriateness in this particular case in that the images of Dōsojin are mainly the result of very local initiatives. They only sometimes get to be housed in "shrines" which take on various characteristics of Shintō. Because they are above all *local*, the Dōsojin cannot really have anything to do with pilgrimage, or so it might be thought. However in Japan it appears that all things are possible. There are about 120 stone Dōsojin carvings of particular excellence around the city of Hotaka in central Japan, which is otherwise famous for its cultivation of green horseradish (*wasabi*). Following the fashion to "go round" to various places, these Dōsojin have attracted the interest of city folk who hire bicycles to go round and admire them.[39] These are tourists, rather than pilgrims, people who come from somewhere else in order to admire, and yet they may perhaps make some kind of personal request to the Dōsojin of a different locality. So here, once again, we reach the very margins of the phenomenon of "pilgrimage," and we also reach the margins of "Shintō."

Somewhere between politics and folklore there is a wide area of religious activity and orientation in contemporary Japan which can fairly be referred to as "Shintō." In these pages the main assumption has been that it is the "shrines" (*jinja*, etc.) which above all define this religious tradition. Since there are in fact very many shrines throughout the whole country which are recognizable institutions and which are grouped together in associations, notably the Association of Shintō Shrines (Jinja Honchō), this is quite a reasonable approach. However Shintō is not just a question of

---

39. Reported approvingly in *Japan Pictorial* 19/1 (1996).

institutions. If we may return briefly to the pilgrimage around the shrines of Shimozuke, the leaflet containing all the information about them also has a short statement on "how to visit shrines," and this gives some indication of the meaning which is considered to underly the practice, and which is espoused by the institutions. Though typical, it is just a little more explicit than the statements which are sometimes seen.

> Here is a simple explanation of how to do o-mairi[40]. First purify your hands and mouth at the water stand (temizuya) and proceed to the front of the main shrine (honden).[41] Offer a coin and ring the bell. The bell has the meaning of attracting the attention of the kami-sama and of cleanly purifying oneself. Making your petition within your breast, do two bows, two claps and one bow. In bowing deeply twice, clapping the hands twice, and at the end making one more bow and then withdrawing, it is most important, above all, to do o-mairi with a grateful heart.

Clearly a dominant level of meaning is to be seen in the wish to receive, and ensure this-worldly benefits. These are all set out in detail, as shown above. However the opportunity is also taken to instruct visitors in the correct manner of visiting a Shintō shrine. Not only that, it is emphasized that, above all, the visit should be carried out with a sense of *gratitude*. That is to say, even while the mood of the visitor may be one of expectation, the complementary attitude of gratitude for favours received is presented as being even more important. Note however that "gratitude" is a value which is also generally current, in Japan, in what is usually referred to by observers as civil religion. The specifically Shintō note is added by the emphasis on ritual and inner purity.

On this background, let us now try to sum up the character of the Shintō pilgrimages. First, the eight "downtown shrines" in Tokyo, like the Seven Gods of Fortune, seem to remain firmly in the area of "primal religion," inserting few explicitly Shintō themes. The only special point about them is that there is a clear emphasis on Shintō *shrines*, and this may be contrasted with the circuits for the Seven Gods of Good Fortune, which are mixed with Buddhism. This aspect is even clearer in the examples from Kyōto. Second, in the Tokyo Ten Shrines Pilgrimage we find a much stronger emphasis on patriotism, with a certain nostalgia for the Meiji Period. Of course, this-worldly benefits are also expected, but this does not seem to be the only meaningful point of this network. It could be taken as a gesture in the direction of the wider civil religion

---

40. That is, here, to perform a visit to a Shintō shrine, although the word is also used more widely in various religious contexts.
41. Usually the building before which individual prayers are offered is known as the *haiden*, behind which a smaller *honden* is situated. In some larger shrines it is also possible to walk round and stand in front of the *honden*, where the *kami* is presumed to reside.

of Japan, but at the same time the connection is made steadily to the Shintō shrines and to their *kami*. Third, those responsible for the Shimozuke shrines in Tochigi Prefecture seem to be interested in educating their public into a Shintō perspective. This-worldly benefits are offered. However at the same time, the importance is emphasized not only of gratitude but also of a pure heart. This is a specific religious teaching, if a rather general one. The same is true for the linkage of sixteen shrines in Shinagawa Ward (in Tokyo), where there is a strong focus on locality and the local *kami*. Fourth, the most stable common feature throughout is the way in which each visit is recorded in a pilgrim's book. In the Shintō contexts however this is not referred to as a *nōkyōchō* which would, if distantly, bring in the association of having a *sūtra* copied. Rather, the term *shūinchō* will be found, which refers to the "seals" or *shūin* of the respective shrines.

In sum therefore, we can see that Shintō shrine circuits show a general continuity with the routes around the Seven Gods of Good Fortune, and therefore beyond these with the Buddhist circulatory pilgrimages. In other words, quite a few Shintō shrines are ready to play the game of pilgrimage circuits, which was originally derived from Buddhism. However they do not provide any support for Buddhist interpretations of life. The Shintō circuits are brought on to the scene at what is regarded here as a shared level of "primal religion," that is, the underlying religious culture which provides a kind of platform for more differentiated teachings. This is characterized by a widely understood symbolic language and religious transactions of various kinds, relating in particular to "this-worldly" benefits. There is no tension here with Shintō, because the Shintō tradition is mainly concerned with this world. However it is expected that people will pray in the Shintō fashion, with the usual hand-claps, and themes are emphasized such as the traditional patriotism of Shintō related to the Emperor (the Emperor Meiji standing in some sense for the whole Imperial Household), the idea that ritual and inner purity are the key to happiness, and the importance of the divinities in one's own neighbourhood. The Shintō circuits contribute particularly to the sacralization of space at the local level, and do so rather more strongly, it may be posited, than the Buddhist pilgrimages which are far more widely based and more widely known.

We have therefore, in Japanese pilgrimages of any kind, a dialectical relationship between the transactional routines which are firmly located within the primal religion system of the country, and the divergent meanings proposed in different religious perspectives. It is evident that through participation in the wider system those responsible for Buddhist temples and Shintō shrines, each in their own ways, are at pains to articulate their own particular systems of meaning. Thus the meanings of pilgrimages to various kinds of divinities can diverge considerably. With this in mind, it is possible to see whether and to what extent the primal system is transcended, for example in terms of personal self-knowledge and development. In the two following chapters we will return to our main subject by considering first the transactions which take place in particular during the Buddhist pilgrimages of Japan, and then the ways in which specifically "Buddhist" meanings are developed and appropriated by the pilgrims.

— Chapter Six —

The Pilgrim's Transaction

A religious transaction in three steps

We now return to the consideration of the Buddhist circulatory pilgrimages which are the main subject of this book. While the pilgrim's journey consists of a numbered series of temple visits it is also important to consider what is done at each individual temple. This follows a more or less consistent pattern. Each visit is brief enough, lasting on average about half an hour, but in this short time a number of ritual actions are performed. The time allotted also allows a few minutes for rest and refreshment, before striking out for the next destination.

As explained in the Introduction, it seems appropriate to think about the circulatory pilgrimages of Japan in terms of three guiding concepts: route, transaction, and meaning. Having considered numerous routes, we are now focusing on "transaction," and in the final chapter we will be thinking about the meaning or meanings of these Buddhist pilgrimages. The idea of transaction is given prominence here because it is a key component of much Japanese religion, especially at what we refer to as the primal level, which cuts across differentiable religious perspectives. Though already discussed more generally elsewhere, the concept of "rites of transaction" is adduced here with special reference to pilgrimage.[1]

Buddhist pilgrimages in Japan are carried out mainly by people who think of themselves in some sense as "Buddhist" but at the same time are normally living their lives in the practical daily world. Most of them are lay people who have a wide range of concerns from day to day and from year to year. They may also participate in other kinds of religious activities, so that their participation in a Buddhist pilgrimage is only one feature of their lives. Large numbers of Japanese people attend Shintō shrines as well as Buddhist temples in the course of the year, and not a few are also drawn to the practices of one or more of the so-called

---

1. See Pye 1996 and Pye and Triplett 2004.

new religions, some of which are by now rather well established. The teachings of the founders, leaders and teachers of these religious groups are quite specialized from case to case, and if taken seriously they often contradict each other. However, there is a widespread assumption on the part of the general public that the shrines and temples to which recourse is made are likely to be of assistance for their own special reasons. They are all competent in some particular way, it is thought. Assistance, indeed, is what is wanted by the majority of the people. They seek success in their business or professional life, reassurance concerning their worries, the healing of their sufferings, and safety in their daily life and journeys. Surely, it is felt, the gods and buddhas will provide these. Or, at any rate, they might. However, this should not be left entirely to chance. Human beings for their part should contribute their devotions and their offerings. A pilgrimage to a number of temples and/or shrines is a sustained and costly example of this.

Since there are two parties to these matters, the human and—in whatever precise sense—the divine, the whole religious activity can be regarded as a *transaction*. This usually involves establishing a relationship, which may be temporary or more long-term, with an appropriate divine agent. These ritually structured relationships may lead the individual further into areas of personal understanding or meaning which have a long-term value, and the question of this more widely reaching significance will be considered later. At the same time, it does not seem odd to those participating, including those who staff the temples, that there is an immediate, even a commercial aspect to the transaction. This is only natural. Whichever side of the relationship is held in view, it is understood that there will always be *quid pro quo*. That is why we refer to it as a transaction.

If we consider the matter in a different perspective, namely with the consciousness that there might be a profound teaching in Buddhism itself which is not evident in daily religious activities, a different question arises. This question would be, given that pilgrimage falls largely into the general field of Japanese religion and shares in its features, where is the Buddhist significance? The matter will be considered later under the heading of the third guiding concept, namely "meaning." We do not mean to imply that "transaction" is without significance. On the contrary, it certainly does have a significance which is generally understood by the participants, even though they do not need to talk or think about it very much. The profounder, specifically Buddhist meaning is more elusive because it only becomes apparent through a dialectical process. To approach it satisfactorily we must first be familiar with the standard transactions of the pilgrim.

The religious transaction carried out at the temples on a pilgrimage route in Japan may be said to have three main aspects which are functionally distinct. The first aspect is that the pilgrim demonstrates in some way that he or she has in fact arrived at the temple in question for the intended visit. The second aspect is an act of devotion, recitation or prayer, based on recommended texts but allowing some individual variation, and usually related to a specific aspiration or petition. The third aspect is the acquisition of proof of the visit, in particular by having a booklet or scroll stamped and inscribed at the appropriate place.

With this transaction in mind, the pilgrim performs a prescribed series of actions at each temple in a given series. The actions vary in accordance with factors such as the time constraints of the visit, whether or not the pilgrims are in a group, and what the specific pilgrimage is about. Arrival at the temple can involve various actions such as rinsing one's hands and mouth, just as at a Shintō shrine, and striking the temple bell where this is permitted. However, the key indication that one has arrived at the temple, as a pilgrim, is the deposition of a simple slip of paper in a box near the main hall of reverence. The importance of these pilgrims' slips (on which more details will be given below) can be seen from one of the terms in common use for referring to the very activity of pilgrimage, namely *fudasho-meguri*. *Meguri* means "going round" as explained earlier, and thus *fudasho-meguri* means, literally spelled out, "going round the *fuda* places."[2] This expression shows that the *fuda* (or *o-fuda*, if we add the honorific prefix) are a key element in what the pilgrim has in mind as he or she does the rounds.

In addition to the pilgrims' slips, other items may also be deposited, for example a hand-copied Buddhist text or a votive tablet (*ema*). Such votive tablets are in common use in shrines and temples all over Japan, and attract much interest, but in the case of pilgrimages they are an extra detail and not essential. There is also scope for variation in the devotional pattern. If the pilgrims are in a group there may be a more substantial recitation of *sūtra* passages than some individuals are inwardly prepared for, or have time for. Other variations relate to the various halls for reverence. On the Shikoku pilgrimage route and its derivatives the crucial element is the hall of Kōbō Daishi, the "Daishidō," while on the Kannon-sama pilgrimages it is of course the Kannon Hall (Kannondō) which is obligatory while again the main hall of the temple, if different, may be visited optionally. When it comes to the collection of a proof that the visit has taken place, the seal or red-ink stamp and freshly written calligraphy which is collected from each temple in a booklet are *de rigueur*. Variously however, these may be applied in a special booklet for the purpose, to a pilgrim's shirt, or on to a commemorative scroll.

---

2. A related term is *fudashojunrei*, as used for example in a leaflet of the association named Edo Fudasho Kai. *Fudashojunrei* means a pilgrimage (*junrei*) round the *fuda* places (*fudasho*).

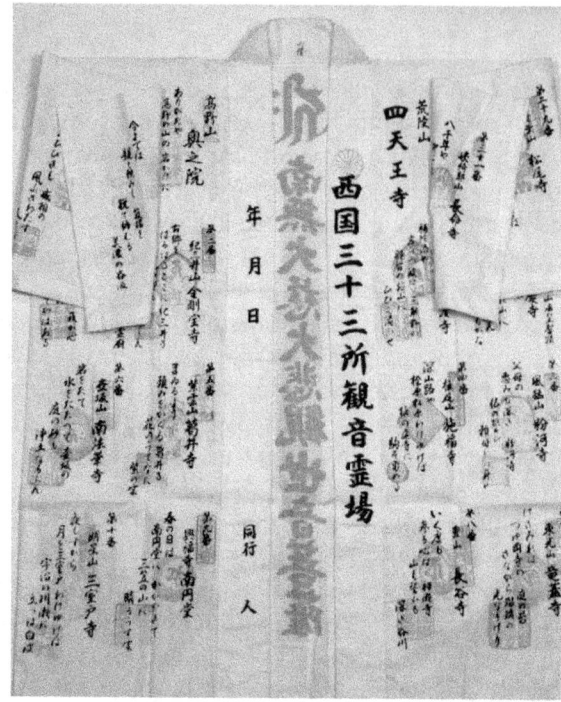

Figure 6.1 Pilgrim's shirt with Saikoku seals and calligraphy. The central calligraphy appears reversed because it shows through from the back of the shirt.

It is the certification itself which is of crucial importance, whichever medium is selected. Even the approach to acquiring it can vary and may sometimes seem quite casual. For example, the seals are often collected by the bus-driver or tour leader while the pilgrims get on with their reciting. This saves time in the case of groups travelling together. Usually the providing office and the hall for devotions are in close proximity, but they are sometimes a little way apart. It is not unknown for an individual to go to a conveniently located office near the main temple to collect the seal in person, while not in fact making an arduous climb to a slightly distant Kannon hall for devotions. Variable details may be added to the act of certification. For example the pilgrim might also buy an amulet, for personal use, or perhaps for a relative or friend. A commemorative photograph taken by a companion on the spot may also be considered as an optional part of this phase of the ritual. However the main evidence of the visit will always be the seal and calligraphy.

With whatever variations and additions, the religious transaction which the pilgrim carries out at each temple visited during the pilgrimage is of central importance. Without it, the travellers would just be going on a recreational walk or tour. Whatever the recreational value of going on pilgrimages may be, and it is surely high, this alone does not correspond

The Pilgrim's Transaction

to the intentionality of the pilgrims. The intentionality, focused in simple devotions, is sandwiched between the symbolic acts of depositing and receiving proof of the visit to each temple. Stated abstractly therefore, the three vital phases of every visit, which can be reinforced in various ways, are as follows:

1. **The pilgrim deposits evidence of the visit.**
2. **The pilgrim performs a devotional act.**
3. **The pilgrim acquires evidence of the visit.**

Religious transaction is not explicitly taught to pilgrims in terms of the threefold analysis presented here. The pattern of ritual action is learned from other pilgrims rather than from temple authorities. However some guidance is occasionally available. In particular, organized groups are often led by qualified guides known as *sendatsu* 先達 who have been round many times and who are therefore experienced in the routines as well as understanding the motivations for pilgrimage. At the same time, not a few of the guidebooks published for use by pilgrims contain brief, informal instructions on what to do, including, not unexpectedly, the points already noted. Even though most behaviour is learned through imitation, such sources reflect traditional practice and provide additional guidance for new generations of pilgrims.³ As a typical example, here are the instructions translated from Hirahata's guidebook to the Kamakura Thirty-three:

1. After entering the temple grounds, first wash out mouth and wash hands at the water stand.
2. Sound the temple gong (only where this is freely permitted).
3. Deposit the pilgrim slip and/or a copied *sūtra* text in the box provided before the main hall.
4. Donate a candle, incense and coins.
5. Direct your thoughts towards the main Buddha of the temple, do a *gasshō* [i.e. fold hands in reverence] and recite a *sūtra* text such as the *Heart Sūtra*, the *Kannon Sūtra*, *The Kannon Sūtra in Ten Stanzas* (*Jikku Kannongyō*), the *Honzon myōgō* [i.e. the "exquisite name" of the main Buddha revered], the *Ekōmon* and so on.
6. At the seal office, pay the required fee and receive the seal in your book, on your scroll or on your shirt.
7. While on pilgrimage you may experience difficulties, unpleasantness, vexation or sadness, but this should all be interpreted as the workings of Kanzeon and be received gratefully in the fervent spirit of *gasshō*. Kindness should be extended to fellow pilgrims and to all those whom one meets on the way.⁴

---

3. The importance of imitative behaviour and its significance for the relationship between supposed norms and variations was explored in my essay: "Vorgabe und Praxis in den buddhistischen Pilgerfahrten Japans," Pye 2005.
4. Hirahata, *Kamakura Sanjūsankasho*, 1990, page 7. In a different text box on the same

This text reflects what can be observed at temples on the pilgrimage routes all over Japan. The author of the guidebook adopts a slightly didactic tone, especially at point (vii), but in general it can be read simply as a reminder of what millions of pilgrims have been doing over decades and centuries. As far as recent times are concerned, it corresponds to what may be observed in the field. The text also illustrates rather well, if only because of the numeration, how the analysis which we seek in "the study of religions" cannot simply be left as what the religious exponents say, but must progress to its own new level of reflection. In this sense, consider the following: (i), (ii) and (iv) could occur at any visit to any Buddhist temple. They also fit with what is expected when visiting a Shintō shrine except that there would then be no temple gong and no incense. Notice also that here the points (i) (ii) and (iv) surround and enclose the act which is specific to pilgrimage, namely the deposition of the evidence of the visit (point iii). At least in its repeated form this is specific to pilgrimage because each one of the temples has to be visited for the pilgrimage to be completed. Points (v) and (vi) represent the second and third phases of the transaction respectively. Point (vii) is an exhortation concerning attitudes which, interesting though it is, lies outside the structure of the visit as such.

The above may be compared with the text of a small leaflet provided at Temple No. 1 of the Shikoku Pilgrimage for pilgrims who are at the beginning of their journey round the eighty-eight temples.

How to Visit the Temple

1. First, before the gate, make one bow, then cleanse the hands and proceed to the main building.
    i) Deposit a pilgrim's slip (those who have prepared a copied *sūtra* should deposit the copied *sūtra*).
    ii) Offer a candle, incense or coins (rather than material offerings).
    iii) Take rosary in the hands, hang it on the index finger of the left hand and the middle finger of the right hand, rub it 4-5 times and then hang it in one loop on the left hand.
    iv) Open *sūtra* book and recite the *sūtras*.
    v) Holding the rosary again on the index finger of the left hand and the middle finger of the right hand, rub it and offer petitions.
2. Then go to the Daishidō [i.e. the hall honouring Kūkai] and repeat 1-5 above, and when finished there, visit any other worship hall.
3. Then go to the temple seal office to collect your scroll, booklet or white shirt with its seals, make a bow at the temple gate and proceed to the next temple.

---

page we find the recommended "attitude to pilgrimage," which is cited in the next chapter below.

The Pilgrim's Transaction

This text illustrates very clearly the three aspects of the transactional ritual explained above, although of course again without providing the exact numeration of our own analysis. The deposition of evidence of the visit is found in item 1(i) and the obtaining of proof of the visit appears under item 3. Note too that in the Shikoku pilgrimage, the act of devotion which is the central part of the transaction is carried out twice, once before the main hall and once before the Daishidō, that is, the hall honouring Kōbō Daishi (Kūkai). So devotions are prescribed in the first instance under item 1 (iii–v) and then again as item 2, being the visit to the Daishidō. Here reverence is paid to Kūkai, who is one's symbolic religious companion on the journey. The buddhas venerated in the main halls of the 88 temples are rather varied, as may be seen in the list given above in Chapter Three, while the pilgrimage draws its consistency from the devotions at the Daishidō.

In sum, while such instructions can be seen to be followed quite consistently by pilgrims on the spot, they do not in themselves provide a clear analysis of the three crucial ritual steps. Whatever the variations, each of these steps is represented in some way or other, every time. Thus there is an underlying structure to the religious transaction at each temple. We now move forward to consider the three aspects of the ritual pattern in a little more detail.

The pilgrim deposits evidence of the visit

Among the various forms of evidence left behind at each temple to show that the pilgrim has been there, the thin slips of paper known as *o-fuda* are the most common. These are understood by most pilgrims to be an essential part of their equipment, normally being carried in a small rectangular box which is part of the standard outfit. The most usual practice is to deposit one such slip in a special box or basket in front of the prayer hall of each temple. The containers are emptied from time to time by temple attendants, which incidentally provides the latter with some idea of the numbers of pilgrims who have passed through. The slips are usually pre-printed with the title of the pilgrimage, or an invocation of Kannon-sama down the centre, leaving marked spaces to left and right for entering personal information by hand. Slips for the Shikoku and related pilgrimages generally also bear an image of Kōbō Daishi. The information entered by hand usually includes the name of the pilgrim, the date of the visit and the intention of the pilgrimage which is currently undertaken. An example of the pattern is therefore as follows (but appearing vertically in Japanese):

For: [to insert name]
Two fellow pilgrims
Dedicatory pilgrimage
Thirty-three places of Saikoku

HAIL KANZEON BOSATSU OF GREAT COMPASSION AND GREAT MERCY
Address.... [to insert]
Name.... [to insert]

By "intention" is meant here dedicated objectives such as the healing of a sickness or safety on a planned journey, either of which may also be sought on behalf of others. Success in business or other enterprise, or just the general welfare of the pilgrim's family are also popular themes. Whatever the variations, the main point is that the pilgrim was in fact present at the temple, bringing his or her aspirations or petitions to the attention of the buddha or bodhisattva revered there. Thus these tiny slips of paper

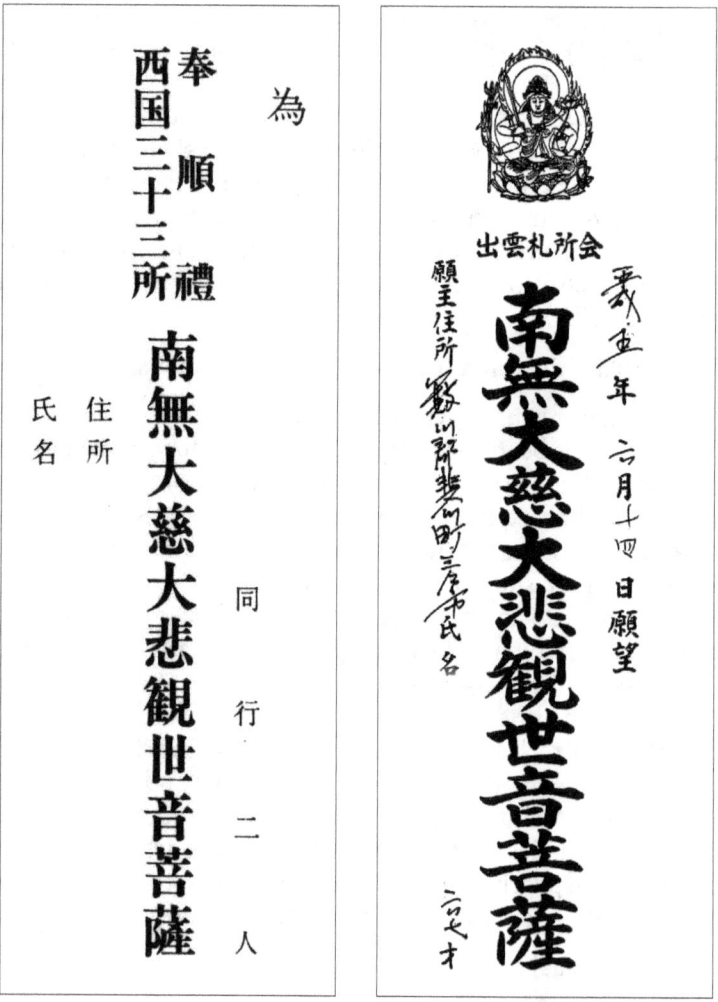

Figure 6.2 Pilgrim slips from the Saikoku Kannon Pilgrimage (left); and the Izumo Kannon Pilgrimage (personal name deleted) (right).

serve as one of the main foci for the whole religious activity of pilgrimage. Circulatory pilgrimage understood as "going round the *fuda* places" means going round a series of temples at which a beneficial transaction can only take place *because the pilgrim was there.*

Most commonly, the pilgrims' slips are white, but pilgrims who have already completed a pilgrimage several times will use slips of different colours. Explanations of these colours vary. In Shikoku I was told by an old man using golden coloured slips that these would be used from the 22nd time onwards. He set it out as follows:

White: first to seventh time.
Red: eighth to thirteenth time.
Silver: fourteenth to twenty-first time
Golden: twenty-second time onwards.

This corresponds to what it says in a leaflet of instructions available at the first Shikoku temple, Ryōzenji.[5] Instructions in a leaflet for the Chita Peninsula pilgrimage of 88 temples are a little different:

First time upwards: white.
Tenth time upwards: green.
Twentieth time upwards: red.
Thirtieth time upwards: silver.
Fiftieth time upwards: gold.
Hundredth time upwards: brocade.

We must remember here that the Chita pilgrimage is much shorter and so can reasonably be visited more frequently. Similar slips, and colours, are used for the Kannon-sama pilgrimages, and here too there seems to be some variation.[6] Hirahata details as many as eight different colours in his guide to the Owari pilgrimage of 336 kilometres, but adds that this is as set out for the example of the Saijō Kannon pilgrimage (1987). In short, information of this kind, even if it gets to be printed on pamphlets or in booklets, does not have any kind of normative authority. It arises above all at the whim of those who print the little batches of pilgrim slips and put them on sale.

The full Japanese word for pilgrim slips in this sense is *osame-fuda* 納 め札, which more literally means "deposition slips." Although there is usually a receptacle for them as described above, it has also been traditional to stick them up on the temple walls. As a result, when going the rounds of pilgrimage temples it is quite easy, and fascinating, to observe the many variations in the *osame-fuda* left by individuals or groups, as they often have a distinctive character. At the Izumo 33 pilgrimage those

---

5. Ian Reader got different information for Shikoku: white 1–4, green 5–7, red 8–24, silver 25–49, gold above 50 times (Reader 2005, 21).
6. Hirahata 1987c.

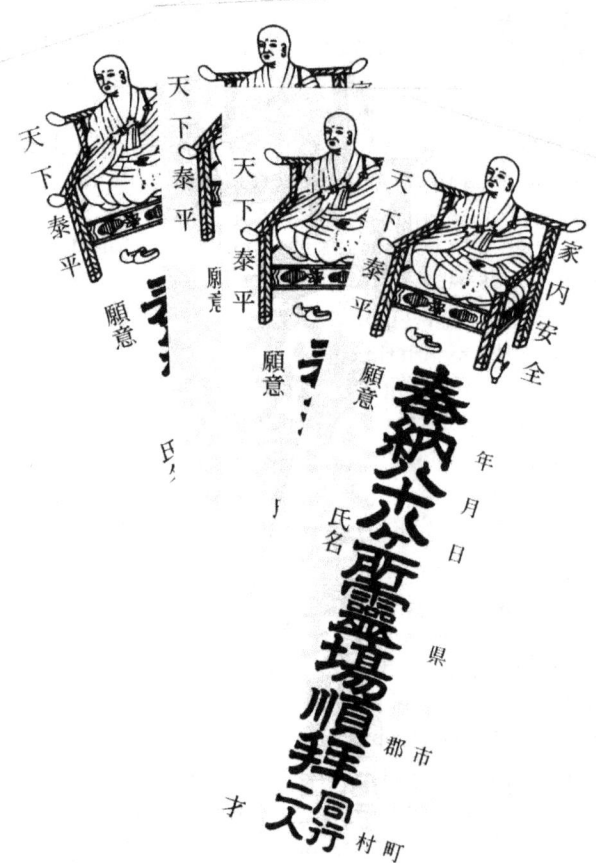

Figure 6.3 Unused pilgrims' slips for the Shikoku pilgrimage.

responsible for the buildings seem to take a delight in leaving as many as possible on display, somehow hanging in huge bunches (see Figure 2.12, on page 60). Presumably because it encourages other pilgrims to follow suit, or to think of carrying out the pilgrimage in the first place, the temple attendants seem to be quite happy about it in this particular case.

A second and most interesting type of traditional pilgrims' slips may be called "commercial pilgrim slips." These do not have religious motifs on them, nor the spaces for name, date and purpose of visit. Rather they show the name of a particular business, in striking, if rather stylized calligraphy, which is usually in black on a coloured ground. Such slips are almost never posted in the usual receptacle but are always pasted upon the walls of the temple, so that these become covered all over with these proofs of visit for the admiration of all and sundry. The Japanese term for pilgrim slips in this sense is *senja-fuda* 千社札, which bears the lit-

The Pilgrim's Transaction

eral meaning of "slips for a thousand shrines." This rather mysterious term is evidently to be correlated with the expression *senjamōde*, which means "visiting a thousand shrines." The occasional explanation for this is that it refers to the practice of visiting a thousand shrines in one's region, especially Inari shrines because they are good for business, on the first "horse" day of the second month. However this practice seems to have lost any separate identity which it may have had earlier, and the number one thousand appears to be nominal. The reality is that representatives of businesses visit selected shrines or temples, and are sent around any well-known circuits. A more obvious term for the same thing is the expression *hōkoku-fuda* 報告札 meaning "advertisement slips." For a while this term could be seen on the monumental gate of the famous temple Sensōji, in downtown Tokyo, albeit on a signboard which did not invite, but specifically *prohibited* their attachment.

Many examples of these *senjafuda* may be found in whole books devoted to them which are published mainly for their design interest. Especially idiosyncratic designs were created in the Edo Period, when they had already become a genre of interest to collectors. Indeed they are the source of design ideas to this day. An interesting example is the "collection of Zeniya Matabei the Second" (Seigensha Dainihenshūshitsu 2004). Some recent examples collected in the field may be seen in colour in *Pilgerfahrt Visuell*.[7]

Compared with the modesty of the ordinary ones, it might be supposed that commercial pilgrim slips are a form of advertising. There is certainly some truth in this. However some considerations speak against an oversimplified understanding, as it seems that there is an effort and cost involved which exceeds the probable benefit. For one thing the businesses concerned are usually very small, and the pilgrims are far from home. Very often, the other pilgrims going round, from far-flung parts of the country, would hardly know where such family shops or businesses are located. Moreover the slips themselves are not very informative, giving little more than a name and a line of business such as "cake shop" or "*sake* supplier." Moreover each slip is quite small and gets crowded out by many others. The employees who bring them round are supposed to find a spare spot for them. As a result they are often pasted up in quite difficult places on the beams of the temple's structure, so that they can only be viewed individually with much craning of the neck. They are put up in these high spots by means of a long, slim-handled brush designed for the very purpose of getting them there. Such brushes are sufficiently characteristic for one of them to have been depicted in a book of patterns for commercial pilgrim slips published in 1920.[8] The brushes, some paste

---

7. Pye and Triplett 2011, 58 (exhibit no.38).
8. Cf. *O-meguri* 22.10 and frontispiece.

and a stock of slips are still carried today, for example by young employees of a small business sent round on the trip for this very purpose. In view of all this, it seems that the advertisement effect could hardly be great enough by itself to warrant the financial investment of the journey.

If advertisement is not the main purpose of these slips, what is? There seems to be little doubt that the purpose is to effect the usual *religious* transaction on behalf of the business. The shop must be protected against fire and theft, and prosperity should be bestowed upon it. The employees' knowledge of Buddhism may be slight and their prayers cursory, or even skipped altogether, as I have often observed. Even so, the main purpose of the pilgrimage is to arrange with the powers of another world for this-worldly benefits to accrue, in this case to the business, in this world.

Apart from the two classic forms described above, a wide variety of ephemera may be seen at the pilgrimage temples which belong in principle to the class of "pilgrims slips" or *o-fuda*, even though they are much larger than normal, or made of wood or of cloth.

One case consisted of a sheet of paper, being somewhat larger than an ordinary pilgrims' slip, with the following text:

(at top, left to right):	Offering
(from right, vertically):	Date: 23.10.60" [= 23. October 1985]
	Hail Daishi Henjō Kongō
	Hail Kanzeon Bosatsu
	Noda City
	Seikō-in Shoraikō [= name of the group][9]

The group of pilgrims mentioned here is apparently a new association (*kō*) of supporters of a temple (Seikō-in) in Noda City, which was making its first joint pilgrimage. Next to this paper, attached to the simple wooden lattice obscuring the inside of the temple, were three divination papers (*mikuji*), intended either to ward off expected misfortune or to ensure the good fortune which they promise.

These ephemera are of immense interest in that they tell us about whole groups of people who jointly undertook a pilgrimage and sometimes, however briefly, why they did so. In From the names it is also possible in principle to gain an impression of the gender spread. However, there is no major issue relating to gender in the study of Japanese pilgrimage since groups may be single-sex or mixed depending on how and why they were formed in the home location. Occasionally a special slip may have a distinctive patriotic flavour, for example, showing the Japanese flag or Hinomaru, which is otherwise not so prominent in the Buddhist pilgrimages. Or again several names may be found altogether, with a summary of

---

9. Cf. *O-meguri* 21.3.

their wishes such as "safety in the home" and "world peace."

The *Heart Sūtra* will be considered again in Chapter Seven, but in this context it is relevant that copied versions of it are also often affixed to hospitable walls and pillars of temple buildings. This works quite well because this short *sūtra* fits easily on to a single sheet of paper. In such cases merit is achieved because of the act of copying, but leaving it behind as a statement of intent on the temple walls shows that in this regard it is similar to the pilgrims' slips. Not only did one copy the *sūtra* out by hand; one also visited the temple in person and offered the *sūtra* as a proof of the particular visit. The copied *sūtras* may also be stuffed into a special box for receiving pilgrims' slips when the temple authorities do not want to have too many things pasted up in the wooden structures.

Another common form of evidence of one's visit, quite familiar to all Japanese people, is the votive tablet or *ema*, which is almost always made of wood. These *ema*, bought on the spot and thematically illustrated, are widely used in shrines and temples which are nothing to do with pilgrimage in the present sense, so that their use specifically in the context of a pilgrimage route is quite continuous with general religious practice. In some cases however, they may provide a particular individual with a reinforcement, or even a substitute, for the standard pilgrim slip. The use of an *ema* almost always implies that benefits in this world are sought, even if they are expressed rather generally.

The pilgrim performs a devotional act

The pilgrim does not only leave his or her own physical mark at the temple visited. The second part of the transaction is, most importantly, a specific act of devotion, combining the appropriate bows, the prayerful folding together of the hands (*gasshō*) and a recitation. The recitation is usually quite brief, though the interest invested in it and the evident piety of the pilgrims may be quite high. In other cases it appears to be cursory, and sometimes it is not clear whether any particular text is recited at all. Well organized pilgrim groups however can be seen and heard chanting in unison, using the appropriate booklets, and often reciting key texts such as the *Heart Sūtra* from memory. These texts will be considered further in Chapter Seven, because they open the door to a level of meaning which lies beyond the immediate transaction. In the transactional context, the pilgrim assumes that the recitation of a short text and/or the offering of silent prayer will provide a guarantee of the delivery of the petition or aspiration which is close to the heart.

In one of the examples of instructions for pilgrims quoted above, the act of devotion included the following suggestions (under point v):

> Direct your thoughts towards the main Buddha of the temple, do a
> *gasshō* and recite a *sūtra* text such as the *Heart Sūtra*, the *Kannon Sūtra*,

The Kannon Sūtra in Ten Stanzas (*Jikku Kannongyō*), the *Honzon myōgō* [i.e. the exquisite name of the main Buddha revered], the *Ekōmon* and so on.

More will be said on the content of these texts in Chapter Seven, but note here that these particular instructions are directed towards a pilgrimage for the bodhisattva Kannon. In the case of the Kannon-sama pilgrimages there is, as far as routine is concerned, just the one obligatory place for performing devotions, namely the Kannon Hall itself. This may not be the main hall of the temple, and any other devotions are optional. Reference to the *honzon myōgō*, i.e. the "exquisite name" of the main buddha revered at the temple is therefore part of the optional devotions. It is of course common for pilgrims to pray before the main hall as well, but it is the visit to Kannon Bosatsu which really counts. And remember, there may not be much time! Another leaflet for a Kannon-sama route suggests that the pilgrim recite a *sūtra* before the "treasure hall," i.e. where Kannon-sama might be housed, or if pressed that he or she simply chant "Namu Kanzeon Bosatsu," i.e. "Hail to the Bodhisattva Kanzeon" (as Kannon is also called).[10] In other words, the *sūtra* in this case would typically be the *Kannon Sūtra* (*Kannongyō*) but in accordance with the regular principle of abbreviation in Japanese religion, the invocatory formula would be sufficient in itself.[11]

The short *sūtras* or *sūtra*-like texts are usually recited to the accompaniment of a small percussion instrument which can be sounded by being tapped against the lower part of the thumb. This helps to keep the rhythm going from character to character, for these texts are all in *kanbun*, i.e. in Chinese text form. The texts are printed in small folding booklets (leporellos)[12] which are convenient to carry and to use and which display variations according to denominational perspective. More will be said on these in Chapter Seven.

In addition to these texts a specific "song" (*go-eika*) may be recited at each temple. In effect this is also a recitation, because the texts of these songs are so short that they can hardly be sung in the ordinary sense of the word. The temple songs usually contain some more or less poetic allusions to the situation of the temple in question in its landscape or to the main buddha who is housed there, to Kannon-sama, and so on. Since the *go-eika* are specific to each temple there are many thousands of them for the various pilgrimages of the whole country. Because they are all different they reinforce the idea that each specific temple has its

---

10. The form Kanzeon is the one which appears in Chapter 25 of the *Lotus Sūtra*, in the Chinese version which is commonly used in Japan. This corresponds to Chapter 24 in Sanskrit manuscripts (of later date than the Chinese versions).
11. The *Kannon Sūtra* is identical with Chapter 25 of the *Lotus Sūtra* in Kumārajīva's Chinese version. Sometimes only the verse portion is used. See further in Chapter Seven.
12. This unnecessarily obscure term for folding booklets is included here because it may be met with in libraries and museums.

own character and must be visited in its own right, even while the connecting thread is provided by Kannon-sama, Kōbō Daishi, Fudō-son, or another. Here in translation is the *go-eika* of Temple No. 8 (Hasedera) of the Saikoku Kannon sequence:

> So many times my heart ascends
> to the temple of the springing stream.
> –mountain and vow alike,
> the river deep below.

This song turns on the name of the temple, Hasedera 長谷寺, here written however as 初瀬寺, which, with the same pronunciation, means the temple of the first springing up of rapid waters. While the resolution, aspiration or vow of the pilgrim rises high up to the mountain on which the temple is situated, the river rushing down its valley below seems all the deeper. As in most of the *go-eika*, the thought is moved forward by loose associations rather than tight grammar, and this is reflected in the style of the translation.

After reciting the *go-eika* and *sūtras*, petitions may be requested and, as seen already, this is without doubt an important part of the pilgrimage. Although the term *kigan* is wide enough to hint at aspirations for the future, which could include some kind of spiritual progress or the development of spiritual powers, what is usually meant by "petitions" here is requests for benefits in this world, the well-known *genzeriyaku*. Apart from being the subject of those short moments of silent prayer, for which there is just enough time, these requests may be recorded in various other ways for the attention of the divinities, buddhist or other. There are various standard forms. A common method is to write petitions on a wooden stick which will then be ceremoniously burned in the temple by the temple priests. This practice, known as a *goma* ceremony, is ultimately derived from India and in some cases is also performed at Shintō shrines. Another way is to write the requests into paper forms provided for the purpose, often showing printed suggestions as to what to pray for, and to hand these in with a donation for inclusion in formal prayers offered by specialists. A well-known and rather popular way mentioned already is to purchase a votive tablet (*ema*), to inscribe one's name and one's heart's desire on the back and then to hang it up on the frame provided for the purpose in the temple or shrine grounds. When people visit other parts of Japan, away from home, they are often interested to see whether there are any particular benefits which they might receive there by means of an incidental visit to a shrine or temple, and this interest is often reflected in travel leaflets. There are whole books on the matter, listing shrines and temples and the particular advantages which their resident divinities offer. Of course Kyōto, the frequently visited temple and shrine capital of the country, lends itself particularly for this treatment.

The idea of "this-worldly benefits" (*genzeriyaku*) has also attracted quite a lot of attention in recent western literature on Japanese religion. This is not surprising in that it is widely current in Japanese religions, and superficially very much in evidence, as every observer on the spot is well aware. Why is it that observers find the idea of such petitionary prayer for recognizable benefits so particularly noteworthy? In the writer's experience of teaching about Japanese religions outside the country, since the late 1960s, the notion has often been received with a certain amount of scorn or been swept aside as unimportant. Yet when western students themselves go to Japan they inevitably come across it for themselves, and may even feel moved to write books about it. It is fair to speculate that the initial cognitive dissonance among students in the western world arises because of a widespread, unreflected presupposition that religion ought really to be about "higher things," not this world but some other world, not the ordinary experience of life but a special experience, not the daily difficulties which may be partly determined by our karma but some quite distinct realm of anticipated enlightenment. But such a polarized view of human aspirations is not appropriate to our subject. Pilgrimage in Japan is in large part about the achievement of merit and therefore the accrual of benefits, which may be first material and only later, perhaps, spiritual.

There remains therefore the question as to how far this level of transactional ritual and petitionary prayer is transcended in a more fully Buddhist direction. To what extent is pilgrimage also about the transformation of ordinary life in a wider perspective. What after all is "benefit"? And what might the results of "merit" be? The monks, nuns or temple assistants who provide the seals and execute the calligraphy do not appear to have very much interest in such questions. The answer depends on the experience and maturity of the individual pilgrims. It is the people who determine the meaning of the pilgrimage for themselves as they leave their offerings and prayers behind on slips of paper or wood. For them it is, in the first instance, a costly practice which is supposed to bring a benefit in return. Yet even though such benefits are this-worldly there is also a threshold of meaning which is crossed by at least some pilgrims in so far as they realize that the value of their pilgrimage transcends the level of this-worldly petitions. We shall return to this matter more substantially in Chapter Seven. It may seem paradoxical, or not, but it is the central act of the religious transaction which provides the matrix for a deepened understanding which might somehow transcend the transactional.

The pilgrim acquires evidence of the visit

Third, evidence of the visit is required. The concluding act of the pilgrim's transaction at each temple is therefore to obtain the temple seal and calligraphy as proof of his or her visit. These may be applied to the pilgrim's book, a pilgrim's shirt or a commemorative scroll. Each one demonstrates that the pilgrim has in fact performed a visit, or in the standard Japanese term for a single visit to a holy place, that he or she has performed *o-mairi* to the temple in question. However in this case it is proof for the pilgrim to take home. When all the commemorative seals have been collected, for example thirty-three for the Saikoku Pilgrimage or eighty-eight for the Shikoku Pilgrimage, it shows that the whole pilgrimage has been completed. Such proof may be a source of satisfaction and reassurance and can be proudly displayed to relatives and friends.

Most pilgrims carry a small booklet with a traditional binding for this purpose, folding or otherwise, which is usually referred to as a *nōkyōchō* 納経帖 in Japanese. The pages are often pre-printed for each temple, showing where the seal is to be entered. Alternatively the pilgrim's white cotton jacket-like shirt may be used, or a spare one taken especially for this purpose. Another highly favoured, but rather expensive medium for the seals is a hanging scroll which bears an appropriate painting in the middle, for example of Kannon-sama herself. Such scrolls may have the right number of fields lightly drawn in, or marked in a provisional underlay, so that the various seals can gradually be assembled in an ordered fashion.

The seals mounted in any of these artefacts are more than just a memento. It is time to look at their exact function. The booklet used for this purpose, the *nōkyōchō*, is sometimes called a *hōinchō* 宝印帖 or "seal booklet." The element *chō* in each of these terms means notebook, or more specifically "register." However the most important clue to the underlying meaning lies in the element *nōkyō*, for this means literally donating a *sūtra*. Donating a *sūtra* means spending money, in this case a small fixed sum, in order to pay for a *sūtra* to be copied, at least theoretically. Copying *sūtras* (*shakyō* 写経), or having *sūtras* copied by someone else, is a religiously meritorious act. As noted already, some pilgrims copy out their own *sūtras*, especially the *Heart Sūtra*, which is short enough to be copied conveniently. However this will not stop them from following the customary practice of making the donation required to get the temple seal in their booklet, or on their shirt or scroll. But the seal is not the *sūtra*. The seal (*hōin* 宝印) and the calligraphic signature of the temple are a kind of receipt for the donation which has been made. The *sūtras* will in fact never be copied by temple priests or their attendants, or at least not in any statistical relationship to the seals issued.

If the practice of paying for the seal and calligraphy of each temple can be explained as a substitute for paying a priest to copy a *sūtra* and thereby acquire merit, such a meaning has no relevance in the case of the Shintō circuits described above in Chapter Five. There the practice may be said to be more akin to stamping a souvenir book with the rubber stamp of historic or remote railway stations. On the other hand, while the use of station stamps in the waiting room costs nothing, a visit to a Shintō shrine will usually be linked to a request for supernatural assistance in some matter or other and therefore is expected to cost something. Getting a Shintō shrine stamp should therefore also be understood as part of the transaction, however lighthearted the mental connections may be.

Even at the Buddhist temples it has to be said that the acquisition of the seal is a heavily abbreviated form of a more substantial activity. It was argued already that such abbreviation is very characteristic of Japanese religion and indeed of Japanese life generally. Accordingly it also tends to become more or less mechanical. Temple priests or other attendants, in particular the wives of temple priests, sit behind a little window and just quickly fill up the appropriate page of the pilgrims' books. Sometimes they smile, and sometimes they just look a little bored. In the 1990's the price was usually 300 yen, though earlier and in less well-known places it had been only 200 yen. By 2012 the price had crept up to 400 or even 500 yen. At this rate a completed book or scroll for thirty three temples, plus three additional ones, could cost 18,000 yen, which is rather a lot of money. In the case of a scroll it still has to be mounted at considerable expense.

Of what does this "seal" consist in detail? Usually it consists of three red imprints from a pre-cut stamp with a wooden handle, upon which is superimposed a hand-written calligraphic motif in black ink. In some cases there are two red imprints. The important regular features are the name of the temple and its number in the pilgrimage series. In some cases, but infrequently, the date is included.

The booklets in which the pilgrims collect their seals are worthy of study in themselves, for the pre-printed pages carry systematic information about each temple, such as its name and address, its number in the series, its tale of origin (*engi*), the denomination, the object of reverence, and the pilgrim's song (*go-eika*). The binding is usually a little festive. There are many variations.[13] In an example from Sendai the booklet also contains at the front a short hymn to Kannon-sama and an explanation of the pilgrimage routes, and at the back a map of the route around Sendai. The titles also often have a common form, adjusted to the specific route for which they were intended, but usually including the key term *nōkyō* explained earlier, as in these examples:

Saikoku sanjūsan reijō nōkyōchō
Bandō sanjūsan kannonreijō nōkyōchō

---

13. Cf. *O-meguri* (Pye 1987) sections 25–27, for an earlier presentation with some black and white illustrations. Further illustrations in colour will be found in Pye and Triplett 2011, items numbers 4–7. Items 4 and 5 are my completed personal books from the Saikoku and the Chichibu Kannon pilgrimages.

Chichibu reijōsanjūyonsho nōkyōchō
Sendai sanjūsan kannonreijō nōkyōchō

These designations mean "*sūtra* donation register for the thirty-three spiritual places of Saikoku," etc. with variations referring to the "Kannon spiritual places" in the case of Bandō and Sendai and to thirty-four temples in the case of Chichibu (for all of which see Chapter Two above).

The seals and calligraphy on shirts, scrolls and in the booklets are all proof that one has made the pilgrimage, or at least that someone has made it on one's behalf. While these proofs have traditionally taken quite clear forms, other informal ways have been found to document and thus "prove" the visit. For decades now photography has played a role. It is usual for Japanese travellers wherever they go to take a photograph of themselves, or to have one taken. This is not just a photograph but a "*commemorative* photograph," the extremely frequently heard Japanese phrase for this being *kinen shashin*. This might hardly seem worth mentioning, but for two reasons. First, the statement is truly justifiable as a specific, ethnic cultural generalization, i.e. to an extent which would not apply to people from all countries. Second, while tourist snapshots are mainly intended for memories, the commemorative photographs taken on shrine and temple visits, and all the more so for pilgrimages to a whole series of temples, contain the important element of reporting that the visit or pilgrimage has been made. They are for proof.

Before the days of mass photography, the postcard culture was more significant than it is today. It flourished at a time when journeys also took longer, so that there was a reasonable chance of a postcard arriving home to the family before the person who sent it! The interplay of travel culture, pilgrimage destinations and "famous places" (*meisho* 名所) in the development of tourist maps from the Edo Period onwards is striking. From the Meiji Period onwards "famous places" naturally came to figure very much in postcard culture, and if only because of the impressive buildings a good proportion of the illustrations show religious sites, the famous temples and shrines of the whole country. Such postcards also take on the function of the proof of a visit, which is what is being considered here. Moreover, at some point in this development postcards were designed which bore, not a photograph of a shrine or temple, but a red-ink print of the commemorative seal or seals, either individually stamped or in some cases pre-printed. In a personal album dating from the early Shōwa Period (1930s), it was possible to inspect no less than 102 postcards of this kind, all stemming from religious sites and evidently intended as documentation of the visits. The similar style of cards from many different religious institutions, and the fact that in many cases they were sold with prefixed postage stamps and special postmarks, indicates that this practice was well established at the time. Only one of them had in fact been sent anywhere, from Temple No.

1 of the Saikoku pilgrimage, at Nachi, to an address in Ōsaka. The others were simply assembled as proof of visits under the handwritten title *Jinja Bukkaku, shūin sutanpu*, meaning "Shrines and Buddhist temples, seals and stamps." This individually devised title combines the "seal" of the Buddhist transaction explained above with the modern word (derived from English) for a commemorative rubber stamp.[14] The range of places, mainly in the Kansai region, indicates a definite interest in the circulatory pilgrimages of Buddhism, for example the Saikoku circuit and the Settsukuni circuit in the Kōbe area. But there is also a clear interest in Shintō shrines, reflecting their public prominence because of the promotion of Shintō by the government at that time. So while this particular collection took on the function of the traditional *nōkyōchō*, its compiler had made up his or her own pilgrimage around a large number of varied religious destinations in pre-war, western Japan. These additional possibilities should not however distract us from the reality that most pilgrims carry a book specifically for assembling the seals and calligraphy of each temple in a particular pilgrimage sequence. This is the norm.

The seals and calligraphy on a pilgrim's shirt are just the same as those in the books. However the shirt provides a space for a large vertical slogan which sums up the devotional attitude of the pilgrim, most commonly for Kannon-sama or for Kōbō Daishi. (For details see further in Chapter Seven). It is said that a pilgrim's shirt with the seals and calligraphy on it may be placed in a coffin when the pilgrim dies, but I have not been privileged to observe this. It could also be placed in the Buddhist house altar for a while, or kept indefinitely somewhere near it. Very occasionally it gets left behind in a house clearance.

Hanging scrolls as proof of pilgrimage

The most impressive form of proof that a pilgrimage has been completed is undoubtedly a large, beautifully mounted scroll on which all the temple seals and calligraphy have been mounted. These scrolls are highly treasured as long as the pilgrim is alive, and indeed they can be most impressive statements of a devotion fulfilled, a pleasure to look upon and to display to others. Like other scrolls, they may be hung on occasions within the *tokonoma*, the cultural alcove in a Japanese room where a flower arrangement or a special vase may stand. Or they may be placed rolled up within the *butsuma*, the small closet-like section in a Japanese style room where the Buddhist house altar is kept, and if so they will be revered along with the memorial tablets of the ancestors and other foci of devotion depending on the denomination.

---

14. It is not certain whether the handwritten title is from the same period as the postcards, although it seems likely.

The Pilgrim's Transaction

If the seals alone can nowadays cost 18,000 Yen for thirty-six temples visited, we have to reckon that the seals for a scroll for the Shikoku 88 pilgrimage, even at 400 yen per temple, is going to cost more than 35,000 Yen. A professional mounting with appropriate backing material, brocade bands etc. will bring the cost up to at least 200,000 Yen – a month's salary for a modest employee. But this does not include the cost of making the pilgrimage itself, i.e. the expenses of the journey. Thus the financial investment creeps up imperceptibly but inexorably. Such scrolls are very costly items.

It is all the more striking that when they show up in second-hand shops or flea-markets, as they very occasionally do after house clearances, the resale value is only four or five thousand yen, a fraction of the original cost. This is because scrolls of this kind, though impressive and in their own way even beautiful, have no value as works of art. Their value lies in the merit which has been achieved. So if the person has died, and the scroll has neither been treasured by a descendant nor ritually disposed of by fire, as many religious artefacts are, there is in effect no value at all. The materials cannot really be recycled, except possibly for the wooden or ceramic cross bars on which the scroll is wound when closed up. The merit has lost its relationship and relevance to any particular persons. With patience therefore it is possible for enquirers to find such scrolls for close examination or exhibition purposes.

In 2005 the writer acquired just such a scroll at a second-hand shop in Kyōto. Great was his joy over this extremely favourable acquisition, which could only have been made possible on account of merit produced by others! Since (as usual) there is no date, name or dedication on the scroll, it can only be speculated that anything up to twenty years may have elapsed since the performance of the pilgrimage, even in the life of an elderly person. The scroll is kept in its original box of *kiri* wood, measures 188cm by 65cm in size and is made of strong paper with a brocaded border and gilded wooden endpieces for rolling it up. The centre-piece is a painting of Kannon-sama, in this case a *Shō-Kannon*, facing to the front, standing on a lotus blossom and bearing a very small erect buddha-image in the crown. Though very simply drawn, this is presumably Amida Buddha, of whom Kannon Bosatsu is sometimes understood to be an emanation. The scroll is complete with the seals and calligraphic names of the temples of the Saikoku Thirty-three Kannon Pilgrimage. The seals therefore document the completion of the pilgrimage by an unknown person. In all, there are thirty-seven seals, including so-called *bangai* temples, that is, temples outside the numbered sequence but relevant to the pilgrimage. At the top centre is No.1 (Seigantoji, at Nachi), to the left and right of it are two *bangai* temples, in the second row are two more *bangai* temples at the outside with Nos. 2 and 3 centred. Below these follow the rest of the temples, all in the correct sequence, from right to left down to No. 33 in the bottom left-and corner. Some similar scrolls have 38 seals, but this pattern with 37 is one of the standard variations. The three seals at the top contain the chrysanthemum symbol of the imperial house (there are sometimes four of these). For this and related examples see also the exhibition catalogue *Pilgerfahrt Visuell* (Pye and Triplett 2011).[15]

There are many variations in the scrolls for the Kannon pilgrimage. In some the bodhisattva is presented with her figure slightly turned and her face looking slightly downwards, thereby conveying an impression of flexible compassion. Other iconographical forms will be found, such as the "Willow Kannon" or the "White Kannon." The arrangement of the lines of seals and calligraphy is also diverse. On a wider scroll the elements (with three seals) can be rather well spaced, with only three temples on each line. In this case a graceful, vertical Kannon-sama is just right for taking up five rows in a central position with five rows above and five rows beneath. This makes room for a total of forty temples, which means that no less than seven extra-numerary places will have been visited. These include the three usual *bangai*: Kazan-in Bodaiji, Gankeiji and Hokki-in, but also give prominent positions to the nationally significant temples: Shitennōji (designated "the first Buddha-dharma of Great Japan"), Zenkōji, Kōya-san and Sensōji. In simpler scrolls the first three *bangai* alone are more usual, as this gives a total of 36 temples which can be arranged with pleasing symmetry. Sometimes the temple seals may be added in a slightly inaccurate order. This reminds us that the underlying purpose is to prove that one was there, no more and no less. However, in the end result the temples are usually in the right order on the scroll (apart from highlighting extra-numerary ones), even if they were not originally visited in the right order.

A scroll in the making may be slightly transparent, so that through it may be seen a temporary extra sheet beneath showing the right fields for the various temples. This helps the pilgrim, and the temple attendant, to know precisely where the seals and calligraphy should go. Incomplete scrolls may be seen in which the temples visited so far are not in sequence, but dotted around the scroll as visits have proved possible. Scrolls are also made for the Bandō and the Chichibu pilgrimages, and in theory can be made for any of the Kannon pilgrimages. In any particular case the seals and calligraphy of the temples will identify the particular route. However the scrolls do not display any other significant differences which would distinguish the various Kannon routes. Very occasionally one may see all the seals and calligraphy of the one hundred temples of Saikoku, Bandō and Chichibu in one single, huge, wide scroll. However this can hardly be more than a commercial display or a boast-

---

15. Exhibit No.8, page 25.

ful gimmick, for it would be very impractical for any ordinary pilgrim to go round the temples carrying such a thing.

In a rather special, discreetly elegant scroll which came to hand, the central figure of the bodhisattva is replaced with the characters for the *nenbutsu* (Namu Amida Butsu) and the seals are accompanied, not with the usual calligraphy but with the text of the temple song (*go-eika*). These had been written in a very fine hand, the work of a single person. In some places it seems as if the seals were put on first and the *go-eika* texts added later, which would have been a very special work to be done with such consistency over the existing seals.[16]

Historically, other elaborate forms of scroll paintings for Kannon-sama have been known. One variation shows the thirty-three Kannon in their various iconographical forms, thus suggestive of the pilgrimage, but without any temple seals being collected. At the centre of one such scroll can be seen the character for "heart" or "mind" (*shin* 心). Such a scroll is an example of the genre of *kanjin* scrolls or paintings which show a varied field of Buddhist iconography or cosmology held together by the "visualization of the mind" (*kanjin* 観心).[17] The underlying concept here is drawn from the "mind-only" (*yuishin* 唯心) tradition of Mahāyāna Buddhism, but the theme is not restricted to schools identified with that. However, while the thirty-three appearances of the bodhisattva are celebrated in the case mentioned, such scrolls have less direct connection with pilgrimage as discussed here. Indeed there is a long-standing tradition of painting Kannon-sama for scroll mounting, independent of pilgrimage. This can be an amateur activity, or it can find expression in works by well-known people such as Okada Mokichi, the founder of the new religion Sekai Kyūseikyō.[18]

The scrolls for the Shikoku pilgrimage are remarkably similar to those for the Kannon-sama routes, considering that they are thought of as quite separate and unrelated pilgrimages. The main difference lies in the sheer size, because there are more temples to be accounted for, and in the cen-

---

16. Illustrated in Pye and Triplett 2011, 33 (exhibit no.17). In a few places it is very hard to be sure that the ink was applied over the seal (though various opinions were taken); it is therefore possible that the *go-eika* were first printed on to the scroll, though of course from a calligraphic original. At the time of writing no similar scrolls are known with which this could be compared.
17. In a simple painting acquired at Mount Kōya in 1973 the central character for "mind" is surrounded by the ten states of possible rebirth. A fine scroll on the same theme is owned by the Zen temple Sengakuji in Tokyo, famous for its tombs of the forty-seven samurai who committed *seppuku* after avenging the death of their insulted lord.
18. His name is usually rendered Okada Mokiti in the context of the religion itself. Facsimiles of his Kannon portraits were donated to the writer and are now in the Museum of Religions at Marburg.

tral image which is usually of Kōbō Daishi. One such scroll in excellent condition acquired by the writer measures no less than 74cm across and 196cm in height.[19] The mounting, which is typical, has an outer deep blue area with gold-coloured brocade, a secondary frame in which strong red dominates, and a strip in golden yellow above and below the central sheet. The sheet bears the portrait of Kōbō Daishi and the seals and calligraphy of each temple. Since there are 88 temples and one extra position for Mount Kōya, the home of Shingon Buddhism, the total effect is stunning. The temple seals and calligraphy are arranged in rows beginning at the top right and ordered horizontally. The first five rows show seven temples each. The sixth and seventh row each have only six of the ordinary temples because the central position is taken up by an entry for Mount Kōya, which extends vertically over two columns. This comes, specifically, from the Oku no In ("the further temple"), which is Kōbō Daishi's mausoleum located at the end of the long trail through the cemetery area of Mount Kōya. Following on down the scroll, rows 8 to 12 are then divided by a painting of an elegant and luxurious baldachin (a ceremonial roof-like structure) which honours Kōbō Daishi who is sitting beneath it. In this section the rows have the entries for two temples each at the right and at the left. Rows 13, 14 and 15 are then reunited as complete rows with seven temples each, the final one being number 88 at the bottom left hand corner.

In other scrolls of similar type the figure of Kōbō Daishi may be positioned slightly differently, so that the position of the seals and calligraphy also varies. However Kōbō Daishi is always there, at the optical centre of gravity with more rows above than beneath. Daishi-sama, as he is usually called, is seated on his chair as a teacher of Dharma, with his shoes neatly placed below. This position is similar to that of the portraits of many Zen masters, but in his case we always see, somewhere in the foreground, the pitcher which is a symbol of the transmission of the teaching "poured from teacher to student like water" and hence his own right to initiate successors in the Shingon tradition.[20]

Less commonly seen is a very nice scroll for the twenty-five temples associated with Hōnen Shōnin surrounding the portrait of the master.[21] He is shown seated on a low mat, holding a rosary for reciting the *nenbutsu* (Namu Amida Butsu), which is the central practice in Pure Land Buddhism. The six characters of the *nenbutsu* are written vertically above his head. The temple seals and calligraphy run from the top right hand corner, being arranged in two uninterrupted rows of four at the top, six rows of two each which are separated by the *nenbutsu* and the portrait, and two further rows of four each in the lower part. This makes

---

19. Illustrated in Pye and Triplett 2011, 28 (exhibit no. 10).
20. This expression was provided by Elizabeth Tinsley, from oral tradition.
21. Illustrated in Pye and Triplett 2011, 33 (exhibit no. 16).

a total of twenty-six temples, which arises because the concluding one is a "special site," namely the temple Seiryūji 青竜寺(青龍寺) which is in the Saitō complex of Enryakuji on Mount Hiei. The mounting is similar to that in common use for the more famous pilgrimages, the blue sections hosting gold-coloured tree peonies (*botan*) and the narrow horizontal strips showing sixteen-petalled chrysanthemums.

These are just examples of the thousands of scrolls which have been assembled by pilgrims and the scroll-mounting trade over the years. Descriptions of the varied secondary characteristics could be multiplied, and the details make a quite fascinating study in their own right.[22] In general, observation suggests that the secondary pilgrimages are more frequently documented by pilgrims' books than by scrolls. However, distinctive pilgrimages do have their own distinctive scrolls. Ready made scrolls are also offered in mint condition (for a very high price) by shops dealing in Buddhist house altars and other accessories, for persons who cannot themselves go on a pilgrimage. In such cases the seals have been collected by commercial tour operators, who are visiting the temples anyway. As religious artefacts these must be regarded as having a devotional status similar to any other scrolls with religious themes not related to pilgrimage. They lack the merit inherent in a scroll on which the seals are personally assembled by a pilgrim. Nevertheless the brochures are very informative.[23] Also, it should be said that the main work of such commercial enterprises lies in supplying the materials and assembling the completed scrolls on their elaborate mountings, which all has to be done properly. The pilgrim usually just carries around the central part which is pre-painted or pre-printed on light paper and could not be hung by itself. It can be carried in a small cylindrical plastic case.

With the consideration of these scrolls we have already begun to enter into the symbolic world which informs the minds of the pilgrims. However, the scrolls are above all a most potent symbol of the pilgrim's *transaction*. They are the finest proof that the pilgrimage was completed. They show that the pilgrim visited the buddhas and bodhisattvas in question, to pay devotion, and at personal cost. The blessings of the buddhas and bodhisattvas have been received and are being brought back to others in the pilgrim's family. By placing the (rolled up) scroll in the Buddhist house altar the matter is also reported to the ancestors, in a display of gratitude and reassurance, so that they too become parties to the transaction.

In conclusion, let it be emphasized once more that it is the combination of the three main steps, in whatever form, which ensures the com-

---

22. More details on the construction and use of scrolls will be found in Pye and Triplett 2011, 59–61.
23. The writer is grateful for much information in this connection from a Kyōto shop specializing in scrolls named Fuji Kōgeisha, located near Kitano Tenmangū.

plete transaction. The pilgrim has taken the trouble to go to the temple in question, he or she demonstrates this overtly, whether praying for something specific or for general benefits, and then is provided with proof of the visit, which is taken to imply that the benefits might indeed accrue. These actions all appear to the Japanese pilgrim to be quite familiar and straightforward. This is because they are part of the common language of Japanese religion in which such actions regularly play an important role. It is also assumed that they belong together and form part of one *single* transaction. The actions themselves are repetitive, and to some observers they might appear to be rather mechanically or almost casually performed. However this is common in ritual behaviour and has no effect on its presumed validity or efficacy. In spite of, or indeed because of the sheer efficiency of the act, the pilgrims and their families expect, or at least strongly hope, that the completion of their side of the transaction will ensure the practical fulfilment of their petitions and aspirations.

In the next chapter we will turn to the question of meaning or meanings which go beyond the transactional level of primal religion. The Buddhist pilgrimages in some sense also offer a route of personal development and it is this aspect which now remains to be explored.

— Chapter Seven —

The Meaning of Japanese Buddhist Pilgrimage

Divergent meanings and Buddhist meanings

In view of the millions of persons who perform Buddhist pilgrimages in whole or in part, for themselves or for others, once only or repeatedly, paying devotion not only to Kannon-sama but also to other buddhas and bodhisattvas, it will be evident that the *meanings* which may be discerned in this practice are multiple. We must also remember that in many cases the sequence to be visited includes temples of various different Buddhist denominations. No one single or "essential" meaning can be extracted, therefore, which might fit these pilgrimages into the doctrinal structures of a particular Buddhist school of thought. At the same time certain emphases in the practice of the pilgrims lead us towards an area of interpretation which is widely recognizable and may be regarded and designated as "Buddhist." Key reference points here are devotion to Kannon-sama and the recitation of the *Heart Sūtra*, and on these more will be said below.

It may seem self-evident from some points of view that "Buddhist" pilgrimage has a "Buddhist" meaning. However there have recently been some academic discussions which might seem to contradict this. For one thing, the attempt has been made to argue that rites, being governed by rules for their performance rather than by concepts, are simply "without meaning."[1] Evidently this position is not and cannot be adopted here, at least not in any extreme form. It may certainly be admitted that ritual activity follows a more or less regular course simply because of the way in which it was performed last time, and the time before, or in other words it is "rules" which dominate, and not some kind of idealized doctrine. Indeed in fieldwork, an answer which is frequently given to the straight question about why somebody does something is that "it is always done like that," and in its way this is an extremely plausible

---

1. See especially Staal 1989.

answer.[2] Yet at the same time, in practice ritual is not "always done like that." As often as not it is adapted and even altered, for both circumstantial and conceptual reasons. Whatever sub-texts or divergent codings may be seen in rites of any kind, it is therefore perverse not to take seriously what the performers of the rites themselves think that they are doing, especially when this too is repeated many times. In a different kind of argument, other commentators refuse to try to identify what is "Buddhist" and what is not, on the grounds that any such attempt is "essentialist" and implies a preconceptualization of Buddhist orthodoxy. This objection sounds as if it is directing respect towards the "actors" in all their variety, i.e. those who say they are "Buddhist"—and that is fine as far as it goes. On the other hand, the broad stream of "Buddhist" tradition has fuzzy edges. In the end it fizzles out into activities which are not "Buddhist" and which can be distinguished from Buddhism. For example, as we have just seen in a preceding chapter, a pilgrimage can be a Shintō pilgrimage and not a Buddhist one. Both of these arguments then, in their severity, are little more than exaggerated academic follies. If they were to be meekly accepted it would be quite impossible to go beyond a superficial description of the pilgrimages introduced in this book.

On the contrary, it is quite possible to observe ritual practices which are similar in some respects but whose meanings diverge. A specific example which has already been described above, in the context of "transaction," is the practice of paying to receive the seal and calligraphy of each of the sacred places visited. In so far as this transaction is similar in Buddhist and pilgrimage Shintō circuits, there is a common meaning which lies in the confirmation that the visits to the sacred places have in fact been made. However, while in Buddhist cases the practice can also be interpreted as a substitute for paying a monk to copy a *sūtra* and thereby produce merit, such a meaning has no relevance at all in the case of Shintō circuits. Of course, the majority of pilgrims are probably unaware of the *derivation* of this dramatically abbreviated Buddhist practice, but nevertheless the seals and calligraphy are incorporated into a book which contains the names of the temples and their central objects of worship, on to a pilgrim's shirt with a central statement of Buddhist loyalty or prayer, or on to a scroll with iconographic depictions. All of these indicate a Buddhist meaning rather than a Shintō meaning. A guide to the Chita Peninsula Shin-Shikoku pilgrimage (introduced in Chapter Three) suggests that it is particularly appropriate to go round in spring and autumn at the time of *higan*, when ancestors are remembered in all Buddhist denominations of Japan. It also says that while people will no doubt have different concerns, some in this world and some in the next,

---

2. Consequently, in fieldwork it is not advisable to ask "why" something is done, and better to elicit any conceptual accompaniment to actions in indirect ways.

they all have in common that they would like to complete the pilgrimage which they have resolved to perform. What we see here is that a Buddhist pilgrimage is presented as functioning on two levels of meaning, one for this-worldly matters and one for more far-reaching questions about the sequence of generations and the deceased. In a sense, even the attention to ancestors is part of the primal religious stratum, but by means of it the Buddhist temples call attention to questions about the wider meaning of human existence. After all, going on such a pilgrimage represents a greater investment of energy and attention than the regular visit to the local cemetery, important though this is.

When summing up the character of the Shintō pilgrimages introduced above in Chapter Five, we noted a rather specific set of values and meanings, including especially an emphasis on purity and gratitude. Even though these values may be met with elsewhere, a specifically Shintō note is added by emphasizing them. As far as the Shintō context is concerned, therefore, this is the meaning. Buddhist meanings are different, and they can also be identified, as will be seen below.

We do not need to assume that the meaning of pilgrimage is "religious" only, in some precise doctrinal sense. Contextually, there are certainly wider motivations to be considered. The religious value or meaning of these might be contested, depending on the point of view. For example, in a postscript to Moriguchi's guidebook to the Izumo Kannon Pilgrimage, we read that when a pilgrim sets out on his or her journey the desire "to see the sights and enjoy the mountains" plays a significant role.[3] The special atmosphere of the spiritual places coupled with the influence of nature, the text continues, leads to a sense that one's heart is being purified.

While an emphasis on purity is clearly promoted by the Shintō *kiyome* (purification) rituals, the "purification" of the heart, or of one's being, is an intention which is not restricted to Shintō alone. Indeed the *yamabushi* 山伏 and related mountain traditions which are conveyed within and between Buddhism and Shintō are known for their emphasis on the "purification of the six roots" (*rokkon shōjō* 六根清浄). In this expression the "six roots" refer to the six sense organs, traditionally listed as eye, ear, nose, tongue, body and mind. By "body" is meant the physical basis of all sensory perception, i.e. physical feeling, which escapes further definition, and by "mind" is meant the organ of conceptual perception, this usually being regarded in Buddhist analyses as the sixth of six senses. It is possible to take *rokkon shōjō* as an entirely Buddhist notion. However it just happens to fit conveniently also with the Shintō concept of purity, while leading one somehow beyond it into the Buddhist area. This probably accounts for its widespread use not only in Shingon Buddhism and

---

3. Moriguchi 1977, postscript on an unnumbered page, apparently by another writer.

among the *yamabushi* of Shugendō, but also among groups of Shintō-oriented pilgrims, for example on the three mountains in northern Japan known as Dewa Sanzan (Haguro-san, Gassan, and Yudono-san).[4] The full phrase recited is *zange zange rokkon shōjō* 懺悔懺悔六根清浄, i.e. "penitence, penitence, purify the six roots."

Another significant strand of meaning, for many religious or semi-religious travellers, lies in the nostalgic connection which can be made with ancient Japanese Buddhist tradition. This is identified less with any particular teaching than with the famous "old temples" (*koji* 古寺) and their various important cultural properties and national treasures. Not a few guidebooks present themselves as *o-meguri* or *junrei*, i.e. circulatory pilgrimage, highlighting famous temples of Nara, Kyōto and elsewhere, but without referring to any of the numbered circuits which have a specific devotional focus. A classic example is Watsuji Tetsurō's *Koji junrei*, first published in 1919 and in a popular pocket format in 1979, the author being a well-known figure in the study of Buddhist art and thought. Another example which has run into many editions is Mizuno Keizaburō's *Nara - Kyōto no koji meguri. Butsuzō no mikata* (1985 onwards). In this case there is an explicit emphasis on the appreciation of Buddhist images, which in their variety can be puzzling and at the same time impressively fascinating for visitors to historic locations. Such books in effect promote a form of "pilgrimage," as we might call it in a metaphorical sense, which seeks a return to "roots" and to a general form of Buddhist orientation, but without requiring a specific ritual or doctrinal focus. On the other hand the national importance of the places and their iconography should not be underestimated. Such journeys are rather popular in the context of friendship and may be undertaken, for example, by two young women who are school or college contemporaries. When a taste is developed for this it does not necessarily lead to a performance of the standard pilgrimages with the standard pilgrim's kit. Rather, the focus is on personal subjectivity, whether sentimental or conducive to greater self-knowledge or spiritual development. The point is illustrated by the suggestive title of a work by Nakagawa Toshio which can be translated as: "A journey of love and heart around 108 temples all over the country" (Nakagawa 1979). The significance of the number 108 lies in the 108 passions which are to be expurgated by visiting these temples one by one. Moreover, by visiting temples where there is a buddha or bodhisattva image which is highly regarded as a work of art, a sensitivity to Buddhist iconography is developed. Such "national treasures" or "important cultural properties," as many of them are, figure regularly in school excursions, and thus contribute to the overall impact

---

4. C.f. Pye and Triplett 2007, and for an illustration of such pilgrims see Pye 2004, frontispiece.

of the "civil religion" of Japan. At the same time, the temples which have important images of this kind are sometimes also part of one or more pilgrimage circuits in the traditional sense, so that interest in visiting other temples later on, perhaps as a "real" pilgrimage, may be awakened. A reflective guide on the Saikoku pilgrimage by Matsuo Shinkū, the incumbent priest of Matsuodera (Saikoku No. 29) clearly builds on this genre, while leading back to the numbered pilgrimages and thus to a kind of orthodoxy or orthopraxy. In the sub-title he speaks of "Walking the Mother of Ways" (Matsuo 1992).

Why does a person decide to go on a pilgrimage at all? This is a significant question because the practice is not obligatory in Buddhism, as it is in Islam (in so far as it is in the power of the individual Muslim). There are many individual reasons, but a common structure found expression on an individually designed pilgrim slip, deposited at a temple in Shikoku. This bore the following three simple Japanese words:

   Arigatō
   Sumimasen
   Dōzo

These mean "thank you," "sorry" and "please." In other words, some things were good: *thank you*; some things went wrong: *sorry*; I would like something to happen for the best: *please*. In these simple words we see an expression of much which underlies Japanese religion at its most general level, and certainly the practice of pilgrimage is in touch with the wider range of Japanese religious attitudes and behaviour.

To some extent the more precise meanings of Japanese Buddhist pilgrimage have already become apparent in the description and analysis of the religious *transaction* which takes place at each temple visited on the route. However this does not at all exhaust the question of meaning, or meanings, for these are single transactions at single temples. Moreover the transactional element is often focused on a petitionary prayer for a particular benefit in ordinary life. Even if the whole pilgrimage is undertaken on behalf of a relative who is ill, or is about to undertake a major foreign journey, this remains at the transactional level characteristic of primal religion. But is there not some *plus* of meaning in the carrying through of a complete pilgrimage linking thirty-three, eighty-eight or some other number of stations? The main perspectives for an answer to this question will appear when we consider three informative areas: (a) indications on the pilgrims' equipment, (b) the buddhas and bodhisattvas who are venerated as foci of meaning, and (c) the kinds of texts which are regularly and enthusiastically recited.

When talking with pilgrims, who are understandably always in rather a hurry to get on with their journey, the answers which they give about how they understand their pilgrimage are indeed most frequently couched in terms of particular intentions or prayers at the level of this-worldly benefits, for these can be briefly stated. However, the weight of evidence from these other areas, which we will now consider, is considerable. All of these indications become extremely familiar, as questions show, to pilgrims proceeding on their journey. There are repetitions at every temple, and yet there is a progression towards completion, so that the pilgrim eventually experiences a new status. This means that a development or even a transformation of consciousness can occur in the course of a circulatory pilgrimage, just as in other pilgrimages to a single goal.

It is here that the main options arise, in the pilgrims' own perspective, for the perception and experience of a meaning which goes beyond the level of the payment for and the receipt of favours. It is extremely relevant in this regard that leaflets and guidebooks regularly mention the *gohonzon*, the *engi* and the *go-eika* for each temple to be visited. The first two of these indicate a supernatural world which is at once a competent partner in a religious transaction *and* a window on transcendence. It will be seen that a frame of reference is found here which links the individual visits and transactions. This frame of reference provides continuity over the whole of a pilgrimage and creates space for the pilgrims' self-understanding to develop. However, before looking at this in detail, we should pay attention to the Buddhist and Chinese background of Japanese Buddhism.

Chinese and Indian perspectives

The main question for us in this chapter is whether there is a meaning or meanings which go beyond those mentioned so far, and which can be identified as "Buddhist." The practice of pilgrimage as known in many societies which historically have no direct connections with Japan was considered briefly in Chapter One, and thematically it becomes a matter for cross-cultural or comparative study. However, for Japan itself it is quite natural first of all to seek more direct clues in the wider tradition of Buddhist pilgrimage in India and in China, the two countries to which Japanese Buddhists above all looked for inspiration. In fact, early knowledge of Buddhism in Japan arrived from the Korean peninsula, in particular from the kingdom of Paekche, but it was not long before an idealized view of the transmission of major teachings from India, via China to Japan was constructed. Within this pattern, the historically motivated journeys of Chinese pilgrims to India was perceived as a model for Japanese travellers in search of "the Dharma," even though they themselves only made it as far as China.

In spite of their general relevance, the Buddhist pilgrimages known in India and China do not display close structural parallels with those of Japan. India is the land of Buddhist *origins* and has its own special foci

The Meaning of Japanese Buddhist Pilgrimage

of pilgrimage which reflect these origins, whereas the countries of East Asia developed alternative forms of pilgrimage in later times after the distinctive forms of Mahāyāna Buddhism had become widely popular. The motif of origin is not quite absent in Japanese Buddhist pilgrimages. It has been seen that every sacred site has its own *engi*, the account of its "affinity" (*en*) or in other words a narrative about why there is a particular reason for going there. Moreover the extra-numerary temples are in some cases included, notably in the Saikoku pilgrimage, precisely because they are connected with the *origin* of the pilgrimage. However the journey to India, and the pilgrimage to various sites connected with the historical Buddha is somehow larger than that. In this case the main purpose of the pilgrimage is to identify oneself with the places of origin, rather in the way in which some Christian pilgrims visit the "Holy Land" in order to be in "those very places," as one might say. This principle is not characteristic of most of the circulatory pilgrimages in Japan, although it does play a role in those of the Pure Land and Shin Buddhist traditions, in which people revisit the locations important in the lives of the founders Hōnen and Shinran.

Japanese pilgrims today are of course aware as a matter of general knowledge that the Buddhist religion arrived in Japan from India via China and Korea. Information on this as a cultural development with special reference to architecture and sculpture is regularly included in school textbooks. The major historical sites and exhibits (as many Buddhist sculptures have become) which illustrate the process of the transplantation of Buddhism to Japan are on the influential itineraries of school excursions. The active Buddhist leaders of the past, for their part, looked mainly to China for their models. Just as the famous Chinese "pilgrims" travelled to India for inspiration and sources, so did Kūkai, Ennin and Dōgen go to China. Even the more evidently Indian influences of esoteric Buddhism were mediated to Kūkai and Ennin by people whom they met in China. Yet they knew that beyond China, in the story of Buddhism, lay India, the very birthplace of the faith.

The first places of pilgrimage in ancient Buddhism were naturally linked with the Buddha himself. In the *Great Nirvāṇa Sūtra* (in Pāli, the *Mahāparinibbāna Sutta*) four places are specifically mentioned as those which a devoted disciple should visit. At the end of the Buddha's life, so it is narrated, the disciple Ānanda asks what could be substituted for the audiences with the Buddha which used to take place when the rainy season was over. Obligingly the Buddha answers that there are four places which may be visited "with feelings of reverence," namely:

> The place, Ānanda, at which the believing man can say: 'Here the Tathāgata was born!' is a spot to be visited with feelings of reverence.

The place, Ānanda, at which the believing man can say: "Here the Tathāgata attained to the supreme and perfect insight!" is a spot to be visited with feelings of reverence. The place, Ānanda, at which the believing man can say: "Here was the kingdom of righteousness set on foot by the Tathāgata!" is a spot to be visited with feelings of reverence. The place, Ānanda, at which the believing man can say: "Here the Tathāgata passed finally away in that utter passing away which leaves nothing whatever to remain behind!" is a spot to be visited with feelings of reverence.[5]

The actual places are Lumbinī (near Kapilavastu), Bodhgayā/Uruvelā, Vārāṇasī (Benares) and Kusinārā. The text then continues that anyone who dies while making a pilgrimage to one of these holy places will after death be reborn in a joyous heaven. This idea is a widely known concept in pilgrimages, evidently one which arose quite naturally to provide comfort to those undertaking a dangerous journey, which is what pilgrimages certainly were in older times. Historically speaking it is not easy to be sure whether these particular places of pilgrimage arose *because* of the sequence in the Buddha's life, or whether the eventual patterning of the life-story was itself influenced later by what had in the meantime become pilgrimage sites. The reason why this is not evident is that the earlier canonical texts simply do not provide any connected story of the Buddha's "life." The two main narrative sequences in the early texts lead into (a) the Buddha's Enlightenment and the first preaching of Dharma, and (b) the Buddha's decease or Nirvana. These two narrative sequences are independent of each other, and it is only later authors who run them together into a single life story. There are entirely plausible, if seldom adduced, reasons for this. Each narrative sequence has its own function in the establishment of the Buddhist religion. The first leads into the ordination of the first Buddhist monks, thereby legitimising the foundation of the monastic community, the *saṅgha*. The second leads into the cremation of the Buddha's body and in particular to the sharing out of the relics, thus legitimising the cult based upon them which was open to the laity. In other words the two narrative sequences explain the beginnings of Buddhism as a religion. In retrospect it can be seen that the places of pilgrimage were the first indications of a connected life pattern, which however was not turned into a single narrative until centuries later.[6]

However even within India it was not possible for all Buddhists to visit these particular places, especially in the early days, and this was no

---

5. Quoted for convenience from the well-known, if now slightly old-fashioned translation by Rhys Davids and Rhys Davids (1966), 153 (Mahāparinibbāna Sutta V, 7–8).

6. I have explained this in more detail in *The Buddha* (1979), but this was written for a very general readership, so that the critical points continue to be overlooked by academics who continue to write the story of the Buddha's "life" in one piece.

The Meaning of Japanese Buddhist Pilgrimage

doubt the reason for the division of the relics in the first place. According to the narrative they were divided after some discussion into eight portions for various Indian kingdoms and other groups. Since each place where a portion of the relics was preserved represented the Buddha's attainment of nirvana, the relics were further divided. In particular, foreign countries came to have their share, as at the famous Temple of the Tooth in Sri Lanka and others from Thailand to Japan. In the same way, cuttings from the *bodhi* tree (the tree of enlightenment) under which the Buddha supposedly sat at Bodhgayā, were also taken to other parts of India and the world to make up for the fact that the very tree of Bodhgayā itself could not be visited by all.

As Buddhism spread to other countries, the other key places associated with the Buddha's own activity were even less accessible for pilgrims from elsewhere. Only a tiny number of intrepid Chinese Buddhists such as Făxiăn[7] (c. 337–c. 422) and Xuánzàng[8] (602–664), managed to see them, and as a result these pilgrims and their records took on a particular importance in the story of the transmission of Buddhism to their own country. But for the overwhelming majority of people the vast distances involved, the economic and political constraints and the sheer hazards of travel made such journeys completely unthinkable. In consequence alternatives were developed to satisfy what is apparently a widespread readiness to travel as an expression of religious devotion. Thus China soon had its three great Buddhist holy mountains: Mount Wŭtái, sacred to Wénshūshīlì (Sanskrit: Mañjuśrī, Japanese: Monjushiri), Mount Pŭtuó, sacred to Guānyīn (Sanskrit: Avalokiteśvara, Japanese: Kannon) and Mount Éméi, sacred to Pŭxián (Sanskrit: Samantabhadra, Japanese: Fugen). Attention may be drawn to a particularly interesting account of Mount Éméi in André Migot's work *Tibetan Marches* (London 1955), where he describes the mountain (there referred to as Mount Omei), as being dotted with pagodas which pilgrims visit along their path to the summit. This is an example of sequential pilgrimage, but is still not quite the same as visiting a series of sites which have equal status in the pilgrimage, for the single, dominating mountain, Mount Éméi itself, remains the main goal. While pilgrimage is again becoming a most significant activity in mainland China, it is the impressive single sites which form the main focus, as for example at the Guānyīn centre Pŭtuó, referred to as the Chinese Potalaka. Circulatory pilgrimage to multiple sites does not seem to have been on the agenda, right up to modern times.

Needless to say these pilgrimages partly owed their existence to the increasing interest in Mahāyāna Buddhism directed towards the great bodhisattva figures, whose cults were developing a dynamic of their

---

7. Wade-Giles transliteration: Fa-hsien.
8. Wade-Giles transliteration: Hsüan-tsang.

own. But there was also another important innovation which occurred with the Mahāyāna. This was that in place of relics of the Buddha himself, should none be available, a text such as the *Lotus Sūtra* could be placed as an object of reverence inside a *stūpa* or *caitya*. A *sūtra*, which conveys the teaching of the Buddha and thus consists of Dharma, may be regarded as representing the Dharma-body of the Buddha himself. For this reason any temple which had a *stūpa* or a pagoda (which developed out of the ancient memorial mound) could become the focus of a pilgrimage directly to it. And of course, while the copying of *sūtras* was itself regarded as being meritorious, every centre of Buddhist cult would want to have its own *stūpa* in which to preserve fine examples, if a patron for its construction could be found.

The Japanese tendency to select mountains as places of recourse in Buddhism was copied from China. In India the basic model had been to leave the village and go into the forest for meditation. However, in China, Korea and Japan the plains were largely cultivated, so that in order to find forests and achieve genuine retreat from the world it was necessary to seek the remoteness of mountains. In the case of Japan there was also another tradition of mountain veneration which has continued to this day, being cultivated by Shintoists, by Buddhists (especially of the Shingon tradition) and by a variety of independent groups which draw on both Shintō and Buddhism for their inspiration. This may all easily be observed on a mountain such as Ontake in central Japan, though the actual climbing of the mountain is arduous enough and should only be attempted with the appropriate clothing and footwear. The existence of this independent tradition of mountain veneration led to the superimposition of Buddhist themes on mountains which were already presumed to be occupied by highly numinous spirits. Some of these spirits take the form of long-nosed goblins known as *tengu* who, once tamed by intrepid wandering monks, are still now propitiated with festivals and marketed, not least for the benefit of the subsequently founded Buddhist temples. Many of the temples for Kannon-sama around Chichibu are set up on the small mountains which surround the city. The "mountain" consciousness, going back to China, is also reflected in the fact that almost all Buddhist temples have not only have their usual temple name ending in *-ji* or *-tera* but also a formal "mountain" name ending in *-san*, even though the latter is little used except on formal sign-boards or in lists of temples.

Now that world travel has become open to many there is increasing interest among Japanese Buddhists in travel to the Buddhist sites of India. However interest in the Indian origins of Buddhism implies a reflective and conscious faith, for it is not really part of everyday religious consciousness in Japan. Moreover, although Buddhism is derived

The Meaning of Japanese Buddhist Pilgrimage

from India, it does not always give an impression of Indian-ness to Japanese people. On the contrary, architecture and iconography in general have taken thoroughly Chinese, Korean and Japanese forms. The modern adoption of Indian architectural and iconographic motifs in some temples implies therefore a conscious effort to set up a new relationship with Buddhist origins in India. Such an intended relationship is often the result of the initiative of a particular priest or leader and may be documented in various denominational contexts from Shingon to the modern Risshō Kōsei-kai. An example would be pairs of paintings which portray the Buddha in the enlightenment position and in the nirvana position. We have seen that these are two important themes for Buddhist origins in India and indeed remain so in the countries of Theravāda Buddhism, while in Japan statues of the Buddha in the reclining nirvana position are rather unusual. To some extent therefore the recent Indianising approach bypasses ordinary religious practice or attitudes. Visits to the sites of these great events in India are of course a form of pilgrimage, and yet they are not understood in the same way as standard forms of Buddhist pilgrimage within Japan. One important feature of Indian religious practice which is very closely related to pilgrimage and indirectly had more influence on Japan is circumambulation (as discussed in Chapter Four).

Although these various points of connection with the Indian and Chinese background are of considerable importance, the particular form of circulatory pilgrimage to multiple sites seems to be specific to Japan. Recently a pilgrimage has been advertized in Japan called the Thirty-three Sacred Sites of Kannon in Korea, designed for Japanese tourists, apparently at the instigation of the incumbent of Temple 17 of the Japanese Shinsaikoku route. This would seem to have no historical basis in Korea but rather to be a very recent construction projected on to Korea in terms of Japanese pilgrimage practice. Advertisements present it as part of the romance of the journey of Buddhism from India to China, to Korea and thence to Japan.

This disassociation is also evidenced, paradoxically, by the interest shown in India by Shin Buddhists. We have seen (Chapter Four) that in Shin Buddhism (Jōdo Shinshū) pilgrimage is theoretically eschewed, on the grounds that is a practice which implies that benefits arise on the basis of one's own merit or self-power (*jiriki*). Shin Buddhist faith by contrast is centred on other-power (*tariki*), that is, on the saving vow of Amida Buddha. Shin Buddhists however do feel able to participate in group journeys to India to visit Buddhist sites. Some staff members of Ōtani University in Kyōto (which is a Shin Buddhist foundation) do this with a clear religious motivation. Recently groups of students have been taken along. A report in *Ōtani Daigaku Kōhō* (No. 124, October 1996) describes the journey as an experience of India beginning at Calcutta and ending in Delhi (where there is a partner institution) but with a clear emphasis on recalling (*omoimegurasu*) the area in which Śākyamuni Buddha lived and taught. The word used here means, more literally, "to cause to circulate in one's thoughts," so that there is a subliminal association with *meguri*. Bodh Gayā as the place of his enlightenment and Sarnath as the place of the "first turning of the wheel of dharma" are emphasized. Such journeys to India may of course merge into tourism as in the case of a Shin Buddhist taxi driver in Kyōto who had visited the Buddha's birthplace at Lumbinī, but not any other main sites such as *Bodh Gayā*. Being interested in mountains, he had also visited Nepal and was planning to climb famous mountains in China. This interest also gives him the excuse to visit Kami-Daigo temple in the south of Kyōto five or six times a year –a strenuous uphill walk which just happens to culminate in a visit to Number Eleven of the famous Saikoku pilgrimage. Thus the Shin Buddhist rejection of pilgrimage as a merit-making activity has fuzzy edges, not least because of the Indian connection.

Clothing, staff, hat

The pilgrims' clothing and equipment, the guidebooks, various objects at the temples themselves, and the devotional booklets used for chanting provide a steady stream of meaningful associations. At each temple the pilgrim is reminded of the buddhas and bodhisattvas who are revered there and of the legends of origin or affinity. Indeed in many cases the temple name alone provides an important link to a central Buddhist concept, as for example in Saikoku No. 12, the "Temple of True Dharma" (Shōhōji 正法寺) or Saikoku No. 17, the "Temple of Six Perfections" (Rokuharamitsuji 六波羅蜜寺). The devotional texts, though short, are of considerable importance because they are recited again and again, so they will be treated in a section of their own below.

When fully clothed in the prescribed way the Japanese Buddhist pilgrim is a striking figure. Most prominent are the whiteness of the clothing, the size and visibility of the straw hat, and the nowadays largely symbolic staff. A whole group of pilgrims so attired is an impressive sight. It is clear that they are engaged in a very special activity which separates them from others for as long as it progresses. The details of the clothing and the equipment already provide indications of how the activity itself is understood.

Many pilgrims do indeed go round with the exact traditional attire. Others however do not. Instead they simply have a white pilgrim's jacket over ordinary clothes, or wear modern leisure clothes and carry the pilgrim's staff only. This does not seem to matter too much. However, even those who go round the circuit in ordinary clothes respond to and to

The Meaning of Japanese Buddhist Pilgrimage

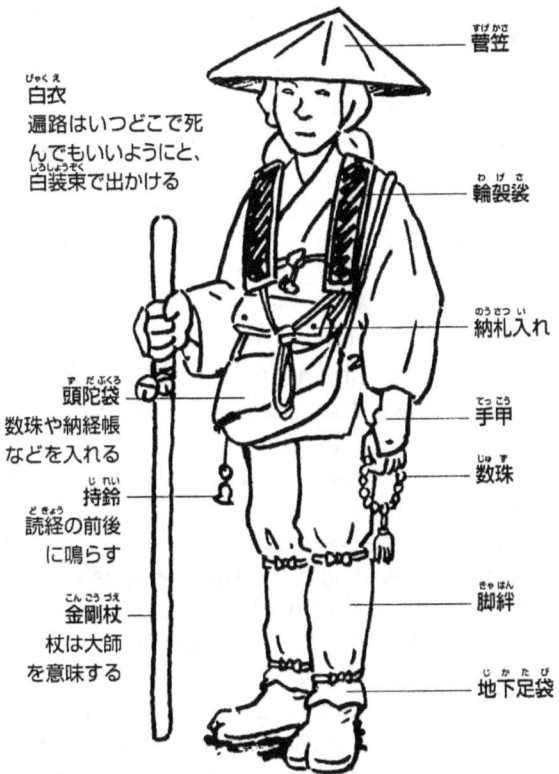

Figure 7.1 Popular sketch of mannequin with pilgrim's attire.

some extent identify with those who are dressed for the part. Moreover the guidebooks and the other literature of encouragement, even tourist advertisements, make considerable play of the traditional image of the pilgrim. At temples near the beginning of a route, mannequins may be seen, reminding people of what they need.

In general, any activities in Japanese life are thought to call for the appropriate attire. Fishermen wear fishermen's gear, even when they are only sitting in rows beside a small rectangular tank to pull out the fish which have been purposely put in for this purpose. Golfers wear golfers' gear. If hiking, one has a rucksack, if going to the office, one wears a tie, and so on. The language of clothing indicates where one thinks that one is at any one moment, and what the purpose of one's current activity is. This is as true for pilgrims as for any others, even if some pilgrims leave the actual wearing of the full attire to others.

At Shikoku No.1, the main temple hall sells a variety of accessories and also boasts a life-size mannequin (female) who is correctly attired as a pilgrim with the appropriate accessories. Other mannequins are set up at shops nearby. The necessities are explained in a free leaflet. In addition to the white shirt or jacket (*hyakue* 白衣) and broad hat made of sedge reeds (*sugegasa* 菅草), white leggings (*kyahan* 脚絆) traditional footgear (*tabi* 足袋) and also white gloves (*tekkō* 手甲)[9] are recommended. As accessories one needs not only the staff (*tsue* 杖) but also the rosary (*nenju* 念珠 or *juzu* 数珠) and the little box (*fudaire* 札入れ or *nōsatsuire* 納札いれ) for carrying pilgrims' slips. These things may be carried in a shoulder bag (*zudabukuro* 頭陀袋) for small personal belongings, though needless to say the last mentioned is easily replaced by modern bags of various shapes and sizes, especially when pilgrims are using motorized transport. An optional extra is the bell (*suzu* 鈴) which may be hung from the neck and announces the passing by of a pilgrim. The whole outfit is impressively completed by a stole (*wagesa* 輪袈裟) which is worn above all during recitation before the buddha halls.

The meaning of the pilgrims' attire is not hard to find. The most important single feature in the interpretation of the pilgrim's clothing is that the white jacket (*hyakue*) symbolizes a funeral cloth. In Japan a body is briefly cleaned shortly after death and then wrapped in a rather large white cloth, over which an ordinary kimono may then be drawn afterwards. The body can then be lifted with straps on the funeral cloth and placed into the coffin. The white jacket, together with the other white clothes, the leggings and traditional footgear (*tabi*) are all reminiscent of such attire. What it means for the pilgrimage is that while travelling one has departed temporarily from normal life. The pilgrim has left the world of ordinary activity but will, normally, return to it. A brief leaflet of instructions from Ryōzenji, the first temple of the Shikoku pilgrimage, asserts this symbolism of the funeral cloth. At the same time it says that the white jacket means that one is offering body and soul to Kōbō Daishi. Moreover it goes on to say that after going round the pilgrimage in the right order one returns at the end to Temple No.1 out of gratitude, and in order to be reborn again from the death of the journey. For this reason, apart from the practical stress of getting round the many temple sites within the time that this provisional death to the world is allowed to last, there is often a certain carefreeness about being a pilgrim. It is not surprising that pilgrimage was popular during the Tokugawa Period, when it was almost the only form of unconstrained travel open to the common people. It is perhaps in this connection that the Shikoku pilgrimage, at least, comes nearest to being amenable to the interpretative categories proposed by Victor Turner, i.e. that the pilgrims pass through a "liminal" barrier and experience a common situation which they share as *communitas* (cf. discussion in Introduction above).

---

9. Also *te no kō* 手の甲. These are meant in particular for covering the back of the hand.

Apart from its colour the white jacket usually has some phrases painted on its back in ink.

In particular, it is common to see there a vertical slogan which sums up the devotional attitude of the pilgrim, most commonly for Kannon-sama:

南無観世音菩薩	Namu Kanzeon Bosatsu
南無大慈大悲観世音菩薩	Namu Daiji Daihi Kanzeon Bosatsu

or for Kōbō Daishi, on the Shikoku routes:

南無大師遍照金剛　　　　Namu Daishi Henjō Kongō

The latter may be prefaced by the seed syllable for the Sanskrit "ōm" or "aum," and at the side it may be accompanied by the phrase *dōgyō ninin* 同行 二人, meaning approximately "two people going round together" or more tightly "two practising together." This refers to the idea that Kōbō Daishi is travelling the pilgrimage together with the pilgrim. *Namu* means "hail to," and *daiji daihi* means "great compassion" referring to the compassion (*jihi* 慈悲) of a bodhisattva. The phrase *henjō kongō* means "widely shining diamond," or more fulsomely "the diamond of universal illumination." The image of a diamond picks up not only the name of the widely known *Diamond Sūtra*, but hints more specifically at the Diamond Mandala, which is one of the two main complementary mandalas in Shingon Buddhism (the other being the Womb Mandala).

Other markings follow the pattern of votive offerings, giving the name of the pilgrimage, the date, the name and place of origin of the pilgrim, the phrase *dōgyō ninin,* and the purpose of the pilgrimage. Occasionally other Shingon Buddhist "seed syllables," which often stand symbolically for particular Buddhist divinities, may also be seen on the jacket. This script, adapted from Sanskrit, is known as *siddham* script, and cannot be read by the majority of pilgrims. People see such script on tombstones, especially on the five-tiered pagoda-style tombstones with their cosmological significance, and it creates an aura of mystery or what might be called internal exoticism. Its use is one of the various justifications for calling Shingon Buddhism "esoteric," in the sense that what you see has to be explained and this requires special knowledge which is not available to all.

The suggested way of writing all these things on pilgrims' shirts was current in guidebooks dating from the nineteenth century at latest.[10] The jacket or shirt is also one of the things which can be adorned with the seals and calligraphy at each temple, as explained previously, and will ultimately be proof that the pilgrimage has been completed as a whole. Sometimes a shirt, like the staff, is deposited at the last temple as a final act of donation. In other cases it may be an extra one acquired especially for giving to a sick or very old relative in preparation for their death-

---

10. Cf. *O-meguri* 13.5.

bed. This means that the pilgrimage has been performed vicariously for another person. The dedication of a shirt in this way, whether for oneself or for another person, shows that the pilgrimage mirrors in life our ultimate passage through death. Even as the pilgrimage is completed, life comes to be understood as transitory, or as "empty," to use the word which occurs in the *Heart Sūtra* itself. Thus the passage through sickness to death, of oneself or another, is opened up to a Buddhist interpretation.

A second focus of meaning in the pilgrim's equipment is the staff (*tsue*), and the standard expression *dōgyō ninin* which is usually written on it, as well as on the shirt as already mentioned above. This is of particular relevance to the Shikoku pilgrimage but is often carried over to other routes by keen pilgrims. It is said that the staff will get worn down by two or three centimetres during the Shikoku pilgrimage, but this would only happen if the pilgrim walks most of the way. The most common interpretation is that the staff represents Kōbō Daishi, who in spirit is performing the pilgrimage together with each individual pilgrim. This gave rise to the standard expression *dōgyō ninin* ("two practising together") mentioned above. This is tantalisingly difficult to translate because it means two people sharing the companionship of the way and at the same time the companionship of "practice" (*gyō*, i.e as in *shugyō*). However, the two people are not current friends or relatives of flesh and blood. Rather it means that each individual pilgrim is going round together with no less than the "great teacher" (*daishi*) himself. The Shikoku guidebooks place some emphasis on this idea of going round together, spiritually, with Kōbō Daishi, and the phrase *dōgyō ninin* also appears on pilgrims' hats and on pilgrims' slips left behind at the temples. If two living people of today go round together then the phrase, as seen on the pilgrim slips, is adjusted to *dōgyō sannin*, that is, *three* people proceeding (or practising) together. A leaflet available recently at temple No. 51, Ishiteji, even bears the title *dōgyō mannin*, "ten thousand practising together," thus emphasizing the community of the numerous pilgrims. The phrase *dōgyō ninin* and its equivalents is characteristic of the Shikoku pilgrimage but may also quite often be seen on pilgrim slips deposited at temples of the Saikoku, Bandō, and Chichibu routes. This is partly because the pilgrims in question may be members of one of the sects of Shingon Buddhism, but there seems to be some simple transference to others as well. That is, people just think it is an expression which you use when going on a pilgrimage. Since the staff represents Kōbō Daishi, it is treated with great respect. On reaching the hostel at night, the lower part of the staff is washed clean of any dirt from the road, taken inside (unlike shoes or sandals, which are of course left outside) and placed in the most formal corner of the room, the *tokonoma*, where otherwise there might be a flower arrangement and a hanging picture scroll or calligraphy. The staff (*tsue*) is also known as a "diamond staff" (*kongōzue* 金剛杖), the diamond being a symbol of the absolute indestructability of enlightenment in Mahāyāna Buddhism and especially in Shingon Buddhism. Another line of thought, occasionally mentioned in ephemeral pamphlets, is that the staff represents a *stūpa*. But what is a *stūpa*? A *stūpa* marks the relics of a buddha, having originally been a mound or cairn. It is not surprising therefore that the *stūpa*, and hence the staff, is to be treated like the Buddha himself, or like Kōbō Daishi (O-Daishi-sama).

The third focus of meaning is the pilgrim's hat *sugegasa* 菅笠. In form it is traditional, and practical, being simply the same as a peasant's hat made of reeds (*suge*) used when working in fields. As a flattish cone it gives protection equally against sudden downpours of rain and against the beating sun. Of particular interest however are the phrases which are commonly painted on it. These are more testing than those on the white jacket. Apart from *saikoku junrei* (for example) giving the name of the pilgrimage, and *dōgyō ninin*, there is usually a verse in four lines which has been current in Shingon Buddhism and in Shugendō since mediaeval times. It runs:

迷故三界城	Through ignorance the three worlds are a prison
悟故十方空	Through enlightenment the ten directions are empty
本来無東西	Originally there is neither east nor west
何処有南北	Where then shall be south and north?[11]

Putting this idea in another way, the difficulty of finding the pathways to a multitude of goals is a transient matter indeed, being directions which human beings look around for in "the three worlds" of past, present and future, which will surely pass away. The real goal however is enlightenment, beyond all thoughts of the points of the compass. Of this the pilgrim's own hat is a constant, if paradoxical reminder.

On most such pilgrims' hats, which have become one of the most well-known symbols of the *henro* or circulatory pilgrimage, there are usually two more lines, which run:

Dōgyō ninin 同行二人 (as explained above)
Namu Daishi Henjō Kongō 南無大師遍照金剛
(Hail to Daishi, the Widely Shining Diamond)

In the Kannon routes Kōbō Daishi is not so emphasized, and so there may be something simpler such as:

Saikoku Junrei 西国順礼 (or in the older form: 西國順禮) which just means Saikoku Pilgrimage.

On a pilgrim's hat the four main lines are truly striking. In effect the pilg-

---

11. Writer's translation. Bohner translated: "Aus dem Irrtum die drei Welten / Aus dem Erwachen die zehntausend Himmel / Im Anfang war nicht Ost noch West / Wo war der Nord, wo war der Süd?" (Bohner 1931). I translate "originally there is..." rather than "was" because the non-being of east and west is a matter of their underlying ontological status, rather than a chronological one, and hence it is timeless and tenseless. This is the text in Gotō 1958 and so on, though variants may be found.

rim carries on his or her own head a perpetual question-mark about being a pilgrim. Even while going round a circuit of temples which is geographically defined, the pilgrims are reminded that the ten directions, like all the phenomena of existence including the various forms of human need and compassionate response, are empty. They are empty, that is, of that persistent thrust to existence which seems to drag living beings on into ever new variations of desire, attachment and suffering. Thus the pilgrim is led through the provisional experience of pilgrimage to an understanding of his or her own being in which these very same provisional forms are disarmed. Admittedly, the extent to which this may be true for any one pilgrim at any particular time along the pilgrimage is very hard to ascertain. As a line of interpretation it may therefore seem to be rather speculative. It is however reinforced by the message of the commonly used *Heart Sūtra*, which will be considered a little later. While the four key lines on the hat have attracted the attention of scholars before, it is surprising but true that their meaning is unfamiliar to quite a few people in Japan who themselves are not going on a pilgrimage. For the pilgrims however they certainly have an existential, if paradoxical relevance. They see them every time they put on their hat or take it off at the end of the day's temple visits.

Instructions for the route

The various guidebooks sometimes give suggestions as to the correct attitude to be adopted by pilgrims. Although these do not provide direct evidence about the pilgrims' subjective experience, they do indicate a certain mental orientation which is not difficult to aspire to and which is evidently taken to heart by many. This has already been touched on during the chapter on ritual behaviour, for there is a close connection. An older guidebook to the Shikoku route (Gotō 1958, but with at least one reprint) contains several pages of advice on these matters.[12] But here is a more recent, and widely distributed short list of recommendations on "the attitude of pilgrimage":

> Above all, chant the name of Kanzeon with deep faith (*shinjin*).
> Go round always only in the spirit of practice (*shugyō*).
> Do not kill any living things.
> Do not flirt with the opposite sex.
> Take medicines (and health insurance card) with you.
> Do not drink *sake*.
> Be humble and do not dispute with fellow pilgrims or others whom you meet.
> Travel lightly and do not carry too much money.
> Do not carry unnecessary luggage.

---

12. I came across this extremely interesting booklet when I was responsible for the Marburg Museum of Religions for a short period (1998-2000). Unfortunately its existence (or relevance) was unknown in the museum when I mounted the exhibition entitled *O-meguri* in Marburg (1987).

Take care to eat healthy food.
When taking up lodging, arrive in good time.
Do not leave your lodging at night time.
To avoid accidents, observe traffic rules.
To ensure the preservation of cultural assets, take care not to start any fire.
Observe the rules (opening times, off limits areas) of each temple which you visit.[13]

Observation suggests that the great majority of pilgrims do follow such suggestions. Internalized on a daily basis they provide a general foundation for more specifically religious discipline and reflections. In effect, they are a bit like instructions for meditation focused on the quietness and neutrality of the place selected for the purpose, and the physical preparedness of the person, on the basis of which meditation as such can take place.

At the very least, a distinction is urged, and largely upheld, between just going around as a tourist and going around as a pilgrim. The pilgrims are instructed to bow when passing through the main gate (*sanmon*) of the temple, and to rinse hands and mouth in the simple, but prescribed fashion at the water stand provided for the purpose. The meaning of this ritual is, simply enough, purification. It means that the dust and pollution of the roads outside are, once again, left behind for the duration of the visit to the temple. After this preparation the pilgrims perform the sequence of acts described in the previous chapter, and they do *not*, typically, go in for other touristic activity. For one thing they do not really have any extra time, but perhaps more importantly they have been encouraged to concentrate on their core actions and devotions, the candles, the recitations and so on. On the last occasion which I was able to observe, a group of pilgrims were travelling in rain all day, but it was quite evident that the attitude to their acts of devotion was completely unaffected by this adversity. It may be believed that although the borderlines may not be quite tightly drawn there is a real and strong sense in which pilgrims feel themselves to be pilgrims and not merely tourists.

The guidebooks are usually presented sequentially in the numbered order of the temples, and it is understood that one would normally visit the temples in that order. This might seem to lend itself to commentary which emphasizes psychological or spiritual growth or development. However indications of this are not so easy to find. On the contrary, there is a tendency for performance of the complete pilgrimage around the circuit to be seen as a single act, like bathing in the Ganges once in a lifetime, as one guidebook puts it.[14] Of course, this contradicts recommendations to go round as many times as possible, which is more typical

---

13. Hirahata's *Kamakura Sanjūsankasho* (1999), 7. This is found on the same page as the instructions on "how to worship" quoted in the previous chapter.
14. Settsukuni Hachijūhakkasho Reijōkai 1987, 3.

of the shorter pilgrimages. The slight emphasis given to the final temple of a series, or to a concluding visit to Mount Kōya in addition to the Shikoku 88, has been noted before, but this emphasis is related to the joy of completion of the whole route. The total degree of merit attained is now rounded out, so to speak, but its accumulation has been evenly spread over the visits to each and every temple on the way. On the whole the equal status of the various temples on any one route seems to operate as something of a brake on the idea of spiritual progress throughout the journey. The guides are simply not set out in a manner which suggests qualitative advance. Moreover the temples do not themselves promote messages to their visitors suggesting that they must be moving forward, at *this* particular temple, to a new stage of religious development.

The suggestive subtitle for one neatly produced series of guides produced by Yamada Eiji 山田英二 can be rendered "Journey from heart to heart," and of course "heart" (*kokoro*) is a term which is widely used to mean sincere, inward feeling. Here it implies a qualitative commitment to the journey, either for one's own sake or perhaps rather for the sake of others, living or dead. Yet it does not really suggest subjective change during the journey. An adult comic style is used for a complete companion to the Saikoku pilgrimage authored by Nagatani Kunio which was put on sale on April 17th (*taian*) 1991.[15] This tells the story of a husband and father who decides to go on a pilgrimage to the surprise and concern but eventually the delight of his family. In short, he returned a better person. Thus there is something of a transformational narrative here, though not one which is representative of a widespread type.

The pilgrims' seal books in some cases also function as mini-guides, giving the basic information for each temple on the right hand page and leaving the left hand page free for the seals and calligraphy. At the same time there is often a very short introduction or postscript which gives an interpretation of the pilgrimage. Such a book for the Sendai Kannon route makes mention of most of the points set out above, including reference to India and China as a general background, all under the heading of "the meaning of pilgrimage" (*junrei no igi* 巡礼の意義).[16]

Four stages in the Shikoku pilgrimage

There is one traditional conceptual pattern which suggests a structured progression in the pilgrim's personal religious development, and that is the idea that the Shikoku pilgrimage can be divided into four stages. It will be recalled (Chapter Three) that these four stages are correlated with the four traditional provinces of the island of Shikoku as follows:

---

15. A *taian* is a day of "great peace," one of the six types of day (*rokuyō*) which are thought by many in Japan to affect one's life for better or worse.

16. Cf. *O-meguri* 26.4.

Awa Province (temples 1–23)   *hosshin*: giving rise to the mind (of enlightenment)
Tosa Province (temples 24–39)   *shugyō*: discipline
Iyo Province (temples 40–65)   *bodai*: enlightenment (*bodai* = Sanskrit *bodhi*)
Sanuki Province (temples 66–88)   *nehan*: nirvana

These are the major stages in the development of a living being towards becoming a buddha. The most mysterious of these may seem to be *hosshin*. It refers to that deep point of resolve when a person conceives of the very idea of the pursuit of "supreme perfect enlightenment," to use a phrase which appears in the *Heart Sūtra*.[17] After setting out on the path of bodhisattvahood, with all its various stages to be mastered and perfections to be practised, it will be discovered that this in turn implies hard discipline (*shugyō*). While the journey may be hard, the pilgrim thinks not only of the temples already visited but of those which are still to come. In due course progress really does seem to be made, and thoughts may turn towards the wider purpose of it all. There may indeed have been a practical purpose, such as to pray for the health of a relative or for the success of some enterprise in the ordinary world. At the same time the atmosphere of the Buddhist temples must surely begin to work on the pilgrim, whose thoughts may turn towards the higher reaches of this religion. If he or she has "conceived the mind" of enlightenment, why should he or she not progress towards that goal? The famous phrase promoted by Kōbō Daishi himself will no doubt come to mind: "attaining Buddhahood in this very body" (*sokushin jōbutsu*). As completion of the pilgrimage is neared, the movement of travel which reflects the movement of life itself will find its peace. The very term *bodhisattva* includes the element *bodhi* meaning enlightenment, and the bodhisattva is a being who is on the point of realizing buddha-hood itself, which is completed by entry into the state of nirvana.

The Japanese term *shugyō* also requires some explanatory comment, for it arises not only in the context of our present theme of pilgrimage but refers also to any strenuous efforts in asceticism in the major denominations of Buddhism. It is especially characteristic of the Shugendō (or *yamabushi*) tradition, for example taking the form of arduous mountain climbing and leaning over perilous cliffs, or standing under cold and powerful waterfalls. These practices are usually undertaken with a view to the attainment of supernormal powers. Generally speaking supernormal powers are regarded in Buddhism as as a mere by-product of progress in the Buddhist way, and only to be used when compassion

---

17. The phrase in Sanskrit is *anuttara samyak sambodhi*, which is maintained in transliteration in the Chinese text for recitation. It is also frequent elsewhere.

demands. In Shugendō, which combines aspects of "esoteric" Shingon or Tendai Buddhism with traditional Shintō-related reverence for the power of mountains, there is a tendency to regard the attainment of such powers as worthwhile ends in themselves. This is not surprising considering the investment of effort involved in their procurement. Moreover, they are of practical value, it is commonly thought, in the areas of clairvoyance and healing. Ideally however, even in Shugendō the strengthening of inner character and spirituality should lead the adept into the higher reaches of Buddhist attainment. In real life, many pilgrims are not really ambitious when it comes to *shugyō*. They prefer to wear ordinary shoes and use regular means of transport. The more strenuous displays of pilgrimage, which involve going round very fast, and in some cases repeatedly, are left to semi-professionals, or would-be professionals, persons who might be getting ready to launch a new religious group under their own leadership.

Looking beyond *shugyō*, the third and fourth stages lie ahead as the real goals of Buddhism: enlightenment and nirvana. There is no expectation that "enlightenment" will suddenly occur at one or other of the temples in the third section, or that the pilgrim will enter a state of nirvana by the latest at temple Number 88. While *shugyō* can easily be understood as a temple by temple battle with physical circumstance, *bodai* and *nehan* are best understood as visions of what could be. They hold out a Buddhist resolution of religious striving which lies beyond the geography of pilgrimage.

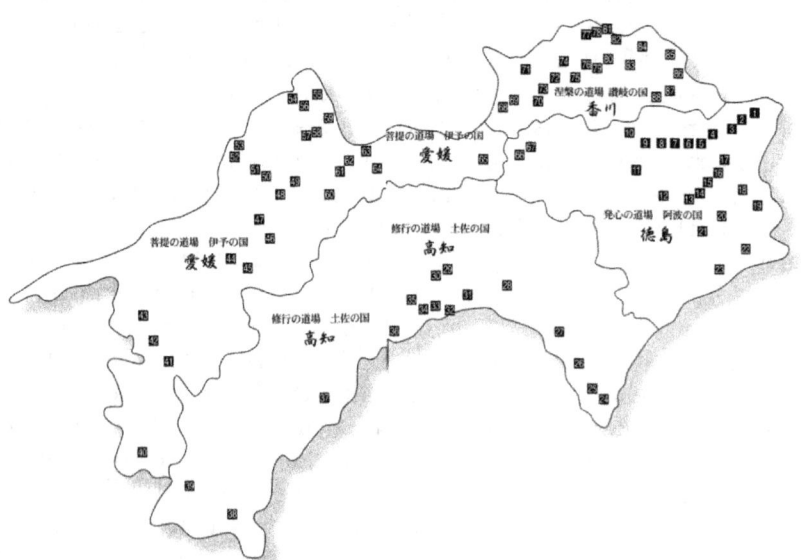

Figure 7.2 Map of the Shikoku pilgrimage showing four provinces and four spiritual stages.

The Meaning of Japanese Buddhist Pilgrimage

It has been seen (Chapter Three) that while the four stages of the Shikoku pilgrimage are usually brought in somehow, there is some question about their importance in the minds of pilgrims today. While they are referred to from time to time in guidebooks and ephemeral documents, they do not really seem to play as prominent a role in the spiritual development of pilgrims as might be imagined. Although I spoke with several hundred pilgrims in Shikoku in 1983, not one of them mentioned any of the four stages of progress, and Ian Reader's impressions just under a decade later seem to be consistent with this.[18] The negative evidence is quite indicative in that a conversation about where people are going, and why, is just about the most relaxed form of "interview" imaginable and therefore would easily allow for these stages to be mentioned if they were really important. External and ephemeral evidence for the four stages is also rather weak. The signposting of the temples along the way does not pick up this theme, and the pilgrims' slips and other accessories make no use of it. It is possible that the idea of the four stages has diminished in importance, and if so the question arises as to why. Two reasons come to mind. First, the use of modern transport has encouraged people to carry out the pilgrimage in sections convenient for the number of days available at any one time, and not necessarily following the numbered order of the temples. Hence the stages are not so compelling as they may once have been. Second, many people do not cherish enlightenment and nirvana as their goals to begin with. Rather, they are more concerned with health, the well-being of their families, in some cases repentance for errors committed, and the repose of their ancestors. These concerns are assured above all, it is felt, not by progress along the way, but by the *completion* of the route, and this can nowadays be achieved more quickly, giving less time for reflection and personal development. Nevertheless, the concept is there in the cultural tradition and seems to recur whenever convenient. Moreover there is a tendency for recent guidebooks to include it more prominently, and this itself is likely to have some impact on the pilgrims.[19] Reference to the four stages in a guide map to the miniature Shikoku pilgrimage at Mount Takao in Eastern Japan (noted in Chapter Three) has no practical purpose, since the route is short, and so, just like the prominence given to the *Heart Sūtra* in the same source it can only make sense as a recommendation to entertain the possibility of a personal transformation. Whatever the varying influence of the idea of these four stages from time to time, it is certainly not just a recent one and is available in the tradition for reflective intepretations when these are sought.

---

18. Reader 2005, 54ff.
19. Reader notes that these four stages are probably a more or less modern construction, while not failing to adopt it in his own listing of the temples (Reader 2005, 52 ff. 273ff.).

Buddhist recitations

It is often assumed that in Buddhism the main form of systematic activity is meditation, but from an early date this has not in fact been so. The recitation or chanting of texts has been a regular aspect of Buddhist practice as far back as this can be traced at all. Without chanting there would be no structured oral tradition and hence no written Buddhist canon as we know it. The main texts chanted in Buddhism are *sūtras* or portions of *sūtras*, a Buddhist *sūtra* being purportedly (but historically speaking not literally) a teaching uttered by the Buddha himself on some specific occasion. In practical religious contexts the *sūtras* are usually accompanied by short verses of an introductory or ancillary kind. Needless to say, these *sūtra* portions and other verses are of the utmost importance in articulating the general perspective of meaning entertained by the pilgrims who use them. The folding devotional booklets used by pilgrims contain a number of standard devotions for recitation. The many variations depend on the denominational orientation or on local decisions taken prior to printing. At the same time there is a general affinity between them all. The booklets on sale at the temples in Shikoku for example, the majority of which are of the Shingon denomination, are very similar to each other. In some cases, in spite of the fact that reproduction is supposedly prohibited, they seem to be pirated editions which are merely printed in different covers, sometimes in different colours. Usually the pilgrim carries a little folding book of devotional texts of this kind. The two key texts to be found in them are the *Heart Sūtra* and the *Kannon Sūtra*, the latter often being abbreviated to the verse part alone. Depending on the particular pilgrimage, other texts are included relating to particular buddhas or other figures to be revered such as Fudō or Jizō. These folding booklets are in principle no different from those which are used in any Buddhist temple services or in devotions before the Buddhist house altars (*butsudan*) which are so widespread in Japan. In the more substantial booklets, the contents vary significantly according to denomination, the *sūtras* presumed to be of greatest importance for the teaching of that denomination being given pride of place. The pilgrim is more likely to be carrying a specialized booklet devised for the route in question, containing not only the texts mentioned but also the special "songs" (*go-eika*) which relate to each individual temple. An appropriate *wasan* (a hymn-like song in occasional use) may also be included: *Fudō-wasan, Jizō-wasan, Zenkōji-wasan*, and so on.

Also very ancient is the practice of chanting very short, slogan-like utterances. There are two Sanskrit terms for such utterances. One term is *dhāraṇi* –or *darani* if transliterated simply from the Japanese. This is usually translated as "spell," and in general it may be said that such spells have a more or less magical quality in that they are directed towards the control of a world external to the person who utters them. The other type, better known in the western world, is the *mantra*. This has a more meditational function, for it addresses the buddha or bodhisattva in the mind of the practitioner, leading to their unity or identity. However, it must be said that in Japanese Buddhism the borderline between the two supposedly differentiable types is not always very clear in practice. The *shingon* (or "true words") of Shingon Buddhism have some of the features of both types (see examples below). Some *dhāraṇi* consist of meaningless syllables, and this emphasizes their spell-like quality. Others, however, do have some meaning. In the case of the "spell" at the end of the *Heart Sūtra* (see below), there is some ambivalence in this regard, for although it has no meaning in Japanese, it does (or from a modern Japanese point of view *did*) have a meaning in Sanskrit. Recitation booklets are more likely to contain *dhāraṇi* or *shingon* if they are oriented towards Shingon Buddhism.

Finally, we should not overlook the associations of the individual names of the temples in Japan.[20] The lists shown in this book may seem rather obscure to the general reader, yet the characters used to write them are full of doctrinal and devotional associations. To give a parallel from western religions, it is rather like looking at numerous names of churches such as Holy Trinity, St. Peter and St. Paul, Church of the Holy Cross, Our Lady of West Lake, Christ the King, and so on. Unfortunately it would disrupt the concept of this book to explain all the temple names which occur here. However many include the name Kannon, and others terms such as *bodai* (enlightenment) and elements such as *jō*, *jaku* or *an*, meaning "peaceful," *hokke* meaning "dharma flower" (i.e. lotus), *nen* as in *nenbutsu*, or *gan* meaning "aspiration." One reason why the characters have been included in the lists in this book is so that those who know Japanese or are learning it will pick up some of these associations. They are certainly significant in shaping the mentality of the pilgrims, who see them again and again.

There now follow some of the typical contents of the recitation booklets in widespread use. First of all there are various short texts which are commonly used to introduce and conclude recitation at the temples. In some of the following examples a short explanatory note has been added beneath the text. It should be remembered that in Japanese these booklets are always printed vertically. Following the most typical opening and closing verses, some examples of the *darani* or *shingon* are given which are typical of the Shingon-shū booklets in particular. Booklets geared to other denominations, or of a more general character, are not likely to include them. Somewhere between the introductory and concluding texts would normally be found the *Kannon Sūtra* and the *Heart*

---

20. Cf. Seckel 1985 for a substantial book on the subject. Unfortunately, while the thematic explanations are valuable, the arrangement is cumbersome and it is not possible to use it as a direct reference work for looking up temple names.

Sūtra, but in view of their moderate length and widespread importance the main treatment of these will follow on afterwards. In addition, brief notes are offered on two special kinds of text which are particularly suitable for the pilgrimage situation, namely devotional songs known as *wasan* and the short "songs" for each temple (*go-eika*).

Kaikyōge
Verses for Opening the Sūtra

Unsurpassed, profound and mysterious Dharma
Difficult to meet with, even in a thousand million ages
This we now see and hear, receive and hold fast
Aspiring to understand the true meaning of Nyorai.

These lines, Verses for Opening the Sūtra, are sometimes found at a later point in the booklets, immediately before the *Heart Sūtra*, because it is indeed the *sūtra* in question. However they often appear at the very beginning of the whole booklet, followed by the other verses presented below, even though these are not a *sūtra* in the strict sense of a text pronounced by the Buddha himself. In such a case it shows that we are looking ahead to the *Heart Sūtra* which is being regarded as the main focus of the whole devotional exercise.

The standard heading is sometimes written out as *Kaikyō no ge* ("verse of opening the *sūtra*") which fits it more easily into modern Japanese syntax. The verse is printed in four lines of seven characters or two lines of fourteen characters. The Dharma, sometimes, but rather misleadingly translated as "Law," is the teaching of a Buddha, which can only be met with very rarely indeed. In fact it can only be heard when a Buddha has recently come into the world, which is traditionally said to occur less frequently than the flowering of the *udumbara*, a mysterious plant indeed. An age is a "kalpa," a Sanskrit term which is often transliterated and not used in normal Japanese. As already seen, the designation Nyorai is familiar in the names of specific buddhas or *tathāgatas*, for example in Dainichi Nyorai (Vairocana Tathāgata), and the "true meaning" referred to here signifies the mysterious, transcendent departure of a Buddha from all the entanglements of karma. In short, it means that the pilgrim is promising to try to understand the nature of Buddhahood by means of the *Heart Sūtra*, which is soon to be recited.

Zangemon
Words of repentance

The bad deeds which I have done hitherto
Arise from time inconceivable and from greed, anger and stupidity
In accordance with body, speech and mind, which bring them forth
Of all of these I now repent.

The Meaning of Japanese Buddhist Pilgrimage

Figure 7.3 Dainichi Nyorai as illustrated in a guidebook.

This heading is sometimes written out as *Zange no mon* ("words of repentance"), which as in the last case, fits it more easily into modern Japanese syntax. For *zange* we also find *sange*, both pronunciations often being indicated in *hiragana* script. The title can also be found as *Sange-ge*, the second *ge* meaning "verse" (the usual translation for Sanskrit *gātha*). The word "bad" used here stands for *aku*, which is often translated in Buddhist texts as "evil." A certain problem arises because the pair *zen-aku* is usually translated smoothly as "good and evil," but in some cases this can lead to questions about the nature of "evil" which are not appropriate to the Buddhist context. The word "evil" is therefore better avoided. Western readers in particular should note that while the term "sin" is not used in Buddhism, there is certainly regular reference to "bad deeds," and the contrast which is sometimes made with Christianity should therefore not be exaggerated. "Greed, anger and stupidity" are otherwise known as "the three poisons." It might be thought that people cannot help being stupid, if their mental facility is not great, but in this context it implies not mere lack of endowment, which itself is not reprehensible, but a *willed* or obstinate stupidity.

Sanki
Three refuges
This disciple (add name here) from now on into all future time
Takes refuge in the Buddha
Takes refuge in the Dharma
Takes refuge in the Sangha

These are the three refuges common to all historic forms of Buddhism.

Sankyō
Three realms
This disciple (add name here) from now on into all future time
Enters the realm of the Buddha
Enters the realm of the Dharma
Enters the realm of the Sangha

The meaning of "realm" (the character also means "boundary") is that after "taking refuge" the disciple or pilgrim is identified as passing through into the realm of the Buddha, the Dharma and the Sangha respectively. As explained orally, the understanding is that it repeats the taking of the three refuges more emphatically and conclusively.

Jūzenkai
Ten precepts
Whoever is a disciple
[Must] through all future time
Not kill living beings
Not steal
Not be sexually incorrect
Not tell lies
Not speak maliciously
Not speak harshly
Not use a double tongue
Not be greedy
Not be angry
Not hold wrong views

The term *jūzenkai* means literally "ten good rules," and some variant formulations may be found.

After these various opening verses there usually follow one or two preferred *sūtra* texts. The *sūtra* for Kannon Bosatsu, popularly known as the *Kannongyō*, is often abbreviated to the verse sections, while the *Heart Sūtra* always occurs in full because it is very short and there are no verses. One may also find others, such as a *sūtra* on Fudō Myōō (see also below) or the shortest of the three *sūtras* relating to Pure Land Buddhism, the *Amida-kyō*, which contains a description of the Pure Land in the West. The choice will depend on the denominational orientation of the pilgrim and the particular pilgrimage being undertaken.

Then may follow the suggestion that a *wasan* relating to a particular bodhisattva, such as Jizō, could be inserted, at the pilgrim's discretion. The booklets usually conclude with a dedication, as follows.

Ekō
Dedication
We pray that this merit may be spread far and wide so that we and all living beings may together realize the Buddha-way.

The term *ekō* is sometimes translated, or rather explained, as the "transfer of merit." A similar verse which is more likely to be found in Shingon booklets than elsewhere runs:

Sanrikige
Verse on the three powers
By the power of my own merits, the power of the assisting grace of the tathāgatas, and the power of the whole realm of Dharma, I abide in widely spread reverence.

Shingon Buddhism provides a context for this because it has a relatively strong emphasis on the idea of achieving merits by one's own strong practice. However Shingon booklets also use the more widely current *ekō* verse. By "reverence" is meant here the somewhat elastic concept of "offering reverence" (*kuyō*) to buddhas and various deceased beings who might need it.

While the above texts will mostly be found in booklets from various denominations, the following *shingon* are typical, as the word implies, of Shingon Buddhism. However, Esoteric Tendai Buddhism (*tendai mikkyō* or *taimitsu*) also makes use of *shingon*. Here are some typical examples of *shingon*.

Hotsubodaishin shingon
The true word of aspiring to the mind of enlightenment
On bōjishatta boda hadayami

Sanmayakai shingon
The true word of the *sanmaya* rule
Onsanmaya satoban

Fukuyō shingon
The true word of widely spread reverence
On abokya hojamani handoma bajirei tatagyata birokitei sanmanda harasaraun

The *Shingon seiten* (a Shingon service book) explains that this may be added when lighting incense or lights, or placing flowers, the merits being offered to all the buddhas.

Gohonzon shingon
There is no specific text here because in the recitation booklet being fol-

lowed at this point we read that one may insert the *shingon* of the main buddha of a particular temple, that is, its *gohonzon*. "It may be repeated as often as one's heart may wish." It is quite likely to be one of the Thirteen Buddhas, see next.

Jūsanbutsu no shingon
Shingon of the thirteen Buddhas
Fudō Myōō: *Nōmaku sanmanda bazara dan kan, etc.*

As these syllables have no literal meaning they are not all written out in full here. The *shingon* for Fudō, shown above, is a short Shingon version, and the Tendai version varies from it. A longer Shingon variant runs: *Nōmaku sanmanda bazara dan senda makaro shada sowataya untarata kanman.* The list usually continues with Shaka Nyorai, Monju Bosatsu, and so on down to Kokūzō Bosatsu. For the Thirteen Buddhas, see also Chapter Four above.

Kōmyō shingon
The true word of shining brightness
(to be repeated three times, seven times, or twenty-one times)
On abokya beiroshanō makabodaramani handoma jinbara harabaritaya un

This is apparently *not* understood to be the *shingon* of a particular buddha. In one recitation book it precedes a position for silent "prayer in the heart."

Finally, a special place must be found for the:

Go-hōgō 御宝号 (or Daishi hōgō 大師宝号)
The honourable treasure-name (of the Great Teacher Kōbō Daishi)
Namu Daishi Henjōkongō

This is the same phrase which often appears on ephemera such as pilgrims' slips deposited at temples, or on the pilgrim's shirt or hat, especially in the context of the Shikoku pilgrimage. Here it is usually repeated three times at the main hall and three times at the Daishi hall, thus making a grand total of 528 times, at least. The posthumous "treasure name" of Kūkai is Kōbō 弘法, the literal meaning of which is "Broad Dharma." With Kōbō Daishi the question of meaning becomes multi-layered. He is revered as the supposed founder of the Shikoku pilgrimage, and as the spiritual companion of the pilgrims as they go round. He is also the authoritative spiritual leader for all entrance into the particular mysteries of Shingon Buddhism. Because of these roles he becomes in many people's minds a supernatural divinity alongside the other Buddhist celestial powers, and consequently one of those who is considered competent to provide benefits. This can be illustrated with a rather large paper amulet (Figure 7.4 below) which shows Kōbō Daishi in his normal portrait position on his teaching chair, with a stylized Sanskrit letter A emerging from a lotus flower.[21] The text in between tells us that it is from temple Number 14 (Kanjizaiji), in Awa province, and then in the larger characters proclaims Kūkai to be Yakuyoke Daishi, that is the "great teacher who wards off bad fortune." So the amulet carries a signification at the level of transactional religion, while also purveying the symbols which would take the believer further into a Shingon Buddhist orientation.

The *shingon* are most frequently shown in syllabic writing, but in older times they were also written in Chinese characters which were used to transliterate Sanskrit terms. To illustrate, here is a *shingon* for Kannon as Jūichimen Kannon, from a small recitation booklet which specifically contains a short *sūtra* devoted to its revelation (see Figure 7.5 below):

On ma ka kya ro ni kya so wa ka
唵 摩 訶 迦 盧 尼 迦 沙 波 訶

In the original booklet, dating from 1881, the slightly older orthography makes the *shingon* look even more determined or even fearsome, than as shown here. In the booklet it is also emphasized that this is the truly correct form of the *shingon*, being the one given in the middle of the "*sūtra*" itself. The original printing is, as in most of the older booklets, vertical. The full title of the *sūtra* is *Bussetsu Jūichimen Kanzeon Bosatsu zuigan sokutoku darani kyō*, which tells us that the *darani* brings immediate advantages in accordance with the vow of the Bodhisattva Kanzeon. These are detailed in the text along the lines of the salvific promises set out in the *Lotus Sūtra* (see further below), from which it is evidently ultimately derived. Thanks are due to an otherwise unidentifiable citizen of Ōsaka, Mr. Yamada Shōsuke, who donated this booklet to all people of faith.

Sūtras, wasan and go-eika

Other significant texts include the *sūtra*s which are short enough to be recited by pilgrims who have little time, hymns of praise (*wasan*) to particular divinities and the temple songs (*go-eika*).

At this point the *sūtra* element can be illustrated with a very short *sūtra* about Fudō Myōō, known as the *Bussetsu shōfudōkyō*, i.e. "The Sūtra on the Holy Fudō, Proclaimed by the Buddha."

> At that time there was a bright king in the great assembly. This great bright king possesses great powers. On account of the virtue of his great compassion he appears in a blue-black form. On account of the virtue of his great concentration he is seated on a rock of diamond. On account of his great wisdom he displays himself in a halo of fire.

---

21. This amulet was previously inserted for purely illustrative purposes into Beatrice Lane Suzuki's *Buddhist Temples of Kyōto and Kamakura* 2013 (edited by the present writer), 123.

Figure 7.4 Paper amulet showing Kōbō Daishi in traditional pose.

Wielding the sword of great wisdom he cuts through desire, anger and foolishness. Holding the rope of concentration, he binds what is hard to lay low. Raising the mind of non-characteristics, and with a body like empty space, he has no abiding. He only deigns to reside in the imagination of living beings. As the conceptions of living beings are diverse, so, in accordance with their thoughts, he produces benefits for them which completely fulfil what they seek. At that time, on hearing this *sūtra* expounded, there was great joy among the multitude, and they trustingly received and revered it.

A few notes may be added on this text. The expression "bright king" is *myōō*, as found in the name of Fudō Myōō, and the brightness is that of illumination as opposed to ignorance. Desire, anger and foolishness are sometimes referred to as the three poisons. Concentration is *sanmai* (三昧, also read *zanmai*), while the rope, being the decisive weapon of a hunts-

The Meaning of Japanese Buddhist Pilgrimage

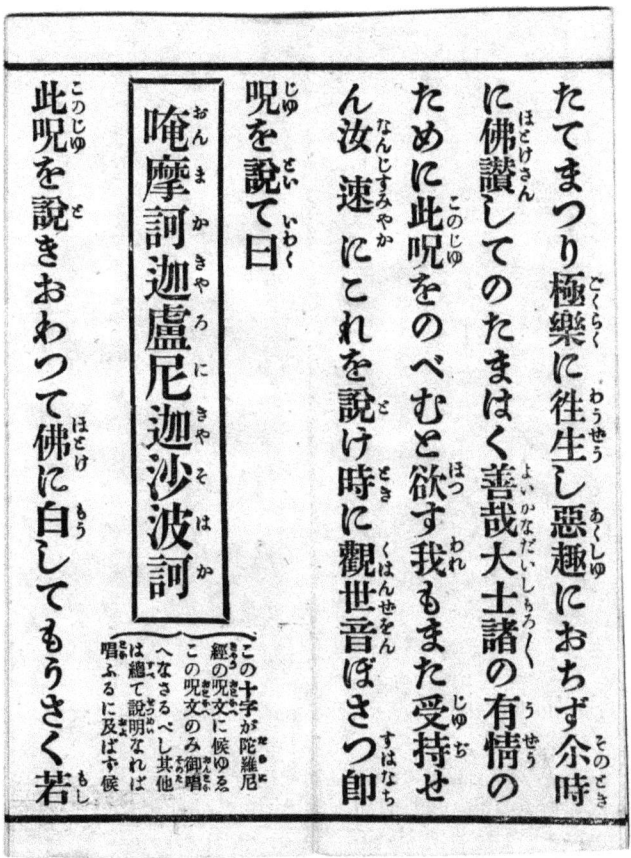

Figure 7.5 A shingon formula (mantra) in a book of pilgrim's devotions.

man who can catch elusive prey,[22] is brought in to imply the power which can go forth from meditative concentration. We see here a combination of the promise of "benefits," using a term which –as will not escape the pilgrims' notice– also appears in the concept of "this-worldly benefits," with the idea that Fudō himself is a being who does not "abide" anywhere, or need anything. This is because he is free from the three poisons, and has achieved the consciousness of non-characteristics, that is, of not being attached to characteristics. Nevertheless he can be represented for living beings, and can reside in their hearts and minds. Indeed, he only deigns to reside in their imaginations, for otherwise he does not abide. This short text is preserved in the Chinese Buddhist canon, but will also be found in Japanized forms, as for example in a booklet called *Reijō junpai shokyō yōshū*, a "collection of all the *sutras* needed for going round the spiritual

---

22. Cf. the rope of Fukūkensaku Kanzeon, Kanzeon of the Rope of Sure Deliverance (Chapter Two).

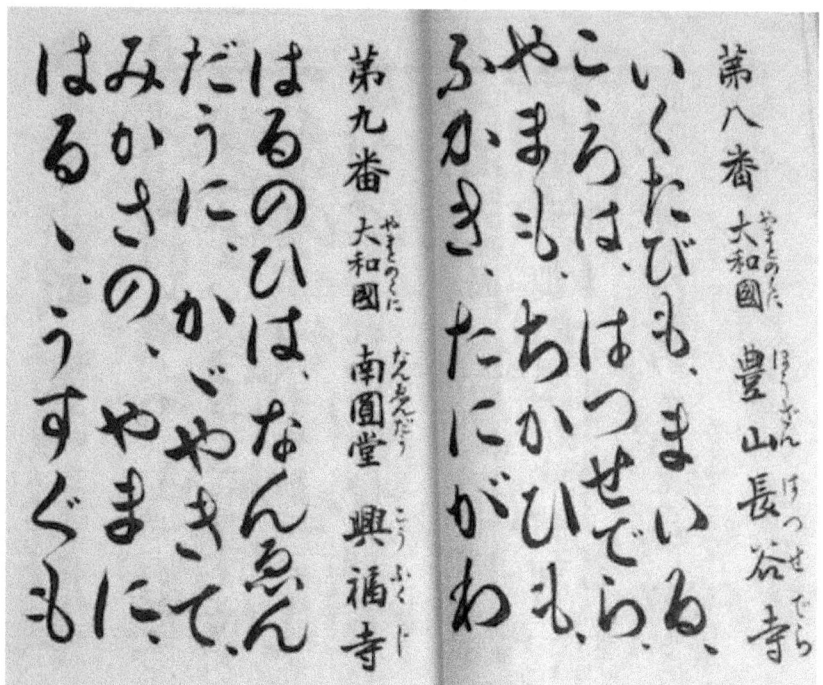

Figure 7.6 Traditional book of the Saikoku *go-eika*, opened at temples 8 and 9.

sites." In such versions, the verbs are interpreted in the present tense, because Fudō Myōō is present in the imagination of the pilgrims now. This is followed in the translation here, except for the opening and closing lines which are standard *sūtra* formulations. The latter are usually understood as being in the past tense, because the *sūtra* is supposed to be something which the Buddha taught at such and such a time. This typically Mahāyāna text was of course not really proclaimed by the historical Buddha, but that is of no importance for the pilgrims. They are interested in Fudō Myōō now.

The short poetic texts or songs known as *go-eika* have been mentioned several times already, and of course these add a further context of meaning, though usually a somewhat diffuse one. Traditionally they have been written or printed in phonetic script (*hiragana*), which is appropriate for traditional Japanese verse, and fine for singing. In modern guides some Chinese characters (*kanji*) are included to bring out the meaning and thus make them easier for modern readers to understand. They are composed in *waka* form, that is, they consist of two parts of seventeen plus fourteen syllables. The seventeen can be further divided into 5+7+5 and the fourteen into 7+7. Consider the *go-eika* of Jōzenji, the Jizō temple of Kuramaguchi referred to in Chapter Four:

The Meaning of Japanese Buddhist Pilgrimage

> *Yado kaete mizoro mo ima ya kuramaguchi*
> *Irikuru hito wo michibiki ni keri*
> A change of lodging, from former Mizoro to present Kuramaguchi,
> All who come in here are given guidance on their way.

Since Jizō Bosatsu was only moved to Kuramaguchi during the Meiji Period, this song must be from the nineteenth century. Many *go-eika* are considerably older however, and their pedigree can hardly be traced. The contents are a far cry from the formal Buddhist texts, and help to provide a feeling that there is some kind of Japanese cultural accompaniment. This is why images of the landscape or other local associations so often play a part, as in the example of Hasedera's *go-eika* already quoted in the previous chapter. Two further examples from the Saikoku Kannon Pilgrimage.

> For temple Number 1:
> *Fudaraku ya kishi utsu nami wa mikumano no*
> *Nachi no o-yama ni hibiku takitsuse*
> Fudaraku and the waves beating on the shore, echoed
> By the waterfalls and torrents in the mountains of Nachi of Mi-kumano.

Nachi, in Kumano, is known as the place of the highest waterfall of Japan, which streams down powerfully yet elegantly, and is regularly honoured by Shintō priests. The first temple of the Saikoku Thirty-three is immediately adjacent to the main shrine of Nachi, in the hills. The shrine itself is announced to this day on its main *torii* (the symbolic gateway) as the shrine of Kumano Gongen (*avatar*). This is one of the three shrines of Kumano, referred to here as *mi-kumano*. Down below near the sea-shore is the temple where, in olden times, the abbot was ritually set adrift in a sealed boat for his last journey, to Fudaraku (otherwise known as Hodaraku), a mythical Pure Land.

> For temple Number 5:
> *Mairu yori tanomi wo kakuru Fujiidera*
> *hana no utena ni murasaki no kumo*
> The entreaties made on our visit are enfolded by Fujiidera,
> Just as we see a purple cloud cradled in the wisteria flowers.

Literally, the purple cloud is in the "calyces" (*utena*) of the flowers, just as floating in the calyx of a lotus blossom is a metaphor for being in the bliss of a Buddhist heaven. The name of the temple itself includes the Japanese word for wisteria (*fuji*), which therefore does not need to be repeated in the second part of the Japanese text. The wisteria blooms at this temple are at their best in early May. Modern guidebooks are likely to include a photograph of the superb blossom, but at other times of the year it is just an association.

For temple Number 19:
> Hana wo mite ima wa nozomi mo
> Kōdō no niwa no chigusamo sakari naruran
> Seeing the flowers, our hopes will flourish now,
> And so too, in the garden of the Kōdō, will a thousand plants.

The formal name of this temple is Gyōganji, but it is also known as the Kōdō, as it is referred to in this song.

We turn now to a type of text which figures in some of the booklets, namely the *wasan* 和讃, meaning a "Japanese song of praise," i.e. one which was originally composed in Japanese as opposed to the formal Chinese (*kanbun*) of the *sūtras*. The *wasan* is a significant form of devotional piety, and some more details on these will be given further below. These have an old tradition. Several well-known *wasan* were composed by Shinran (1173-1263) to sum up salient points of his teaching (that of the Jōdo Shinshū) in an accessible and memorizable form, and these are used to this day, though the Japanese of course no longer seems at all modern. Other *wasan* of uncertain provenance and pedigree are directed towards particular bodhisattvas or divinities, as may be seen in titles such as *Jizō wasan* or *Benzaiten wasan*. Particular denominations may have a preferred *wasan* such as the *Shingon anjin wasan*, a hymn for settling the mind (*anjin*).

Three *wasan* contained in a booklet for the Saikoku and related pilgrimages (*Shokoku reijō sanjūsansho shobutsu eika shū*), which mainly contains the regular *go-eika*, are as follows.

(i) *Sai no kawara Jizō wasan*

There are various *Jizō wasan* and in this case the term *kawara* draws attention to the dried bed of a river in which stones are piled up to commemorate *mizuko*, i.e. children lost through miscarriage or abortion. Though demons may knock them over in the night, Jizō is said to come around and pick them up again. The *wasan* concludes with the acclamation of Jizō of Long Life: "Namu Enmei Jizō Daibosatsu."

(ii) *Enkō Daishi Kurodani wasan*

The title of this *wasan* refers to Hōnen Shōnin (here named Enkō Daishi) and refers to the temple of Kurodani where Hōnen resided after leaving the Tendai centre on Mount Hiei. This temple, named Konkaikōmyōji, is number 24 in the Twenty-five Spiritual Places of Hōnen Shōnin referred to in Chapter Four and on the pilgrim's scroll described in Chapter Six. The *wasan* tells of the fleeting nature of human life and the consequent importance of the *nenbutsu* which alone can assist us. The *wasan* is recommended in a booklet for pilgrims, but according to informants is used mainly on special occasions, for example at meetings of a *wasan* association held in the temple.

The Meaning of Japanese Buddhist Pilgrimage

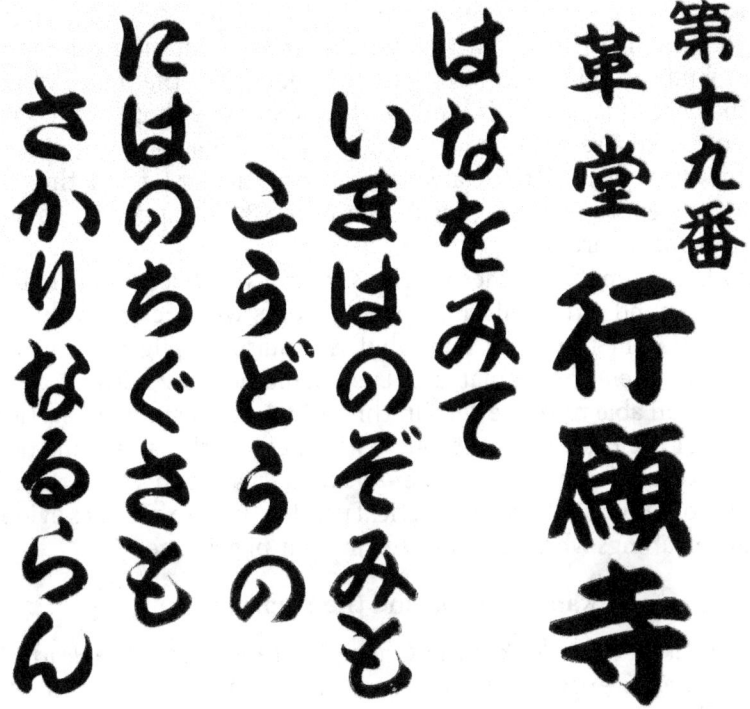

Figure 7.7 Handwritten pilgrim's song pinned on temple entrance of Saikoku No. 19.

(iii) *Nachisan betsugan wasan*

The title of this *wasan*, "Special Aspiration at Mount Nachi" recalls the location of temple Number One of the Saikoku pilgrimage route, Seigan-toji, of which the *go-eika* was given just above. It opens with the statement that Kanzeon (Kannon) appeared at the great waterfall of Nachi and its shrine in order to help all people in the world of suffering.

Of course, not all *wasan* have a direct relation to pilgrimage. The culturally influential Rinzai monk Hakuin (1689-1796) composed a *wasan* on *zazen*, beginning with the impressive words "Living beings are buddhas from the beginning. Just as, with water and ice, there is no ice apart from water, so there are no buddhas apart from living beings."[23] While this is included in a collection of texts for the use of anybody interested in Rinzai Zen, we should remember that various Rinzai temples are numbered among the temples of the pilgrim routes. It is difficult to draw sharp lines here.

Another short folding text entitled *Bodai wasan*, with the longer title of *Hotsubodaishin kūkenshō* inside it, was published by an individual person

---

23. Translated from a modern Rinzai *sūtra* booklet from 2001 (Zen bunka kenkyūsho, Hanazono Daigaku), which refers to the *wasan* as *Hakuin Zenji Zazen wasan*.

in Ōsaka for the benefit of his ancestors, that is, for their attainment of enlightenment.[24] The text, with a Zen Buddhist orientation, refers to the "pure land" as being within us and concludes with the image of punting the boat of *hannya* (wisdom) until we reach the shore of nirvana. It is mentioned here because it is analogous to a book of pilgrims' *go-eika* which was dedicated to the ancestors of a particular person, thus illustrating the endless overlapping details of the Buddhist culture in which the pilgrimages are set.

To what extent do all these various texts give evidence of what goes on in the mind of the pilgrims? The booklets which contain them are extremely numerous, and many but not quite all pilgrims carry one along with them for regular use. Even some of those without a booklet are often able to recite certain things by heart, especially particular *shingon*, or the *Heart Sūtra*, although others evidently cannot and do not try. On balance, it may be confidently stated that the booklets are sufficiently common, and in such practical use, for them to count as evidence for the meanings which pilgrims see in their pilgrimage.

Kannon-sama and the *Kannon Sūtra*

We now take a closer look at the *Kannon Sūtra* and then at the *Heart Sūtra*, both of which are of central importance in the pilgrim tradition. Although the bodhisattva Avalokiteśvara was originally presumed to be male in ancient India, the Chinese form Guānyīn eventually took on more feminine characteristics and was mainly brought in such a form, via Korea, to Japan. Guānyīn, in Japanese Kannon, is also known as Kanzeon, this being the form of her name which actually appears in the most important, and popular *sūtra* in which she occurs, the *Lotus Sūtra*. In Kumārajīva's Chinese version of this *sūtra*, which is the one in common use, Kanzeon is the subject of Chapter 25. This chapter is itself frequently regarded as a *sūtra* in its own right, and is so known as the *Kannongyō*. Kannon-sama also appears as Kanjizai in the introductory lines of the *Heart Sūtra*. But Kanzeon and Kanjizai are simply accepted as slightly mysterious alternatives to the ubiquitously popular name Kannon-sama. Kannon-sama is by far the most prominent among all the buddhas and bodhisattvas in the devotion of pilgrims. Kannon-sama may be set up in the temples of almost any denomination, and it has already been noted that she is quite popular in the Zen Buddhist tradition. She even appears in the relatively exclusive tradition of Shin Buddhism as one of the two companions of Amida Buddha, though the temples of this tradition play no part in the usual pilgrimage circuits.

---

24. No date, but the printing shows that it is from the first half of the twentieth century.

The main iconographic figures of Kanzeon, or Kannon, were already introduced in Chapter Two. Let us recall that while the formal designations of the images are diverse, Jūichimen Kanzeon, Nyoirin Kanzeon, etc., these are all, for the pilgrim, simply Kannon-sama. This may reasonably be compared with the way in which devotion to the Virgin Mary works out in Catholic culture. Very often, devotion is couched in terms of a particular appearance of Mary such as La Virgen de Guadalupe in Mexico, or Nossa Senhora Aparecida in Brazil, to mention merely two which are of great importance in Latin America, or indeed others which emphasize a particular function such as "consolation." These forms all bring Mary close to the local identities and religious sensibilities of the people. But at the same time it is always the same Mary, just the Virgin Mary. The situation is quite comparable in the case of Kannon-sama. The well-known iconographic forms, being fewer in number than the thirty-three forms referred to in the Kannon chapter of the *Lotus Sūtra*, are representations which are known to be, paradoxically, at once prominent in the imagination and secondary as regards the deeper reference. In the innumerable temples of Japan other forms will also be found, some of great antiquity and some more modern. More recently we find statues of a Kannon-sama who is able to provide assistance with an easy birth, or we find her as Mizuko Kuyō Kannon who, like Jizō Bosatsu, cares for infants lost through miscarriages or abortions. Another common theme is Kannon-sama holding a fish, displaying her ability to help in getting a good catch. This "Gyoran Kannon" is traditional but has now become a general good-luck theme displayed on hanging scrolls and so on. A notable recent form is Heiwa Kannon, or Peace Kannon, reflecting the widespread desire since the end of World War II simply to be blessed with political peace in the world. One of these has been set up in recent times in the beautiful gardens of the Rinzai Zen temple Tenryūji at Arashiyama, Kyōto. These may all be seen as varying versions of Kannon-sama which reflect the different needs of the people, which is just how this bodhisattva is presented in the Kannon chapter of the *Lotus Sūtra*. But all of these forms, whether ancient or modern, are representations of one and the same Kannon-sama. If there is any difference between Kannon-sama and the Virgin Mary in this respect it is that the concept of Kannon-sama's adoption of appropriate forms has been consciously articulated in the text of *The Kannon Sūtra* itself. How far this is appropriated depends on the general education and reflective ability of the individual devotees.

Kannon-sama is brought close to the people in many ways, recently for example in comic-style children's books. An example from the well-known publishing house Aoyama Shoin contains a number of moralizing stories in comic form with an evidently seriously Buddhist didactic intent. It includes the text of the Kannon Chapter of the *Lotus Sūtra* in

Japanese translation and a postcript "for mothers" which recommends both faith (*shinkō*) in Kannon-sama and the pilgrimage of the thirty-three temples dedicated to her. To reinforce this identification the thirty-three temples are listed with an indication of their different types of Kannon statue, their addresses, a map showing their whereabouts in the Kinki region of Japan, instructions on how to get there and the *go-eika* of each temple.[25]

The connection between this-worldly benefits and other-worldly perspectives is worked out through the figure of Kannon-sama with particular transparency. As it says in the conclusion of a pamphlet about the Edo Kannon pilgrimage circuit, "Hail to Kanzeon who gives us peace and safety in this world and in the world hereafter." While the teaching of Buddhism in general addresses the problem of suffering and its resolution, as famously in the four noble truths, we see in this instance a dialectic between what people want in terms of the reduction of suffering here and now, and what is best for them in a further perspective. This dialectic, which is particularly characteristic of Mahāyāna Buddhism, is clearly articulated in the figure of Kannon-sama, as may be seen in the text of the *Lotus Sūtra* itself.

Chapter 25 of the *Lotus Sūtra*, entitled "The Chapter of the Widely Open Gate" (J. *Fumonbon* 普門品)[26] includes both prose and verse, but the recitation books often include only the verses and these alone are referred to simply as the *Kannon Sūtra* (*Kannongyō*). The result is that pilgrims do not necessarily have a precise idea of what is in the full text of the *sūtra*. Before looking at the verses, it may be recalled that it is the prose section which contains reference to the thirty-three ways in which the bodhisattva could appear for the salvation of many different kinds of beings. These are listed in patterns such as: "To those who are to be saved by the form of Brahma, he teaches the Dharma by changing himself into the form of Brahma," or "To those who are to be saved by the form of a householder, he teaches the Dharma by changing himself into the form of a householder," or "To those who are to be saved by the form of a wife of a rich man, a householder, a state official or a brahmin, he teaches the Dharma by changing himself into the form of a such a wife."[27] It is notable that many of the forms listed are those of Indian divinities or of

---

25. *Manga Saikoku Sanjūsan Fudasho—Kannon Junrei*, Tokyo (Aoyama Shoin) date and editor unknown.

26. In full: "The chapter of the widely open gate of the Bodhisattva Kanzeon." Other translations will be found. This is chapter 25 according to the Chinese counting. The Bodhisattva is usually referred to as Avalokiteśvara in English presentations of the *Lotus Sūtra*.

27. Cf. various English translations such as: Katō, Soothill and Schiffer 1971 and Hurvitz 1976.

mythical creatures of various kinds. However there are enough different kinds of human beings for most to be included somehow, including children. In any case, the effect of the list is to imply that it could go on and on to cover all living beings of any kind. The number thirty-three is not in fact mentioned, though it can be worked out by adding up all the variations, including four kinds of wives mentioned above and also the four kinds of Buddhist disciples, monk, nun, layman or laywoman. It is perhaps not surprising therefore that the temples of any one circuit of thirty-three will simply have whichever of the seven main iconographical forms (explained in Chapter Two) happens to be housed there.

The listing of all these ways in which Avalokiteśvara (i.e. Kanzeon) can appear to save various beings is set in the context of an exchange between another bodhisattva named Akṣayamati and the Buddha himself, in which the Buddha is explaining the wonderful saving abilities of Avalokiteśvara. A characteristic feature of this account is that salvation from fire, flood, cyclones, demons and evil robbers predominates in the first part. Particular attention is given to the case of a caravan of merchants proceeding along a dangerous road and threatened by bandits. It is here that we learn that the merchants should invoke loudly the name of the bodhisattva, using the phrase: "Hail to the Bodhisattva Avalokiteśvara," which comes out in Japanese as *Namu Kanzeon Bosatsu*. It will be readily noticeable that this phrase is paralleled in the *nenbutsu* so prominent in Pure Land Buddhism and Shin Buddhism, which runs *Namu Amida Butsu*, and indeed these are only two of a number of such invocations to various bodhisattvas and buddhas which can easily be repeated by devotees.

The benefits of rescue from various conceivable disasters may be summarily referred to as this-worldly salvation, whereas in the listing of the thirty-three forms of Avalokiteśvara the idea of salvation slides almost imperceptibly into the teaching of Dharma. The latter is referred to as the bodhisattva's "power of skilful means." That is, there is a movement from this-worldly benefits towards the more far-reaching, other-worldly value or meaning of the Buddhist Dharma itself.[28] This will be most clearly understood when the whole *Kannon Sūtra* is read, but in practice many recitation books restrict themselves to the verse section, no doubt in order to save space and indeed, for the pilgrims themselves, time. In the verses, the emphasis may seem to be more clearly on immediate salvation from disasters and physical threats. Nevertheless, it should be noticed that as they proceed there is an increasing emphasis on the transcendental "wisdom" of the bodhisattva. What is commonly referred to in brief as the "wisdom" of a bodhisattva is that insight into

---

28. The dialectics of all this are explained more fully in Chapter Four of my *Skilful Means* (1978, 2003) entitled "Mythology and skilful means in the *Lotus Sūtra*" of which see the section "Transformations of a bodhisattva."

the emptiness of all phenomena (i.e. their nature of being empty of "own being," and thus without persistent ontological status), which in turn can bring relief from attachments, and hence from suffering. So this is coupled with compassion which

> like a beautiful expansive cloud,
> sheds the Dharma-rain of deathlessness
> and extinguishes the flames of the passions.

Exactly the same connection is made at the beginning of the *Heart Sūtra*, but before turning to that we will consider the verses of the *Kannon Sūtra* in more detail.

At this point in the Chinese text the designation Kanzeon changes to the simpler Kannon (we are using Japanese rather than Chinese pronunciations here) and, as we have seen, it is precisely as Kannon that the bodhisattva is known to the pilgrims in Japan. Variations in other translations such as "Cry Regarder" (Katō *et al.*) and "Sound-Observer" (Hurvitz) offer a literal translation of the characters used for the name. This procedure is not altogether unjustified, but is not followed here because in the meantime these Chinese characters have come to form a single proper noun. A translation or supposed restitution back into the Sanskrit "Avalokiteśvara" is also misleading. When all is said and done, these verses are not found in all manuscript traditions and versions of the *Lotus Sūtra*, but they are found in the Chinese version of Kumārajīva which is that followed in the pilgrims' recitation books. In an English translation male forms are preferable in that the verses pre-date the Chinese gender transformation of Guānyīn; but we should remember that the language of the original verses is not really gender-specific, and that Japanese users regard Kannon mainly as female. The verses are as follows:

> Hear the deeds of Kannon
> Which are well matched to every quarter.
> His broad vow is as deep as the ocean,
> His time-span is inconceivable.
>
> Serving many thousand billions of buddhas
> He conceived a great, pure vow.
> I will tell you about it in brief.
>
> Hearing his name, seeing his body,
> And recollecting him in mind are not in vain,
> For this can extinguish all sufferings of existence.
>
> If an evil-doer wishing harm
> Pushes someone into a great pit of fire
> Let him be mindful of the power of Kannon
> And the pit of fire will turn into a pool of water.

The Meaning of Japanese Buddhist Pilgrimage

Or if someone is in the current of a great sea
Threatened by dragons, fish and demons
Let him be mindful of the power of Kannon
And the waves will not submerge him.

Or if someone is on the peak of Mount Sumeru
And people wish to push him down
Let him be mindful of the power of Kannon
And he will be held safe in the air like the sun.

Or if someone is chased by an evil person
And is falling down off Mount Diamond
Let him be mindful of the power of Kannon
And not a hair of his head will be harmed.

Or if someone is surrounded by bandits
Each with a sword ready to strike
Let him be mindful of the power of Kannon
And they will forthwith turn their minds to mercy.

Or if someone is suffering by regal command
And on the point of death by execution
Let him be mindful of the power of Kannon
And the sword will break into pieces.

Or if someone is imprisoned, bound by the neck,
With arms and feet in shackles,
Let him be mindful of the power of Kannon
And he will be released without hindrance.

If anyone wishes to harm the body
With spells and curses and poisonous herbs
Let us be mindful of the power of Kannon
Which will send them all back to their source.

Or if someone meets evil *rākṣaṣas*
Poisonous dragons or any kinds of demon
Let him be mindful of the power of Kannon
And they will immediately not dare to hurt him.

If someone is surrounded by evil beasts
Their tusks sharp and their claws to be dreaded
Let him be mindful of the power of Kannon
And they will quickly flee far far away.

If there are lizards and snakes, vipers and scorpions,
Breathing poison and burning with smoke and fire,
Be mindful of the power of Kannon
And hearing one's voice they will run away by themselves.

When thunder peals and lightning flashes
And clouds send out hail and torrential rain
Let us be mindful of the power of Kannon

And it will immediately dry up and be dispersed.

When living beings are weighed down with adversity
And countless pains afflict their bodies
The power of the wonderful wisdom of Kannon
Can save the world from its suffering.

Endowed with supernormal powers
And widely practising the skilful means of wisdom
In all the lands of the ten directions
There is not a region in which he does not manifest himself.

All the various kinds of bad tendencies
Birth in the hells, and among the demons and beasts,
The sufferings of birth, old age, sickness and death,
All these will be brought along to extinction.

We should always revere him and pray to him
Who has true vision, pure vision,
The vision of broad and great wisdom
The vision of compassion and the vision of mercy.

A light of immaculate purity,
A sun of wisdom which breaks down all darkness,
He is able to tame the winds and fires of disaster
And illumine brightly the whole wide world.

The compassionate body of the precepts thunders
And the exquisite intention of mercy, like a great cloud,
Pours out the sweet dew of Dharma rain
And extinguishes the flames of the passions.

If someone stands accused before judges
Or fears for his life in the midst of an army
Let him be mindful of the power of Kannon
And a host of enemies will be put to flight.

Exquisite voice, the voice of one who regards the world,
Voice of Brahma, voice of the tide of the sea,
His voice surpasses these worldly voices.
For this reason he should always be called to mind.

You should never for one moment let doubt arise.
The pure and holy Kanzeon,
In suffering, distress, death or disaster,
Can provide a point of reliance.

He is adorned with all possible virtues,
He regards living beings with eyes of compassion,
The ocean of his accumulated merit is immeasurable,
And for this reason he should receive reverence.[29]

---

29. Author's translation. To avoid very cumbersome renderings and in an attempt

The Meaning of Japanese Buddhist Pilgrimage

This text is usually chanted at a steady speed, and is not a subject for reflective commentary or interpretation on the spot. However, a frequently repeated text works on the imagination over a long period, and brief elucidation is therefore appropriate here. It is immediately evident that the earlier stanzas are setting out the desperate situations in which people might find themselves, while the later ones form an invitation to praise, a kind of doxology. This balance is slightly disturbed by the stanza beginning "If someone stands accused before judges" which is similar in pattern to the earlier ones and belongs with them in terms of its content. It is therefore possible that it was displaced in the text at an early stage in the transmission. The desperate situations are all summed up in the stanza which begins "When living beings are weighed down with adversity," and this then redirects us towards the vision of a more fundamental salvation from suffering, which in Buddhism is the summary existential problem underlying all others. We then hear of the great wisdom and compassion of Kannon in a manner which is reminiscent of the opening of the *Heart Sūtra*. It is because of his practice of the perfection of wisdom, or insight, that Kannon (Kanjizai) is able to give release from "all sufferings," as they are summed up there. There is some ambiguity in the phrase "the voice of one who regards the world," for seen in isolation this is none other than the name Kanzeon, which at the beginning of the *sūtra* is usually, if mysteriously, translated as "he who sees the cries of the world." But here it is compared with other voices, the voice of Brahma and the voice of the tide of the sea. Insofar as "His voice surpasses these worldly voices," the idea is picked up that a buddha, or a great bodhisattva, is a "world-conqueror" in a spiritual sense. This is a common epithet (as *jina*) both in the older Buddhist scriptures and in the Jaina tradition where the spiritual heroes are also called *jinas*.[30] In a final occurrence the term Kanzeon does occur as a title or name, and this makes a link with the prose sections of the *sūtra*.

Sometimes the attempt is made to list and illustrate 33 different iconographical forms of Kannon, even though these are found neither in the 33 Saikoku temples nor with any precise correlation to the verses of the *Lotus Sūtra*. Among these some have established themselves in the wider imagination and are most likely to be seen in paintings, examples being:

Byakue Kannon	白衣観音	(White Robed Kannon)
Gyoran Kannon	魚藍観音	(Kannon with a Fish Basket)

---

to match the succinctness of the original, any male pronouns are used with an inclusive intention.

30. Though the Jaina scriptures in the form known to us today are much later, the origins of the religion predate Buddhism, and it is probable that the term *jina* was taken over by Buddhists as an expression of a rival claim to authority.

Ryūzu Kannon 竜頭観音 (Dragon's Head Kannon)
Yōryū Kannon 楊柳観音 (Willow Tree Kannon)

The White Robed Kannon is regarded as that form of the bodhisattva who appears specifically to nuns, and is shown firmly seated on a rock of meditation. It is also said that he, or in this case she, emerged from a white lotus. The variation Kōō Byakue Kanzeon Bosatsu 高王白衣観世音菩薩 is particularly noted for facilitating progeny and for safe childbirth.[31] Kannon "with a fish basket" may be shown holding just such a basket with a large fish in it. This seems to promise a good catch, which features regularly in lists of this-worldly benefits. However there is some ambivalence, because the same Kannon is thought to ward off threatening dragons, fish and evil demons which might be met with at sea, a theme found in the verses of the *sutra*. In this case Kannon-sama is shown standing firmly on a rather fierce looking fish. The Kannon with a dragon's head is one who has the positive power of the dragon to disperse other evil spirits. In the name Yōryū Kannon *yōryū* refers to two kinds of willow trees, the river willow and the weeping willow. This Kannon is shown holding a sprig of willow. The image suggests that Kannon moves flexibly like a flowing willow tree, in accordance with the wishes of many kinds of living beings. This accords in general with the characterization of the bodhisattva found in the *sutra*.

The idea of setting up thirty-three images of the bodhisattva on one spot was referred to in Chapter Two under the concept of miniaturization, and this is well established as an act of meritorious piety. In such cases the Saikoku pilgrimage itself sets the tone and the images match their iconography. Some time during the brief Meiwa years (1764–1772) of the Edo Period (1600–1868) a group of "believers" from Ōsaka sponsored just such a set of Kannon statues, but for the Shingon temple Dainichiji 大日寺 in Shikoku. Since this temple is No.4 of the Shikoku Eighty-eight, we see here a neat interlocking of the two main pilgrimages, via the figure of Kannon. The statues, though extremely beautiful, are not a major focus of the temple, but they are arranged in such a way that pilgrims pass them as they go from the main hall to the Daishidō. A notice board reminds them of Kannon-sama's *shingon: On arorikya sowaka* and asserts that for those who recite it Kannon-sama will fulfil all the heart's wishes (*shinganjōju* 心願成就) at any time and in any place, "which is

---

31. An image with this name, said to be the only one in Japan, was brought from China in 1655 and placed in a side hall in the grounds of the temple Kannonji 観音寺 to one side of the famous Kyōto shrine Kitano Tenmangū. Kannonji is dedicated to Jūichimen Kannon, the "real buddha" (*honjibutsu*) behind the Shintō divinity of Tenmangū, Sugawara Michizane. It counts as No. 31 in the Rakuyō series. In the special Byakue Kanzeon Hall there is also a miniature collection of the thirty-three Saikoku Kannon, just in front of the image, but barely visible behind a curtain.

to say that Kannon-sama changed herself into thirty-three forms and promised to save all those who pray to her." The notice board goes on to explain that this is set out in the chapter on Kanzeon Bosatsu in the *Lotus Sūtra* and that this is the same as the *Kannongyō*, i.e. the *Kannon Sūtra*. In practice the Shikoku pilgrims are usually in too much of a hurry for more than a slight pause in front of the complete set of statues, yet the connection is made.

The prominent position of Kannon-sama in the minds of pilgrims is reinforced by references at the centre of the pilgrims' slips deposited at the temples (see previous chapter), and especially with the phrase Namu Daijidaihi Kanzeon Bosatsu 南無大慈大悲観世音菩薩 or "Hail to Kanzeon Bosatsu of Great Compassion and Great Mercy." Here the compact term *jihi* 慈悲 which is commonly translated as "compassion" is spread out into its component parts for extra emphasis.

Some of the booklets contain a short additional text with the title "Kannon Sūtra in Ten Lines," also sometimes referred to as "Kannon Sūtra on Long Life in Ten Lines" (*Enmei jikku kannongyō*).

Jikku kannongyō

Kannon Sūtra in Ten Lines

Kanzeon!
Hail to the Buddha!
With the Buddha is our affinity[32]
With the Buddha is our link
Linked to Buddha, Dharma, Sangha
With unchanging joy and pure in self
Call every morning on Kanzeon
Call every evening on Kanzeon
The calling arises from the mind
The calling is not separate from the mind

Finally, if there is not enough time to recite all of the verses from the *Kannongyō* then at least the following may be recited:

May peace and protection be granted in this world and the world to follow.
Namu Kanzeon.[33]

The *Heart Sūtra*

However pilgrims do not need to rely only on the *Lotus Sūtra* for their understanding of Kannon or Kanzeon Bosatsu. There is an obvious cross-

---

32. Literally "cause" (*in* 因), but this has various non-relevant meanings in English.
33. This appears as the conclusion of a guidebook to the Edo Thirty-three, and elsewhere.

reference from the Kanzeon of the *Lotus Sūtra* to the Kanjizai Bosatsu of the *Heart Sūtra*, and indeed these are both the same Kannon-sama in the popular mind. Handwritten copies of the *Heart Sūtra* are offered both at temples of the Kannon pilgrimage routes and temples of the Shikoku Eighty-eight and related pilgrimages.

It is through this association that the transactional level of votive offerings and this-worldly benefits may come to be transcended in a further religious sense. While the "*Kannon Sūtra*" (*Kannon-gyō*) was incorporated into the *Lotus Sūtra*, the meaning of a believer's relationship to Kannon-sama is best understood in terms of the underlying concepts of Mahāyāna Buddhism in general. In other words, we should always include the *Heart Sūtra*'s reference to Kanjizai in our minds when we are thinking about the Kannon pilgrimages. Notably, this is the Kannon Bosatsu who is immediately introduced as "practising the perfection of insight, giving release from all sufferings," as will be quoted in full below.

We turn therefore last of all to this *Heart Sūtra*, which is almost the shortest of *sūtras*.[34] Its very brevity is no doubt one of the reasons why it has been copied and recited as much, if not more than any other. Though short, its text is pungent and powerful. While being a standard recitation for pilgrims who owe allegiance to Shingon Buddhism, having pride of place in their devotions as they go around the eighty-eight sacred places of Shikoku, it is widely used in almost all the Buddhist pilgrimages of Japan. It also takes on a life of its own in guidebooks and popular commentaries penned by Buddhist leaders of most denominations. In such cases the title is often abbreviated to: *Hannya Shingyō* (*Prajñā Heart Sūtra*). Here is the text as commonly used in Japan (writer's version).[35]

Maka Hannya Haramitta Shingyō

Mahāprajñāpāramitā Heart Sūtra

When the Bodhisattva Kanjizai was practising the deep *prajñāpāramitā* he perceived the five constituents each to be empty and gave release from

---

34. The shortest is presumably "The Perfection of Insight in One Letter," i.e. in the letter A, which is supposed to sum everything up in one syllable (see Conze 1973, 201). Unfortunately however, unlike the *Heart Sūtra*, this shortest of *sūtras* does not tell us what is being summed up!

35. This translation, from Xuánzàng's Chinese version, goes back to 1982 and has frequently been made available in unpublished form. The male pronoun "he" is used in the first line because the text predates the iconographic gender shift. Sanskrit terms (shown in italics) are only used here to replace Sino-Japanese transliterations. Thus *prajñā* is written with the two Chinese characters 般若 (bō-rĕ, Japanese *han-nya*) which approximately transliterate it; whereas "heart" (*hṛdaya*) is written with one Chinese character 心 (xīn, Japanese *shin*) which translates it, as in *Hannya Shingyō*, the title of the *sūtra* in Japanese pronunciation.

The Meaning of Japanese Buddhist Pilgrimage

all sufferings. Śāriputra, form is not other than emptiness and emptiness is not other than form. The very form is emptiness, the very emptiness is form. The same is true for feeling, perception, striving and consciousness. Śāriputra, all these factors have the mark of emptiness. They do not arise and they do not cease, they are not polluted and they are not cleansed, they do not increase and they do not decrease. Thus in emptiness there is no form, and no feeling, perception, striving or consciousness. There is no eye, ear, nose, tongue, body or mind; no form, sound, smell, taste, sensation or concept; no world of sight, and so on, up to no world of mind. There is no ignorance and no doing away with ignorance, and so on, up to no doing away with ageing and death. There is no suffering, no accumulation, no cessation, no path. There is no knowledge and no attainment. Because of this non-attaining, and because he relies on the *prajñāpāramitā*, a bodhisattva is free of hindrances in spirit. Because he is free of hindrances in spirit he is without fear. He is far removed from all upsetting daydreams, and he finally perfects nirvana. All the buddhas of the three worlds, because they rely on the *prajñāpāramitā*, attain *anuttara samyak sambodhi*. Know therefore the *prajñāpāramitā*. This is the great divine spell, the great illuminating spell, the unsurpassed spell, the unequalled spell. It is able to do away with all sufferings, being truth and not illusion. Therefore I proclaim the spell of the *prajñāpāramitā*, and I proclaim it thus: *gate, gate, paragate, parasamgate, bodhi svaha*.

Prajñā Heart Sūtra

This text, being Xuánzàng's Chinese version of the *sūtra*, is the one widely used, and learned by heart, in Japan. Do pilgrims in Japan understand these words? It depends on which ones. The word *bodaisatta* (corresponding to Sanskrit *bodhisattva*) is somehow understood, even though it may seem a little complicated when compared with the more widely current *bosatsu*. The word *prajñāpāramitā*, which in Japanese takes on the sound *hannya haramitta*, is not really understood as "perfection of insight," though the more studious may know that it is one of the "six perfections" of a bodhisattva. In the main, it is "understood" in so far as it becomes familiar. And indeed this applies to the whole text.

It is, after all, not exactly a straightforward text. Paradoxically it negates the main concepts of Buddhism. Beginning with the words "Śāriputra, form is not other than emptiness and emptiness is not other than form" the Buddha himself is presumed to be speaking. He is therefore presented as giving a version of his teaching which sets a question mark, or rather a mark of negation, over some of the central concepts of traditional Buddhism. The reason for this is that some of the well known formulae upon which Buddhist followers had come to rely, such as the four noble truths—of suffering, its cause (here the "accumulation" of karma), its cessation and the path thereto—had themselves come to be potential obstacles in a spiritual sense. So a paradoxical dialectic is set up in which Buddhist teachings, though needed, are also relativized through being negated. The formulae which are thus negated are the five constituents of existence, the six senses with their organs, their objects and the "worlds" or realms which thereby arise, the twelve factors of dependent origination (but here abbreviated to a mention of the first and last) and the four noble truths. The purpose of these negations lies in the removal of spiritual obstacles. In longer *sūtras*, this is all set out in lengthy discourse, but here we have it in a nutshell, the heart of the matter, the "heart" of the perfection of insight, or (in more widely current English terminology) the heart of the bodhisattva's perfection of "wisdom."[36] It is only on the basis that the bodhisattva perceives the five constituents of existence each to be "empty" that he could "give release from all sufferings." In this sense the workings of compassion arise from insight into the true nature of things. What does it mean to say that the five constituents are "empty"? The five constituents had been taught to be form, feeling, perception, striving and consciousness. These are the factors of every individual existence. But they are themselves transient, that is they are "empty" of substantiality. They are without ultimate ontic persistence. To perceive this, indeed to practise this perception in consciousness, is to be liberated like a bodhisattva, so the text is telling us. But the straightforward formulations of Buddhist teaching are themselves couched in terms of existence as normally understood, so they too are declared to be empty of substantiality. Not many religious texts tell us such things about the teachings of their own tradition! Yet this is what the pilgrims are reciting all the time.

The *Heart Sūtra* has its location in the wider literature of Mahāyāna Buddhism. In particular it is notable that the passage running from "Śāriputra, form is not other than emptiness..." down to "...and no attainment" is paralleled in the *Great Prajñā Sūtra*, that huge text which takes up three whole volumes of the printed Buddhist canon.[37] In temples it fills large heaps of the folded *sūtra* texts used in recitation, and so great is the amount of sheer text that it can never be recited sentence by sentence. Instead it is recited symbolically by having the beginnings and the ends of each booklet shouted out while all the folded pages are showered through the air in a wonderful display of concertina-like virtuosity. Zen Buddhists seem to be especially good at performing this practice, which is known as *tendoku* 転読, "turning and reading," but it

---

36. Unlike Edward Conze (*passim*) the present writer regularly avoids the expression "wisdom" because it is too diffuse, suggesting wise sayings or a general state of mature reflection. Here it is a technical term meaning insight into the true nature of things as empty, nirvanic, etc.

37. T223, 223a.

The Meaning of Japanese Buddhist Pilgrimage

is carried out with verve by Tendai and Shingon adepts as well. After the passage mentioned, which is about half of our text, the *Great Prajñā Sūtra* has a continuation in the same vein: "There is no stream-winning, no fruit of stream-winning," etc. This refers to the "fruits" of attainment," a "stream-winner" being one who attains the Buddhist path and will not slip back. Following "...they do not increase and they do not decrease" the *Great Prajñā Sūtra* adds "This *dharma* of emptiness has no past, no future and no present." This is a reference to the three worlds of past, future and present, in terms of which all existents are supposed to exist according to the Sarvāstivādins, whose teachings were rejected by the exponents of the Great Vehicle (the Mahāyāna). So the teaching of emptiness enables us to escape being caught in the snares of existence. The thought of the very short and very long texts is in principle consistent. What is not clear is the sequence of development. Apparently the "*Prajñā Sūtra*," which may first have been the variant in 8000 lines, grew and grew, like most *sūtras*. Indeed, like the proverbial turnip "it grew and grew till it could grow no longer," and then once again a really short summary was required which apparently crystallized around a representative section of text. But we do not need to pursue the intricacies of such textual developments here,[38] for the pilgrims are, frankly, not interested. They recite the *Heart Sūtra*, their *Hannya Shingyō*, many times. As they continue on their way, from temple to temple, they become more and more familiar with it. Step by step they internalize the meaning. It is one of the ways in which the "practice" of *hannya*, in the sense of insight into the true nature of things as "empty," can be internalized.

Summing up this whole chapter, it is safe to say that the Buddhist pilgrimages can be distinguished along these lines from similar pilgrimages which do not bear any such Buddhist meaning. At the same time we must not forget that not all pilgrims will "practise" their way into the central meaning of the *Heart Sūtra* as explained here. Others will remain at the level of transactional religion. Even some group leaders (*sendatsu*) may largely acquiesce in the transactional level of understanding, while some will make an effort to guide the pilgrims who have no specialized knowledge into a greater "respect for the buddhas" and thus step by step into the further meaning. So at the transactional level, the continuities with non-Buddhist pilgrimage are quite marked, but at the level of further meanings, the divergences become increasingly apparent.

---

38. More details may be found in the works of Edward Conze, *The Short Prajñāpāramitā Texts* (1973), *The Prajñāpāramitā Literature* (1978), etc. and Lewis Lancaster *Prajñāpāramitā and Related Systems* (1977).

— Chapter Eight —

General Conclusions

Are the pilgrimages Buddhist?

In these general conclusions a few points are raised, or revisited, which may be of interest to those who are studying other pilgrimages or who are interested in the methodology of the study of religions as a discipline. If any readers prefer to end with the preceding chapter, in particular with the *Heart Sūtra*, that will also be quite satisfactory.

By considering pilgrimage on three levels, in terms of "route," "transaction" and "meaning," we have been able to approach an answer to the question as to how these numerous and complicated pilgrimages may be regarded as "Buddhist." For various reasons the answer to a question such as "Are the pilgrimages Buddhist?" may not be immediately evident. However, by working through a description and an analysis of the phenomena, we have arrived at the answer that while there are many common features in Japanese circulatory pilgrimage there are also divergences in symbolism and recitation practice which help us to identify those which are tendentially "Buddhist" and those which are not.

Underlying both the question and the answer is a more general question about what could count as "Buddhist" or "Buddhism" to start with. Buddhism is a historically complex tradition which can be met with in many forms, and quite often historians or observers become impatient with such questions. Some have sought to answer it in one easy sentence such as that if such and such a group says it is "Buddhist," then it is. By analogy, in our particular case, one might say that if the pilgrims say they are Buddhist, then they are. Observers who take this approach feel, in one sense rightly, that they are not called upon to set up essentialist norms of their own concerning what counts as "Buddhist," and what does not. However this matter can easily be treated too lightly. The question should not just be decried and avoided. Buddhists do tell us what is "Buddhist," to be sure, but on the other hand there are serious marginal cases, and in recent times there have been those who would claim the well-sounding label "Buddhist" for the marketing of teachings and practices which really diverge most significantly from historic forms of Buddhism. So, just as with other religions, there are justifiable questions about the coherence of the various religious patterns or systems and the extent to which they fit into a diachronic sequence or a synchronic pattern of apparently related phenomena. Serious historians or students of religions really need to think about these matters more carefully than is often done. In this book it has been implied from the outset that most of the circulatory pilgrimages in Japan are in at least some sense Buddhist. However this is not self-evident, and the situation is to some extent obscured by the complexities which have been explored above. In all brevity, let us consider the main aspects of this problem as part of the general conclusions to be drawn.

First, the circulatory form of the pilgrimages described here appears to have no close parallels in other Buddhist countries such as India or China. The model of pilgrimage found in the early texts of Buddhism is based on revisiting sites of importance in the life of the historical Buddha himself, and this has only been picked up in a secondary way in Japan. It is of course true that single-goal pilgrimages to major temples, such as Zenkōji, have analogies in the Buddhism of other countries, but as was set out in the Introduction these are analogous to single-goal pilgrimages in other religions too, which can easily be recognized as distinctive.

Second, the pilgrimages are not really required by the specific teaching of any particular Buddhist denomination within Japan itself, such that doctrinal lineage, at least, would identify them as Buddhist. Of course, Kōbō Daishi is central to the Shikoku pilgrimage, but Shingon Buddhism does not *depend* on this particular practice. The text for Kannon-sama is part of the *Lotus Sūtra*, which is a dominant text in Tendai and Nichirenite Buddhism, but the doctrinal architecture of these, as it might be called, does not include pilgrimage. The only qualification to this might be that in Tendai Buddhism the *sennichi kaihōgyō* is thought to derive, indirectly, from the practice of meditation by means of continuous walking (*jōgyō zanmai* 常行三昧). Even here however, Rhodes has already pointed out that the two practices have little in common beyond the fact that a lot of walking is involved.[1]

Third, circulatory pilgrimage as a popular religious activity[2] has developed its own dynamic in what are evidently non-Buddhist contexts. The pilgrimages focused on the Seven Gods of Good Fortune (*shichifukujin*) can hardly be said to be Buddhist in conception, even though some or all

---

1. Rhodes 1987.
2. The word "popular" here simply means that people like it.

the divinities may be lodged in Buddhist temples, for example Zen temples. The motivation and intentions of those going round is avowedly transactional and this-worldly. Sometimes Shintō shrines form part of these circuits, and there is no perceived tension of meaning at all. This is because the intentions remain at the transactional level. Furthermore we have seen several cases of straightforwardly Shintoist imitations of Buddhist circulatory pilgrimage. These involve visiting designated Shintō shrines which have no Buddhist connections whatever. In these cases the various strands of meaning are built up with symbols and values which are espoused by the representatives of Shintō, and not of Buddhism. A world independent of Buddhism is envisioned, as in much of modern Shintō since the Meiji Restoration.

Fourth, many of the practices commonly associated with pilgrimage, notably petitionary prayer, overlap with general features of Japanese religious life. The ordinary religious transactions effected with particular spiritual beings, buddhas or bodhisattvas, are often not so different from those carried out at Shintō shrines with the divinities (*kami*) worshipped there. In daily life such religious activities are perceived by many as a continuum. Only at certain points does the meaning of the pilgrimage seem to crystallize in a more clearly or fully Buddhist sense. This consideration does not only apply to pilgrimage. The same might be said for other activities which contribute to the complex make-up of Buddhism as it is actually lived out in various Asian countries. Funeral rites and reverence for ancestors, for example, are almost inseparable from "Buddhism" in some situations. Yet these matters do not flow automatically from the complex of teachings and practice which can be identified as early Buddhism, or indeed from the more developed teachings of its many later scholastic exponents. The question about the status of pilgrimage in Buddhism is analogous.

Fifth, it should never be forgotten that in almost all varieties of Asian Buddhism there is a certain tension or dialectic between the perception of life characteristic of Buddhism and the many religious activities and concepts with which Buddhism has come to be associated. This may sometimes seem to be confusing, and yet in the long term, for Buddhists, it is more like a liberating dialectic. Putting it in Mahāyāna terms, the "compassion" of the bodhisattvas adopts countless forms and invites participation in numerous activities, which all tend in their own way and their own time towards "the Buddha way." Thus, what may not at first seem to be "Buddhist" to a casual observer can *move* in a Buddhist direction for the persons involved. This dialectic is found in early Buddhism but is quite typical of Mahāyāna Buddhism. It should always be taken into account in matters of interpretation. These ambiguous elements of religious culture, as we might perceive them in observation, are the "skilful means" of Buddhist communication. On the other hand, not everything or anything which does not seem to be Buddhist can be claimed to be somehow Buddhist underneath. Some things are just not Buddhist at all. In other words, a certain amount of judicious appraisal is needed unless we are to fall into utterly arbitrary views.

Sixth, circulatory "Buddhist" pilgrimage in Japan is evidently full of various interrelated meanings. For some who go round it is little more than a healthy leisure activity with simple participation in some of the general forms of Japanese religion. The connections with tourism and the desire for leisure, the commercial interests of the travel industry and the features of the transport infrastructure have often been pointed out. At the temples themselves, transactions at the temples involve the payment of relatively small sums of money in exchange for expected this-worldly benefits (*genzeriyaku*) for oneself or one's family. Yet for others, the meaning may be more transformational. There is no doubt that the personal experience of pilgrims is deepened as they reflect,

Figure 8.1 Iconic depiction (*miei*) of Nyoirin Kannon Bosatsu from Saikoku No. 18 (Rokkakudō, Kyōto).

during the journey, on family hopes and on gratitude to their ancestors, on the sequence of life and death of which they themselves are part. In the Buddhist understanding, the ups and downs of this life are thereby set into a more relative perspective. If travelling from one place to another reflects the difficulties and efforts of life, the completion of the pilgrimage makes the onward passage through death seem possible.

To sum up, the individual transactions performed by pilgrims at every stage of the journey are continuous with the myriad comparable religious actions performed at many other Buddhist temples, Shintō shrines and other religious foci all over Japan; but taken together they can come to assume a more specific direction and a more comprehensive intention. The interpretation of single ritual actions by themselves does not exhaust the meaning of these pilgrimages as a whole. We have seen that there can be a dimension of *Buddhist* meaning, going beyond the merely transactional, into which the pilgrim may mature in the course of his or her pilgrimage, whether gradually or even suddenly. For many pilgrims the meaning of their activity is focused particularly in the *Heart Sūtra* with its paradoxical negations of common Buddhist formulae. Some might consider that this text itself represents a departure from earlier phases of Buddhist tradition. In the "great vehicle" (Mahāyāna) perspective however it is a deeply Buddhist text which enables innumerable followers, ordained or lay, to access a more subtle level of understanding. When the picture is thus fully considered it seems fair to describe most of the pilgrimages which have been introduced here as Buddhist. By this is meant that, in the long run, whatever else may be going on, and without entering into denominationally oriented differences of doctrine, it is Buddhist meanings which are dominant. This is true for at least some of the pilgrims some of the time, even if it is not true all the time for all those who are going round from temple to temple. In drawing this conclusion we do however distinguish the Buddhist-oriented pilgrimages from those which are located almost entirely on the level of transactional religiosity, notably the trips around the Seven Gods of Good Fortune, as well as those which promote specifically Shintō themes. These counter-examples provide a clear indication that it is possible to give a reasonable answer to the question about whether the pilgrimages described above are "Buddhist" as follows. Most are and the others are not. Within those pilgrimages which in general may be regarded as Buddhist, the Buddhist meanings will be accessed more persistently and more successfully by some pilgrims than by others.

Postscript on the general theory of pilgrimage

This assessment fits in with the more widely conceived theoretical orientation provided in the Introduction. it will be recalled that a three-step model of pilgrimage was proposed dealing with (i) the route, (ii) the transaction and (iii) the meaning. We have seen that it is not possible to separate these entirely, and indeed hints about the later steps were built in as the presentation progressed. Yet these three organizing concepts amount to a clear, inductively gained model of the phenomenology of pilgrimage which is particularly relevant to the cases studied. This model seems to be potentially relevant to other cases of pilgrimage, whether circulatory or not. Indeed there is a corrective value here vis-à-vis widespread assumptions about pilgrimage, which lies in two things. First, we place much less emphasis than usual on the *goal* of pilgrimage in favour of the *route*. The very fact that the goals are multiple means that the route which links them takes on a greater importance. Second, this in turn opens up the possibility of a progression in the pilgrims' consciousness, or to use the term favoured by René Gothóni, even a transformation. To use a religious term, it may be viewed as a spiritual progression. This is not to say that a single-goal pilgrimage cannot be a moving experience for the pilgrim. It is usually intended to be. But in the cases studied here the sheer extension of the route around all the temples in the sequence holds the potential for steadily increased familiarization with the meanings which are symbolically extended.

As far as the first corrective is concerned, it means that in any study of pilgrimage it is important to reflect on the relationship between the route and the goal or goals for the particular case. In this regard some precision is required, and one misunderstanding in particular should be avoided for the cases under study here. What counts as "a pilgrimage"? The general definition offered in the Introduction is maintained also for these cases, namely that "Pilgrimage is the deliberate traversing of a route to a sacred place which lies outside one's normal habitat." There may seem to be some tension here, in that this study has been devoted to examples of sequential pilgrimages which begin at a Number 1 and end at a Number 33, 49, 88 and so on. The first temples (or shrines) do of course represent a starting point, and the final numbers in any sequence represent a conclusion to that sequence. At the very first temple, or in shops adjacent to it, some of the accessories required can still be purchased. At the last temple, these very same items, staffs, hats, and so on, may be left behind to indicate completion of the sequence, since they are no longer needed. So we might jump to the conclusion that the pilgrimage "only" consists of going round the numbered temples. However this perception would not be quite right, as we are reminded by the general definition of pilgrimage, because the pilgrim will also be departing from and returning to his or her home or "normal habitat." The journey there, and the journey back (albeit from a different place) are parts of the overall "pilgrimage." This can be seen from the fact that some of the things needed for the circulatory part, which is avowedly the main part, will be taken as luggage when departing from home, and the things which are taken back as evidence of the sequence of visits will be taken back to the home (and *not* left at the last temple). The farewells and greetings, though not ritualized in the cases studied, also illustrate this point. A particular nuance is added by the fact that the complete scrolls with calligraphy and seals still have to be mounted on to permanent surrounds, before they can be proudly hung in the *tokonoma*, the focal point of the best room in the house.

As to the second corrective point, this is not the place to enter into a new debate on terminological questions relating to "religion," "religiosity" and "spirituality," which have often been tossed around most carelessly in recent years. To use the word "spiritual" here is simply to take seriously the self-understanding of those pilgrims who do think that they are somehow getting somewhere, apart from just as far as to the next temple or the last temple of the sequence. The pilgrim's initial concern is quite naturally with the route and with the location of the temple destination or destinations. But attention then shifts to the religious actions which are performed at these various destinations, as is summed up above under the concept of transaction. From there comes, or may come, a further progression to the question of the meaning or meanings which the journey holds for individual pilgrims. These meanings may even relativize the value of the journey as such, as we have also seen. This progression of consciousness, or spiritual progression, does not have to be literally chronological, though individual pilgrims will have their own time-scale of inner development. It refers to a process which may take place in fits and starts, or it may even be present as a multilayered perception more or less from the beginning.

A further major theoretical orientation emerged in the field and found confirmation in the detailed analysis. This was set out in Chapter Six, which was devoted in particular to the matter of transaction. The transaction as such takes place at each of the temples which is visited, and it was found that it could be analysed in three simple phases. First, the pilgrim initiates the visit and deposits evidence for it. Second, he or she performs a devotional act which accords with the symbolism and conceptions of the pilgrimage in question. Third, he or she acquires evidence of the visit to take away. This analysis should not be confused with the overall theory, or practice, of pilgrimage. It is only a part of it. Nevertheless, attention is drawn to it as it may be quite relevant to the acts performed in the context of other pilgrimages, at their respective goals, whether single or multiple.

These theoretical reflections are relatively simple; but simple theory is not necessarily bad theory. Moreover, there are certain important ram-

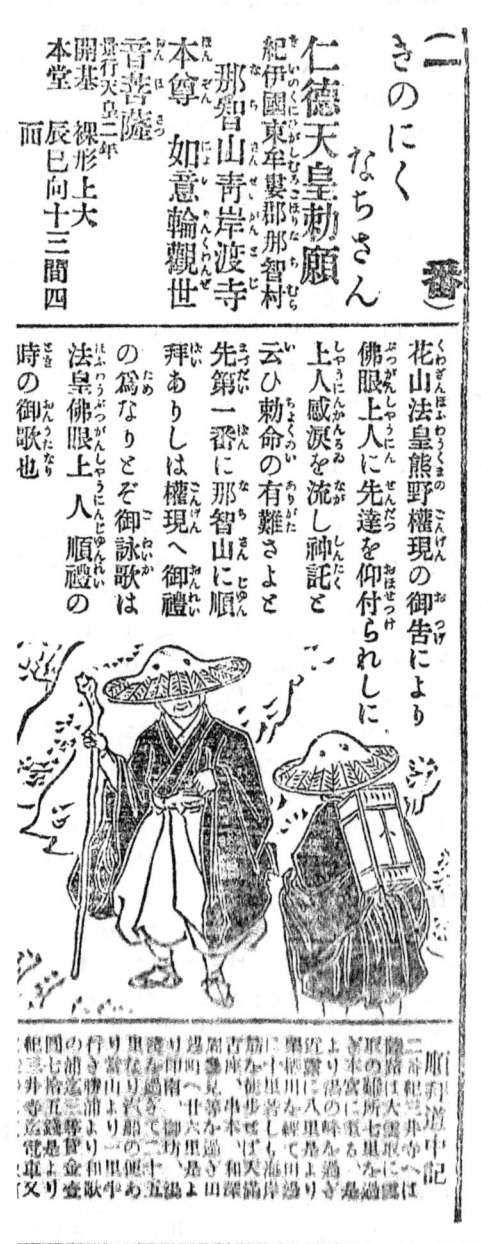

Figure 8.2 Traditional illustration of pilgrims with details of Saikoku No 1.

ifications which go beyond the subject of this book. First, the area of transaction is thought to be a key feature of what is regularly designated by the present writer as the "primal" religion of Japan, that is, the unified field of religious culture and behaviour in which the great majority of the population shares. This means that it is here that the specific religions meet in daily practice of many kinds. The centre of gravity of the idea of circulatory pilgrimage lies here, which explains, analytically, why the easily understood patterns favoured in one religious orientation (Buddhism) can easily be transferred to another one (Shintō). This view of Japanese religious culture is admittedly an observer's view, or to use a popular terminology, an "outsider" view. The question of meanings on the other hand, addressed in the previous chapter, inevitably gets very close to the understanding of "insiders," that is, participants in the pilgrimage system. This is phenomenologically necessary. Moreover attention was drawn to the way in which Buddhist interpretations can easily manage a variety of expressions of "Buddhism," whether simple or subtle, as "skilful means," or provisional constructs. Pilgrimage itself is just such a construct. Since these pilgrimages are located within the wider range of Japanese religious activity, theoretical questions about "syncretism" also arise. Syncretism is understood here to be a dynamic process of an ambiguous nature, and thus distinct from a straightforward synthesis in which nothing would be left to be contested. The option of divergent meanings arising in the context of a coherent field of religious behaviour, by contrast, is one which is entirely consistent with such an understanding of syncretist situations and processes.[3]

Finally, the research underlying this presentation, as an exercise in the study of religions, has been operating in terms of description, characterization, analysis and interpretation. The last mentioned has been very specifically intended to serve the task of analysis, including analytical explanation. Rarely have we moved into matters of *correlational* explanation, which would demand the formulation of different questions, sociological and psychological and other. These might be specific questions relating to the economics of pilgrimage, the demography of age and gender, power struggles between various denominations, the geography of religion, and so on. Explanatory theories are a type of theory which depend on prior knowledge of a particular field, although they are often advanced without it. This presentation has attempted to provide such basic knowledge to start with, and to present it in a stable, analytical, and in that sense theoretical framework.

---

3. For the writer's use of the term "syncretism" see "Syncretism versus synthesis" in: 2012b and other references given there.

Bibliography

Note. Some Japanese books do not have authors or editors in an individualised sense, but are written on the authority of an institution such as a pilgrimage society, which may also be the publisher. This is reflected in some of the details given below. In Japanese titles only proper names have been capitalized.

Asakusa Nadokoro Shichifukujin Kai (editorial authority).
- 1979. *Asakusa Nadokoro Shichifukujin Mōde.* Tokyo: Asakusa Nadokoro Shichifukujin Kai. (N.B. In this title, the pronunciation *nadokoro* is prescribed for 名所 (otherwise *meisho*) meaning nameworthy or famous places.)

Bhardwaj, Surinder Mohan.
- 1973. *Hindu Places of Pilgrimage in India.* Berkeley: University of California Press.

Blacker, Carmen.
- 1975. *The Catalpa Bow.* London: George Allen and Unwin.

Blyth, R. H.
- 1952. *Haiku*, vol. 4, Autumn-Winter. Tokyo: Hokuseidō Press.

Bocking, Brian.
- 2001. *The Oracles of the Three Shrines: Windows on Japanese Religion.* London: Routledge/Curzon.

Bohner, Alfred.
- 1931. *Wallfahrt zu Zweien. Die 88 heiligen Stätten von Shikoku.* Supplement XII der Mitteilungen der deutschen Gesellschaft für Natur- und Völkerkunde Ostasiens). Tokyo and Leipzig: DGNVO and Asia Major Verlag.

Conze, Edward.
- 1973. *The Short Prajñāpāramitā Texts.* London: Luzac and Co.
- 1978. *The Prajñāpāramitā Literature.* (2nd Edition Revised and Enlarged), Bibliographica Philologica Buddhica Series Major I. Tokyo: The Reiyūkai.

Edo Fudasho Kai (editorial authority).
: 1993. *Shōwa shinsen Edo sanjūsan Kannon fudasho annai.* Tokyo: Edo Fudasho Kai.
: 2000. *Shōwa shinsen Edo sanjūsan Kannon fudasho annai.* Tokyo: Edo Fudasho Kai.

Eliade, Mircea.
: 1959. *The Sacred and the Profane. The Nature of Religion.* New York: Harcourt, Brace and World.

Enbutsu, Sumiko.
: 1990. *Chichibu. Japan's Hidden Treasure.* Tokyo: Tuttle.

En no Gyōja Reiseki Fudasho Kai (editorial authority).
: 2002. *Shugen no seichi. En no Gyōja reiseki fudasho junrei*, Ōsaka: Toki Shobō.

Farmayan, Hafez and Elton L. Daniel, trans. and eds.
: 1990. *A Shi'ite Pilgrimage to Mecca 1885-1886. The Safarnâmeh of Mirzâ Moḥammad Ḥosayn Farâhâni.* London: Saqi Books.

Fukuda, Tsuneo.
: 1981. *Chichibu junrei no hitoritabi.* Tokyo: Gendai Shorin.

Gauntlett, John Owen and Robert King Hall.
: 1974. *Kokutai No Hongi. Cardinal Principles of the National Entity of Japan.* Newton, MA: Crofton Publishing.

Gotō, Shinkyō.
: 1958. *Shikoku junrei.* Wakayama City: Shikoku Reijō Sanpaihōsankai.

Gothóni, René.
: 1994. *Tales and Truth: Pilgrimage on Mount Athos Past and Present.* Helsinki: Helsinki University Press.
: 2000. *Attitudes and Interpretations in Comparative Religion.* Helsinki: Academia Scientiarum Fennica.

Gothóni, René, ed.
: 2005. *Pilgrims and Travellers in Search of the Holy.* Bern: Peter Lang.

Hayami, Tasuku.
: 1970. *Kannon shinkō.* Tokyo: Hanawa Shobō.
: 1975. *Jizō shinkō (Hanawa Shinsho 49).* Tokyo: Hanawa Shobō.

Hayashi, Takashi and Mamoru Murakami.
: 1983. *Kitamine no hito. Hieizan sennichi kaihōgyōsha Utsumi Shunshō.* Tokyo: Kōsei Shuppansha.

Heissig, Walther.
: 1970. "Die Religionen der Mongolei." In *Die Religionen Tibets und der Mongolei*, edited by Giuseppe Tucci and Walther Heissig. Stuttgart: Kohlhammer.
: 1980. *The Religions of Mongolia.* ET of Heissig 1970 by Geoffrey Samuel. London: Routledge.

Hirahata, Ryōyū (also read as Yoshio).
: 1980. *Aizu Kannon reijō.* Chōshi: Manganji Kyōkabu.

Bibliography

    1985. *Bandō sanjūsankasho*. Chōshi: Manganji Kyōkabu.
    1987a. *Kamakura Sanjūsankasho*. Chōshi: Manganji Kyōkabu.
    1987b. *Owari Kannon junrei*. Chōshi: Manganji Kyōkabu.
    1987c. *Saijō Kannon junrei*. Chōshi: Manganji Kyōkabu.
    1992. *Wakariyasui Saikoku sanjūsankasho*. Chōshi: Manganji Kyōkabu.
    1999. *Kamakura Sanjūsankasho*. Chōshi: Manganji Kyōkabu.
    And numerous similar titles.

Hoffmann, Ute.
    2004. "Pilgertourismus im Aufschwung. Die Wallfahrt zu den 88 Heiligen Stätten in Shikoku." *OAG Notizen* 2: 10–25.

Hoshino, Eiki.
    1981. *Junrei. Sei to zoku no genshōgaku*. Tokyo: Kōtansha.
    1997. Pilgrimage and peregrination. Contextualising the Saikoku *junrei* and the Shikoku *henro*. In *Japanese Journal of Religious Studies* 24(3–4): 271–299.

Hosokawa, Gyōshin.
    1983 *Shinran. tsuketari Rennyo no tabi: koji junrei gaido*. Kyōto: Hōzōkan.

Hurvitz, Leon.
    1976. *Scripture of the Lotus Blossom of the fine Dharma, translated from the Chinese of Kumārajīva*. Buddhist studies and translations. Records of civilization, Sources and Studies 94. New York: Columbia University Press.

Inoue, Kazu.
    1924. *Kōryō to kannon reijō junpai jikki*. Tokyo and Ōsaka: Seikadō Shoten.

Jakuhon (see Murakami Mamoru).

Jingū Shichō (editorial authority).
    1979. *O-Isemairi*. Tokyo: Jingū Shichō.

Kakinoki, Kenji and Yasuo Seki.
    1991. *Shinano sanjūsan fudasho meguri*. Matsumoto: Kyōdo Shuppansha.

Kantō Sanjūroku Fudōson Reijōkai (editorial authority).
    1999. *Kantō sanjūroku Fudō reijō gaido bukku*. Iwase: Kantō Sanjūroku Fudōson Reijōkai Jimukyoku.

Katō, Bunnō, trans.
    1971. *Myōhōrengekyō. The Sūtra of the Lotus Flower of the Wonderful Law*. Revised by W.E. Soothill and Wilhelm Schiffer. Tokyo: Kōsei Publishing.

Kinki Sanjūroku Fudōson Reijōkai (editorial authority).
    1986, 1991. *Kinki sanjūroku Fudōson reijō*, Ōsaka: Toki Shobō.

Kitazawa, Natsuki and Ken Shimizu, (et al.)
    2008. *Worshipping Kannon: Treasures from the Thirty-three Pilgrimage Sites of Western Japan*. Nagoya: Nagoya City Museum. See Nara National Museum 2008.

Knott, Kim.
    2005. *The Location of Religion: A Spatial Analysis.* London and Oakville, CT: Equinox Publishing.

Kobayashi, Shigeru.
    1993. *Saikoku 33kasho reijō meguri,* Tokyo: Nichiji Shuppan.

Koji Kenshōkai (editorial authority).
    1979, 1992. *Kinki sanjūroku Fudōson.* Ōsaka: Koji Kenshōkai. (= Shimoyasuba 1979, 1992).

Kouamé, Nathalie.
    1997. "Shikoku's local authorities and *henro* during the golden age of the pilgrimage." *Japanese Journal of Religious Studies* 24(3–4): 413–425.
    2000. *Initiation à la Paléographie Japonaise à travers les Manuscrits du Pèlerinage de Shikoku.* Paris: Langues et Mondes.
    2001. *Pèlerinage et société dans le Japon des Tokugawa: Le pèlerinage de Shikoku entre 1598 et 1868.* Paris: École française d'Extrême-Orient.

Kubota, Nobuhiro.
    1985. *Sangaku reijō junrei.* Tokyo: Shinchōsha.

Kurashige, Ryōkai.
    1982. *Echigo junrei sanjūsankasho.* Niigata: Shinseiin.

Kyōto Shinbunsha (editorial authority).
    1979. *Shin Saikoku reijō. Junrei no tabi.* Kyōto: Kyōto Shinbunsha.

Lancaster, Lewis.
    1977. *Prajñāpāramitā and Related Systems. Studies in Honor of Edward Conze.* Berkeley, CA: Institute of Buddhist Studies.

Ludvik, Catherine.
    2006. "In the service of the *Kaihōgyō* practitioners of Mt. Hiei." *Japanese Journal of Religious Studies* 33(1): 115–142.
    2007. *Sarasvatī. Riverine Goddess of Knowledge. From the Manuscript-carrying Vīṇā-player to the Weapon-wielding Defender of Dharma.* Leiden: Brill.

Maeda, Takashi.
    1971. *Junrei no shakaigaku.* Kyōto: Minureba Shobō (= Minerva Shobō).

Mano, Yukie.
    1993. *Chita Shikoku 88-kashomeguri kanzengaido.* Nagoya: Kaietsu Shuppansha.

Matsuo, Shinkū.
    1992. *Saikoku fudasho furumichi junrei.* Tokyo: Shunshūsha.

Migot, André
    1955. *Tibetan Marches.* London: Rupert Hart-Davis.

Mizuno, Keizaburō.
    1985. *Nara-Kyōto no koji meguri.* Tokyo: Iwanami Shoten.

Bibliography

Moriguchi, Ichisaburō.
   1977. *Izumo no reijō sanjūsanban fudasho meguri.* Matsue: San'in Chūō Shinpōsha.

Murakami, Mamoru, trans.
   1987. *Shikoku henro reijōki* (by Jakuhon). Tokyo: Kyōikusha.

Nakagawa, Toshio.
   1979. *Ai to kokoro no terameguri.* Tokyo: Keimei Shobō.

Nara National Museum (editorial authority).
   2008. *Worshipping Kannon: Treasures from the Thirty-three Pilgrimage Sites of Western Japan.* Special Exhibition at Nara National Museum and Nagoya City Museum August 1 to September 28, 2008 and October 18 to November 30, 2008. Nara: Nara Kokuritsu Hakubutsukan.

Niizuma, Hisao.
   1996. *Shinran Shōnin nijūyohai junpai.* Ōsaka: Toki Shobō.

Nishigaki, Seiji.
   1983. *O-Isemairi.* Tokyo: Iwanami Bunsho.

Pye, Michael
   1978. *Skilful Means. A Concept in Mahayana Buddhism.* London: Duckworth.
   2003. *Skilful Means. A Concept in Mahayana Buddhism.* 2nd edition. London: Routledge.
   1983. "Suffering and health in Mahayana Buddhism." In *World Religions and Medicine,* edited by David Goodacre, 24–31. Oxford: Institute of Religion and Medicine.
   1987. "This-worldly benefits in Shin Buddhism." In *Gilgul, Essays on Transformation, Revolution and Permanence in the History of Religions, Dedicated to Zwi Werblowsky,* edited by S. Shaked, D. Shulman and G. G. Stroumsa, 192–202. Leiden: Brill.
   1987. *O-meguri. Pilgerfahrt in Japan.* Schriften der Universitätsbibliothek Marburg 31. Marburg: Universitätsbibliothek Marburg.
   1996a "Shintō, primal religion and international identity." *Marburg Journal of Religion* 1(1): 3.
   1996b. "Syncretism: Buddhism and Shinto on one island." In *Religions in Contact: Selected Proceedings of the Special IAHR Conference held in Brno, August 23-26, 1994,* edited by I. Dolezalova, B. Horyna and D. Papousek, 159–162. Brno: Czech Society for the Study of Religions. New edition as "Buddhism and Shintō on one Island" in 2013b.
   1997. "Perceptions of the body in Japanese religion." In *Religion and the Body,* edited by Sarah Coakley, 248–261. Cambridge: Cambridge University Press.
   1999. "Methodological integration in the study of religions." In *Approaching Religion,* 1. edited by Tore Ahlbäck, 188–205; Åbo, Finland: Donner Institute. Republished in 2012a.
   2000. "Japans buddhistische Pilgerwege." In *Japan Reiseland: Beiheft zur gleichnamigen Ausstellung der Staatsbibliothek zu Berlin8.Juli bis 26. August*

2000. edited by Helga Dreßler-Wormit, 75–98. Berlin: Staatsbibliothek zu Berlin – Preußischer Kulturbesitz.

2002a. "Won Buddhism as a Korean new religion." *Numen* 49(2): 113–141.

2002b. "Traces of Shinran Shōnin." In *Resonanzen. Schwingungsräume der praktischen Theologie, Gerhard Marcel Martin zum 60 Geburtstag*, edited by Constanze Thierfelder and Dietrich Hannes Eibach, 215–224. Stuttgart: Kohlhammer.

2004. *The Structure of Religious Systems in Contemporary Japan: Shintō Variations on Buddhist Pilgrimage*. Occasional Papers 30. Marburg: Centre for Japanese Studies, University of Marburg.

2005a. "The way is the goal. Buddhist circulatory pilgrimage in Japan with special reference to selected artefacts." In *Pilgrims and Travellers in Search of the Holy*, edited by René Gothóni, 163–181. Bern: Peter Lang.

2005b. "Vorgabe und Praxis in den buddhistischen Pilgerfahrten Japans." In *Im Dickicht der Gebote: Studien zur Dalektik von Norm und Praxis in der Buddhismusgeschichte Asiens*, edited by Peter Schalk, 353–373. Stockholm: Stockholm University.

2005c. "Japanilaisen uskonnollisuuden sähkösiä heijastumia." In *Pyhä media*, edited by Johanna Sumiala-Seppänen, 146–166. Jyväskylä: Atena Kustannus.

2013a. *Strategies in the Study of Religions*, Volume 1, "Approaches and Positions." Berlin: Walter de Gruyter.

2013b. *Strategies in the Study of Religions*, Volume 2, "Religions in Relation and Motion." Berlin: Walter de Gruyter.

Pye, Michael, ed.

1993 *Macmillan Dictionary of Religion*. London: Macmillan. Republished 1994, New York: Continuum.

Pye, Michael and Triplett, Katja.

2004. " Religiöse Transaktionen: rational oder irrational?" In *Workshop Organisation und Ordnung der japanischen Wirtschaft IV. Themenschwerpunkt: Wahrnehmung, Institutionenökonomik und Japanstudien*, edited by W. Pascha and C. Storz, 27–38. Duisburg: Institut für Ostasienwissenschaften, Universität Duisburg-Essen.

2007. *Streben nach Glück. Schicksalsdeutung und Lebensgestaltung in japanischen Religionen*. Religiöse Gegenwart Asiens/Studies in Modern Asian Religions, vol. 1. Berlin: LIT-Verlag.

2011. *Pilgerfahrt Visuell. Hängerollen in der religiösen Alltagspraxis Japans*. Veröffentlichungen der Religionskundlichen Sammlung der Philipps-Universität Marburg Band 5. Marburg: Diagonal-Verlag.

Reader, Ian.

1987. "From asceticism to the package tour – the pilgrim's progress in Japan." *Religion* 17: 133–148.

1988. "Miniaturization and proliferation: A study of small-scale pilgrimages in Japan." *Studies in Central and East Asian Religions* 1: 50–66.

1993. *Sendatsu and the Development of Contemporary Japanese Pilgrimage.* Nissan Occasional Paper Series No. 17. Oxford: Nissan Institute of Japanese Studies.

2005. *Making Pilgrimages. Meaning and Practice in Shikoku.* Honolulu: University of Hawaii Press.

Rhodes, Robert
1987. "The Kaihōgyō practice of Mt. Hiei." *Japanese Journal of Religious Studies* 14(2-3): 185–202.

Rhys Davids, T.W. and C.A.F. Rhys Davids.
1966. *Dialogues of the Buddha.* 5th Edition. Translated from the Pali of the Dīgha Nīkaya. London: Luzac and Co, for the Pali Text Society.

Saikoku Yakushi Reijōkai (editorial authority).
1989. *Saikoku yonjūkyū Yakushi junrei (with a guide to the fuda places by Shimoyasuba Yoshiharu).* Ōsaka: Toki Shobō.

Sakai, Usaku.
1960. "Les pèlerinages au Japon." In *Les Pèlerinages*, edited by Anne-Marie Esnoul, *et al.*, 342–359. Paris: Éditions du Seuil.

Sakurazawa, Takahira.
1978. *Shinshikoku Okutama reijō hachijūhachi fudasho.* Tokyo: Musashino Kyōdoshi Kankōkai.

Satō, Hisamitsu.
2004. *Henro to junrei no shakaigaku.* Kyōto: Jinbun Shoin.
2006. *Henro to junrei no minzoku.* Kyōto: Jinbun Shoin.

Satō, Takashi.
1989. *Echigo sanjūsan Kannon fudasho junrei no tabi.* Niigata: Niigata Hōjigyōsha.

Satō, Tatsugen and Wakō Kaneko.
1989, 1996. *Shichifukujin.* Tokyo: Mokujisha.

Seckel, Dietrich.
1985. *Buddhistische Tempelnamen in Japan.* Stuttgart: Steiner-Verlag-Wiesbaden.

Seigensha Dainihenshūshitsu, ed.
2004. *Senja Fuda. Nidai Zeniya Matabei Korekushyon.* Kyōto: Seigensha.

Settsukuni Sanjūsankasho Reijōkai (editing society).
1982. *Settsukuni sanjūsankasho reijō annai chizu.* Kōbe: Settsukuni Sanjūsankasho Reijōkai.

Settsukuni Hachijūhassho Reijōkai (editing society).
1987. *Settsukuni hachijūhassho junrei chizu.* Kōbe: Settsukuni Hachijūhassho Reijōkai.

Shima, Kazuharu.
1983. *Gyōdō ni ikiru.* Tokyo: Kōsei Shuppansha.

Shimoyasuba, Yoshiharu (text) and Koji Kenshōkai (editorial authority).
   1979, 1992. *Kinki sanjūroku Fudōson*. Ōsaka: Koji Kenshōkai.
Shimoyasuba, Yoshiharu (text) and Tōkai Sanjūroku Fudōson Reijōkai (editorial authority).
   1986. *Tōkai sanjūroku Fudōson junrei*. Ōsaka: Toki Shobō.
Shinbutsureijōkai (editorial authority).
   2008. *Kami to hotoke no michi wo aruku*. Tokyo: Shūeisha.
Sōma, Dai.
   1982. *Ōmi 33-kasho*. Ōsaka: Hoikusha, Kara Bukkusu/Color Books.
Staal, Frits.
   1989. *Rules without Meaning: Rituals, Mantras and the Human Sciences*. Toronto Studies in Religion, vol 4. New York: Peter Lang.
Statler, Oliver.
   1984. *Japanese Pilgrimage*. London: Pan Books.
Stegerhoff, Renate.
   1990. *Wallfahrt als Ausdruck andiner Volksfrömmigkeit*. Unpublished MA Dissertation, Marburg University.
Stevens, John.
   1988. *The Marathon Monks of Mount Hiei*. Boston, MA: Shambala.
Suzuki, Beatrice Lane.
   2013. *Buddhist Temples of Kyōto and Kamakura*. Edited by Michael Pye. Eastern Buddhist Voices, vol. 5. Sheffield: Equinox Publishing.
Takemura, Toshinori.
   1994. *Kyō no o-Jizō-san*. Kyōto: Kyōto Shinbunsha.
Takizawa, Jō, *et al.*, eds.
   1973. *Kawasaki Daishi Fukkō Sanjūnen no Ayumi*. Kawasaki: Kawasaki Daishi Henshō Sōsho Kankōkai, Heigenji.
Tanaka, Yasuhiko.
   1990. *Kyō no fukujin meguri*. Kyōto: Kyōto Shinbunsha.
Teeuwen, Mark and Fabio Rambelli, eds.
   2003. *Buddhas and Kami in Japan. Honji Suijaku as a Contemporary Paradigm*. London: Routledge.
Tōbu Bijutsukan, Kyōto Bunkahakubutsukan, Nihonkeizaishinbunsha, eds.
   1996. *Saikoku sanjūsansho – Kannonreijō no shinkō to bijutsu*. Kyōto: Nihonkeizaishinbunsha.
Tōdō, Kyōshun.
   1988. *Jōdoshūnai ni okeru soseki junpai nit suite. Toku ni Reitaku Annaiki ikō*. Tokyo: Jōdo shū Press.
Tōkai Sanjūroku Fudōson Reijōkai (editorial authority).

1986. See Shimoyasuba Yoshiharu.

Turner, Victor and Edith Turner.
   1978. *Images and Pilgrimages in Christian Culture: Anthropological Perspectives.* New York: Columbia University Press.

Van Gennep, Arnold.
   1960. *The Rites of Passage.* Chicago, IL: Chicago University Press. First published 1908.

Watanabe, Katsumi.
   1989. *Kunisaki rokugō manzan reijō meguri. Usa Jingū to sanjūsan reijō junpai no tabi.* Oita: Kunisaki Rokugō Manzan Reijō Kai.

Watsuji, Tetsurō.
   1979. *Koji junrei.* Tokyo: Iwanami Shoten. First published 1919.

Yamada, Eiji.
   1979. *Edo sanjūsan kannon meguri.* Tokyo: Daizō Shuppan.

Yanagawa, Keiichi and Kiyomi Morioka, eds.
   1979. *Hawai nikkeishūkyō no tenkai to genkyō.* Tokyo: Tokyo University.
   1981. *Hawai nikkeijinshakai to nihonshūkyō.* Tokyo: Tokyo University.

Yoshinari, Isamu, ed.
   1996. *Nihon reichi-junrei sōkan (Rekishi Tokuhon Bessatsu 29).* Tokyo: Shinjinbutsuōraisha.

Index of Temples and Shrines

A

Akechidera 51
Akechiji 51–2
Amabiki Kannon 47, 66
Amaterasu Kōtai Jingū 164
Anaoji 42, 45
Ankōji 112
Anrakuji 47, 50, 84
Anshō-in 135
Anyō-in 47, 50, 63
Anyōji 135
Arakidera 51
Asahiji 61
Asakusadera 41
Asakusa Kannon 47–8
Asakusa Shrine 158
Atsuta Jingū 9, 145, 163
Awata Jinja 172
Ayako Tenmangū 172

B

Betsuganji 63
Bokuunji 51–2
Budarakuji 63
Butsumokuji 85
Butsunichi-an 62
Byōdōji 84, 107, 143

C

Chibadera 48, 50
Chikurinji 84
Chinnōji 116
Chion-in 127
Chionji 126
Chishaku-in 107, 112
Chisoku-in Chūzenji 47, 50
Chōdaiji 61
Chōfukuji 61
Chōhōji 42, 45, 67
Chōkeiji 61
Chōkenji 144
Chōkōji 51–52
Chōkokuji 47, 59–61
Chōmeiji 42, 46
Chōmyōji 123
Chōrakuji 61
Chōsen-in 51, 53
Chōsuiji 61
Chūzenji 47, 50

D

Daienji 51, 53
Daigoji 71, 114, see also Kami-Daigoji
Daihōonji 108
Daijiji 51–2
Daikakuji 50, 112
Daikōji 85
Daikokuji 143–4
Daikokusha 174
Daikōmyōji 107
Dainichiji 84, 91, 252
Dairokuten Sakaki Jinja 169

279

Daishidō 78, 105, 120, 183, 186–7, 252
Daishōji 113
Daitokuji 143
Daizenji 107, 117, 119
Dendengū 162
Dōjidō 51, 53
Dōryūji 86
Dōshū-in 112–3

E

Ebisu Shrine 147, 149–51, 154–6
Eifukuji 51, 85
Eiheiji 35, 112–3
Eiheiji Tokyo Betsuin 69
Eikandō 126, 135, 142
Engakuji 60, 62, 64
Engyōji 42, 45, 67
Enkōji 84
Enmeiji 63, 85
Enmyōji 85
Enpukuji 48, 50
Enryakuji 114, 130, 132, 146, 205
Entsūji 61
Enyūji 51, 53
Eyamisha 173

F

Fudōji 112
Fudōmyōōji 112
Fujiidera 42, 44–5, 84, 241
Fuji no mori Jinja 144, 172
Fukuōji 62
Fuonji 61
Fusaiji 61
Fushimi Inari Taisha 139, 143–4, 164
Futaarayama Jinja 176

G

Gakuenji 61
Gandenji 47, 50
Gankeiji 31, 41, 43, 46, 202
Gankōji 61
Gekū (Ise) 146
Genkūji 126
Gōdoji 51, 53
Goeidō 129
Gofukuji 54
Gokadō 51

Gokoku Jinja 176
Gokō no Miya 144, 172
Gokurakuji 63, 83
Gonjōji 126
Goō Jinja 172
Goryō Jinja 170, 172–3
Gōshōji 86
Gumyōji 47, 50
Gyōganji 38, 42, 45, 55, 242

H

Hachiman Daimyōjin 145
Hachimangū 53, 162–3
  Tomioka 166
  Usa 53
Hakusan Jinja 66, 166–7, 170
Hantaji 85
Hasedera 30–31, 33, 41–2, 45, 47,
  49–50, 63, 70, 139, 195, 241
Hase Kannon 47, 70
Hashidatedō 51, 53
Hashidateji 51
Heian Jingū 133, 163
Heikenji 98
Henshōji 143
Hie Jinja 166
Higashi Honganji 9, 127–9
Hikawa Jinja 166
Hinokumo Jinja 164
Hiraide Raiden Jinja 176
Hirano Jinja 164
Hirose Jinja 164
Hirota Jinja 164
Hiyoshi Taisha/Jinja 130, 164, 173
Hiyoshisha 173
Hōchōji 51–2
Hōgonji 42, 46
Hōji 143
Hōjuji 85
Hōkaiji 63
Hōkanji 108
Hōki-in 41
Hokki-in 30, 41, 43, 46, 202
Hokkeji 42, 45
Hōkokuji 63
Hōkongō-in 108
Hōmyō-in 93

Index of Temples and Shrines

Honda Hachimangū 156
Hōnenji 126
Honganji 9, 127–9
Hongwanji 128, see also Nishi Honganji
Honkokuji 122–3
Honmanji 123
Honnōji 123
Honpōji 123
Honryūji 123
Honzenji 123
Hōon-in 112
Hōonkōji 126
Hōrakuji 112
Hōrinji 84, 107–8, 162
Hōsenji 51, 53
Hoshigamiji 61
Hoshigayaji 47, 50
Hoshinoya Kannon 47–8
Hōshōji 52–3
Hotsumisakiji 84
Hōunji 52–3
Hōzanji 112
Hyakumanben Chionji 126

I

Ichibatadera 59, 62
Ichibataji 62
Ichihime Jinja 172
Ichijōji 42, 45
Ichinomiyaji 86
Idoji 84, 91
Iinuma Kannon 48
Iiyama Kannon 47
Iizumi Kannon 47
Ikisu Jingū 159
Ikukunitama Jinja 164
Imado Jinja 169
Imaizumi Yasaka Jinja 176
Imakumano Jinja 172
Imakumano (Kannonji) 42, 45, 136
Imamiya Jinja 170, 172–4
Imamiya Ebisu Shrine 151
Imamiyabō 51–2
Inari Shrine/s 139, 143, 145, 153, 156, 164, 173, 191
Inarisha 173

Ise Jingū 1, 9, 14, 72, 126–7, 145–6, 159–10, 162, 164–5
Ishifudadō 51
Ishiki Yomizu Hachimangū 162–3
Ishiteji 85, 97–8, 222
Ishiyamadera 42, 45
Isonokami Jingū 163
Isshinji 126
Itsukushima Jinja 135, 152
Iwadono Kannon 47, 52
Iwaidō 51
Iwakuraji 61
Iwamadera 42, 45
Iwamotoji 51, 84, 91
Iwanouedō 51, 53
Iwashimizu Hachimangū 163
Iwayadō 54
Iwayaji 62, 85, 112–3
Iyadaniji 85
Izanagi Jinja 164
Izumo Taisha 1, 9, 14, 53–4, 57, 59–62, 69, 72, 141, 150, 163–4, 188–9, 209
Izuru Kannon 47

J

Jakkōji 123
Jigenji 51–2
Jikōdera 47, 50
Jikōji 47
Jingū, see Ise Jingū
Jinne-in 85
Jinushisha 173
Jionji 47, 50
Jishuinarisha 173
Jissō-in 112
Jitsusō-in 112
Jizōji 84, 100, 117
Jōban-in 117
Jōchiji 64
Jōdoji 85
Jōeiji 61
Jōjuin 63
Jōkō-in 122
Jōkōmyōji 63
Jōmyōji 63
Jōonji 61
Jōrakuji 51–2, 54, 84

Jōrinji 51, 53
Jōruriji 85
Jōsenji 51–52
Jōsōji 61
Jōzenji 117, 240
Jufukuji 61, 63
Jūrakuji 84
Jūrinji 126

K

Kaburaiji 112
Kachiodera 42, 45
Kaizōji 63
Kakurinji 84
Kameido Tenmangū 166–7
Kameyama Jinja 164
Kamidaigoji 42, 45, 71, 112, 218
Kamigamo Jinja 117
Kamigoryō Jinja 133
Kamo Wake Ikazuchi Jinja 163
Kamo Mioya Jinja 163
Kaname Kannon 47
Kanda Shrine (Myōjin) 166–8
Kandaijin Jinja 172
Kandōji 61
Kanjizaiji 85, 237
Kannondō 65, 78, 183
Kannonji 42, 45, 51, 53, 61, 85–6, 95, 136, 252
Kannonshōji 42, 44, 46
Kanzeonji 47
Kasamoridera 48, 50
Kasamoriji 48
Kashihara Jingū 163
Kashima Jingū 159
Kasuga Jinja/Taisha 163–4, 172, 174
Katori Jingū 159
Katsuōji 42, 45
Katsuoji 126
Katsurakawa Sokushōmyōō-in 112
Katsura Jizōji 117
Kawasaki Daishi 98–9
Kechiganji 52
Kegonji 37, 43, 46, 137
Kenchōji 63
Kenninji 108
Kenshindō 131

Kichijōji 85, 91
Kikusuiji 52–3
Kimiidera 42, 45
Kimiisan 43
Kimpusenji 121
Kinshōji 51–2
Kinzōji 86
Kirihataji 84
Kishima Jinja 162
Kisshōin Tenmangū 172
Kisshōji 85
Kita-in 148
Kitamuki Kannon 47
Kitamukizan Fudō-in 112
Kitano Tenmangū 55, 133, 162, 205, 252
Kitsushōji 85
Kiyomizudera 42, 45–6, 48, 50, 61, 112–3, 126, 133, 135
Kiyomizuji 61
Kiyomizu Kannon 48
Kiyosumi-dera 122
Kiyotakidera 47, 49
Kiyotakiji 47, 49–50, 84
Kiyozumidera 122
Koami Jinja 169
Kōanji 61
Kobayashidera 51
Kōdai (Kōtai) Jingū 162–4
Kōdō Gyōganji 42, 45, 242
Kōenji 85
Kōfukuji 39, 63, 114
Kokawadera 42, 45
Kokubunji 84–6, 112
Kōmineji 84
Kōmyōji 47, 50, 61, 63, 126–7
Kongōchōji 84
Kongōfukuji 84
Kongōhōji 42, 45
Kongōji 61, 99
Konkaikōmyōji 126, 242
Kōnomineji 84
Konpira Shrine 72, 80, 101, 140–1, see also Kotohira Shrine
Konponchūdō 130, 132
Konsenji 83
Konzōji 86
Kōonji 85

Index of Temples and Shrines

Kōryūji 162
Kōsanji 37
Kōshō-in 86
Kōsokuji 63
Kōtai Jingū 146, 162, 164
Kotohira Shrine 80, see also Konpira Shrine
Kōtoku-in 63, 70
Kōyamaji 86
Kōzōji 48
Kuhonji 63
Kumadaniji 84
Kumano Hayatama Taisha 146
Kunikakasu Jinja 164
Kuramaguchi Jizō 117, 240–1
Kyōōgokokuji 108
Kyōonji 63
Kyōzenji 112
Kyūshōji 51, 53

M

Maegamiji 85
Makinoodera 42, 45
Makioka Jinja 164
Mandaraji 85
Manganji, 47, 50, 56, 62, 64, 110
Manpukuji 61
Manshu-in 112
Mashiko Kannon 47
Matsunoo Shrine 164
Matsunoodera 42, 45
Matsuo Jinja 164
Matsuodera 211
Meigetsu-in 64
Meiji Jingū 163
Meisekiji 85
Meoto Daikokusha 174
Mibudera 116
Miidera, 42, 45, 65, 68, 71, 114, 147
Mii Shrine 154
Mimurotoji 33, 42, 45
Minami Hokkeji 42, 45
Minedera 61
Mineji 61
Mizusawadera 47, 50
Mokujikidera 135
Moto Ise Kono Jinja 165

Motoyamaji 40, 85
Mudōji 112, 133
Munakatasha 173
Myōdenji 123
Myōganji 123
Myōkakuji 123
Myōkanji 54
Myōkenji 123
Myōkō-in 63
Myōōdō 112, 133
Myōō-in 63
Myōonji 51
Myōrakuji 94
Myōrenji 123
Myōshinji 162

N

Nachi Shrine 23, 243
Nagaoji 86
Nagaoka Tenmangū 172
Nagoji 48
Naikū (Ise) 146, 162, 164
Nakayamadera 42, 45, 54, 95, 112–113
Nakodera 48
Nakoji 48, 50
Nako Kannon 48
Namegawa Kannon 48–9
Namekawa Kannon 48
Nan'endō 41, 42, 45
Nankōbō 85
Nanzenji 49
Nariaiji 42, 45, 165
Narita-san 99–100, 113
Naritasan Ōsakabetsuin Myōō-in 112
Negoroji 86, 112
Nenbutsudō 127
Nezu Jinja 166-7, 170
Nichirinji 47, 50, 98
Nichizengū 164
Nikaidō 126–7
Ninnaji 97, 108, 112-3, 162
Nishi Honganji 9, 117, 127–8
Nishinomiya Jinja 151
Nison-in 126
Niu Kawakami Jinja 164
Nogi Jinja 144
Nosakaji 51–2

Nyakuōji 172
Nyoirinji 112–3

O

Ofune Kannon 52
Oginodō 51
Oguraji 61
Ōji Jinja 166–7
Okadera 42, 45
Okazaki Jinja 172
Ōkuboji 86
Oku no In 130, 204
Ōmidō 47
Ōmiwa Jinja 164
Ongakuji 51, 53
Onjōji 42, 45, 68, 71
Onoterusaki Jinja 169
Onsenji 114
Onzanji 84
Orihimesha 173
Ōsakabetsuin Myōō-in 112
Ōsaki Jinja 176
Ōshima Jinja 164
Otebanji 51
Otehandera 51
Ōtori Jinja 169
Ōyaji 47, 49–50
Ōya Kannon 47
Ōyamato Jinja 164
Ōyashiro (Izumo) 163–4

R

Raiden Jinja 176
Raikōji 63
Rakuhōji 47, 50, 66
Reiun-in 107
Rendaiji 61
Rengeji 61, 112
Renjō-in 63
Rokkakudō 42, 45, 55, 67, 262
Rokudai-in 95
Rokuharamitsuji 42, 45, 116, 133, 218
Rokujidō (of Shitennōji) 126–7
Rokuson no Ō Jinja 172
Ryōanji 142, 150, 153, 162
Ryōsenji 82
Ryōzenji 81, 83, 189, 220
Ryūgaiji 42, 45
Ryūhō-in 63
Ryūhonji 123
Ryūkōji 85
Ryūsekiji 51, 53
Ryūsenji 112
Ryūshakuji 132
Ryūshō-in 48, 50

S

Sai-in (Kasuga Jinja) 172
Saikōji 51–2
Saimyōji 47, 50, 54
Sairinji 85
Saizenji 51–2
Sakaki Jinja 169
Sankakuji 85
Sanzen-in 112
Sashiro Kannon 47
Satakeji 47, 50
Sefukuji 42, 45
Seigandoji 42, 45, see also Seigantoji
Seiganji 62, 126–7, 131, 135
Seigantoji 23, 33, 42, 45, 146, 201, 243
Seigensha 191
Seikyōji 107
Seirinji 126
Seiryūji 49, 68, 126–127, 205
Seiwa-in 55
Sekkeiji 84
Senbon Shakadō 107, 116
Sengakuji 203
Sengensha 66
Senju-in 61, 63
Senkōji 61
Sennyūji 107
Sensōji 41, 43, 47–50, 154, 158, 191, 202
Senyōji 48
Senyūji 85
Shakadō (Senbon) 107, 116
Shiba Daijingū 166–8
Shiba Jinmyō-sama 167
Shidoji 86
Shiki Shrine 66
Shimabuji 51–2
Shimo Goryō Jinja 170, 172
Shimogamo Jinja 133

Index of Temples and Shrines

Shinagawa Jinja 166–8
Shinjō-in 58
Shinnyodō 133, 135, 139
Shinpukuji 51–2
Shinshōji 84, 113
Shinyakushiji 114
Shippōryuji 112
Shiraiwa Kannon 47
Shiramineji/Shiromineji 86
Shiramine Jingū 172
Shirasagi Jinja 176
Shirayama Kannon 51
Shitaya Jinja 169
Shitennōji 14, 43, 55, 110, 112–4, 126–7, 130–1, 156, 202
Shizudō (of Tōdaiji) 126
Shōbōji 47
Shōfukuji 47, 50
Shōgenji 130
Shōgo-in 112
Shōhōji 42, 45, 47, 50, 143, 218
Shōjōke-in 126
Shōkokuji 47, 107, 142, 147, 149, 153
Shōren-in 112
Shōrinji 51–5
Shōrin-in 126
Shōryūji 84
Shōzanji 84
Shusshakaji 85
Sōgenji 94
Sōhonzan Chion-in 107–8, 127
Sōjiji 42, 45
Sokushōmyōō-in 112
Sugawara-in Tenmangū 172
Sugimotodera 47, 60, 62–4
Sugimoto Kannon 47
Sugimotoji 47, 50
Suika Tenmangū 173
Suisenji 52–53
Suitengū 169
Sumadera 95
Sumiyoshi Jinja/Taisha 156, 164, 169
Sunzuji 62
Suwa Shrine (Daimyōjin) 145

T

Tachiki Kannon 47
Taga Jinja/Taisha 164
Taihōji 85
Taimadera 126
Tairyūji 84, 112
Taisanji 85
Taishōgunsha 173
Taiyūji 112
Taizanji 85
Takahata Fudō 99
Takakuradera 48, 50
Takebe Jinja/Taisha 164
Takidani Fudōmyōji 112
Tanba no Yosa no Miya 165
Tanemaji 84
Tanigumisan 37
Tanjōji 126
Tashiro Kannon 47
Tatsueji 84
Tatsuta Jinja 164
Tenjinsha (Kameido) 166
Tenmangū
  Kitano 55, 133, 162, 205, 252
  Ayako 172
  Kameido 167
  Kisshōin 172
  Nagaoka 172
  Sugawara-in 172
  Suika 173
Tennōji 86
Tenryūji 156, 162, 245
Toba Jizō 117
Tōdaiji 64, 126
Tōdō (Mt. Hiei) 130
Tōfukuji 107, 113
Tōji 45, 108
Tōkeiji, 64
Tokujōmyō-in 137
Tokurin-an 117
Tomioka Hachimangū 166
Toyokuni Jinja 172
Toyouke Daijingū 146
Tsubosakadera 42, 45
Tsukikagedō 51
Tsukinowadera 126
Tsukiyomisha 173
Tsūshōji 134

U

Unbenji 85
Usa Hachimangū 53
Ushibusedō 51
Utsunomiya Futaarayama Jinja 176

W

Wakamiya 174
Wakamiyasha 173
Waraten Jingū 172

Y

Yakuōji 84
Yakuriji 86
Yakushiji 114, 175–6
Yamadera 132
Yamizosan 47
Yanodō 51
Yasaka Jinja 133, 164, 176
Yasakaji 85
Yashimaji 86
Yasukuni Shrine 165
Yasuzumi Jinja 176
Yōhōji 123
Yokawa (of Mt. Hiei) 67, 122, 130
Yokomineji 85
Yōmeiji 61
Yoshimi Kannon 47
Yoshiminedera 31, 42, 45
Yoshino Jinja 164
Yoshizaki Betsuin 129
Yūseiji 123
Yushima Jinja 170

Z

Zenjibuji 84
Zenjōji 61
Zenkōji 41, 43, 62, 137, 202, 230, 260
Zenkokuji 150
Zenrakuji 84
Zenrinji 135
Zentsūji 86
Zuisenji 63

General Index

The following indications are used to assist in the differentiation of Japanese proper nouns: auth. –author name; city –city name; mt. –mountain; pn. –name of person (other than an author); pln. –place name; pref. –prefecture; prov. –province (traditional); ward –city ward. Temple and shrine names are listed in a separate index.

A

abbot 97–9, 241
abbreviation (in religion) 10, 17, 65–7, 75, 92–3, 96, 98, 120, 194, 198, 208, 230, 234, 256
abortion 109, 115, 119, 242, 245
Ācāla 91
adept 10, 132–3, 228, 257
advertisement 11, 96–7, 100, 148, 151, 165, 175, 191–2, 217, 219
affinity 11, 46, 149, 155, 213, 218, 253
  day 11, 99, 117, 155
ageing 136, 255
agent (divine) 182
Aichi (pref.) 113
Aizen Myōō 104
Aizu region 57, 68
ajari 132–3
ajisai-matsuri 170
Aki no kuni (prov.) 152
Akṣayamati 247
aku (evil) 233
Allgäu 20

altar (Buddhist) 65, 200, 230
  Christian 20
  house altar (*kamidana*) 172
Amahashidate (pln.) 165
Amaterasu 145, 162–5
ambiguity 142, 261, 267
ambivalence 158, 231, 252
Amida 70, 83–7, 90–2, 108–9, 124, 127, 129, 131, 135, 201, 203–4, 217, 234, 244, 247
Amidadō 126, 135
Amitābha 124, 127
amulet 18, 162, 175, 184, 236–8
analysis 5–6, 15, 17, 25, 185–187, 211, 259, 265, 267
Ānanda 213–4
ancestors 1, 71, 74, 103, 119, 200, 205, 208–9, 229, 244, 261, 263
anger 232–4, 238
animal/s 115, 119, 135, 144, 161
annai 10, 54, 70, 159
annaisho 64
anniversary 94, 107–8, 125, 166

anthropology 15, 21, 58, 76
anzan 169, 176
Aoyama Shoin 245–246
Aparecida 245
appearance/s
  of bodhisattvas 11, 29, 116, 167, 203, 237, 243, 246–7, 252
  of buddhas 87, 105
  of Mary 245
apron/bib 96, 116
Arashiyama (pln.) 107, 161–2, 245
architecture, 9, 18, 137–8, 213, 217, 260
arduous 10, 17, 66, 100, 110, 121, 133, 140, 148, 160, 184, 216, 227
arigatō 96, 211
aristocracy 31, 113, 116
armour 35–36, 38, 87, 151
arms (many) 38, 43, 158
artefacts 24–5, 43, 197, 201, 205
Asahi Shinbun 144, 148
Asakusa (pln.) 41, 47–8,
  Kannon 47
  Shichifukujin 149, 154, 157–8
ascetic/s 4–5, 9, 10, 80, 94, 110, 121, 142, 227
Ashigara (mt.) 32
Ashikaga shogunate 156
Ashuku Nyorai 108
association/s
  pilgrimage 64, 94–5, 121, 134, 136, 169, 175, 183, 192
  shrines 177
  tourism 99, 155
  wasan 242
Association of Shintō Shrines 177
astrology 108, 123–4, 161
asuras 135
Athos (mt.) 12
Atsuta Daimyōjin 145
attainment 12, 79, 105, 138, 152, 214–5, 226–8, 244, 255–7
  no-attainment 255–7
attire (of pilgrims) 220
aum 221
Auroville 22
auspicious 123, 149, 151, 154
Avalokiteśvara 29, 215, 244, 246–8

avatar 167, 241
avert (malfortune) 87, 144, 169, 176
avoidance
  of disease 39
  of harm 176, 225
Awa (prov.) 57, 78–9, 83, 227, 237
Awara (city) 129
Ayodhya 22

B

Bandō Kannon circuit 3–4, 32–3, 46–50, 54–6, 60, 64, 66, 68–9, 72, 74, 110, 198–9, 202, 222
bangai 30–31, 41, 43, 59, 62, 72, 94, 157, 201–2
banner/s 117, 131, 165
Bantō 32, see also Bandō
Bashō 132
Basilica 17
Batō Kannon/Kanzeon 36, 39–40, 42, 53, 65, 85, 87, 115
Bavaria 20
bead/s 97, 136
behalf of 116, 188, 192, 199, 211
bell 178, 183, 220
Benares 17, 214
benefit/s (this-worldly) 5–6, 8, 12, 39, 65, 67, 105, 109, 117, 119–20, 127, 131, 133, 141, 143–4, 147, 155–6, 160, 162, 169–72, 175–6, 178–9, 192–3, 195–6, 206, 209, 211–2, 216–7, 236, 238–9, 246–7, 252, 254, 262
Benten, see Benzaiten
Benzaiten 15, 68, 104, 131, 135–6, 142–4, 147, 149–53, 155–8, 242
bhagavant 106
Bhardwaj, Surinder 14
bib *see* apron/bib
birth
  Buddha 120
  Dengyō Daishi 130
  easy 245
  year of 108
  in hells 250
Bishamon/ten 85, 91–2, 104, 136, 147, 150–1, 155–6

General Index

Biwa, Lake 15, 54, 65, 68, 71, 130, 142, 147, 152
Black Stone 18, 22
Blacker Carmen (auth.) 133–4
blessing/s 100, 133, 136, 153, 205
blue-black Fudō
Blyth, Reginald Horace (auth.) 115
bō 86
boat 159, 173, 241, 244
Bocking, Brian 163
Bodai wasan 243
bodai 79, 227–8, 231
Bodaiji 41–3, 45–6, 202
Bodhgayā 214–215, 218
bodhi 79, 227, 255
  tree 215
bodhisattva/s 2, 6, 11, 21, 29–30, 34–5, 38–9, 66–7, 78–9, 82, 86–8, 91–2, 98–9, 103–6, 108–9, 115–16, 119–23, 127, 134–5, 145, 153, 157, 167, 175, 188, 194, 202–3, 205, 207, 210–11, 215, 218, 221, 227, 231, 235, 237, 242, 244–8, 251–2, 254–6, 261, *see also* Bosatsu
body 109, 119, 133, 171, 209, 220, 227, 232, 238, 248–9, 255
  of Buddha 214, 216
  compassionate 250
  image 43
  national (*kokutai*) 14
  transformation 145
Bohner, Alfred 12, 15, 75–6, 79–81, 223
bokefūji 136
book/let/s
  devotional texts 33, 43, 57, 106, 186, 193–4, 218, 230–2, 235–7, 239–40, 242–4, 246–8, 253, 256
  of pilgrims, for seals 18, 26, 37, 40, 43, 48, 62, 65, 72, 94, 108, 122, 124, 131, 134, 136, 149, 154, 159–61, 167–8, 174, 179, 183, 185–6, 197–9, 200, 205, 208, 226
  see also guidebook
bō-rě (han-nya) 254
Bosatsu/Daibosatsu 87, 106, 121, 123, 255
  Fugen 107

Jizō 36, 67, 84–5, 88, 91, 92, 97, 100, 103, 107, 109, 115–6, 131, 177, 241–2, 245
Kanjizai 254
Kannon 36, 49, 56–7, 59, 87, 92, 108, 116, 121, 145, 194, 201, 234, 254, 262
Kanzeon 84–7, 91–2, 109, 188, 192, 194, 221, 237, 247, 252–3
Kokūzō, 84, 88, 92, 108, 236
Miroku 84, 88, 92, 107, 154
Monju 84, 88, 92, 107, 109, 236
Myōken 123
Seishi 108
Shikoku Bosatsu statistics 92
Shinpen 121
botan 205
Brahma 246, 250–1
Brazil 245
brilliance of state 166
brocade 94, 189, 201, 204
Bùdài 154
Buddha/s, *see also* Nyorai
  Amida 70, 124, 127, 131, 201, 217, 244
  as Nyorai 86, 92
  future 88, 104–5, 154
  Great (Daibutsu) 70
  historical (also putative) 70, 79, 87, 105, 120, 213–6, 218, 223, 230, 232, 234, 237, 240, 247, 253, 255, 260
  Jizō as buddha 119
  Medicine 59 (Yakushi), 114
  Miroku 154
  rarity of 232
  Śākyamuni 87, 105, 119, 155, 218
  Thirteen 103, 106–9, 236
  Vairocana 145
  Yakushi 114, 175
buddha/s 106 *and passim*
  gods and buddhas 1, 105, 117, 144, 146, 182
  metaphysically real 252
  stone buddhas 68, 100, 134–5
buddhahood 54, 105, 109, 152, 227, 232
Buddha-way 235, 261
Buddhism/Shintō 14, *see also shinbutsubunri*
Bunkyō-ku (ward) 66, 166, 170

business 56, 171, 190–2
    success 144, 151, 155, 169, 176, 182, 188
butsu 87–8, 103, 106
butsudan 230, see also altar
butsuma 200
Buzan-ha 30, 45–6, 50, 70
Byakue Kannon/Kanzeon 251–2
byōki heiyu 176

C

cairn 223
caitya 216
calamities 87
calendricity 123, 144, 170
calligraphy 16, 58, 162, 190, 203, 222
    for pilgrim's record 18, 26, 41, 43, 48–9, 72, 126, 134, 136, 167, 173, 175, 183–4, 196–204, 208, 221, 226, 265
calvary 19
catalogue 44, 48, 94, 106, 129, 161, 202
cathedral/s 19–21
Catholic 20, 22, 245
celestial beings 6, 29, 86, 91, 105, 116, 135, 158, 236, see also divinities
cemetery 1, 22, 106–7, 109, 115, 204, 209
certification 184
cessation 255–6
Chalma 22
Chan 154
chant/ing 106, 193–4, 218, 224, 230, 251
chapel 20, 157
Chiba (pref.) 56–7, 64, 99, 122
Chichibu (city) 4, 32, 148, 155, 216,
    Kannon pilgrimage 4, 26, 32–4, 46, 48–9, 51–2, 54, 56, 58, 60, 68–9, 72, 74, 198–9, 202, 222
chikamichi 80, 96
Chikubushima (pln.) 15, 135, 142, 152–3
childbirth 117, 144, 252
children 39, 115–7, 119, 175, 242, 245, 247
Chilson, Clarke 94
China 13, 29, 91, 116, 145, 153, 212–3, 215–8, 226, 252, 260
Chinese
    overseas 29
    figures 116, 117, 154, 215
    pilgrimage 212–3, 215

terms 34, 86, 88, 91, 104, 116, 150, 154, 176, 248, 254
texts 38, 194, 227, 237, 239–40, 242, 244, 246, 248, 254–5
traditions 144, 147, 154, 244, 248
Chita Peninsula pilgrimage 37, 40, 93–4, 189, 208
Chiyoda Ward 165–6
Chizan-ha 45, 50, 107–8
chō (distance) 167
chō (notebook) 197
choice 17, 57, 167, 234
Chōshi (city) 56, 64
Christ 19, 20, 231
Christian/ity 11, 19, 21, 213, 233
chrysanthemum 170, 202, 205
Chūgoku region 58
church/es 16, 19–20, 22, 71, 128, 231
circuit/s (general) 4, 9, 44, 106, 124–5, 131, 139, 143, 146, 148–9, 208, 210–11, 224–5
    Kannon (various) 26, 31, 33, 41, 54–5, 57, 59, 60, 62, 69, 72, 200
    Fudō, 111–3
    saintly founders 120–7
    Shichifukujin 154–9
    Shikoku 75–102
    Shintō-based 159–80, 261
    Yakushi 113–4
circulation 6–8, 66, 73–4, 81, 103, 117, 133–5, 156, 159, 165
circulatory 1–2, 4–6, 8–11, 16, 19–22, 24, 29, 32, 60, 71–2, 74, 103, 116, 119–20, 124–5, 128, 130, 132–3, 135, 137–8, 140, 144, 146–7, 158–60, 162, 166, 168, 179, 181, 189, 200, 215, 218, 210, 212–3, 217, 223, 259–62, 264–5, 267
circumambulation 81, 97, 136–9, 145, 217
civil religion 178, 211
clairvoyance 228
clockwise 81, 97, 137–8, 158
cloth sack
clothing 12, 17, 216, 218–20
coffin 200, 220
cognitive dissonance 196

coin/s 68, 99, 150, 178, 185–6
collection
  of fees 71, 81, 129
  by pilgrims 43, 94, 97–8, 129, 133, 134, 136, 154, 160–1, 163, 168, 172, 175, 183–4, 186, 191, 197–8, 200, 203, 205
  collectors 10, 191
colour 33, 41, 100, 190, 204–5, 230
  pilgrims' slips 94, 189
commemoration 31, 40, 43, 54, 62, 99, 107, 126, 131, 144, 149, 154, 159, 162–3, 168–9, 173, 183–4, 197, 199–200, 242
commentary 225, 251, 254
commercial 8, 12, 27, 67, 82, 147, 151, 161–2, 169, 182, 190–1, 202, 205, 262
communitas 11–12, 17, 220
community 11, 115, 117, 214, 222
companion/s 26, 76, 184
  of Shinran 128–9
  spiritual 3, 105, 187, 222, 236
company (business) 148, 151, 162
  employee/s 191–2
compassion/ate 2, 87–8, 105, 139, 145, 188, 202, 221, 224, 227, 237, 248, 250–1, 253, 256, 261
competition 55, 57, 171
completion 4, 6–10, 17–19, 21, 52, 62, 68, 72–4, 79–80, 86, 96, 99, 101–2, 114, 120, 133, 138, 140, 146, 154, 159, 163, 170–5, 186, 189, 197–8, 200, 201–2, 205–6, 209, 211–12, 221–2, 225–7, 229, 263–4
Compostela 18, 20–21
Conze, Edward 254, 256–7
copying (sūtras) 58, 161, 179, 183, 185–6, 193, 197, 208, 216, 254
correlation (with Shintō) 53, 145–6, 157
cosmology 104, 203, 221
cost/ly 12, 17, 24, 26, 108, 144, 161, 170, 182, 191, 196, 198, 201, 205
cremation 214
crossroads 115, 130–1
cult/s 78, 88, 100, 109–10, 152–3, 214–6

D

Daibokuten 156
daibosatsu 84, 88, 121, 242
Daibutsu 70
Daigoha 70
Daihannyakyō 142
daiji daihi 221, 223
Daikoku/ten 136, 142–4, 149–50, 154–5, 174
daimoku 122
Dainichi Nyorai 84–5, 87, 89, 91–2, 108, 145, 232–3
Daishi (meaning) 227
  Dengyō 130, 145
  Enkō 242
  Ganzan 67
  Jikaku 132
  Jishō 131–2
  Kenshin 131
  Kōbō 3, 4, 15, 68, 75, 78–99, 101, 103, 105, 120, 130–1, 139, 183, 187, 192, 195, 200 204, 220–3, 227, 236, 238, 260
  Tendai 145
  Yakuyoke 237
Daishidō 78, 105, 120, 183, 186–7, 252
  meaning 78
Daniel, Elton L. 18
darani 230–1, 237
Davids, Rhys 214
dead, realm of 30, 117
death 30, 54, 115, 129, 249–50, 255
  anniversaries 107–8, 125
  of pilgrim 13, 214, 220–2, 263
  on cross 19
deathlessness 248
dedication (of pilgrimage) 187–8, 201, 222, 235, 244
definition of pilgrimage 11, 16, 18, 264
deity
  tutelary 115
  wrathful 150
  harvest 153
  see also divinity/ies
Delhi 218
deliverance 36, 39, 239

Demachi (pln.) 142–3, 152
demon/s 39, 151, 242, 247, 249–50, 252
Dengyō Daishi (pn.) 130, 145
denki/denpa 162
denomination/s 1, 9, 30, 35, 41, 49–50, 52, 60–61, 65, 69–71, 82, 95, 107, 110, 113–4, 121–4, 127–8, 131, 137, 141, 155, 198, 200, 207–208, 227, 230–1, 235, 242, 244, 254, 260, 267
denominational 14, 34–5, 41, 44–6, 49, 68–71, 101, 107, 109–10, 121, 127, 136, 145, 194, 217, 230, 234, 263
department store 13, 169–70
deposition (by pilgrim) 24, 97, 183, 186–7, 189, 211, 221–2, 236, 253
destiny 123, 169, 176
detachment 154
deva/s 104, 116, 135, 150
devotional
  acts 10, 13, 19, 20, 21, 31, 33, 41, 97–100, 133, 138–40, 147, 158, 177, 183–4, 187, 193–6, 265
  aids 41, 205, 218, 225, 245
  attitudes 46, 49, 65, 67–8, 75, 78, 91–2, 96, 98–9, 104–5, 108–9, 121, 123, 125, 133–4, 156, 165, 185, 193, 200, 207, 213, 215, 221, 225, 231, 224, 245
  texts, *see* booklets
Dewa Sanzan (mt.) 9, 145, 210
dhāraṇi 230–1
Dharma 121, 204, 212, 214, 218, 232, 234–6, 246–8, 250, 253
  Dharma-body 216
  Dharma flower 231
  Dharma King 31
  Dharma rain 248, 250
dharma of emptiness 257
dialectic/al (Buddhist) 5, 21, 179, 182, 246–7, 256, 261
diamond 221–3, 237, 249
Diamond Sūtra 221
directions, ten 223–4, 250
divination 192
divine, the 182, 255
  agent 255
  persons 121

divinity/ies 1, 180, 195, 242, *see also* deity, gods and buddhas, *shin-butsu*
  agricultural, 39, 65, 115, *see also* deity
  Buddhist 4, 24, 92, 100, 103–6, 122, 221, 236–7,
  daimyōjin 145
  female 135, 152
  fertility 115
  good fortune (seven) 147–59, 260
  Indian 242
  kami 9, 121, 122, 145, 173, 261
  local 24, 167
  north pole 122
  protective 96
  Shintō 159, 162–3, 174–5, 179, 252
  ten/tiān 91–2
  thirty 145
  wayside 115, 177
  wealth (Inari) 156
dō (hall) 34, 104–5, 131
doctrine/doctrinal 17, 131, 138, 144, 207, 209–10, 231, 260, 263
  in Shin Buddhism 70, 127–8, 131
Dōgen (Zenji) 4, 103, 124, 213
dōgyō ninin 221–3
  sannin/mannin 222
donation 67, 115, 185, 195, 197, 199, 203, 221, 237
Dōsojin 115, 177
dove (completion) 154
Dōzo 211
dragon 152–3, 249, 252
dual occupancy 9, 14, 22–4, 216
Duquenne, Robert 153

E

East Asia 104, 124, 151, 153, 213
eastern Japan 3, 32, 81, 98, 113, 128, 159, 175, 229
east nor west 223
Ebisu (–gami, –ten) 147, 149–51, 154–6
Echigo 54, 128
  Kannon route 58
economic/s 13, 17, 32, 74, 82, 101, 115, 166, 176, 215, 267,
Edo 3–4, 53, 154, 166

General Index

Edofudashokai 55, 70, 183, 253
Kannon pilgrimages 55, 69, 246
Period 32-3, 46, 48, 55, 64, 76, 95, 119, 142, 148-50, 159, 160, 191, 199, 252
Egypt 18
Ehime Prefecture 78, 85, 96, 134
eight
  gods of good fortune 169
  shrines 169, 170, 172-3, 175-6, 178
eighty-eight (Shikoku) 75, 79-101, 183, 186, 197, 252, 254
ekō 235
Ekōmon 185, 194
electricity shrine 162
Eleven-faced Kannon 35, 65, 87
Eliade, Mircea 13
Ely 21
ema 65-6, 124, 162, 168, 183, 193, 195
Éméi, Mount 215
Emperor (Tennō) 168
  Go-Hanazono 156
  Go-Shirakawa 54, 119
  Hirohito 166
  Kazan 31, 41, 43
  Meiji 166, 179
  Ōjin 156
  Reigen 120
  Uda 113
Empress Suiko 130
emptiness 88, 91, 248, 255-7
empty 21, 67, 222-4, 238, 248, 254, 256-7
Enbutsu Sumiko (auth.) 32, 34
Enchin (pn.) 71
engi 11, 22, 46, 119, 198, 212-3
Church of England 20-21, 71
Enkō Daishi 124, 242
enlightenment 79, 83, 105, 138, 196, 223, 227-9, 231, 235
  of parents/ancestors 54, 244
  of the Buddha 79, 120, 214-5, 217-8
Enma-ō 30, 116
enman wagō 169
Enmei Jizō 84, 88, 242
Enmei Kannon 253
enmusubi 169, 174, 176
Enmyō Jizō 84, 88, *see also* Enmei Jizō
ennichi 11, 99, 155

Ennin 71, 132, 213
En no Gyōja 103-4, 110, 121
En no Ozuno 121
Enoden (railway) 157
Enoshima (pln.) 135, 152, 157-8
Enshū region 53
enthronement ceremonies 165
entrepreneur 81, 58
enumeration 36, 103, 120-1, 134-5, 138, 146, *see also* numeration
ephemera/al 24-26, 48-9, 169, 192, 229, 236
esoteric 109, 213, 228
  Tendai 71, 235
  Shingon 109, 121, 221
essentialism 245, 207, 208, 259
essentialism (insider) 145
ethnology, 16, 20, 58
Etō-ku (ward) 166
evil/s 39, 233
  persons/demons 247-9, 252
exhibition/s 16, 20, 44, 169
  by author 7, 12-13, 25, 161
existence
  constituents 256
  divinities etc 78
  human 67, 209, 224, 248, 251 256-7
  previous 105
existential situation 38,
existents 257
exoticism 221
expense 17, 18, 27, 53, 95, 99, 115, 120, 197-8, 201
experience
  of pilgrim 21, 185, 196, 212, 218, 220, 224, 262, 264
  of researcher 11, 26, 80
explanatory theory 6, 267
extinction 87, 96, 137, 250
extra-numerary temple 30-31, 43, 46, 59, 62, 72, 94, 130-1 *see also bangai*
eye/s 38, 250
  opening ceremony 99
  thousand 35-6
eyesight 59, 105

293

F

faith 9, 14, 16–17, 20, 29, 35, 70, 119, 125, 213, 216–7, 224, 237, 246
Farâhâni, M. M. H. 18
Farmayan, Hafez 18
Fǎxiǎn 215
fee/s 71, 139, 161, 175, 185
female 115, 135, 149, 152, 167, 177, 219, 248
feminine 29, 244
fēngshuǐ 176
fertility 115, 177
festival/s 140, 142, 162, 170, 174, 216
fieldwork 24–2, 207–8
fifteen *shaji* 156
fiftieth circulation 189
fire 237
 ritual disposal 201
 protection 151, 192, 225, 247–9, 250
fish (good catch) 151, 245, 249, 251–2
five
 Benzaiten sites 152
 constituents 254, 256
 flower festivals 170
 happinesses 143–4
 virtues 114
flames 91, 110, 48, 250
floats (festival) 174
flower/s 126, 134, 154, 170, 200, 222, 231, 235, 237 241–2
foci (religious) 9, 22, 97, 104, 110, 123, 169, 189, 200, 211–2, 263
foetuses 115, 119
folklore 16, 177
footsteps, follow in 3, 120
forest 216
fortune 147, 151–3, 160, 175, 192
 bad 192, 237
 eight shrines of 169
 family 119, 166
 opening 123, 144, 155, 171, 176
 seven gods of, *see* Shichifukujin
 sack of 150
 ship of 150
 telling 170
forty-eight mountains 121

forty-eight temples/vows 127
Forty-nine Yakushi 103, 109, 114
forty-ninth day 107
forty-seven samurai 203
foundation 30–31, 55, 59, 80, 94–5, 98, 103, 114, 124, 130, 132, 136, 156, 162, 166, 214, 216–7
foundational story 11, 29, 46
founder/s 1,3, 30–31, 35, 41, 75, 79, 103, 120–1, 131, 138,145, 182, 203, 213, 236
four
 lands of Shikoku 3, 75, 78–80, 226
 places of pilgrimage 213
 seasons 154–5
 stages 78–80, 83, 98, 226–9
 truths 246, 255–6
fudasho 70, 95, 121, 183, 246
 meaning 97
fudashojunrei 183
fudasho-meguri 183
Fudō/-son 4, 84–5, 91–2, 97, 99–100, 103–5, 107, 109–114, 132–3, 145, 156, 195, 230, 234, 236–40
fūfu enman 174–5
Fugen Bosatsu 107, 215
Fuji (mt.) 66, 159
Fujiwara family 174
Fukakusa-ha 127
fukū 39
fuku 147, 161, *see also gofuku*
Fukuchiyama (city) 100
Fukuda Tsuneo, 33
Fukui (pref.) 35, 129
Fukūkensaku/ Fukūkenshaku 36, 42, 39, 239
Fukumairi 169
Fukuoka (pref.) 93
Fukurokuju 153–7
Fukushima (pref.) 57, 68
fukuun shugo 175
Fumonbon 246
funeral, 106–7, 220, 261
Fushimi (pln.) 117, 139, 143–4, 164
fūsui (fēngshuǐ) 176

General Index

G

gakumon geinō 169
gan (aspiration) 231
Ganges 225
Ganzan Daishi 67
garments 3, *see also* clothing
Gassan (mt.) 9, 210
gasshō 185, 193
gate/s, 10, 23, 71, 152, 169, 186, 191, 225, 241, 246, *see also mon, torii*
gātha 233
Gauntlett, J.O. 14
ge (verses) 232–3
geinō 169
Gekkai Shōnin 95
gender 192, 248, 254, 267
  Kannon 29, 248, 254
generation/s 71, 127, 146, 185, 209
Genji clan 71
Genkū 124
Gennep, Arnold van 11
genre/s 33, 78, 163, 191, 203, 211
Genroku Era 81
genzeriyaku 6, 147, 162, 195–6, 262
geography/ical 5, 9, 17, 32, 48, 55, 59, 62, 72, 95, 110, 114, 138, 158, 167, 224, 228, 267
German pilgrimage 20
ghost/s, hungry 116, 119, 135
Gifu (pref.) 113
Gion Festival 174
gloves 220
goal/s 22, 73–4, 265
  goal/route/way 6–8, 16–17, 19, 21–22, 24, 223, 264
  multiple 7, 10, 19, 121, 264
  objective 109, 223, 227–9
  single 8, 10, 18, 19 21, 101, 122, 139, 160, 215, 260, 264
  single/multiple 14, 21, 74, 212
  typology/diversity 22
goblins (*tengu*) 216
Gochi Kyōdan 108
god/s 1, 4–5, 68, 91, 104, 105, 117, 135–136, 141, 142, 144, 146–9, 146–60, 147–8, 151–2, 153,154–5, 157–8, 162, 166, 168–9, 174, 175 176, 178–9, 182, 260, 263
Gods of Good Fortune *see* Shichifukujin
goddess, 15, 142, 144, 148, 151–3, 157–8
go-eika 33, 43, 120, 129, 194–5, 198, 203, 212, 230, 232, 237, 240–4, 246
gofuku 143–4
gogekōshiki 129
Go-Hanazono, Emperor 156
gohei 66
gohonzon 82, 86–7, 91–2, 99, 104, 109, 155, 212, 235–6 *see also* Honzon *myōgō*
gōkaku tassei 176
Gokuraku 108
golden 153, 189, 204–5
goma 133, 195
gong 100, 185–6
Gongen 167, 241
Good Friday 19
goriyaku meguri 143
Go-Shirakawa, Emperor 54, 119
Gothóni, René 12, 264
Gotō, 223–224
gratitude, 81, 104, 139, 168, 178–179, 185, 205, 209, 220, 263
Great Vehicle 21, 79, 105, 257, 263, *see also* Mahāyāna
Greece 12
greed 232–4
green slips 189
Guadalupe 17, 245
Guānshìyīn 29
Guānyīn 29, 215, 244, 248
guidance
  of departed 109, 115
  of pilgrims 97, 185, 241, 257
guide (persons) 80
guidebook 8, 15, 25, 33–4, 55–8, 65, 68, 70, 76, 82, 94–7, 113–4, 121, 128–9, 134, 146–7, 158–9, 165, 185–6, 189, 208–12, 218–9, 221–2, 224–6, 229, 233, 240–1, 244, 253–4
  map as guide 10, 32–3, 98, 229
gyakumawari 18, 72, 81
gyō 222

Gyoen 165
gyōja 121
Gyoran Kannon 245, 251

H

Habikino City 165
habitat, normal 11, 16, 18–19, 22, 74, 264
Hachifukujin 169
hachijūhakkasho 75, 94, 96, 98–100, 25
Hachiman (and shrines) 53, 145, 156, 163, 166, 173, 175–6
Hachiōji (pln.) 98, 165
hagiographical 78
Hagurosan (mt.) 9, 210
haiden/honden 178
haiku 115, 132
Hail 188, 192, 194, 221, 223, 246–7, 253
hajj 17–18, 21
Hakone-yama (mt.) 32
Hakuin Zenji 243
halberd 174
hall, for Daishi, Kannon etc. 4, 14–15, 54, 78, 103, 105, 129, 183, 194, 252
Hall, R. K. 14
Hamamatsu (city) 53
hands 38, 178, 183, 185–6, 193, 225
han'ei 166
hanging scroll/s 18, 25, 73, 125, 129, 160, 162, 164–5, 175, 190, 197, 222, 245
Hankyū railway 148
Hannō City 148
hannya 109, 244, 255–7
  Hannya Shingyō 254–7
  Hannya Sūtra (Great) 142, 257
happiness 119, 136, 150, 153, 161, 173, 176, 179
happinesses
  five 143–4
  seven 87
harae (o-harae) 140
harmony 114, 131, 169
hassha (eight shrines, various) 169, 172–3, 175
hat (pilgrim's) 3, 74, 218, 220, 223–4, 236, 264
hatsumōde 149
Hawaii 155–6

hayamawari 114
Hayami Tasuku (auth.) 30, 116–7
Hayashi Takashi (auth.) 132
healing/s 6, 18, 22, 105, 114, 141, 155, 182, 188, 228
health/y 59, 107, 119, 141, 144, 169, 176, 224–5, 227, 229, 262
heart, 20, 92, 146, 173, 175, 178–9, 193, 193, 195, 203, 209–10, 226, 236, 239, 252, 254–6
  by heart 244
Heart Sūtra, 67, 105, 185, 193, 197, 207, 222, 224, 227, 229–32, 234, 244, 248, 251, 253–7, 259, 263
heaven/ly 91, 104, 144, 214, 241
Heian Period 32, 116, 119, 174
Heike clan 71
Heisei Era 43, 114, 161, 175
Heissig, Walther 49, 153
Heiwa Kannon 245
hells 88, 116, 119, 135, 250
henjō 192, 221, 223
henjō kongō 221, 236
henro 77, 80–1, 96, 99, 163, 223
hidden 41, 44, 135
Hieizan (mt.) 35, 67, 71, 114, 122, 126–7, 130, 132–3, 145–6, 205, 242
higan 208
hikifuda 151
Hikosan (mt.) 9–11, 53
Hindu pilgrmage 17
Hino City 99
Hinomaru 192
Hirahata Ryōyū (auth.) 56–8, 62, 64, 96, 185, 189, 225
Hirohito, Emperor 166
Hiroshima (pln.) 81
hisshō kigan 176
hitoritabi 33
Hodaraku 241
Hoffmann, Ute 12, 76
hōgo 236
hōin/chō
Hōjō Tokimune (pn.) 62
Hokkaidō 57–8, 98, 113, 121
Hokke-shū 122–3
hokke 231

General Index

hoko 174
hōkoku-fuda 191
Hokuriku region 8, 57
holy, various 2, 16, 18–19,
   Kannon 35, 38, 250
   mountains 215
   sites/places 74, 103, 123–4, 197, 214, 267
   Holy Land 213
honden 178
hondō 104
Hōnen 4, 103, 124–7, 131, 204, 213, 242
honjibutsu 145, 252
honji suijaku 141
Honmon Hokke-shū 123
honsha 10
Honshū 57, 59, 80–81, 96
honzan
   eighteen (Shingon) 109
   sixteen (Nichirenite) 122
Honzanshugen-shū 45, 70, 113
honzon see gohonzon
Honzon myōgō 185, 194
hōō 31
hope/s 25, 67, 149, 206, 242, 263
horse/*ema* 66
horse day 191
Horse-headed Kannon 36, 39, 65, 115
Hoshino Eiki 8–9, 16, 76, 78
Hosokawa Gyōshin 128
hospitality 124
hosshin 79, 227
Hossō-shū 45, 70
Hotaka (city) 177
Hotei-son, 131, 154–6
hotoke 106, 108, 146
Hōtoku Inari 156
Hotsubodaishin 235, 243
hṛdaya 254
hundred
   reverences 138–9
   shrines 159,
   temples 4, 32, 46, 52–3, 57, 68, 202
   seven hundred days 132–3
   hundredth day 107–8
   hundredth time
Hurvitz, Leon 246, 248

husband and wife 174
hyakudo 138–9
hyaku-sha-mairi 159
hyakue 220
hydrangea 170
hymn/s 198, 230, 237, 242
Hyōgo (pref.) 55, 95, 109–10, 113, 126, 136, 146

I

Ibaragi (pref.) 128
Ichigaya (pln.) 150
iconography/ic 104, 106, 110, 116, 134–5, 154, 203, 208, 210, 217
   Kannon 29, 34–6, 38, 41–3, 49–50, 52, 67, 87, 202–3, 245, 247, 251–2, 254
igi (meaning) 226
ignorance 223, 238, 255
Ikinashima (pln.) 96
Iksan (city) 138
illness 30, 139, 144, 211
illusion 255
image/s 8, 15, 41, 43–4, 59, 87, 100, 103–4, 117, 120, 130, 142, 145, 158, 177, 187, 201, 204, 210–1
   hidden 41, 44, 158
   Kannon 41, 49–50, 52, 65–8, 105, 201, 245, 252
   miei 31, 129 *and figure captions*
imitation/s 32, 46, 57, 64–6, 75, 77, 92–6, 107, 119
   behaviour 185
   local 4, 58, 66
   Shintoist 160, 168, 261
immeasurable (merit) 250
immovable 91, 109, 110
immurement 133
imperial, household etc. 55, 113, 159, 163–6, 168, 174, 179, 202
Imperial Household Agency 165
incense 185–6, 235
India 14, 22, 70, 137, 139, 151, 195, 212–8, 226, 244, 260
Indian 29, 104, 142, 145, 150–1, 153, 212–3, 215–8, 246
indigenous 22
Indonesia 21

informant/s 25, 49, 65, 125, 139, 242, *see also* insiders
Inland Sea 3, 93, 101, 152
insiders 267, *see also* informants
instructions 34, 94, 175, 187, 189, 193–4, 220, 246
  route 224–5
  temple visit 185
intention/ality 5, 13, 17, 24–6, 74, 96, 104, 110, 119, 125, 148, 185, 187–8, 209, 212, 261, 263
interlacement 14–15
interviews 26, 71, 166, 229
Inuyama (city) 113
invention 44, 68, 109, 120, 134, 136
invocation 187, 194, 247
Irima (city) 148
Ise-mairi 9, 160
ishibotoke 100, 134
ishidan 140
Islam 21, 17–18, 211
island/s (minor) 93, 96, 155
  for Benzaiten 15, 142, 152–3, 157
ittai 43
Iwate (pref.) 57
Iyo (prov.) 78–9, 85, 134–5, 227
Izu Peninsula 54, 57, 59, 64–5

J

jacket 197, 218, 220–1, 223
Jaina tradition 251
jaku 231
Jakuhon (pn.) 81
Java 21
Jerusalem 17, 22
Ji-shū 62, 69–70, 82, 131
-*ji* 34, 82, 95, 144, 216
Jichiidai 175
jihi 221, 253
Jikaku Daishi 132
Jikku Kannongyō 185, 194, 253
Jimon-shū (-ha, sect) 45, 50, 71
-*jin* 145, 147, 155
jīna 251
jingū 144, *see also* in names
jinja 144, *see also* in names
Jinja Honchō 177

jiriki 127, 217
Jishō Daishi (pn.) 131–2
Jizō (Bosatsu, -son, -sama) 67, 84–5, 88, 91–2, 96, 100, 107, 109, 115–120, 131, 230, 235, 240–2
  abortions 109, 115, 119, 242, 245
  forty-eight 119–20
  six 4, 36, 103, 116–20, 135,
  wasan 230, 242
  wayside, 115, 117, 177
Jizō-bon 117
jōbutsu (*sokushin*) 109, 227
Jōdo Buddhism 41, 69–70, 113, 124–8, 142
  Jōdo 124
Jōdo Shinshū 109, 128, 131, 217, 242
  see also Shinshū
Jōdo-shū 49–50, 61, 69–70, 95, 107–9, 113, 124–5, 131,
Jōdo-shū Seizan-ha 70
jōgyō zanmai 260
jūhachihonzan 109
Jūichimen Kannon 35–7, 42–4, 50, 52–3, 65, 84–7, 91, 237, 245, 252
Jūichimensenju Kannon 42
jūnishi 124
junpai 8, 57, 134, 146, 239
junrei 8, 33, 48, 56–7, 64, 78, 95, 121, 136, 183, 210, 223, 226, 246
junreisha 163
Juntei Kannon 36, 39–40, 42, 52
Jurōjin 149, 153–7
jūroku honzan 122
jūsanbutsu 106, 107, 236
jūsanishibotoke 135
jūsanmairi 107
jussha meguri 165
jūyōbunkazai 98
Jūzenkai 234
juzu 136, 220

K

Ka'aba 18
Kagawa (pref.) 78, 85, 109, 126
kaidan (-*meguri*) 137
Kaihōgyō (*sennichi kaihōgyō*) 4, 132–3, 260
Kaikyōge (Kaikyō no ge) 232–3

General Index

Kailash (mt.) 17, 22
kaiun chōfuku 176
Kakinoki Kenji (auth.) 54
kāla 150
kalpa 232
Kamakura 8, 31–2, 53, 57, 59–60, 62–3, 70, 119, 122, 148, 152, 157–8, 185, 225, 237
kami 9, 66, 121, 123, 141, 148, 168, 171, 173, 178–9, 261, see also named *kami*
  and buddhas 141–2, 145–6,
  Benzaiten 152
  Daimyōjin 145
  Ebisu 151, 156
  Inari 156
  Ōkuninushi 142, 150
  ujigami 168
kamidana 172
kaminariyoke 176
Kanagawa (pref.) 32, 99
kanai anzen 176
kanbun 194, 242
Kanda Myōjin 166–7
Kaneko Wakō (auth.) 148
kanjin 203
Kanjizai 67, 244, 251, 254
kankokuheisha 163
Kannon/-sama 11, 16, 77–8, 84, 87–8, 91, 93, 96, 101, 103, 108–10, 114–6, 120–2, 124, 130–1, 135–6, 141, 145–6, 150, 153–5, 157–8, 165, 183–5, 188–9, 193–5, 197–203, 207, 209, 215–7, 221, 223, 226, 230–1, 234, 237, 241, 260, 262
  circuits (with variations) 2–6, 29–74
  hall 15, 34–5, 49, 54, 78, 105, 139, 183–4, 194, 252
  iconographical types 35–6, 251–2
  Kannon-sama, usage 29, 35, 44
  pilgrimage map 2, 30, 56, 73
  sūtra 244–53
Kannongyō 35, 185, 194, 234, 244, 246, 253
kannonreijō 198–9
Kanpei Taisha 163
kanpeisha 163–5
Kansai region 46, 72, 99, 115, 117, 120, 164, 200

Kantō region 32, 66, 99, 113–14, 128, 149
Kanzeon 29, 35–40, 42–4, 50, 52–3, 84–7, 91–2, 109, 185, 188, 192, 194, 221, 224, 237, 239, 243–8, 250–4
Kapilavastu 214
karma 119, 135, 196, 232, 255
karuṇā 105
Kashiwara (pln.) 165
Kataragama 22
katatagaeyoke 176
Katō Bunnō (auth.) 246, 248
kaun 166
Kawachi (prov.) 156
Kawagoe (ciy) 148, 155, 158
kawara 242
Kawasaki (pln.) 98–9
Kawazu (town) 64–5
Kazan, Emperor 31, 41, 43, 46, 202
Keifuku Railway 162
Keiō Railway 99
ken (prefectures) 54, 146
kenjaku 39
kenkō chōju 169
kensaku 39
Kenshin-dō 131
kenzaku 39
Kichijōten 92, 153–4
kigan 176, 195
Kigensetsu 163
kimono 174, 220
kindergartens 126
kinen shashin 199
king
  bright king (*myōō*) 91, 104 106, 109–10, 237–8
  Dharma King 31
  of the dead 30, 116
Kinki region 110–13, 136, 246
  Fudō circuit 111
kit (of pilgrims) 220
Kita-ku (ward)
  Kyōto 117
  Tokyo 166
Kita-hossō-shū 45, 70
kiyome 209
Kiyomori (Taira no) (pn.) 119

299

Knott, Kim 13
kō (association) 95, 192
Kōbe (city) 54–5, 95, 110, 119, 136, 151, 200
Kōbō Daishi 3–4, 15, 68, 75, 78–80, 92, 94–9, 101, 103, 105, 120, 130–1, 139, 183, 187, 195, 200, 204, 220–3, 227, 236, 238, 260
Kōchi (pref.) 78, 84, 101
Kogi Shingon-shū 50
koji 210
Kokawa Kannon-shū 45, 70
kokka no ryūshō 166
kokoro 226
koku 3, 80
  measure 150
kokuheisha 163
kokumintaiiku 68
kokushi 127
kokutai (national entity) 14
Kokūzō Bosatsu 84, 88, 92, 108, 236
Kōmyō shingon 236
kongōzue 223
Konya 22
Kōō Byakue Kanzeon 252
Korea/n 13, 29, 34, 138, 153, 212–3, 216–7, 244
Kōrien (city) 99–100
kōtsū anzen 169, 176
Kouamé, Nathalie 15, 76
kouke 169, 176
Kōya/-san (mt.) 1, 4, 14, 41, 43, 45, 50, 70, 81, 79–80, 86, 101, 109–10, 113, 130, 139, 202–4, 226
Kubota Nobuhiro (auth.) 9
Kūkai (pn.) 3, 75, 79, 91, 104, 121, 186–7, 213, 236–7
Kumano 4, 81, 121, 145–6, 150, 172, 241
Kumārajīva 38, 194, 244, 248
Kunaishō 165
kuni 54, 59, 80, 95, 152
Kunisaki Peninsula 53–4
Kurashige Ryōkai (auth.) 58
Kurodani (pln.) 126, 242
Kurotani (pln.) 127
Kurozumikyō 9
Kurube (city) 126–7

Kusinārā 214
kuyō 235, 245
Kyō 120, 149, 155, 161
Kyōgyōshinshō 70
kyōji 91
Kyōraku Hassha 172
kyōun yakuyoke 169
Kyūseikannon-shū 45, 70
Kyūshū 9–11, 53, 93, 137

L

Lhasa 17, 22
liberation 256, 261
lightning, averting 176, 249
liminality 11, 17, 220
lineage, doctrinal 260
linkage/s 120, 122, 149, 160, 166, 168–71, 179
living beings 29, 38–9, 67, 87, 105, 115–6, 119–20, 127, 135, 224, 234–5, 238–9, 243, 247, 250–2
locality 13, 33, 146, 170, 177, 179
location/s 14, 56, 58, 66, 88, 95, 98, 109, 117, 128, 151–2, 160, 165–6, 167, 192, 210, 213, 243, 265
lodging/s 34, 93, 225, 241
longevity, 88, 116–7, 242, 253
lotus
  blossom 201, 231, 237, 241, 252
  pond 156
  temple 30
Lotus Sūtra 29, 35, 38, 55, 67, 87, 121–2, 145, 152, 194, 216, 237, 244–8, 251, 253–4, 260
Lourdes 17, 21–2
luck 148, 155, 169, 176, 245
Ludvik, Catherine 133, 153
Lumbinī 214, 218
lute 142, 153, 158

M

magical (spells) 230
Mahābhārata 14
Mahākāla 150
Mahāparinibbāna Sutta 213–214
Mahāprajñāpāramitā Heart Sūtra 254, see also Heart Sūtra

General Index

Mahāyāna 21, 29, 79, 88, 104–5, 203, 213, 215–6, 223, 240, 246, 254, 256–7, 261, 263
mahrib 18
mairi > *o-mairi*
Maitreya 88, 154
Makashikan 116
male
  male–female 115, 177
  male to female 29, 244
  pronouns 248, 251, 254
mandala/s 79, 221
manga 33, 78, 246
Mañjuśrī 88, 215
mannequin (figure) 219
Mano Yukie (auth.) 94
mantra 106, 231, 239
map/s 8, 10, 12, 18, 20, 24–5, 32–3, 58, 78–9, 81, 93, 97–8, 101, 122, 128, 137, 161, 167–9, 198–9, 229, 246
maps as figures
  Kamakura Shichifukjin 157
  Saikoku 2, 30, 33, 73
  Shikoku 7, 77, 83, 228
  sites for Hōnen 125
  Six Jizō 118
marathon 133, 140
Marburg 21, 25, 203, 224
market/ing 8, 13, 98, 144, 151, 174, 216, 260
marriage 174–6
Mary 19–20, 68, 245
Matsuo Bashō (pn.) 132
Matsuo Shinkū (pn.) 211
Matsura Sayohime (pn.) 152
matsuri 170
Matsuyama (city) 81, 97
maturation 6, 263
  maturity 196
mausoleum/a 22, 30, 41, 79, 130, 139, 204
  imperial 146, 156, 165
mawaru/mawari 7, 18
meaning/s 5–6, 13, 15, 18, 25, 59, 72, 75–6, 79, 99, 101, 104, 108–9, 129, 145, 156, 161, 178–82, 193, 196–7, 206–257, 25–267

igi 226
syllables 231
Mecca 12–13, 17–18, 21–2
medicine 224
  Buddha 59, 109, 114
meditation/al 19, 3, 60, 69, 88, 142, 216, 225, 230–1, 239, 252, 260
meguri/ meguru 7–10, 25, 54, 98, 100, 117, 128, 130, 134, 137, 143, 149, 155–7, 159, 162, 165, 167–9, 176, 183, 210, 218
Meguriyasui Hajijūhakkasho 96
Meiji
  Emperor 166, 179
  government 56, 168
  Period 62, 64, 91, 98, 141, 145–6, 151, 167–8, 175, 178, 199, 241
  Restoration 60, 148, 166, 261
meisho 7, 158, 199
meisui 8
Meiwa Era 252
member/s
  family 18, 62, 70, 113
  group 71, 122, 217
memento 97, 152, 197, 222
memorial 67, 216
  tablets 200
memory 115, 129, 193, 242
  popular 22
  nationalist 165
merchants 64, 247
mercy 188, 249–50, 253
merit/s 17, 58, 67, 70, 4, 109, 124–5, 127, 137, 145, 193, 196–7, 201, 205, 208, 216–8, 226, 235, 250, 252
method/ology 16, 24–7, 259, *see also* ephemera, explanatory theory, fieldwork, informants, interviews, philology
metsuzai shōzen 137
Mexico 17, 19, 22, 245
Mezu Kannon 39
michi 146
michibiki 241
Michizane (Sugawara) (pn.)162, 252
Mie (pref.) 113, 146
miei 31, 36–40, 89–91, 129, 143, 262

Migot, André 215
mikkyō 71, 109, 235
mikuji 170, 192
Mílèfó 88, 154
Mimuro-ha 45
Minami-ku (ward) 117
Minato-ku (ward) 166
miniature
  pilgrimages, 4, 19, 21, 48, 65-8, 92-4, 96-101, 137, 229, 252
  votive tablets 168
miniaturization 65-6, 68, 92, 252
minibus 17, 26
Minobu-san (mt.) 1, 122
miracle 11
Miroku Bosatsu 84, 88, 92, 107, 154
mirror (in temple) 65
miscarriage 242, 245 *see also* abortion
misfortune 192
Mishimamachi (pln.) 68
Miura (city) 68, 155
Miyagi (pref.) 57
Miyako Shichifukujin 149
mizuko 119, 242, 245
Mizuno Keizaburō (auth.) 210
modifications 139
Móhēzhǐguān 116
monasticism 113, 122, 150, 214
money 13, 129, 174, 197-8, 224, 262
Mongolia/n 149, 153-4
Monju Daibosatsu 84, 92, 107, 109, 236, *see also* Monjushiri
Monjushiri 88, 215
monk/s 30, 59, 81, 86, 94, 113-4, 122, 132-3, 135, 137, 142, 154, 196, 208, 214, 216, 243, 247
monzeki 112-3
Moriguchi Ichisaburō (auth.) 60, 209
Morioka Kiyomi (auth.) 156
mother/s 115, 152, 211, 24
  Kannon 139
  Mary 68
motivation/s 5, 25, 41, 96, 101, 162, 185, 209, 212, 217
motorization 15, 220
mound 66, 216, 223
Mount, *see* Ashigara, Athos, Dewa

Sanzan, Diamond, Éméi, Fuji, Hakone, Hiei, Hiko, Kailash, Kōya, Minobu, Nachi, Ontake, Pǔtuó, Sumeru, Takao, Wǔtái
mounting of scrolls 198, 201, 203-5, 200, 265
mourning 107
multifocal 19, 21
Murakami Mamoru (auth.) 81, 132
Muromachi Period 32, 55, 113, 148
Musashino region 55, 57
museum 16, 20, 30, 44, 203, 195, 224
music 151
Muslim 12-13, 18, 21, 211
myōgō 185, 194
Myōhō Renge Kyō 122
Myōken 123-4
Myōō 104
  Aizen 104
  Fudō 84-5, 91-2, 99, 103-5, 107, 109-13, 132-3, 145, 156, 234, 236-8, 240
  meaning 91, 104, 106
Myōon Benzaiten 142-3, 152, 158
mystery/ies 221, 232, 236
mystical 21-22
mythical, 87, 104, 241, 247
mythological/ly, 78, 87, 52

N

Nachi/-san 23, 33, 150, 200-1, 241, 243
Nadachi (town) 54
nadokoro 158
Nagano (pref.) 41, 54
Nagaokakyō (pln.) 127
Nagatani Kunio (auth.) 33, 226
Nagoya (city) 16, 44, 57, 94, 99, 113
Nakagawa Toshio (auth.) 210
Namikiri Fudō 84, 91
Namu 221
  Amida Butsu 129, 203-4, 247
  Daishi Henjō Kongō 221, 223, 236
  Enmei Jizō Daibosatsu 242
  Kanzeon Bosatsu 194, 221, 247, 253
  Myōhō Renge Kyō 122
Nara 8, 16, 30, 44, 59, 64, 71, 107, 109-10, 114, 121, 126, 146, 165, 174, 210
narrative 18-19, 30, 33, 213-5, 226

General Index

nationalism 165-6
negation/s 255-6, 263
nehan 79, 87, 227-8, *see also* Nirvana
Nehan Shaka Nyorai 84, 86-7
nen 231
nenbutsu 124, 126, 128-9, 203-4, 231, 242, 247
nenju 220
Nepal 218
network 1, 14, 54, 113, 128, 131, 146, 178
new religions 1
New Year 32, 143, 149, 155, 161, 168-71
Nichibunken (IRCJS) 32, 46
Nichiren 1, 104, 121-3, 131, 137-8
Nichirenite, 106, 121-3, 150, 260
Nichirenshū 122
Nichizō 123
Nihi Nyoirin Kanzeon 43
Nihon Hyaku Kannon 32, 46
Niigata Prefecture 54
Niizuma Hisao 128-9
Nijūshihai/yohai 129
Nine Walis 21
nineteenth century 15, 24, 33, 54, 56, 73, 141-2, 159, 166, 221, 241
nippon rettō 14
Great Nirvāṇa Sūtra 213
nirvana, 79, 83, 86-7, 119-20, 214-5, 217, 227-9, 244, 255
nirvanic 256
Nishigaki Seiji (auth.) 9, 160
noble truths 246, 255-6
Noda (city) 192
nōkyō 197-8
nōkyōchō 48-9, 160-1, 179, 197-200
non-Catholic 19
non-duality 88
normative 41, 101, 189
norm/s 62, 101, 128, 185, 189, 200, 259
North Pole Star 123
north-east quarter 176
nōsatsuire 220
Nossa Senhora 245
nostalgia 3-4, 5, 54, 58, 146, 178, 210
numeration 63, 72, 101, 132, 157, 169, 186, *see also* enumeration
numinous spirits 216

nun/s 196, 247, 252
Nyoirin Kannon/Kanzeon 35-6, 42-3, 52-3, 145, 245, 262
nyorai (meaning) 86-7, 106
Nyorai
  Ashuku 108
  Amida 70, 83-6, 90-2, 108-9
  Dainichi 84-5, 87, 89, 91-2, 145, 232-3
  Daitsūchishō 85, 87, 92
  Shaka 83-5, 87, 92, 107, 145, 236
  Yakushi 4, 43, 59, 84-7, 90-2, 103, 105, 107-8, 109, 114, 175

O

Ōbaku Zen 70
o-bon 116-7
Oda Nobunaga (pn.) 132
offering/s 12, 66-8, 81, 96, 100, 116, 133, 168-9, 175, 178, 182, 186, 192-3, 196, 220-1, 235, 254
Ogose (city) 148
o-harae 140
Ōjin Tennō 156
Okada Mokichi (Mokiti) 203
o-kage 96
ōkami/Ō-kami 152
Okayama (city) 81
Okayama (pref.) 126-7
Okinawa (pref.) 58
Ōkuninushi 142, 150, 174-5
Okushū pilgrimage 57
Okutama (pln.) 95
ōm 221
o-mairi 8-10, 65, 67, 116, 147, 156, 158-60, 163, 169, 173-4, 178, 197
  Hachiman Hassha Mairi 175
  Hassha Fukumairi 168-9
  hyakudo-mairi 138-9
  hyakusha-mairi 159
  Ise-mairi 9, 160
  Jūsanbutsu-mairi 107
  jūsanmairi 107
  Kōbō-mairi 94
  rokudō-mairi 116
  Shichifukujin Mairi 149, 155
  Shimozuke Hassha Mairi 175
o-meguri 21, 25, see also *meguri*

Omei, Mount 215
Ōmi Kannon pilgrimage 54, 70, 130, 152
Ōmi no kuni (prov.) 152
Ōmoto 9
Omuro 97, 108
Ontake (mt.) 9, 216
ontic 256
ontological 223, 248
ordination 113, 128, 137, 214
origination 137, 256
  dependent 256
  of good 137
orthodoxy 128, 147, 208, 211
orthopraxy 211
Ōsaka 3, 20, 54–5, 81, 95, 99, 107, 110, 113–4, 121, 126, 128, 130, 136, 146, 148, 151, 156, 165, 168, 200, 237, 244, 252
osame-fuda 189
Ōtani-ha 127–9
Ōtani University 217
otherness of pilgrims 12
otherworldly 247
otome kannon 68
Ōtsu (city) 68, 110, 127
outfit 134, 187, 220
outsider/insider 267
overlap/ping 244, 261
  circuits 55, 110, 149
  divinities 109, 120
  with *o-mairi* 9
Owari Kannon circuit 57,189
Oxford pilgrimage 20
Ōyama (pln.) 99
Ozuno (En no) 121

P

Pacific
  coast 53
  War 64, 95, 142
pacification 108, 166
Paekche 212
pagoda 98, 130, 215–6, 221
paint, red 174
painting/s 16, 18, 66, 110, 129, 197, 201, 203–5, 217, 251
Palace, Imperial 165, 167

Pāli 213
pamphlet/s, 20, 59–60, 81, 94, 117, 136, 145, 149, 154–5, 162, 188–9 170, 223, 246
Paradise 108
paradoxical 17, 21, 79, 146, 196, 217, 223–5, 255–6, 263
parallel/s 6, 19–20, 55, 120, 138, 153, 165, 212, 231, 247, 256, 260
pāramitā 105
parents 54, 119
participant/s 5–6, 93, 140, 182, 267
  observation 24
participate, 217
participation 261
  pilgrims 1, 32, 67, 70, 82, 96, 133, 181–2, 217, 262
  temples/shrines 55, 69–70, 114, 123, 141, 148, 166, 171, 179
partner/ship (*enmusubi*) 69, 174–6
passion/s 19, 39, 91, 96, 110, 210, 248, 250
pasting up 159, 190–1, 193
path/s, 227, 255–7
  meaning-related 7, 19–21, 77, 79, 96, 146, 223, 227, 255–7
  site-related 10, 23, 67–8, 96, 115, 139, 161, 177, 213
patriarch/s 103, 116, 121, 134, 132
patriotic/ism 159, 162, 165, 168, 178–9, 192
pawaa 147
Payne, Richard K. 76
peace
  inner 79, 116, 227, 231, 246
  world 193, 226, 245–6, 253
Peace Kannon 245
Peninsula
  Chita 93–4, 189, 208
  Izu 54, 59, 64
  Kunisaki 53
penitence 210, see also *zange*
peonies (*botan*) 205
perfection/s 227
  of compassion 105
  of insight 67, 251, 254–6
  six 218, 255

General Index

ten 105
Peru 23
petition/s *see* prayer/s
phenomenology/ical 6, 13–14, 17, 264, 267
phenomenon/a
  in field 15, 77, 119, 132, 138, 145, 159–60, 177, 259–60
  Buddhist view 21, 67, 88, 224, 248
philology 24–5
photograph/s
  commemorative 184, 199
  as data 24–5, 58, 65, 98, 132
piety 31, 69, 193, 242, 252
  filial 152–3
Pilgerfahrt/en 7, 21, 25, 185, 202
pilgrim slips 24, 26, 41, 60, 65, 76, 94–5, 97, 183, 187–93, 196, 220, 222, 229, 236, 253
pitcher 204
plan/planning 26
poisons, three 233, 238–9
pole
  north 123
  south 153
political/ics 14–5, 32, 64, 68, 71, 119, 159, 163, 166, 177, 215, 245
pollution 225
popular religion (term) 177, 260
population 1, 3, 22, 32–3, 64, 134, 136, 141, 161, 267
postcard/s 199–200
poster/s 12, 151, 172
posthumous names 3, 124, 131–2, 236
Potalaka 215
power/s
  competitive 23, 71, 109, 119, 166, 267
  of route 22–3
  other/own 124, 127, 217,
  spiritual 11–12, 104–5, 192, 195
  sites/spots 14–15, 18, 80, 147
  supernormal 106, 109–10, 121, 227, 228, 227–9, 247–8, 250–2
  three 235
practice/s 12, 15, 60, 66, 69–70, 108–9, 185, 193, 207–8, 211, 217, 222, 224, 235, 257, 259–60, 265, 267

ascetic 5, 9–10, 110, 121, 132–3, 227
bodhisattva 67, 105, 227, 250–1, 256–7
circulatory 31–2, 71–2, 76, 81, 117, 122, 124–5, 131, 134, 144, 159
circumambulation 81, 97, 136–9, 145, 217
Muslim 21
Shintō 159–78, 191
various ritual 58, 98, 105, 119, 124, 129, 187, 196–7, 199, 204, 208, 230, 257, 260–1
practitioner/s 53, 67, 121, 133, 139, 231
pradakṣiṇa 137
prajñā 105, 109, 254–7
prajñāpāramitā 254–5, 257
pratyekabuddha 135
prayer/s 26, 65, 67–8, 104–5, 116, 149, 171–4, 178–9, 187, 192–6, 208, 235–6, 250, 253
  for pilgrims 20
  petition/ary 9, 107, 131, 136, 139, 141, 148, 162, 166, 168, 172, 176, 178, 183, 186, 188, 193, 195–6, 206, 211–2, 261
  sticks 133
precept/s 12, 234, 250
pregnancies 109
preparation/s 13, 17, 183, 186, 221, 225
prescribed
  ritual 9, 73, 183, 187, 218, 225
  sequence 17, 19, 72–3, 136
prescription/s 76
price 198, 205, *see also* cost/ly
priest/s
  Buddhist 26, 34, 41, 49, 68, 95, 119, 122, 125, 127, 139, 148, 195, 197–8, 211, 217
  Catholic 20, 22
  Shintō 140, 165–8, 175, 241
Prince Shōtoku 78, 113, 130–1
Pritchard, John 20
promotion/al 15, 20, 58, 80, 121, 124, 125, 134, 136, 139, 149, 156, 165, 167, 169, 172, 200, 209, 210, 226–7, 263

305

proof/s of visit 18–19, 48, 74, 76, 155, 175, 183, 185, 187, 190, 193, 197, 199–200, 205–6, 221
propitiation 216
protection (various divinities) 18, 39, 96, 99, 115, 119, 145, 151–2, 171, 175, 192, 253
Protestant/Catholic 20
province/s 3, 30, 54, 57, 78, 80, 83–5, 128, 134, 175, 226–8, 237
provisional 145, 220, 224, 267
public transport 13, 118, 134
Pure Land 108, 124, 234, 241, 244
Pure Land Buddhism 41, 43, 69–70, 82, 109, 124, 127, 131–2, 142, 204, 213, 234, 247
Pure Waterfall 49
purity 137, 248, 250, 253
  Kanzeon of 36, 39, 250
  Shintō 173, 178–9, 209
purification 100, 140, 142, 175, 178, 209–10, 225
Pŭtuó (mt.) 215
Pŭxián 215

Q

quarter/s (cosmic) 105, 176, 248
quintessence 122

R

railway/s 3, 10, 26, 34, 44, 48, 56, 67, 72, 77, 81, 83, 93, 95, 100, 117, 131, 136, 155, 167, 169, 198
  Enoshima 157
  Hankyū 148
  Keifukuden 161–2
  Keiō 99
  Musashino 55
rākṣasas 249
Rakuchū 134
Rakuhoku 134
Rakunan 134
Rakusai 55, 57, 70, 134
Rakusaikannonreijōkai 55
Rakutō 134
Rakuyō 54, 124, 131, 252
Rambelli, Fabio 141

Randen (railway) 161
Reader, Ian 12, 15, 65, 76, 79, 91, 93, 189, 229
rebirth 36, 115–17, 119–20, 124, 135, 203, 214, 220
receipt 161, 197, 212
recitation 43, 57, 136, 142, 183, 185–6, 193–5, 207, 210–11, 218, 220, 225, 227, 230–57, 259
  daimoku 122
  nenbutsu 124, 126, 204,
red 204
  apron 96
  pilgrim slips 189
  seals 94, 129, 160, 162, 165, 168, 183, 198–9
  shrine structures 152, 174
refuges 234
Reigen, Emperor 120
reijō 11, 82, 98, 147, 198, 239, 242
  in pilgrimage names 29, 32, 54, 75, 95, 99, 107, 130–1, 136, 146
Reijōki 81
Reitaku (pn.) 125
Reiyūkai 9, 122
relic/s 137, 214–6, 223
relocation 55, 62, 166
Rennyo Shōnin (pn.) 128–9
repentance 229, 232–3
Rhodes, Robert 132, 260
Rikuzen (prov.) 152
Rinzai Zen 59, 64, 142, 243
  Rinzai-shū 52–3, 61, 107–8, 113, 131
  temples 49, 54, 60, 69, 70, 82, 124, 142, 143, 149, 153, 156, 245
Risshō Kōseikai, 9, 122, 217
Risshū 95, 108
Ritsu-shū 108
rites/ritual 206
  meaning 5–6, 11, 207–8, 182, 196, 207–10, 224–5, 263
  of transaction 5–6, 169, 181–206
  post–mortal 152, 201, 261
  yearly 1
ritual actions/pattern 10, 17, 73, 109, 133, 142, 181, 184–5, 187, 207–8
ritualization 5, 142, 165, 178–9, 241, 265

riyaku 162, *see also genzeriyaku*
rokkon shōjō 209–210
rokudō 115–6, 120
Rokuhi Nyoirin Kannon 43
Rokujizō 117, 119, *see also* Jizō
rokuyō 226
romantic/ism 55, 83, 77, 96
rope 36, 39, 238–9
rosary 97, 126, 136, 186, 204, 220
route/s *see* circuits, goals, *junpai, junrei*
rú lài 86
run/ner, long distance 133
ryōen 175
Ryōzan (pn) 94
Ryūjin 152–153
ryūshō (*kokka no*) 166
Ryūzu Kannon 252

S

sacred places/sites 1, 8–11, 13–14, 16–18, 20, 22–4, 30, 54, 59, 72, 79, 120, 138, 140, 208, 213, 217, 254, 264 *see also* space/sacralization
  image 129
  mountains 66, 133, 145, 215, *see also* Mount
sacrifice 152–3
Safarnâmeh 18
safe delivery 169, 176
safety 188, 193, 246
  at sea 151
  family/home 119, 176, 193
  journey/traffic 100, 141, 169, 176, 182, 188
Saga (pref.) 110
Sagami (prov.) 152
Sagyō-ku (ward) 117
Sai no kawara 242
sai (Saikoku) 2
Saichō 130
Saigoku 3, 29, *see also* Saikoku
Saijō Kannon pilgrimage 57, 189
Saikō (priest) 119
Saikoku, 2–4, 11, 15–16, 23, 26, 29–33, 36–9, 41–6, 48, 54–7, 65–9, 71–5, 78, 82, 87, 103, 110, 114, 120, 127, 130, 137, 139, 146, 148, 150, 165, 184, 187–8, 195, 197–202, 211, 213, 218, 222–3, 226, 240–3, 246, 251–2, 262, 266
sainanyoke 176
saintly figures 4, 30, 120–1, 124
Saitama (pref.) 66, 155
Saitō (on Hieizan) 130, 205
Sakai Usaku (auth.) 81, 159
Sakai Yusai (*ajari*) 132
Sakamoto (village) 130
sake 191, 224
sakura (cherry blossom) 170
Sakurai (city) 30
Sakurazawa Takahira (auth.) 95
Śākyamuni 87, 105, 119, 155, 218
salvation 11, 105, 109, 124, 237, 246, 251, *see also* save
  this-worldly 247
Samantabhadra 215
sambodhi 227, 255
samurai 203
Sanchi 22
sand/s
  cone 66
  from temples 94, 97–9
sandals 99, 222
sange 233
Sangha/*saṅgha* 214, 234, 253
sanja takusen 163
sanjūbanjin 145
sankei 158
Sanki 234
Sankyō 234
sanmai (*zanmai*) 238, 260
Sanmen (Kannon) 84, 87
sanmon 225
Sannō-sama 167
sanpai/sha 99, 146, 163
Sanrikige 235
Santiago 17
Sanuki (prov.) 78–9, 85, 227
sanzon ittai 43
Sarasvatī 151
Śāriputra 255–6
Sarnath 218
Sarvāstivādins 257
Sasaguri (pln.) 93

Satō Hisamitsu (auth.) 16, 82
Satō Takashi (auth.) 54, 58
Satō Tatsugen (auth.) 148
save, 29, 116, 217, 246, 247, 250, 253, see also salvation
saviour 78
Sayohime 152
Scheidegg (pln.) 20
school excursions 210, 213
scroll/s, hanging 18, 25, 41, 43, 62, 72–3, 108, 125–6, 129, 131, 142, 159–60, 162–5, 175, 183, 185–6, 197–205, 208, 222, 242, 245, 265
sculpture 19, 68, 138, 150, 213
sea 57, 91, 110, 151, 241, 249–52
  Inland 3, 93, 101, 152
  Japan 53, 128, 150,
seal/s 18, 49, 62, 72–3, 94, 144, 160, 165, 168, 170–3, 175, 183–86, 196–205, 208, 221
  in books 2, 26, 48, 65, 134, 136, 161, 168, 179, 197–8, 200, 226
  on scrolls 41, 43, 73, 126, 129, 162–3, 197, 265
season/s 32, 65, 116, 154–5, 169–70, 213
Seckel, Dietrich 231
sect/s 9, 35, 46, 70–1, 75, 95, 108, 121–2, 124, 127, 222
seed syllable 221
seichō kenzen 176
Seishi Bosatsu 108
Seizan Jōdo denomination 70
Seizan Kokushi (pn.) 127, 131
Sekai Kyūseikyō 1, 203
Seki Yasuo (auth.) 54
Sendai (city) 53, 66–7, 69, 198–9, 226
Sendai Kannon pilgrimage 53, 66–7, 69, 198–9, 226
sendatsu 76, 185, 257
senility prevention 136
senjafuda 191
senjamōde 191
Senju Kannon/Kanzeon 35–6, 38, 42, 50, 52–3, 84–7
Senjujūichimen Kanzeon 42–3
Senjusengen Kanzeon 35, 42–4
Sennichi Kaihōgyō 132, 260

Senryūji-ha 45
Senshu Kanzeon 50, see also Senju kanzeon
senzodaidai 71
seppuku 203
Setonaikai 3, 93
settai 12
Settsukuni (prov.) 54, 95, 200, 225
seven 148–9, 158
  buddhas (Yakushi) 84, 87, 91
  calamities 87
  forms of Kannon 36, 38, 247
  happinesses 87
  Mongolian old men 149, 154
  Seven Gods of Good Fortune 4–5, 68. 91, 104, 135–6, 142, 144, 147–60, 166, 168–9, 174, 176, 178–9, see also Shichifukujin
seventh
  day after decease 107–8
  of month 149, 155
  time round 189
shaji 136, 144, 156
Shaka Nyorai 83–7, 92, 107, 145, 236
shakyō 197, see also copying (sūtras)
Shichibutsu 84, 87, 91
Shichifukujin 5, 91, 147, 149–50, 155–8, 160–1, 168, 171, 173, 176, 260, see also Seven Gods of Good Fortune
Shichimenzan 122
Shiga (pref.) 136, 142, 146
Shiga Shōrin (pn.) 98
Shikoku 3–4, 7, 12, 14–15, 26, 33, 40–41, 56–7, 65, 68, 72, 75–92, 101–2, 103, 105, 113, 120, 127, 134, 140–1, 183, 186, 197, 201, 203, 211, 219–22, 224, 230, 236, 252–4, 260 see also Shin Shikoku circuits
  four stages 226–9
  imitations 92–6
  map 7, 77, 83, 228
  miniatures 96–100
  pilgrims' slips 187–90
Shima Kazuharu (auth.) 132
shima 152

General Index

Shimoyasuba Yoshiharu (auth.)110, 113–4
Shimozuke Eight Shrines 175–6, 178–9
Shin Buddhism (Shin-shū) 9, 69–71, 109, 124, 127–31, 141, 213, 217–8, 244, 247
Shin Shikoku circuits 37, 93–5, 99, 208
shin (heart, mind) 203, 254
shin (*kami*) 148
Shinagawa-kun (ward) 168, 179
Shinano Kannon pilgrimage 54, 57
shinbutsu 1, 105, 117, 141, 144, 146
shinbutsu bunri 117
shinbutsu shūgō 1
Shinbutsureijōkai 146
Shin'etsu region 8
shinganjōju 252
Shingon Buddhism 1, 3–4, 14, 49, 52–4, 61–2, 68–71, 75, 79–80, 82, 86, 95–8, 106–10, 113, 121, 127, 130–1, 136, 139, 142, 156, 204, 209, 216–7, 221–3, 228, 230–1, 252, 254, 260
  Buzan-ha 30, 45, 50, 70
  Chizan-ha 45, 50, 107–8
  Daigo-ha 45, 70
  Daikakuji-ha 50
  devotion/devotees 41, 78, 101, 103, 139, 235–7, 257
  Gochi Kyōdan 108
  Kazan-in-ha 46
  Kogi Shingon-shū 50
  Mimuro-ha 45
  Omuro-ha 108
  Sennyūji-ha 107
  Tōji-ha 45, 108
shingon 106, 231, 235–7, 239, 244, 252
Shingon anjin wasan 242
Shingyō 254, 257
shinjin 224
Shinjuku-ku (ward) 150
Shinkansen 81
shinkō 35, 246
Shinnen-bō (pn.) 81
Shinpen Daibosatsu (pn.) 121
Shinran Shōnin (pn.) 127–9, 131, 213, 242
Shinsaikoku pilgrimage 130–1, 217

Shinshū 70–71, 131, 217, 242, *see also* Jōdo Buddhism/Jōdo Shinshū
Shintō 4–5, 9–10, 14–15, 22–3, 55, 59–60, 66, 97, 139–57, 181, 183, 186, 195, 198, 216, 228, 241
  meanings 208–9, 228, 261, 263, 267
  national/patriotic 9, 162–8, 200
  pilgrimages 159–79, 197, 208–9
  shrines, various 1, 10, 14–15, 55, 59, 68, 80, 91, 117, 130, 133, 143
  and Buddhism 1, 5, 15, 24, 53, 60, 72, 80, 91, 123, 135–6, 141–2, 208–9, 216, 252, 261, 267
Shinzei Shōnin (pn.) 132
ship of good fortune 150–1, 173
shirt/s, of pilgrim 18, 131, 183–6, 197, 199–200, 208, 220–2, 236
Shitamachi Hachifukujin 169
Shō Kannon/Kanzeon 35–8, 42–3, 50, 52–3, 70, 85–7, 201
shōbai hanjō 169, 176
Shōdoshima 93
Shōfudōkyō 237
shōgun 62, 148
shogunate 156, 166
Shōkokuji-ha 107
shop/s 13, 165, 191–2, 201, 205, 220, 264
Shoraikō 192
Shōtoku Taishi 78, 104, 113, 130–1
Shōwa Era 54–5, 69–70, 95, 166, 199
shōzen 137
shrine/s *see* Shintō *and* Index of Temples and Shrines
Shugendō 4, 9–11, 53, 80, 110, 113, 121, 142, 210, 223, 227–8
Shugen-shū 45, 69, 113
shugo 175
shugyō 79–80, 222, 224, 227–8
shūin 65, 163, 179, 200
shūinchō 161, 179
sì 34
sickness 6, 176, 188, 221–2, 250
siddham script 221
silver 189
sin 137, 233
six

Amidas 135
Jizōs 4, 36, 103, 116–20, 135
Kannon 36–7, 120, 135
ornaments 43
perfections 255
realms 115–6, 119–20
roots 209–10
senses 209–10, 256
types of day 226
sixteen
  head temples 122–3
  petals 205
  shrines 168, 170–2, 179
  temples (Seizan) 127
skilful means 29, 247, 250, 262, 267
Skog, K. M. 76
snake/s 152–153, 249
social 11, 15, 96, 115–16, 128, 131
socio-political 32
sociological 11, 16–17, 267
sōhonzan 131
Sōka Gakkai 9, 122
sokushin jōbutsu 109, 227
Son/-son (meaning) 88, 106
song/s
  go-eika 33, 43, 120, 129, 194–5, 198, 203, 232, 237, 240–3
  wasan 43, 230, 232, 242
Soothill, W. E. 246
Sot'aesan 138
Sōtō-shū/Zen 35, 49–50, 52–3, 60–1, 65, 69–70, 82, 112–3, 124, 131
South Pole Star 153
space
  empty 238
  sacred 13–14, 19, 138
  sacralization of 13–14, 79, 130, 145, 179
Spain 18
spatial identity 134
spell/s 230–1, 249, 255
spirit/s 14, 108, 119, 135, 152, 216, 252, 261
  spirit (attitude) 171, 185, 224, 255
spiritual
  companion 3, 15, 105, 222
  development 12, 20–21, 79, 109–10,

133, 195–6, 210, 225–6, 228–9, 236, 256, 264–5
  places 11, 14, 16, 29, 32, 41, 48, 69, 75, 81–2, 97–9, 101, 110, 113, 119, 125–7, 136, 146–7, 199, 209, 239, 242
  power/s 11–12, 104, 147, 251
spirituality 60, 147, 222, 228, 265
sponsoring 161, 252
spring/s 133
  hot 57, 114
  season 32, 126, 208
Sri Lanka 22, 215
Staal, Frits 207
staff
  pilgrim's 15, 218 , 220–3, 264, *see also* stick, pilgrim's
  temple 41, 131, 182,
stages of journey 26, 263
  four 78–80, 98, 101, 226–9
stamp/ing 62, 108, 129, 149, 160–1, 168–71, 174, 183, 197–200
stanzas 185, 194, 251
star, 123, 153–4
station/s
  pilgrimage 19, 26, 103, 121, 143, 158–9, 211
  railway 44, 64, 67, 72, 94–5, 99, 117, 130–1, 150, 152, 155, 161, 169, 175, 198, 211
stations of the cross 19–20
statistics 15, 82, 92, 197
Statler, Oliver 76, 80
statue/s 11, 16, 92, 135, 137, 217
  Benzaiten 157–8
  En no Gyōja 121
  Fudō 110, 113
  Jizō 100, 115, 117, 119
  Kannon/Kanzeon 67, 69, 71, 116, 245–6, 252–3
  Kenshin Daishi 131
  Kōbō Daishi 98–9
  Miroku Bosatsu 154
  Nichiren 137–8
  Sot'aesan 138
  Yakushi 91
Stegerhoff, Renate 23
Stevens, John 133

General Index

stick
  pilgrim's 3, 74
  prayer 133, 195
stole (*wagesa*) 220
stone/s 66, 68, 92, 96, 98–9, 140, 142, 153, 242
  image/s 66, 68, 100, 115, 134–5, 177
  inscription 32, 68
  marker 139–40
storehouse 88, 91
straw hat/sandals 99, 218
stūpa 151, 216, 223
subjectivity 4, 210, 224 226
substitution 46, 66, 92, 193, 197, 208, 210, 213
suchness 86
suehirogari 175
suffering/s 67, 119, 182, 224, 243, 246, 248–51, 254–6
Sugawara no Michizane (pn.) 162, 252
sugegasa 220, 223
Suiko, Empress 130
Sumeru, Mount 249
Sumida River 154
sumimasen 211
suna/fumi 94, 97–9
Sunni 18
superimposition 14–15, 216
supernatural
  assistance 104, 121, 160, 198, 212
  divinity 236
supernormal powers 109–10, 227, 250
Suseri hime no mikoto 174
sūtra-copying 197, 208, 216
sūtra/s 33, 161, 179, 183, 185–6, 194, 195, 199, 208, 230, 232, 234, 239–40, 242–3
  Amidakyō 234
  Diamond 221
  Fudō 234, 237–8
  Hannya (*Daihannyakyō*) 162, 256–7
  Heart 67, 105, 185, 193, 197, 207, 221, 224, 227, 229–32, 244, 248, 251, 253–7, 259, 263
  Kannon 35, 38, 58, 122, 136, 145, 152, 185, 193–4, 230–1, 234, 237, 244–8, 253

Kannon Sūtra in Ten Stanzas 185, 194, 253
Lotus 29, 35, 38, 55, 67, 87, 121–2, 185, 194, 216, 237, 244–7, 251–4, 260
Mahāparinibbāna Sutta 213–4
Mahāparinirvana
Sūtra of Brilliant Golden Light 153
Suwa Daimyōjin 145
suzu 220
Suzuki, Beatrice Lane 122, 237
sword (of Fudō) 91, 110, 238
syllable/s 221, 231, 236–7, 240, 254
syncretism, 23, 167, 267
synthesis 267

T

tabi (footgear) 220
tabi (journey) 8, 159
taboo 167
taian 226
taimitsu 235
Taira no Kiyomori (pn.) 119
taisha (as term) 163–4
Taishi (Shōtoku) 104, 130–1
Taishō Era 41, 60, 146
Takahashi Yohei (pn.) 58
Takamatsu (pln.) 81, 126
Takao (mt.) 98, 229
takarabune 150–1, 173
Takarazuka Line 148
Takashimaya Dept. Store 169
Takemura Toshinori (auth.) 117, 119–20
Takizawa Jō (auth.) 99
talisman/s 108, 144, 161–2
tamagushi 175
Tama River 95
Tamonten 151
Tanaka Yasuhiko (auth.) 107
Tannishō 70
tariki 127, 217
tathāgata/s 86–7, 106, 137, 213–4, 232, 235, see also Nyorai
Teeuwen, Mark 141
tekkō 220
temizuya 178
ten, see also Ten

directions 223-4, 250
perfections 105
precepts 234
states 203
thousand together
Ten, *see also* ten
  Happy Kannon 136
  Shrines (Tokyo) 119, 165-8, 178,
  Stanzas/Lines (Sūtra) 136, 185, 194, 253
ten (celestial beings) 91-92, 104, 142, 150-1, 156,
Tendai (Buddhism) 4, 35, 67-71, 116, 130-2, 145-7, 228, 235-6, 257, 260
  Jimon-shū 45, 50
  Shinzei-shū 132
  temples 33, 41, 45-6, 49-50, 54, 61, 67-70, 82, 110, 113, 126-7, 147, 242,
tendoku 142, 256
tengu 216
tenka taihei 148
Tenkai (pn.) 148
Tenkawa Ō-kami 152
Tenna Era 54
Tennō, *see* Emperor
Tennōji (pln.) 130
Tenri (city) 22
Tenrikyō 1, 9
Tenshō Kōtaijin 145, 162
tera (-dera) 34, 82, 216
Teramachi (pln.) 117, 123
terminology
  theoretical 16, 265, 267
  emic 145, 256
Thailand 215
thanks (pilgrims) 93, 96, 137, 173, 211, 237
theory/ies 6, 11-16, 25, 27, 65, 263-7
Theravāda 217
thirteen
  Buddhas 103, 106-9, 114, 236
  shrines 161-2
  stone buddhas 134-5
thirteenth anniversary 108
thirty deities 145
thirty-third anniversary 107-8

thirty-three
  Kannon forms 38, 121, 203, 245-6, 252-3
  Kannon sites 11, 15-16, 29-32, 41-71, 94-5, 120, 139, 185, 187, 197-9, 201, 211, 217, 241, 246-7
thirty-four
  Kannon sites 32, 46-53, 199
thirty-six Fudō 97, 103, 109-13, 156
this-worldly *see* benefits (this-worldly)
thousand
  days 132-3
  shrines 191
thousand-armed 35-6, 38, 87
thousand-eyed 35-6
three
  divinities 163
  islands (Benzaiten) 152
  mountains (Dewa) 9, 210
  poisons 233, 238-9
  powers 235
  refuges/realms 234
  three step transaction 181-5, 187, 205-6
  worlds 223, 255, 257
thunder shrine 176
tiān 91, *see also* ten
Tinsley, Elizabeth 204
Tlaxcala 19
Tōbe (pln.) 97
Tōdō Kyōshun (auth.) 125
Tōbu Art Museum 16
Tochigi (pref.) 110, 128, 175-6, 178-9
Tōdō (on Hieizan) 130
Tōhoku region 113, 132
Tōkai pilgrimages 113, 130, 136
Toki Shobō 128
Tokimune (Hōjō) (pn.) 62
tokonoma 200, 222, 265
tokuban 59
Tokudō Shōnin (pn.) 30-31, 41, 43, 59
Tokugawa
  Ieyasu (pn.) 149
  Period 15, 166, 220
Tokushima (pref.) 57, 78, 83
Tokyo (Tōkyō) 3, 32, 41, 43, 53, 55, 66, 69, 95, 98-9, 114, 152, 191, 203

General Index

Kannon route 56
Shichifukujin 148–50, 154, 157
Sixteen Shrines 179
Ten Shrines 119, 165–8, 178
Eight Shrines 169–70, 178
tombs
  Nine Walis 21
  Imperial family 164
  47 samurai 203
tombstones 221
Tooth, Temple of 215
torii 10, 23, 68, 123, 142, 149, 169, 241
Tosa Province 78–9, 84, 227
tour/ism 5, 7–8, 12, 34, 46, 71, 93, 95, 101, 113–4, 134–5, 155–6, 159, 162, 177, 184, 199, 219, 262
  pilgrim/age 5, 12, 26, 82, 93, 99, 170, 184, 205, 217–8, 225
tracks/traces (of founders) 4, 120–29
transaction/al 5–6, 25, 66–7, 73, 159–61, 169, 179–87, 189, 191–3, 195–9, 200–1, 203, 205–6, 208, 211–12, 237, 254, 257, 259, 261–5, 267
transcendent/al 88, 106, 212, 232, 247
transcending 67, 136, 180, 196, 254
transference
  of meaning etc 18, 77, 125, 144, 160–2, 222, 267
  of merit 235
transformation/s
  meaning 5, 262
  personal 6, 12, 196, 212, 226, 229, 264
  supernatural 31, 55, 145, 221, 247–8
transient 222–3, 256
transliteration, 164, 215, 227, 230, 232, 237, 254,
transmission 133, 204, 212, 215, 251
transplantation 156, 213
transport 3, 13, 25–7, 34, 54, 57, 72, 74–5, 80–82, 113, 118, 130, 134, 161, 220, 228–9, 262
treasure/s 16, 44, 194
  name 236
  national 43–4, 154, 210
Triplett, Katja 5, 25, 94, 123, 129, 152, 173, 181, 191, 198, 202–5, 210

truths, four 246, 255–6
tsue 220, 222
Tsugaru Straits 57
Tsukuba (pln.) 98
tsutsuji 170
Turner, Edith 11, 23
Turner, Victor 11, 23, 220
tutelary deity 115
twelve
  branches 124
  factors 256
  Myōken sites 123
  sub-shrines (Kasuga) 174–5
twenty-four
  Companions of Shinran 129
  Jizō 119
twenty-five
  Amaterasu sites 165
  Hōnen sites 124–6, 204, 242
twenty-year rebuilding (Ise) 165
type/s of Kannon image 41–3, 49–50, 52
typology 22

U

Uda Tennō (pn) 113
udumbara flower 232
Ueno Park 152
Ugajin 152–3
ujigami 168
Uka no Mitama (deity) 153
ultimate/ly 21, 105, 109, 221–2, 237, 256
ume (plum) 170
uni-directional/focal 8, 10–11, 18, 159
unifocal 18
urban 3, 33, 54–6, 95, 149, 158, 176
Uruvelā 214
Utsumi Shunshō (*ajari*) (pn.) 132
Utsunomiya (city) 175–6

V

Vairocana 145, 232
Vaiśravaṇa 151
value
  evidential 6, 25–6, 75–76, 264
  religious 17, 41, 109, 124, 131, 159, 178, 182, 184, 196, 201, 209, 228, 247, 265

van Gennep, Arnold 11
Vārāṇasī 214
vehicles, blessing of 100
Venerable Sot'aesan 138
venerable one (*son*) 88, 106, 154
veneration 137, 154, 157, 187, 211
  ancestors 103
  mountains 216
verse/s 230, 232–5, 240, 246
  four lines 223
  Kannon Sūtra 58, 194, 230, 246–51, 253
  opening 232
via dolorosa 19
vicarious pilgrimage 222
victory, certain 176
vidyārāja 106
Vimalakīrti 88
Virgin Kannon 68
Virgin Mary 17, 19–20, 245
virtue/s 105, 114, 144, 150, 171, 237, 250
vision/s 22, 228, 250–1
visualization 203
votive offerings 67, 116, 221, 254
  tablets 24–6, 55, 65–6, 124, 152–3, 162, 168, 183, 193, 195
  texts 67
vow/s 52, 120, 127, 195, 217, 237, 248

W

Wa–shū 95, 113, 127, 131
wagesa 220
Waipahu Soto Zen Temple 155
waka 240
Wakayama
  City 126
  Prefecture 80–81, 93, 101, 109–10, 146, 150
Wali/Walisongo 21
walking/walkers 20, 27, 34, 71, 93, 96–8, 100, 129, 135–6, 138, 142, 146, 158, 161, 175, 178, 184, 211, 218, 260
Wallfahrt 12, 15, 75
war
  Hachiman 175
  Ōnin War 55

Pacific War 64, 95, 142
pre–/post-war 14, 55, 64, 68, 160, 163–5, 177, 200, 245
warring spirits 116, 119, 135
wasan 43, 230, 232, 235, 237, 242–3
Watanabe Katsumi (auth.) 53
water /s 8, 18, 91, 99, 133, 152, 178, 185, 195, 204, 225, 243, 248
  babies 119
waterfall 23, 49, 110, 227, 241, 243
Watsuji Tetsurō (auth.) 210
waves (cut by Fudō) 91
Wénshūshìlì 88, 215
Westminster Abbey 22
wheel
  of wishes 35
  of Dharma 218
white
  old man 149, 153
  pilgrim's attire 3, 186, 197, 218, 220–1, 223
  pilgrim slips 94, 189
  snake 152–3
White Robed Kannon 202, 251–2
Willow Kannon 202, 252
wisdom 88, 109, 152, 155, 237–8, 244, 247, 250–1, 256
wish/es 153, 178, 193, 252
  fulfilled 139
  wheel of 35
womb mandala 221
women 20, 64, 68, 140, 210
Won Buddhism 138
wooden artefacts 107, 150, 168, 192–3, 196, 201
wood-block prints 46
world 250–3, 255
  detachment from 154, 216, 220
  other 192, 196, 208, 212, 231, 246–7
  peace 193, 245
  secular 10
  symbolic 205
  this world/ly 162, 179, 181, 192–3, 195–6, 208, 220, 227, 243, 246, 250–1, 261 *see also* benefits (this-worldly)
World War II 165, 245

General Index

worship 9, 92, 97, 100, 143, 155, 168, 171, 174, 186, 208, 225
wrathful deity 150
Wǔtái (mt.) 215

X

Xuánzàng 215, 254–5

Y

Yabuki Machi (pln.) 68
Yakuno Kōgen (pln.) 100
Yakushi Nyorai 4, 43, 59, 84–7, 90–2, 103, 105, 107, 109, 114, 130, 175
Yakushi Pilgrimage 130
Yakushirurikō Nyorai 43
yakuyoke 169, 176
  Daishi 237
  Yakushi Nyorai 84, 87
Yama 116
yamaboko 174
yamabushi 4, 10, 121, 142, 209–10, 227
Yamada Eiji (auth.) 53, 55, 70, 226
Yamada Shōsuke (pn.) 237
Yamadera (pln.) 132
Yamagata (pref.) 9, 132
Yamashina-ku (ward) 31, 117
Yamato (prov.) 30, 152, 164

Yanagawa Keiichi (auth.) 156
Yokawa (Mt. Hiei) 122, 130
Yokohama (city) 98
Yōryū Kannon 252
Yoshino (pln.) 4, 110, 121, 164
Yudono-san (mt.) 9, 210
Yuimakyō 88
yuishin 203
Yumefukujin 176
Yusai (*ajari*) (pn.) 132

Z

zange 210, 233
Zangemon 232
zazen 124, 243
Zen (Buddhism) 68–70, 109, 154–5, 203–4, 244, 256, 261
  Ōbaku 70
  Rinzai, 49, 59–60, 64, 69–70, 88, 113, 124, 142–3, 147, 149–50, 153, 156, 243, 245
  Sōtō 35, 49, 60, 65, 69–70, 88, 113, 124,
Zeniya Matabei (pn.) 191
Zenshin-Kō 95
Zhìyǐ (pn.) 116
ziarah 21

www.ingramcontent.com/pod-product-compliance
Lightning Source LLC
Chambersburg PA
CBHW052051230426
43671CB00011B/1873